Integrative
Body–Mind–Spirit
Social Work

Integrative
Body–Mind–Spirit
Social Work

An Empirically Based Approach to Assessment and Treatment

Mo Yee Lee
Siu-Man Ng
Pamela Pui Yu Leung
Cecilia Lai Wan Chan

OXFORD
UNIVERSITY PRESS

2009

OXFORD

UNIVERSITY PRESS

Oxford University Press, Inc., publishes works that further
Oxford University's objective of excellence
in research, scholarship, and education.

Oxford   New York
Auckland   Cape Town   Dar es Salaam   Hong Kong   Karachi
Kuala Lumpur   Madrid   Melbourne   Mexico City   Nairobi
New Delhi   Shanghai   Taipei   Toronto

With offices in
Argentina   Austria   Brazil   Chile   Czech Republic   France   Greece
Guatemala   Hungary   Italy   Japan   Poland   Portugal   Singapore
South Korea   Switzerland   Thailand   Turkey   Ukraine   Vietnam

Published by Oxford University Press, Inc.
198 Madison Avenue, New York, New York 10016

www.oup.com

Oxford is a registered trademark of Oxford University Press

Library of Congress Cataloging-in-Publication Data

Integrative body–mind–spirit social work : an empirically based approach to assessment
and treatment / Mo Yee Lee . . . [et al.].
    p.   cm.
ISBN 978-0-19-530102-1
1. Social service.   2. Mind and body.   I. Lee, Mo Yee.
HV41.I523 2009
361.301—dc22
2008038388

9 8 7 6 5 4 3 2

Printed in the United States of America
on acid-free paper

Contents

Part III: Applications and Treatment Effectiveness

Part IV: Learning and Using Integrative Body–Mind–Spirit Social Work in Practice

Foreword

Mo Yee Lee, Cecilia Chan, Siu-Man Ng, and Pamela Leung have made a wonderful contribution to social work practice by bringing together insights from Eastern thought (especially Buddhism, Daoism, and Traditional Chinese Medicine), Western holistic and systemic theories, complementary and alternative therapies, and social work trends in cultural competence, spiritual sensitivity, and the strengths perspective. The practice framework in this book is both practical and profound. The authors present it vividly, approachably, and realistically through clear guidelines for practice, wise clinical vignettes, empirical evidence, and self-disclosure about their professional and spiritual journeys. Integrative Body–Mind–Spirit Social Work is a significant breakthrough in social work practice.

The authors describe their approach using the metaphor of a healing wheel. The body–mind wheel spins in a healing process on the foundation of spirituality. They define spirituality in a broad sense to encompass and integrate all aspects of the person in the process of searching for meaning and purpose, growing through joys and adversities, striving to live compassionately, and connecting with humankind and the universe. While they draw insights from Eastern religions and philosophies, they do not attach their practice approach to any particular religious beliefs. They bring out the core principles and key ingredients for helping skills and techniques, such as treatment planning, assessment, body-focused therapies, meditation, visualization, grief work, forgiveness, and therapeutic support groups.

Lee, Chan, Ng, and Leung explain how their approach is fully committed to professional social work values and ethics. Integrative Body–Mind–Spirit Social Work builds on the particular strengths, beliefs, and support systems of clients. It engages the inner wisdom and environmental supports of clients in order to nurture resilience, empowerment, and transformation. The authors give moving accounts of ways that clients develop a meaningful life by transforming illnesses, traumas, losses, and conflicts into occasions for learning, growth, and enhanced relationships.

Previous authors have encouraged efforts to incorporate Eastern thought into social work frameworks for cross-cultural application (e.g., Brandon, 1976; Canda, 2002; Canda & Furman, 1999; Chung & Haynes, 1993; Keefe, 1975; Imbrogno & Canda, 1988; Kissman & Maurer, 2002; Koening & Spano, 1998). This book builds on some of these and also introduces many ideas and practices that have barely been considered within conventional social work previously. As one of the people who has advocated for the mutual learning of East and West in social work, I am very happy and enthused about this book as the most thorough, detailed, and practical contribution of this kind to date.

This accomplishment was catalyzed by the authors' extraordinarily creative international collaborations with the Center on Behavioral Health, affiliated with the University of Hong Kong. During my visits there, I have been impressed with the innovative programs linking social workers, psychologists, and others in clinical practice, community organizing, teaching, and research. The Center adapts traditional Eastern philosophy and healing traditions to connect with contemporary practice and research in social work, mental health, and holistic health around the world. All of the authors have a rare combination of strengths in practice-based skills, empirically based knowledge, and philosophically based wisdom. This comes through clearly in their book.

The logo of the Center well symbolizes the authors' approach to Integrative Body–Mind–Spirit Social Work. It is shaped like a human heart and based on the Chinese character meaning "mind." In traditional East Asian thought, the mind is centered in the heart region. This cultural difference between East and West first struck me about 30 years ago in South Korea during a visit to a Buddhist temple. During my conversation with a monk, we frequently referred to the mind. As a matter of habit, I gestured toward my head while, to my surprise, the monk gestured toward his heart. I learned that the Eastern concept of the heart–mind reflects a centeredness and connectedness of body sensation, feeling, thinking, and spirit. Further, by accentuating the heart shape in the logo, the Center emphasizes the importance of compassion in service.

Lee, Chan, Ng, and Leung manifest compassionate and holistic mind in their Integrative Body–Mind–Spirit Social Work approach. Drawing on Daoist philosophy and Traditional Chinese Medicine, they explain how seemingly opposite or conflicting qualities within and between persons can be harmonized through social work practice. Drawing on Buddhist philosophy, they show how clear awareness, meditation, loving kindness, and compassion can help clients transform suffering into healing and growth. While recognizing the important contributions of conventional social work for strengthening a healthy ego, they point out the limitations of an overly individualistic and separated concept of self. The authors describe how Integrative Body–Mind–Spirit Social Work can help clients to integrate, expand, and transcend the individual self while deepening life meaning and purpose, resolving broken relationships, and realizing the interconnected nature of all things.

Integrative Body–Mind–Spirit Social Work gently encourages readers to shift out of narrow cultural, religious, scientific, and ideological assumptions. At the same time, it honors diverse traditions, ways of knowing, and techniques of helping. I am certain that this book will inspire readers with new insights for social work practice that come from the meeting of East and West.

— Edward R. Canda, PhD, Professor
The University of Kansas School of Social Welfare

Preface and Acknowledgments

We have been previously trained in and used cognitive-behavioral approaches, solution-focused approaches, structural and strategic family therapy approaches, and so on in our work with clients and families. We, of course, have greatly benefited from learning and using these approaches in our professional practice. At the same time, we increasingly realize not only the "strengths," but also the "shadows," of these approaches. We witness clients and families who get stuck describing and verbalizing their problems, solutions, dreams, and visions. We wonder whether there is more than therapeutic dialogue as the primary medium of change in treatment. We witness clients desperately searching for meaning in their lives in the middle of chaos in life, mostly relational, but also material. However, spirituality appears to be a distant part of conventional social work practice. Since 2000, the Center on Behavioral Health at the University of Hong Kong has embraced empirically based treatment approaches from Eastern and Western traditions in developing a holistic model that integrates body, mind, and spirit in treating individuals and families. Since then, we have been surprised by the many positive changes in our clients.

Integrative Body–Mind–Spirit Social Work attempts to expand beyond existing social work practice models and integrate a more holistic orientation based on Eastern philosophies and therapeutic techniques to create effective, positive, and transformative changes in individuals and families. This book was written for helping professionals, psychologists, social workers, therapists, and graduate students with an interest in an integrative holistic and strengths-based approach in their professional practice with clients and families. We provide a pragmatic, step-by-step guide from assessment to termination about how to capitalize on participants' strengths in a holistic manner to assist their efforts to do something different and beneficial in their lives.

The organization of the book aims to help readers to understand, learn, and use the model in their practice. To achieve that end, the book is broadly divided into four sections. Part I consists of Chapters 1 and 2. The discussion systematically introduces the philosophical foundation of Integrative Body–Mind–Spirit Social Work, which forms the conceptual framework of the model. These chapters describe the assumptions and beliefs of the model as well as a practice framework that elucidates Integrative Body–Mind–Spirit Social Work's views on problem causation, problem maintenance, and change mechanisms. Part II includes Chapter 3 to Chapter 9. This section provides a pragmatic, step-by-step description of assessment and treatment techniques that use an integrative and holistic perspective. We systematically describe assessment, treatment planning, and treatment techniques pertaining to mind, body, and spirit while maintaining a focus on the body–mind–spirit connection in treatment. Part III, Chapter 10 to Chapter 14, describes five studies that provide empirical support to Integrative Body–Mind–Spirit Social Work as a viable practice approach in bringing about changes in clients. Part VI, consisting of Chapters 15 and 16, is a discussion regarding ethical issues and tips for learning Integrative Body–Mind–Spirit Social Work.

Appreciation must first go to Joan Bossert, Vice President and Publisher; Maura Roessner, Editor of Social Work; and Mallory Jensen, Associate Editor; and all the other wonderful staff at Oxford University Press. Their enthusiastic support for the book has made this book a reality. We deeply appreciate Edward R. Canda for reviewing our manuscript and encouraging our efforts to develop Integrative Body–Mind–Spirit Social Work. Carol Zhong and Hok Hei Tam have provided invaluable professional editorial assistance to our team. As a team, we are all inspired by the incessant commitment of Professor Cecilia Chan, the Director of the Centre on Behavioral Health, to develop and promote an integrative holistic approach in working with clients and families.

Cecilia Chan is appreciative of Jonathan for his support. Pamela Leung is grateful to her husband, Lewis, and her two children, Angela and Henry, for their continued support. Siu-man Ng is grateful to his wife, Rosita, for her relentless support and encouragement. Mo Yee Lee is especially thankful for her mother, Sho Yean Chan, who has given her the greatest gift of life; Kwok Kwan Tam for sharing his passion; and her two children, Tze Hei and Hok Hei, for showing her how to be curious and playful about life.

Lastly, we are deeply indebted to the clients and families we met who have inspired and surprised us with their trust, willingness to work, and courage to change. They impressed us with their perseverance through hardship and trauma, their resilience in difficult moments, and their optimism while enduring pain. They have renewed our faith in the meaning of our work and have given us hope in the power of change. They have been our greatest teachers.

This acknowledgment was written soon after the cyclone in Burma and the earthquake in Sichuan, China. Three hundred thousand people lost their lives in these two disasters, and millions lost their homes. Life is truly not always within our control. Yet, in the trauma and pain of loss and suffering, there were amazing stories of selfless dedication to serving others and inspiring stories pertaining to community mobilization for mutual help and community resettlement with international participation and local innovations. In every loss, there is gain. A balanced and connected view of the world introduces new possibilities for change, passion, and hope.

Mo Yee Lee
Siu-Man Ng
Pamela Pui Yu Leung
Cecilia Lai Wan Chan

List of Contributors

Professor Deborah Akers, PhD
Visiting Assistant Professor, Department of Anthropology, Miami University, Ohio.

Prof. Cecilia L.W. Chan, BSocSc, MSocSc, PhD, RSW, JP
Si Yuan Professor in Health and Social Work, Director, Centre on Behavioral Health, Professor, Department of Social Work & Social Administration, University of Hong Kong, Hong Kong.

Ms. Yu-Ting Chen, RN, MSN
Instructor, School of Nursing, Chang-Gung University, Tao-Yuan, Taiwan.

Dr. Y. T. Fu, MBBS (HK), FRCR (UK) FHKCR, FAMHK
Deputizing Consultant, Department of Clinical Oncology, Queen Elizabeth Hospital, Hong Kong.

Mr. Andy H.Y. Ho, BA Hons, GradDipEd, MSocSc, PhD Candidate, MFT
Research Officer, Centre on Behavioral Health, University of Hong Kong, Hong Kong.

Dr. Rainbow, T.H. Ho, Ph.D., A.D.T.R., C.M.A.
Registered Dance/Movement Therapist (USA), Certified Movement Analyst (USA)
Assistant Professor, Centre on Behavioral Health, University of Hong Kong, Hong Kong.

Dr. Judy W.C. Ho, MBBS (HK), FRCS (Ed), FCSHK, FHKAM (Surg), FRCS (Eng), FACS
Consultant, Honorary Clinical Associate Professor, Department of Surgery, Queen Mary Hospital, University of Hong Kong, Hong Kong.

Dr. Fei-Hsiu Hsiao, RN, PhD
Associate Professor, Department of Nursing, College of Medicine, National Taiwan University, Taipei, Taiwan.

Ms. Yu-Ming Lai, RN, MSN
Instructor, School of Nursing, Chang-Gung University, Tao-Yuan, Taiwan.

Ms. Stephanie S.M. Lau, BSocSc Hons (HKU), MFT Candidate
Research Assistant, Department of Psychiatry, University of Hong Kong, Pokfulam, Hong Kong.

Dr. Antoinette M. Lee, BSocSc Hons (HKU), PhD (CUHK)
Reg. Psychol. Assistant Professor, Department of Psychiatry, Queen Mary Hospital, University of Hong Kong, Hong Kong.

Professor M. Y. Lee, PhD
Professor, College of Social Work, The Ohio State University.

Dr. Pamela P.Y. Leung, BSW, PhD, RSW
Assistant Professor, Department of Social Work & Social Administration, University of Hong Kong, Hong Kong.

Dr. S.M. Ng, BHSc (ChiMed), MSc (PsySW), PhD
Assistant Professor, Department of Social Work & Social Administration, University of Hong Kong, Hong Kong.

Ms. Venus Y.H. Tang, BSocSc, MSocSc Candidate
Research Coordinator, Centre on Behavioral Health, University of Hong Kong, Hong Kong.

Ms. Elaine Y. L. Tsui, Msc (Bath), BSc (London)
Health Psychologist, Centre on Behavioral Health, University of Hong Kong.

Dr. T. K. Yau, MBBS (HK), FRCR (UK), FHKCR, FHKAM (Radiology)
Consultant, Department of Clinical Oncology, Pamela Youde Nethersole Eastern Hospital, Hong Kong.

Ms. Clarissa N. Wang, BA, MPhil Candidate
Research Coordinator, Centre on Behavioral Health, University of Hong Kong, Hong Kong.

Professor Amy Zaharlick, PhD
Associate Professor, Department of Anthropology, The Ohio State University.

Introduction: The Coming of Integrative Body–Mind–Spirit Social Work

> Denise was a teacher at an elementary school. Nicole, her 6-year-old daughter, was born with a muscular condition, and she periodically experienced involuntary muscular spasms that could be painful and traumatic for her and the family. Nicole was easily agitated and frustrated, which led to temper tantrums both at home and at school. Because of her emotional problems, Nicole received treatment from a play therapist for more than 1 year, but Denise observed little improvement. So, she chose to consult a therapist who also practiced Reiki as part of a holistic approach to treatment. Besides engaging Nicole in play therapy, the therapist held family sessions and taught Denise to use massage and other body process work to calm Nicole down when she was upset. The therapist also helped Nicole to use simple breathing and imagery to make her feel better. Together, Denise and her husband explored the meaning of being the parents of Nicole, who can be testing sometimes. They began to realize that, although the muscular condition has been a challenge for them as well as for Nicole, it has forced them to learn to be more accepting of limitations in life but, paradoxically, also more appreciative of being a parent. They also felt more connected to each other as a couple, as well as to other people who are dealing with different adversities in life.

Social work has traditionally dealt with a wide range of psychosocial, interpersonal, and mental health problems for individuals and families. Social work practice with individuals and families in the twenty-first century has accumulated years of experience, expertise, knowledge of human behavior, and change. Decades of outcome research has provided evidence of the efficacy of social work treatment and psychotherapy (Lambert & Ogles, 2004; Lebow, 2006). Despite its efficacy, social work practice has been challenged on many fronts, such as the flourishing of semi-professionals including, but not limited to, therapists using alternative and complimentary therapies, self-help groups, addiction counselors, and life coaches, all of which are a testament to the rise of nontraditional or complimentary methods to help people effectively change. This is also indicative of clients' aspiration for something other than that which traditional social work treatment and therapy can offer. Public interest in alternative treatment and therapies has grown since it was initially evaluated in 1993 by Dr. David Eisenberg at Harvard Medical School. He documented that almost one-third of Americans were using complementary/alternative medicine and spending nearly $13 billion in out-of-pocket expenses (Eisenberg, Kessler, & Foster, 1993). By 1998, these figures had grown to 42% in utilization and $30 billion in expenditures (Eisenberg et al., 1998). Within the field of social work, just in the past decade, there has been a tremendous increase in awareness among professionals and scholars regarding limitations of an increasingly specialized and also compartmentalized approach to social work treatment that downplays the role of spirituality (e.g., Abels, 2000; Becvar, 1988; Bullis, 1996; Canda & Furman 1999; Carroll, 1997; Crompton, 1998; Patel, Naik, & Humphreys, 1997; Van Hook, Hugen, & Aguilar, 2001). A conventional bio-psycho-social construction of the self and human existence, as espoused by the ecological perspective (Germain & Gitterman, 1980) and person-in-environment perspective (National Association of Social Work, 1999), is inadequate for meeting the challenges of human needs in the twenty-first century, as more and more people come to realize we are more than biological, social, and psychological beings—we are also spiritual and habitual beings (e.g., Bullis, 1996; Canda & Furman 1999; Cowley, 1993; Loehr & Schwatz 2003).

A HISTORICAL REVIEW OF THE DEVELOPMENT OF SOCIAL WORK: HOW SOCIAL WORK BECAME "OUT OF SYNC"

The social work profession has traditionally taken a more holistic or integrative view in conceptualizing a client's problem and the change process. The Code of Ethics of the National Association of Social Workers (1999) states that, "A historic and defining feature of social work is the profession's focus on individual well-being in a social context and the well-being of society. Fundamental to social work is attention to the environmental forces that create, contribute to, and address problems in living" (p. 1). This person-in-environment perspective provides an overarching practice framework that unifies diverse areas and specializations of social work practice. Germain and Gitterman (1996), in describing an ecological perspective to the life model practice of social work, also stated that

> From a holistic view, people (and their biological, emotional, and social processes) and physical and social environments (and the characteristics of those environments) can be fully understood only in the context of relationship between and among them, in which individuals, families, and groups and physical/social environments continually influence the operations of the other. (p. 6)

Despite the recognition of the dynamic interplay of biological, psychological, and social domains in human behaviors and life stressors, the discussion does not include spirituality as an issue of concern or a domain of the human experience, in spite of the well-documented influence of spirituality in the lives of many clients (Bullis, 1996), especially around client issues of bereavement, grief, and illness (Nakashima & Canda, 2005).

The early development of the social work profession was promoted by pioneers who had strong spiritual motivations for services, although they did not focus on religious terminology or institutions to express them services, although they did not focus on religious terminology or institutions (Stroup, 1986). Religious and charity organizations heavily influenced the early development of the Charity Organization Society, in which the respect for individual self-worth and dignity and the values of passion and care formed the core values and ethics of social casework practice (Reamer, 1992). For instance, Jane Addams, an icon of the settlement house movement, was affiliated with the Presbyterian Church and the Congregational Church; these faiths at least partly fueled her commitment to serve the poor (Stroup, 1986). In contrast, social work practice, as contrived nowadays, largely separates spirituality from the other domains of human experiences and has avoided discourse regarding spirituality until quite recently.

One cannot appreciate the dilemmas encountered by social work practice without understanding its development, which cannot be divorced from its socio-historical context. Social work practice with individual and families utilizes a wide range of knowledge developed at different points in history to handle human problems. Such knowledge is constantly changing and evolving, for it is facilitated or constrained by the values of the people and the available knowledge at the time regarding human behaviors and the change process, which is affected by the particular historical-cultural context at the time (Donzelot, 1979; Johnson & Sandage, 1999; Green, 1998; Lee, 1996). Despite the presence of religious influence on early pioneers of our profession, the early practice of social work heavily utilized knowledge from psychotherapy in providing treatment for individuals and families. The Greek word *therapeuein* means *to heal*. Therapy is, in a broad sense, a social practice that has an explicit goal of healing or enhancing psychosocial well-being in individuals and families. Traditionally, "healing" functions are mainly fulfilled by religious organizations and the community. As a result of the decreasing religious influence after the Renaissance, human problems could no longer be solely explained or resolved by religious authorities that, traditionally, have had a strong hold on people's lives (Donzelot, 1979). Likewise, industrialization and urbanization lead to broken kinship ties and fragmented communities (Beit-Hallahmi, 1987). Social work emerged in the 1900s as a legitimate and secular substitution, primarily because of its adherence to the values associated with modernism and secularism (Cushman, 1995; Donzelot, 1979).

In order for us to fully appreciate the assumptions and beliefs regarding a client's problems and change process, a review of the development and characteristics of social work practice approaches and perspectives is helpful. Social work practice with individuals and families has traditionally been under the influence of many diverse schools of thought regarding practice. Broadly speaking, these are the action-oriented approaches and the reflective–expressive approaches. Different approaches focus on one or a combination of social forces, psychological forces, biological impulses, or an individual's behavior in understanding and treating individuals' problems.

Reflective–Expressive Approaches

Social work, especially in its early development, heavily utilized knowledge from psychotherapy in providing therapy for individuals and families. These approaches primarily include the psychodynamic approaches (Freud, 1923/1961), cognitivism (e.g., Beck, 1976, Beck, Rush, Shaw, & Emery, 1979; Ellis, 1996), and the existentialism and humanism schools of practice (e.g., Frankl, 1967; Lantz, 1993; Rogers, 1961). Ego psychology (e.g., Goldstein, 1995; Hartmann, 1939), object relations theory (Mahler, 1968), and self-psychology (Kohut, 1971, 1977) built upon existing Freudian psychoanalytic theory but refined and modified its concepts. These theoretical perspectives have exerted, and will continue to exert, significant influence on today's social work practice with individuals and families.

Different reflective–expressive approaches focus differently on psychological forces, biological impulses, other internal processes, and the individual's behavior in understanding and treating individual and familial problems. There is, however, a unifying focus on expression of feeling and reflection about self, others, and one's situation to bring about internal changes. These approaches assume that internal changes or insight development will lead to enhanced awareness, behavioral changes, and new modes of functioning in individuals, without the necessity of specific action agendas.

Action-Oriented Approaches

The early practice of casework as rooted in philanthropic origins was predominantly action-oriented: Social workers directly and crudely provided guidance for clients to resolve difficulties in their lives—for example, offering information and advice from personal perspectives. Such a practice orientation further developed into the problem-solving approach and task-centered approach that originated within the social work profession (LeCroy & Goodwin, 1988). Helen Harris Perlman's problem-solving approach represents a social work-based, psychologically sophisticated, action-oriented approach to social work with individuals and families, in which the client's need for self-direction is recognized and supported (Perlman, 1957). The task-centered approach, developed by William Reid and his associates, (e.g., Reid & Esptein, 1972; Tolson, Reid, & Garvin, 1994) represents yet a more recent development of action-oriented approach in social work practice. These approaches focus on helping clients to learn, practice, and implement specific problem-solving actions relevant to their problems. Actions/tasks are usually explored, learned, discussed, and rehearsed in the sessions and undertaken between sessions. Instead of social workers providing direct information and advice, these approaches focus on clients' self-direction and participation in the problem-solving process. Therapists assist clients while they are rehearsing problem-solving actions during the interviews, and such an effort is supported by a strong therapeutic alliance. Techniques usually include building rapport, helping clients to identify problems, planning and reviewing specific problem-solving actions/tasks, employing enactment and directives, reinforcing constructive behavior, constructing new and beneficial forms of actions/skills, rehearsing those actions/skills, and providing feedback (Reid, 1998).

Despite differences in action-oriented approaches, there is an implicit assumption of linearity between problems and solutions; that is, if one can understand the cause of the problem, one will be able to use the specific therapeutic techniques as suggested by an individual theory to solve the problem and attain the status of health for individuals and families.

Current Development

The more current development of social work practice and theories are influenced by the ideas of systems perspective (Bateson, 1972, 1979), feminist theories (e.g., Chodorow, 1978; Cowley, 1993; Goorich et al., 1988; Worell & Remer, 1992), and social constructivism (e.g., Neimeyer & Mahoney, 1993; Rosen & Kuehlwein, 1996). Instead of assuming a linear relationship between problems and solutions or assuming the existence of an objective "problem reality" that can be scientifically assessed and treated, these approaches focus on circularity, reflexivity, multiversity, and diversity in assessment and treatment. These perspectives provide other important metaphors for working with families and individuals.

The Organizing Perspective: Person-in-Environment Perspective

Despite differences in their views of problems and the change process between action-oriented approaches, reflective–expressive approaches, and more current theories, such as systems perspective and social constructivism, the social work profession has developed a distinct "person-in-environment" perspective to guide our assessment and intervention in social work treatment, regardless of specific practice theories or areas of specialization (NASW, 1999). The development of a "person-in-environment" perspective is very much influenced by the psychosocial/ecological perspective. Helping professionals, primarily influenced by psychodynamic approaches, behaviorism, and existentialism, focuses predominantly on psychological forces, biological impulses, other internal processes, and the individual's behavior in understanding and treating individuals' problems. However, the role of the individual's relationship to the environment in determining behavior is either minimized or not recognized in assessment and treatment. The social work profession distinguishes itself from other helping professions in that it adopts a more integrative or holistic perspective as the core principle of professional practice. Building upon concepts of ego psychology and also focusing on the interrelationship between the person and the environment, Florence Hollis developed the psychosocial perspective in social work practice, in which an individual's behavior is perceived as influenced by both psychological and social factors (Hollis, 1964). More recently, Germain and Gitterman (1980, 1996) developed the life model of social work practice that utilizes an ecological perspective in viewing and helping clients and families. An ecological perspective focuses on the interrelationship between individuals and their broader ecological environment and the implications of such a relationship on social work practice. The life model practice "is not simply a conglomerate of little bits from each of the earlier specializations, but a reconceptualized practice that reflects the continuous transactions among individual, collective, environmental, and cultural processes in human development and functioning, and integrates the modalities required to improve or sustain those transactions" (Germain & Gitterman, 1996, p. ix). A psychosocial/ecological perspective underlies the social work perspective of "person-in-environment" (Saari, 1992) that has been recognized by the National Association of Social Work as the overarching perspective in social work practice (NASW, 1999).

Views of Problem Formulation and Clients' Change

Despite the diverse foci of social work treatment approaches, the values of scientificism, rationalism, individualism, and humanism provide meta-frames that underlie most social work treatment approaches with individuals and families. They usually share some or all of the following characteristics or beliefs in resolving human problems of living: (1) Individuals and/or families should take an active stance to control, master, and overcome their problems. (2) The individual's or family's well-being, empowerment, and self-actualization are the ultimate concerns of social work treatment. (3) Social work professionals should fully consider the mutual interaction between the person (and the biological, emotional, and social processes) and physical and social environments (and the characteristics of those environments) in social work treatment. (4) We can, and should, develop "scientific" methods to resolve human problems of living, based on empirical or rational knowledge. (5) The therapeutic process should rely on sensory information defined by the physical plan of reality rather than the spiritual realm of existence to seek cures for human troubles. (6) Human problems of living can be alleviated through a treatment process in which both client and therapist participate together. (7) The social work professional is professionally trained to develop expertise on dissolving human problems (Lee, 2005).

Despite a preference for an ecological perspective in viewing a client's problems and change process, the social work profession continues to downplay the spiritual dimension as an integral part of the human experience. Similarly, the social work profession attempts to distance itself from the values and motivations expressed by our founding pioneers that were intimately connected with religious and spiritual traditions. Canda (1997) delineates three broad historical phases that describe the shifting relationships between the social work profession and spirituality: (1) Sectarian origin (colonial period through early twentieth century, (2) professionalization and secularization from the 1920s to 1970s, and (3) resurgence of spirituality since the 1980s. Pioneers who had strong spiritual motivations for services promoted the early development of the social work profession, although they did not focus on religious terminology or institutions. From the 1920s onward, however, social work increasingly distanced itself from spirituality. This development is largely related to the social work profession's aspiration for professionalism, along with other professions such as medicine and law. Dr. Abraham Flexner did not endow professional status to social workers in 1915 at the National Conference of Charities and Corrections because of concerns regarding a lack of a systematic, scientific knowledge base to govern social work practice (Dinermen & Geismar, 1984). The development of social work practice and knowledge became increasingly influenced by a knowledge-building paradigm dominated by positivism, scientificism, and rationalism, a privileged knowledge paradigm esteemed by professionals and academia in the West. Spirituality does not have a natural "marriage" with the values, aspirations, and epistemology upheld by the social work profession. Common reasons for excluding any discourse around spirituality include, but are not limited to, the following concerns: (1) As a profession, social work should be objective and value-free; (2) the concept of spirituality is too vague to be consistent with a scientific professional base for social work practice, knowledge and/or research; (3) religion or spirituality primarily addresses ideas of supernatural or private experiences that should not be brought into the public domain of social work agencies; and (4) religions can be dogmatic, rigid, oppressive, and judgmental, which may violate the client's self-determination (Clark, 1994; Sullivan, 1994; Weisman, 1997). During this period, NASW and Council of Social Work Education (CSWE) were established as inclusive, secular, professional organizations. CSWE's curriculum policy guidelines in the 1950s and 1960s referred to clients' spiritual needs in nonsectarian terms; these references were eliminated in the CSWE guidelines of the 1970s and 1980s. As a profession, social work chooses to build its professional base upon scientific and humanistic traditions and "divorces" itself from spirituality. The trend of increased specialization in social work treatment parallels the downplaying of the role of spirituality. Specialization constitutes one hallmark of professionalization that usually represents increased rigor of professional practices, based on rigorous and refined professional knowledge. In doing so, however, social work treatment becomes more and more compartmentalized, so that clients and families are categorized based on presenting problems rather than being viewed as connected and whole beings.

One can never overestimate the contributions of values associated with scientificism, rationalism, humanism, and individualism to social work practice. Social work, as practiced today, has a solid knowledge and practice base that is supported by empirical evidence. The current movement regarding empirical-based practice signifies the profession's aspiration for integrating practical, ethical, and evidentiary concerns into a critical, systematic, and scientific process of building social work knowledge (Gambrill, 2003; Gibbs, 2005). These advances serve to demystify the treatment process for individuals and families, to expand our understanding of humankind as biological, psychological, and social beings, as well as to regulate unethical healing practices of all kinds. Likewise, the individualistic and humanistic thinking that underlies the Social Work Codes of Ethics (NASW, 1999) directs a focus onto an individual's dignity, equality, freedom, autonomy, and self-worth as a self-actualizing being who aspires to growth, fulfillment, and destiny. These values represent a fundamental shift that emancipates a person from years of traditional stronghold of collective existence, sacrifices, and social injustice.

The dilemmas encountered by social work, paradoxically, come from the strengths and contributions of the approaches. Canda and Furman use the phrase "soul loss and soul retrieval" to describe the changing phenomenon (Canda & Furman, 1999). Kenneth Wilber, who is a psychologist studying consciousness and who is at the forefront of the integral movement, speaks convincingly of the dilemmas of "partial truths" (Wilber, 2000). The crucial question is not about which approach is the best or most accurate but about which aspects of human experience or consciousness that different schools and traditions of social work treatment attempt to address. The metaphor of yin–yang, as coined by ancient Chinese philosophy, interestingly provides useful insight into the current dilemmas of mainstream social work practice. Yin and yang metaphorically represent two contrasting forces in nature that are constantly striving for balance but also complementing each other's existence. Yin and yang are inseparable in the sense that there is a cybernetic equilibrium of the yin in the yang and vice versa. The essence of this metaphor is the concept of balance, interrelationship, and complementarity. Social work treatment with individuals and families can be perceived as a reaction to the traditional, communal, religious, and mystical practices of addressing the human problems of living. By adhering to the values of scientificism, rationalism, individualism, humanism, and divorcing itself from other forces, the development of social work practice is bound to be "out-of-balance" at some point, as it will miss the potential contribution, or the reality presented, by the excluded dimensions. A closer examination of the treatment approaches and assumptions of diverse social work treatment models reveals several neglected, yet fundamental, dimensions of human experiences.

Where is spirituality?

While contriving major social work treatment models, mainstream social work practice has downplayed spirituality as a significant domain of human experience. Instead, the focus has been on the cognitive, behavioral, and affective domains of human experiences. Such a phenomenon is likely to be a consequence of social work practice being positioned as a secular solution to the human problems of living in contrast to the religious or mystical solutions that dominated society prior to the Renaissance. Values of scientificism further collude with the historical context to downplay the importance of spirituality in addressing problems of living. The quest for a scientific understanding of human behavior and change relies more on observable and measurable sensory information defined by the physical plane of reality than utilizing the spiritual plane of existence in the treatment process (Slife, Hope, & Nebeker, 1999). Also, flourishing alternative therapies are signals to the field of social work practice that we may be missing something obvious that plays a significant role in helping people effectively change.

There has been an explicit revival of professional interest in spirituality and social work. Early on, in the 1980s, social work scholars such as Max Siporin advocated the inclusion of spiritual aspects in addition to the bio-psycho-social perspective in understanding human needs and development and social work practice. Just in the past decade, there has been an increasingly visible discourse among social work professionals and scholars regarding limitations of a compartmentalized approach to social work treatment that downplays the role of spirituality (e.g., Abels, 2000; Becvar, 1988; Canda & Furman,

1999; Crompton, 1998; Patel et al., 1997). The CSWE's current curriculum policy guidelines also recognize religious and spiritual diversity as legitimate topics for social work education (Russel, 1998). Such a development is likely to be the result of growing awareness within the social work profession, as well as other helping professions, regarding limitations of the existing practice paradigm, as well as feedback from consumers of social work services. Research in the last decade shows that around 88 percent of mental or medical health clients want the spiritual dimension to be included as part of their treatment (Bullis, 1996; Fitchett, Burton, & Sivan, 1997; Koenig, 2002). There is also increasing empirical evidence that supports the positive impact of spirituality on the client's well-being. For example, spirituality is positively associated with increased resilience to stress and lower levels of anxiety (Pardini, Plante, Sherman, & Stump, 2000) and has been shown to moderate the negative effects of emotional adjustment and physical symptoms of stress (Kim & Seidlitz, 2002). Larry Dossey, a physician by training, has devoted much of his professional career to researching and writing about the role of spirituality in healing and medicine (Dossey, 1985, 1993, 1996, 1997, 2001). The increasing interest in, and attention to, mindfulness therapy (Goleman, 2003; Langer, 1990; Segal, Williams, & Teasdale, 2001), practices based on Buddhism (Brazier, 1997; Canda & Smith, 2001), and Daoism (Johanson & Kutz, 1994; Koenig & Spano, 1998; Yip, 2004) is indicative of growing diverse voices within the field of mental health and social work practice that recognize the notable role of spirituality in effecting positive changes in individuals. In addition, increasing efforts have been focused on documenting, for example, the effectiveness of a mindfulness approach in improving the individual's psychological and/or physiological well-being among depressed populations (Teasdale et al., 2000), cancer patients (Brown & Ryan, 2003), and patients with systemic hypertension (Schneider et al., 2005).

A disconnected view of person, environment, and/or services

Descartes, in his book *Meditations on First Philosophy*, established the proposition that the soul, or the self, is a pure, thinking being that could conceivably exist independently of a body (Descartes, 1641/1990). The proposed view of self constitutes the source of the Cartesian dualistic doctrine of the existence of two distinct domains: one thinking, one extended. The mind–body dualistic thinking from Descartes's view of the self still permeates everyday Western thinking, including the quest for scientificism and rationalism. Further supporting the dualistic thinking is the form of scientific inquiry that necessitates reductionistic thinking, in which phenomena are broken down into the smallest possible parts to be studied for precise understanding, prediction, and control. Scientific methods also emphasize linear thinking, which implicates cause and effect relationships among different domains and variables in order to explain human behavior and resolve human problems (Katz, 1985). A strong emphasis on the application of the rational mind, through logic, has created the trend toward reductionism and fragmentation, not only in physical science, but also in the understanding of human being. Influenced by Cartesian dualism is a functionalist and reductionist view of consciousness. In essence, consciousness is portrayed as an emergent property of classical computer-like activities in the brain's neural networks that involves neuronal circuits oscillating synchronously in the thalamus and cerebral cortex: it is viewed as a linear and deterministic process (e.g. Churchland, 1986; Dennett, 1991; Churchland & Sejnowski, 1992).

The resulting development of social work practice with individuals and families certainly echoes such a compartmentalized trend. For instance, clinical social work practices that are influenced by psychoanalysis and ego psychology focus on intrapsychic forces and internal processes and action-oriented treatment approaches, such as task-centered social work practice, emphasize changes in observable behaviors and ignore the "black box." Cognitive therapy assumes the primacy of cognitive processes over emotional and behavioral processes. Social work treatments influenced by such a perspective focus on identifying and changing the distorted thinking processes and beliefs of a person. The body process of individual clients receives little attention in a cognitive-based approach. Consequently, the conceptualization of a person is of one who has distinctively separate and interrelated cognitive, behavioral, and affective domains, but not as a whole, connected, human being. In addition, there is a clear disconnection between spirituality and other domains of human experiences in most social work treatment approaches. The advent of a systems perspective (Bateson, 1972, 1979) should challenge the fundamental assumptions of social work practice because of its emphasis on interrelationships and connection among systems and the recursive feedback process. Even so, the impact of a systems perspective is felt more in working with families (e.g., Haley, 1990; Minuchin & Fishman, 1981; Munichin, Nichols, & Lee, 2007) than working with individuals. In addition, the focus of therapeutic intervention pertains primarily to the cognitive, behavioral, and affective domains rather than the body or spirituality of the person.

The power of dualistic thinking influences the development of social work practice with individuals, despite convincing evidence of a mind–body connection. Psychosomatosis is a long-recognized phenomenon in the health and mental health fields, but the term carries a negative connotation, which is indicative of how our society views the mind–body connection (Weil, 1995). Research on biofeedback (Green & Green, 1977) provides indisputable evidence of complex, recursive relationships between our mind and body. Dr. Larry Dossey (1993, 2001) explores and provides elaborate evidence regarding how spirituality and our mind intersect with our body functions and mental health. Dr. Daniel Siegel (1999) focuses his research on the convergence of neurophysiological development, attachment theory, and interpersonal relationships. Dualistic thinking and the reductionistic method of inquiry may be helpful for professionals in developing and testing knowledge and practice models, but it limits our vision of a more holistic perspective and our potential use of different interventions to assist clients and families in the process of change.

The trend of disconnection can even be observed in our service system, despite the overarching person-in-environment perspective of social work practice. For example, in spite of the common co-occurrence of mental health and addiction problems in clients, the conventional service systems pertaining to mental health and chemical dependency treatment are separated in both their orientation of treatment and the service delivery structure. Such a disconnection creates coordination and collaboration challenges at best, and conflict and discontinuity in treatment at worst.

A narrow interpretation of mind and body

In addition to a disconnected view of a person, many mainstream social work practice approaches adhere to a narrow view of the mind. The reflective–expressive approaches of social work practice with individuals and families emphasize expression of feelings and reflection about self, others, and one's situation to bring about internal changes, which lead to enhanced awareness, behavioral changes, and new modes of functioning in individuals and families. Action-oriented social work practice approaches usually focus on helping clients to learn, practice, and implement specific problem-solving actions relevant to their problems. The focus of these orientations is either on insight development or on identification of the cause of the problem by the conscious and rational mind, as well as the attainment of specific behavioral outcomes that solve the presented problems. Cognitivism and behaviorism constitute two primary theories that heavily influence the development of social work treatment approaches, such as behavioral management and cognitive-behavioral approaches. The focus of conventional cognitive therapies is on a conscious mind that is supposed to think and converse rationally (Beck, 1995; Beck et al., 1979; Ellis, 1996; Meichenbaum, 1977, 1995). Likewise, the primary focus of behaviorism is on behaviors and actions performed by the body, but not the body itself.

Such narrow focuses exemplified by these social work treatment approaches can be a result of limited knowledge regarding the human mind and body at the time of theory development. Such a development was also influenced by the values of scientificism, which promote and prefer rationality and observable phenomena to the more subtle and recursive human processes that do not easily lend themselves to be examined by a straightforward input–output paradigm to establish treatment effectiveness (Gondolf, 1997). The power of the body–mind process that hypnosis, biofeedback, psychosomatic phenomena, mindfulness practices, and spontaneous healing suggest is recognized, although much is still unknown, not to mention the complex, recursive relationships between our mind and body, in relation to our health and mental health, that remain uncharted. The problem with a reductionistic method of inquiry is not only that it leads to the differentiation of mind and body but, unfortunately, to the dissociation of the mind and body (Wilber, 2000). A peculiar consequence is the "loss of consciousness" in the study of psychology or human experience in that we investigate brain states and behavior but not how a person *experiences* the world (Chalmers, 1996; Velmans, 1996). Wilber (2000) vividly describes the dilemma: "We are then faced with two apparently absolute but contradictory truths: the truth of immediate experience, which tells us unmistakably that consciousness exists, and the truth of science, which tells us unmistakably that the world consists only of arrangements of fundamental units that possesses no consciousness whatsoever, and no amount of rearranging these mindless units will result in mind" (p. 174). Emerging scientific efforts to expand our understanding of the mind and consciousness are currently underway, and much is waiting to be debated and unveiled (Wilber, 2000). The Tucson Conference "Toward a Science of Consciousness" clearly represents a landmark of such concerted efforts to explore creative ways that heal fragmentation and lead to a more comprehensive and integrative way of understanding human consciousness (Hameroff, Kaszniak, & Scott, 1996). However, it is clear that a narrow focus on the mind as a rational mind, observable behavior as the sole representative of body processes, and the dissociation of the mind and body does not help social work practitioners and therapists to explore and utilize other treatment orientations that may otherwise be beneficial and helpful in the process of change.

Downplay of body processes

With the exception of gestalt therapy (Kepner, 1993) and movement or dance therapy, most social work practice models with individuals and families emphasize cognition more than the body as a source of change. Again, this is likely to be a consequence of the Cartesian dualistic doctrine and Decartes's view of the self as a purely thinking being. Johnstone (1992) provides a forceful argument for the bodily nature of the self and suggests that Descartes neglected the "felt body" when formulating his proposition. In fact, psychology recognizes the limitation of cognitive processes, especially at the preverbal stage of development when an infant has not yet acquired the ability of spoken language. Instead of having explicit memory, an infant acquires implicit memory, which recalls experiences in the form of behavioral and emotional learning, and that implicit memory influences a person throughout his or her life in powerful ways (Siegel, 1999). Body processes, however, are not used by practitioners who adopt behavioral approaches that focus on observable and measurable behaviors. Classical works by influential therapists such as Carl Rogers (1961), Fritz Perls (1969), E. T. Gendlin (1979), and Alexander Lowen (1967, 1973) address the "ongoing psychophysiological flow" and the power of the body on the mind. There have also been recent efforts within therapy to reclaim the importance of body processes in treatment (Caldwell, 1997; Kutz, 1997). In spite of these developments, body processes are still not part of mainstream social work practice.

The focus on self

The value of individualism significantly shaped current social work practices that emphasize the self as an autonomous, independent entity that constitutes the center of change in the search for individual well-being, self-fulfillment, personal growth, and self-actualization (Doherty, 1995; Singer, 1970). The Social Work Code of Ethics (1999) clearly identifies "dignity and worth of the person" as one of the core values embraced by social workers throughout the profession's history and also constitutes the foundation of social work's unique purpose and perspective. There is also an optimistic assumption that clients should and can control and master their own lives, despite problems of living (Katz, 1985; Sue et al., 1998). In addition, the "self" is not just the vehicle for change but also contains the solution to problems of living, provided the "self" is perfected through the self-actualization process. Influenced by these ideas, symptom reduction represents one end of the continuum of therapy goals that focus on emancipating an individual from problems, which limit the free expression of an autonomous "self." Self-actualization represents the other end of the continuum of therapy goals, the end that is directed at personal growth and positive expression of a "self" that can freely express human worth, freedom, dignity, and beauty. The individualistic and humanistic views adopted by social work practice have certainly aided millions of clients in effecting desirable changes in their lives. However, several fundamental assumptions of such a view also limit our perception of the self and possible therapeutic goals and interventions.

The problem of a forever actualizing self.   The assumption that people should and can control their lives results in a treatment paradigm that prefers the language of accomplishment, mastery, and gaining over the language of letting go, accepting, and going with the flow. Although there are times or situations in a person's life that will benefit from an active attitude of mastery and control, there are other scenarios that call for a person to let go and to accept. Erikson, in his conceptualization of life stages, emphasizes that each life stage transition involves gains and losses (Erikson, 1963). A systems perspective proposes that change is constant in all systems, including human systems (Bateson, 1972, 1979). There will be natural "ups and downs" in our clients. A treatment language that emphasizes both mastery and the process of letting go should more fully capture the essence of human experiences. Such a language will also expand our therapeutic repertoire in assisting individuals.

Self as an "autonomous," independent entity that exists separatel. The conventional understanding of the "self" by social work practice mostly conceptualizes the "self" as a core, autonomous, independent entity that directs an individual's desires, behaviors, and emotions. Such a view, however, has been increasingly challenged by social work professionals who take a more holistic orientation. Siporin (1986) claimed that predominant social work theories neglected the person's spiritual side by emphasizing self-fulfillment and self-actualization on a personal or ego level (rather than a transpersonal level). Kenneth Wilber (2001), a psychologist, convincingly speaks about the problem of creating an imaginary boundary between the "self" and the "not-self." This boundary not only creates a sense of self-identity for individuals but also leads to polarities, oppositions, and conflicts. Such a "closet" definition of the self contrasts with the teachings of Buddhism, which views the boundary between the "self' and the "not-self" as an illusion created by the human mind. A different view of the self and the relationship between the self and its environment will allow therapists and clients to address problems of living in more creative ways.

Self as containing solutions to problems of living. The other assumption involves the view of self as containing solutions to problems of living. Life in the twenty-first century is crazier than ever—more disjointed, disconnected, scattered, and objectified than we have ever experienced. There is increasing recognition of the limitations of a view of the self as containing solutions to problems of living because so much of our present-day problems relate to the self being disconnected, disjointed, and scattered (Butler, 2003). Cultural critics speak of a larger self: a self that is connected to others, to our community, and to our environment. Others speak inspirationally about a deeper self with purpose (Schwartz, 1995). A crucial question for social work professionals to address is how to respond to "the crisis of self" in the twenty-first century.

THE INTEGRAL MOVEMENT

In recent decades, different organizations and movements, especially in the fields of medicine, healthcare, and psychology, have been developed in an effort to expand their narrow focus of inquiry to a more holistic view and embrace diverse traditions and methods of knowing. Integration takes on slightly different meanings in different disciplines, but they all share a vision of expanding beyond a scientific, reductionistic understanding to an open and holistic worldview that embraces atomistic, logical, empirical, analytical, interpretative, dialectical, dialogical, and network-oriented ways of knowing (Dossey, 2001; Shannon, 2002; Wilber, 2000; Weil, 1995).

The "integral" medicine or healthcare movement that is rapidly developing today has moved beyond early attempts in this area, known as "holistic," "allo-pathic," "alternative," and "complementary," to provide a wider scope and stronger empirical research to effectively relate its practices to comprehensive models of human experience and healing. As described by Dr. Scott Shannon, Medical Director of the McKee Center for Holistic Medicine, the movement from *alternative* to *complementary* to *integrative* is reflective of the chrono-logical stages that have occurred within the paradigm shift in health care, in that an integrative approach to health care is seen as central instead of just being peripheral or "alternative" (Shannon, 2002). The integrative paradigm is a process of transformation that expands beyond physical/biochemical view of illness and health based on the scientific knowledge and also embraces ancient wisdoms, which emphasize holism. The Principles of Holistic Med-ical Practice, developed by the American Holistic Medical Association, are built upon the following beliefs and values: (1) The self is multidimensional where body–mind–spirit are interconnected as a whole with no dividing line. (2) People are self-guided, self-corrected, and have innate abilities to heal and move toward balance on all levels, whether physical, mental, or spir-itual. (3) The web of life does not exist in isolation, and we constantly create an active, biochemical exchange with our environment. (4) All liv-ing things move to become more complete and whole. In essence, such an approach recognizes the interconnectedness of body–mind–spirit, a systemic and network-oriented view of the individual and his or her environment, and the inherent strengths and healing abilities of individuals to become whole and complete (Shannon, 2002).

The National Center for Complementary and Alternative Medicine was established by the U.S. Congress in 1998 as one of the 27 institutes and centers that make up the National Institutes of Health. The Foundation for Integrative Medicine, founded by Dr. Andrew Weil and the American Holistic Medical Association, represents notable efforts within the medical profession in this new pursuit. The journals *Alternative Therapies in Health and Medicine* and *Integrative Medicine* provide professional forums for the advancement and dissemination of knowledge in this area.

In the field of psychology, Kenneth Wilber, who is in the forefront of the "integral psychology," attempts to use an "all level, all quardrant" approach to study human consciousness (Wilber, 2000). Wilber perceives that a sane integral approach should attempt to honor, acknowledge, and incorporate the enduring truths of all ages—pre-modern, modern, and postmodern—into an ongoing study of the evolution of human consciousness. This inclusive, integral, and nonexclusionary approach embraces the world not just merely as a perception (modern view) but also as an interpretation that is constructive, contextual, and aperspective (Wilber, 2000). Wilber is not alone in the quest of an integrative journey. Transpersonal psychology, developed from the works of Anthony Sutich, Abraham Maslow, Alan Watts, Michael Murphy, Elmer Green, and Alyce Green, attempts to develop a psychology that embraces transcendent experiences and transcendent values, which go beyond a narrow vision of the self, individuality, or self-actualization. Anthony Sutich, inspired by the ideas of Maslow, described transpersonal psychology as an emerging "fourth force" in understanding human beings and change. The Association for Transpersonal Psychology and the *Journal for Transpersonal Psychology* were both founded in 1969.

Within the social work profession, the Society for Spirituality and Social Work was established in 1990. The current curriculum policy guidelines of the CSWE recognize religious and spiritual diversity as legitimate topics for social work education (Russel, 1998). The trend is promising for spirituality to become a more integral part of social work education and practice.

A SMALL ACT OF BALANCE: LOGICAL–ANALYTICAL VERSUS HOLISTIC SYSTEMS OF THOUGHTS

The "sin of missions" paradoxically parallels the significant contributions and advancements of current social work practice because its practices (or any specific traditions of practice) oftentimes only address "partial truths" of human experiences (Wilber, 2000). The nature of social work practice with individuals and families characterized by mainstream social work is inevitably a product of its socio-cultural-historical context, which prefers the language of secularism, scientificism, rationalism, humanism, and individualism to the language of spirituality, connectedness, and recursiveness. In contrast, social work practice, as a profession, addresses problems of living as experienced by individuals and families who are whole, not fragmented, beings. The dilemma of "partial truths" can be understood within the philosophical and epistemological tradition of the Greek civilization, which had a strong influence on the logical–analytical system of thought of modern science.

One important characteristic of the ancient Greeks was their idea of self in that power was primarily located in the individual (Morris, 1994). The Greeks defined happiness as, "the exercise of vital powers along lines of excellence in a life affording them scope" (Hamilton 1930/1973, 25). The focus on individual power and personal freedom was further manifested by the Greek's tradition of debate (Lloyd 1991; Nakamura 1964/1985). Individuals were encouraged to freely express their opinions and ideas with a great sense choice and a lack of social constraint (Morris, 1994). The philosophical and epistemological tradition of the Greek civilization also has significant influence on modern thoughts. Greeks had a strong sense of curiosity about the world, and they assumed that the world could be understood by discovering the underlying rules (Gaderma, 2002; Lloyd 1991; Stace, 1969). The Greeks created models and developed assumptions of physical causes to understand the nature of objects and events in the world. They constructed these models by categorizing objects and events and generating rules about them for the purpose of systematic description, prediction, and explanation (Cromer 1993; Gaderma, 2002; Toulmin & Goodfield 1961). Greeks perceived that the world was consisted of discrete objects, each with their particular "properties" and could be categorized by reference to their universal properties (Burnet, 1964; Gaderma, 2002; Hansen, 1983). These properties were observable and could be understood independent of their context (Nakamura 1964/1985). The underlying focus on individual object, causality, empirical formal logic, categorization, and discreteness form the basis for the modern, Western, analytic system of thought that promotes scientificism, rationalism, and individualism. Such an analytic system of thought gives rise to a method of knowing, which supports the detachment of object from its context, a focus on attributes of the object based on categorization, a preference for using rules to understand phenomena, the use of formal logic, and avoidance of contradiction (Nisbett, Peng, Choi, & Norenzayan, 2001).

The development of the social work profession and its knowledge base for practice is inevitably a product of a system of thought that characterizes the civilization from which it originated. Consequently, despite an overarching person-in-environment perspective adopted by the social work profession, social work practice research pertaining to a holistic framework is often lacking. In addition, spirituality within a more holistic perspective of treatment was largely absent from the discourse of the social work profession until recently, partly because the nature of spirituality does not lend itself well to observation and dissection. Conventional social work treatment models, such as cognitive-behavioral approaches, task-centered, problem-solving, and/or solution-focused approaches, and so on, all have a narrow focus on "mind" as the source of cognition and "body" as the source of observable behaviors. The fragmentation that characterized not just the clients but also the service delivery systems is consistent with the categorization and rule-based understanding of objects. Likewise, a focus on individuals' power and rights easily gives rise to the current narrow focus on the "self" without a more connected vision of the self embedded in a larger environment.

Wilber (2000) used the term "flatland" to describe the shadow of the logical–analytical system of thought, where everything is reduced to become an object that can be measured, but, in doing so, sacrifices value, meaning, and wholeness, resulting in a "disenchantment of the world," as phrased by Max Weber. The logical–analytic system of thought underlying mainstream social work was fundamentally influenced by Greek civilization. Other civilizations, however, have embraced more holistic, connected, and dialectical methods of knowing and practices, beliefs, and philosophies in healthcare. Examples include, but are not limited to, Ayurveda (Indian culture), herbal medicine (African culture, Chinese culture, Indian culture, Hispanic culture, Native Hawaiian culture, Hurdle, 2002), and medicine wheels (Native culture, Johnson & Cameron, 2001).

The development of Integrative Body–Mind–spirit Social Work is primarily influenced by a holistic system of thought and Eastern philosophies. Chinese civilization had played a central role in the civilizations of East Asia, including Japan and Korea, and the civilizations of Southeast Asia. In contrast to the Greeks' focus on individual power and freedom, Chinese civilization focuses on reciprocal social obligation and collective existence (Chu, 1985; Tamura & Lau, 1992; Triandis, 1995). Individuals exist as part of a large, complex, hierarchal, and generally harmonious society. Group expectations guide and regulate individual behaviors and roles (Chan & Leong, 1994; Munro, 1985). Social harmony is highly esteemed, and individuals are not supposed to transgress the group-defined boundaries of duties or expectations. At the same time, confrontation, individual expressiveness, and debate are largely discouraged (Ho, 1993; Munro, 1985). Such a pattern of social organization parallels the Chinese system of thought, which is more holistic in its essence (Nisbett, 1998; Peng & Nisbett 1999). Chinese people believe that "the world is a collection of overlapping and interpenetrating stuffs or substances" (Hansen, 1983, p. 30). In addition, the individual entity was not a primary conceptual starting point used to understand relationships between objects and events because of inseparable relationships among them (Moser, 1996; Munro, 1985). A consequence of the Chinese assumptions about continuity and the importance of the context is their concern with the fundamental relatedness among objects and events and the consequent alteration of objects and events by the context in which they are located (Logan, 1986; Moser, 1996). There is much less focus on context-free categories and rules to understand the world.

The holistic perspective that only the whole exists and the parts are linked relationally, like "the ropes in a net (Munro, 1985), is related to a Chinese orientation for practicality as a method of knowing. "There is no thought of *knowing* that did not entail some consequences for action" (Munro, 1969, p. 55). Such practicality was based on intuition, experience, outcomes, and empiricism, which is fundamentally different from the analytic tradition of creating formal models or theories based on scientific investigation. Such a practical orientation also accounts for technological advances in China that include, but are not limited to, the invention of irrigation systems, ink, porcelain, the magnetic compass, the Pascal triangle, the paddle-wheel boat, immunization techniques, astronomical observations, acoustics, and so on. (Logan, 1986, p. 51).

The analogy of left and right brain has been used to describe the dualistic depiction of holistic versus analytic, continuous versus discrete, field versus object, relationships versus categories and rules, dialectics versus foundational principles and logic, experience-based knowledge versus abstract analysis, and premodern versus modern, and so on (Nisbett, Peng, Choi, & Norenzayan 2001; Shannon, 2002; Wilber, 2000). There are fundamental differences in how each understands the world, organizes social life, and develops knowledge and understanding. Acknowledging the fundamental differences, however, should not prevent us from searching for a more balanced and inclusive way to address the dilemma of "partial truths." A paradigm engendered by a network-oriented and more holistic perspective provides a beneficial and alternative perspective for social work professionals to contemplate, revisit, and reflect on existing strengths and loopholes of social work practice so that we can celebrate our strengths and address "omissions." The yin–yang metaphor postulates that contrasting forces in nature are constantly and naturally striving for balance and complementing each other's existence. Yin and yang are inseparable in the sense that yin exists in yang and yang in yin. There is always continuity, flow, and contradictions among different forces characterized by balance, interrelationship, and complementarity. In other words, there are always "similarities in differences" and "differences in similarities" (Bahm, 1998). The current effort within the social work profession to address spirituality is just a live example of the dynamic interplay of contrasting forces and perspectives. In a way, this book can be perceived as part of a balancing force that tries to address current developments in social work practice with individuals and families.

THE COMING OF INTEGRATIVE BODY–MIND–SPIRIT SOCIAL WORK

Integrative Body–Mind–Spirit Social Work attempts to expand beyond existing social work practice models and to integrate a more holistic orientation based on Eastern philosophies and therapeutic techniques to create effective, positive, and transformative changes in individuals and families.

This approach was developed and consolidated by experienced psychologists, medical professionals, social workers, and therapists at the Center on Behavioral Health in Hong Kong. The Center on Behavioral Health was established in 2001 by the Department of Social Work and Social Administration, in collaboration with the Faculty of Medicine, the University of Hong Kong, to provide a holistic therapeutic approach for promoting mental, emotional, and behavioral well-being of the community. The Center embraces empirical-based treatment approaches from Eastern and Western traditions in developing a holistic model that integrates body, mind, and spirit in treating individuals and families. Meditation practice, which is an integral part of Integrative Body–Mind–Spirit Social Work, has also been adapted for treating trauma survivors with substance use problems (Lee, Zaharlick, & Aker, 2009). The Ohio Department of Mental Health sponsored the project.

Integrative Social Work does not rebuke existing therapeutic knowledge and practices. Instead, such an approach builds on existing knowledge and practices of social work practice but at the same time addresses challenges and dilemmas encountered by social work practice in the twenty-first century. The development of Integrative Social Work was informed by Eastern philosophies, especially the yin–yang theory, Buddhism, and Daoism. The yin–yang theory, the oldest of these schools of thought, engenders a dynamic systems perspective on understanding individuals and the world. Philosophical Daoism and Buddhism provide important concepts and useful practices for enhancing mind–body and human–nature harmony. Traditional Chinese Medicine (TCM), which is strongly influenced by the yin–yang perspective and Daoism, also provides a systems perspective on health, disease etiology, and a multidimensional treatment approach, and it informs the practices of Integrative Social Work.

PURPOSE AND ORGANIZATION OF THE BOOK

The organization of the book aims to help readers understand, learn, and use Integrative Body–Mind–Spirit Social Work in their practice. To achieve that end, the book is broadly divided into four sections. Part I consists of Chapters 1 and 2. The discussion systematically introduces the philosophical foundation of Integrative Body–Mind–Spirit Social Work, which forms the conceptual framework of the model. These chapters describe the assumptions and beliefs of the model as well as a practice framework that elucidates on Integrative Body–Mind–Spirit Social Work's views on problem causation, problem maintenance, and change mechanisms. Part II includes Chapters 3–9. This section provides a pragmatic, step-by-step description of assessment and treatment techniques that use an integrative and holistic perspective.

We systematically describe assessment, treatment planning, treatment techniques pertaining to mind, body, and spirit while maintaining a focus on the body–mind–spirit connection in treatment. Part III, Chapters 10–14, describes five studies that provide empirical support to Integrative Body–Mind–Spirit Social Work as a viable practice approach in bringing about changes in clients. Part VI, consisting of Chapters 15 and 16, is a discussion regarding ethical issues and tips for learning Integrative Body–Mind–Spirit Social Work.

GUIDING BELIEFS OF THE BOOK

Before describing the assumptions, values, and practices of Integrative Body–Mind–Spirit Social Work, it is important that we explicitly share our beliefs and positions while writing this book. We firmly believe in a strengths-based perspective in social work treatment; we see empowering clients and families as the primary and ultimate goal of social work treatment; we adopt such a perspective when we develop our model; and we attest to an isomorphic process of recognizing and utilizing our individual strengths in collaboratively developing Integrative Social Work. Consequently, we encourage readers to thoughtfully identify their strengths and integrate them in the process of learning this model as well as providing treatment for clients and families.

A point of clarification is that Integrative Social Work does not attempt to integrate differences between philosophies or practices based on Western and Eastern traditions, nor does it claim a comprehensive discussion of philosophies and practices of the East. We take an open and reflexive position in exploring and including methods of treatment that are effective, empirical-based, and consistent with a holistic view of being, as well as the professional ethics of social work treatment. Although the approach is influenced by Eastern philosophies, we respect spiritual diversity in clients and readers. Religious conversion does not have a place in the discussion.

A book on social work treatment or therapy is helpful only to the extent to which readers interpret the meaning and applicability of the approach. We sincerely hope that readers of the book take a reflexive position in understanding Integrative Social Work and at the same time reflect upon their personal values and orientation of practice, as well as professional knowledge and experience. The reader is the only person able to determine how the described approach, including its assumptions and techniques, can be beneficially applied to, and integrated in, his or her practice to create positive changes in clients and families.

Prior to the discussion of Integrative Body–Mind–Spirit Social Work, we would also like to share with readers our journey of developing and learning the approach. We believe that the more transparent we are about our learning, the more helpful it would be for readers to better understand the development of Integrative Body–Mind–Spirit Social Work in beneficial ways.

HOW TO CREATE BENEFICIAL CHANGES IN LIFE: MO YEE'S JOURNEY

I first realized the anguish as well as hope of life when I was still in my high school and was a mentor to a special class of visually impaired students who were junior to me. All 12 students were visually impaired, but several of them were also mentally or physically challenged. I grew up with them for 4 years with laughter and tears. Life is not equal for everyone, but I found out that we can make life better if we all work together. I decided to choose social work as my major in my university years.

Being curious, I went to India for a 6-week study tour after my graduation and prior to my first job at a family service agency. In the slum area and particularly in the House for the Dying in Calcutta, I had another unforgettable understanding of life that lasts with me for a long time. I served lunch for people who knew to receive food only by kneeling. I stood quietly beside the bed of a person who just came to the House in the morning and died within 3 hours because of extreme starvation and illness. I also saw families who brushed their teeth and cooked their food using water from the street ditches. Meanwhile, I witnessed a Brother who gave a big hug to a man with leprosy, while I was appalled by the disfiguration of his hands and face and quietly debating whether to drink the sweet tea that this man had just prepared for me. Problems of living can happen at so many levels: the individual, family, and society level. Life can be drastically different for people but there are always ways to make life better.

As a young and novice therapist, I worked with a wide range of client problems ranging from depression, anxiety disorder, bipolar disorder, suicidal attempts, parent–child problems, marital problems, teenage pregnancy, child neglect, and child abuse, just to name a few. Needless to say, it was emotionally overwhelming for a 20-something social worker. I relentlessly sought for more training in working with clients and families, hoping to discover, learn, and master some "miracle" techniques to effectively help clients and families to address their diverse, and sometimes, dizzying problems of living. Of course, in my twenties, I probably did not realize that creating change in life requires more than techniques. Life is far more complex and fascinating than that.

I finally decided to pursue my master's degree at the University of California, Los Angeles (UCLA), and then PhD at the University of Toronto in search of some answers to a simple question that has inspired me since a young age, that is, how to create beneficial changes in people's life. Meanwhile, I received clinical training at the Hincks Institute, Toronto, and later the Brief Family Therapy Center at Milwaukee. At the same time, I continued my clinical practice primarily with children and families during these years.

(continued)

(continued)

My early practice was more influenced by a problem-focused approach to social work treatment. Like many skilled social work professionals, I helped families and clients to understand their presenting problem and find a way to solve them. I benefited from structural and strategic approaches to family therapy. I learned from neuorlinguistic programming, object relationships, attachment theories, cognitive-behavioral approaches, and so on.

A significant shift in my clinical practice happened when I was exposed to solution-focused brief therapy when I was receiving my postgraduate Clinical Fellowship at the Hincks Institute in Toronto. We all learn from our clients and they are our best teachers. I still vividly remember a 26-year-old client who was a single mother with a 6-year-old boy. She was referred by the school to attend treatment. The presenting problems as mentioned by my client included difficulty in handling her child, who never listened and destroyed almost anything. In her own words, most children are angels after they fall asleep. However, Tom kicked her even when he fell asleep. He, further, had a history of setting fire and touching a young girl who was 2 years younger than him. Tom was also having problems at school and had just been suspended. My client lost her job as a salesgirl six months ago, and she was on welfare since then. She also had a diagnosis of bipolar disorder. In the first session, she appeared to be very guarded, blunt, and vigilant. She was totally negative about any possibility of a positive change in her life or in her son's behaviors.

Later I found out that I was the fourth therapist that my client had contacted with. She appeared to have a history of dropping out from therapy after the first two or three sessions. For some reason, she continued to see me, and by the fourth session, she shared with me something that I still remember until today. She said that she dropped out from treatment not because she did not need it. She realized that she needed help. However, she usually cried desperately after sessions with previous therapists because what they discussed in sessions was mostly about her problems in handling Tom, Tom's behavioral problems, and her own problems. She felt so depressed and helpless after these sessions and cried so badly that she did not want to come back again.

I "noticed" the power of language in creating and sustaining change. Problem-talk, with the best intention, can still reinforce the problem reality just because clients recite it over and over again. I realize that it is more helpful to focus on what clients do well than on what they are lacking. These are simple things, but it takes a lot of discipline for professionals to stay focused, stay simple, and respect clients as the expert of their life and listen intensely for their strengths and resources. My first book published by the Oxford University Press is *Solution-Focused Treatment with Domestic Violence Offenders: Accountability for Solutions*. It is a collaborative effort with the Plumas Project in California that serves domestic violence offenders since 1991 using a solution-focused approach.

Meanwhile, my search for answers to the question "how to create beneficial changes in people's life" has not stopped. One thing I realize is the potential limitation of a

(continued)

(continued)

sole focus on language in solution-focused brief therapy. Not minimizing the power of language, I wonder whether there is more to it as I also witness clients and families get stuck with verbalizing their solutions, dreams, and visions. Professor Cecilia Chan, a long time acquaintance, invited me to participate in the work of the Center on Behavioral Health to explore and develop a treatment approach that cross-fertilizes Western techniques and Eastern philosophies and practices in creating changes in clients and families. Such collaboration proved to instigate another significant shift in my vision and practice with clients. Working with the clients at the Center affords our team the opportunity to develop an integrative approach that addresses body–mind–spirit in a holistic manner. The Eastern philosophies and practices of a yin–yang perspective, Daoism, Buddhism, and TCM allow me to personally revisit conventional social work practice, especially in terms of our view of problems, the process of change, and the role of bodywork and spirituality. I am of course still greatly influenced by a solution-focused and strengths-based approach in social work treatment. Readers can probably find imprints of these approaches when reading the book. However, such perspectives are now weaved in a more holistic body–mind–spirit holon of our existence.

While finishing up this book, I am involved in a research at Amethyst House, which is a treatment center for homeless women with substance abuse problems. The study is funded by the Ohio Department of Mental Health to examine the effects of meditation practice on the mental health outcomes of trauma survivors. As an academic in addition to being a therapist, I view research as an integral part of the development of Integrative Body–Mind–Spirit Social Work. We need empirical evidence to examine its effectiveness as well as fine qualitative studies to carefully explore and delineate the mechanisms of change.

This is an evolving journey, and I am pretty sure that there will be no finite answer to my question about how to create beneficial changes in people's life. However, I find myself being privileged to be part of this process and journey.

SUI-MAN'S STORY

I was trained in psychiatric social work at Manchester University, UK, in the early 1990s. The training proved to be extremely useful in the formulation of my base mental health practice model. After familiarizing myself with Western assessment, diagnosis, and treatment modalities, I pursued training in TCM at the Hong Kong Baptist University. Also, Buddhism and Daoism have been my long-time interests, and I have been regularly practicing *taiji* and meditation for about 10 years. I gradually put the bits and pieces together, reshaped myself, and developed my integrative practice model.

As I reflect on my personal process of learning Integrative Social Work, I am of the opinion that congruence and true assimilation are of paramount importance. After all, Integrative Social Work is about integration. In the learning process,

(continued)

(continued)

beginners are naturally fascinated by various indigenous health wisdoms and practices and will try out various new things. I did this as well. I found that at one point I had to reduce and simplify so that the techniques could be integrated into clinical practice. Perhaps Buddhism is a good example. To "know" Buddhism can be a lifetime pursuit. One can easily find literature on Buddhism, some ancient and some contemporary. However, reading extensively may not necessarily be translated into practice. If a person wishes to practice Buddhism, she or he may be better off not reading too much. She or he should devote her or his time and effort in everyday real-life practice. To me, as time goes by, Buddhism has been reduced to four words only: loving kindness, compassion, joy, and nonattachment. These principles guide my personal life, including my clinical practice.

PAMELA LEUNG

I started my clinical practice when I was a social worker in Hong Kong in a pioneer community rehabilitation service center for people with chronic illness, in 1994. At that time, psychosocial treatment for people with chronic illness (except mental illness) had just started to develop in Hong Kong. Professor Cecilia Chan was my mentor in this pioneer field of developing psychosocial intervention for people with cancer and their families in the community. With her guidance, I read extensively into mind–body medicine, holistic health, and complementary healing practice, adopting a Chinese medicine approach. I attended courses on *qigong*, meditation, acupressure, and Reichian healing. In addition, as a Christian, I was fascinated by the wisdom of Buddhism and Daoism and how they viewed and approached problems in life. Integrating Eastern health practices and philosophies with Western therapeutic techniques, Professor Chan and I conducted psychoeducational groups for cancer patients and started intervention studies for this integrated body–mind–spirit approach in Hong Kong. Later, I extended my work to families of people who had had heart attacks, strokes, or spinal cord injuries, as well as parents of children with chronic health conditions. Throughout my work, I witnessed people grow from life crises and experience a fuller life than they had before. What is more, I found that, in my clinical encounters, people facing more severe crises experienced more personal growth and transformation. Some of my clients were terminal cancer patients who were committed to helping and encouraging other people, even in the last days of their lives as their bodies wasted away. I have also met people with severe stroke magically recovering and becoming active advocates of patients' rights. One of our clients was a young lady who became quadriplegic as a result of a car accident. Her whole body was immobilized except for her head; she was dependent on others for every aspect of daily living. As a result of her energized spirit and charisma, she was able to attract people from different walks of life to join her in doing volunteer work for other people with physical disabilities.

(continued)

(continued)

Such enlightening stories are numerous. I was touched by these people who taught me about resilience and human dignity, who have validated my belief in human potential, strength, and compassion. I realized that, even when there is no cure, healing and personal transformation is always possible. The stories of these patients informed me that spirituality played an important part in their healing process. I am convinced that there is meaning and a life lesson to be learned in every instance of human suffering. The inspiration from these patients has shaped my belief and practice. Since then, I have focused my intervention on people's strengths and helped them to search for meaning in the midst of loss.

This strength- and meaning-focused orientation not only became the guiding principle for my professional work but also became a constant source of support and encouragement for me in my personal life. My daughter was born premature, with a cleft palate and Pierre Robin Syndrome. The latter is a defect with a recessed jaw that may cause breathing difficulties and suffocation. She was hospitalized for almost 2 months after her birth and required intensive medical care. During that period, I stayed in the post-natal intensive care unit of the hospital every day. I saw newborn babies with various birth defects, suffering, but also striving for survival. Looking at these babies, I realized not only how fragile life is but also how strong it is. I appreciated that life is embraced with courage and perseverance from the first day of birth. When I saw my daughter's suffering, I was hurt, but at the same time, I believed that it was God's blessing to let her experience the challenge. I told her when she was older how brave she was when she was a small baby and that she was endowed with the courage to cope with life challenges. I was also grateful to God for giving me a special child. I have learned to give unconditional love and be a loving parent. I learned how cherished life is.

Another time, when I had been working very hard at work, I was infected with tuberculosis. I underwent a 6-month treatment during which I had to take many pills and tolerate the side effects of nausea and fatigue. The feeling of being sick and tired was unpleasant. I experienced a low mood for the duration of the treatment. Yet, this experience has been very valuable and meaningful to me. I have a deeper understanding of suffering and empathy. Having been a patient, I understand how it feels to be sick, tired, and depressed. I realized that suffering cannot be taken away; it can only be experienced. I believe that empathy is the acknowledgment that one may never understand how another person feels in his or her situation but that one can accept unconditionally and respect how he or she feels. I found compassion to be the essence of empathy and healing. My own illness experience has helped me to be more empathetic and gave me more ideas about what may be helpful or inspiring for a person who is ill. In addition, the illness reminded me to reorient my goals and to adjust my lifestyle and my coping.

After recovering from tuberculosis, I started my own journey of self-discovery. I started to think about how I would like to lead my life, both professionally and personally. I joined different workshops on personal growth. I developed a deep curiosity and interest in the body–mind–spirit connection and the use of humanistic and

(continued)

(continued)

experiential approaches. I continuously participated in workshops and training in the Satir model and learned from Dr. John Banmen and Dr. Maria Gomori on how to do family reconstruction and to facilitate personal transformation. I was impressed by the healing power of experiencing intimacy and authenticity with myself and with others. I started to connect with others using not only my mind but also my spirit. I started to integrate even more body work and spirituality into my therapy with the help of my new learning. I also learned from Dr. Bennet Wong and Dr. Jock Mckeen of the Haven Institute of British Columbia the use of Reichian breathing, bodywork, and energy theories on emotional healing. The experience of unifying the body and mind through breathing, emotional expression, and authentic dialogue with others was a transforming experience for me. It also expanded my intervention repertoire.

I started my doctoral training in 2003 and studied the phenomenon of human beings turning suffering into growth and meaning making. I found that doing research is a way of documenting and integrating clinical experience into knowledge and is a rewarding experience. During my doctoral training, I read Buddhist psychology extensively and engaged in the regular practice of mindfulness meditation and yoga. Unlike learning Western therapy approaches, which require more extensive use of the mind, Eastern approaches require the learner to engage in total body–mind–spirit integration. After all, the process of developing my own integrative model was both a journey of personal growth and of professional enrichment. I am grateful to all my teachers and my patients and clients, who taught me so much in the process.

THE SEARCH FOR SPIRITUAL PEACE: CECILIA CHAN

University days awakened me, as I was exposed to socialist ideals and the search for freedom in the Hippie movement, and I witnessed the socioeconomic and political oppression in colonial Hong Kong in the 1970s. I also learned about barefoot doctors who provided community health services for the weak and disadvantaged people in China. Actively participating in social advocacy and collective action through the study of social work, I was committed to social justice and total personal development.

At my internship agency, my supervisor was a Rogerian counselor. He offered me 20 sessions of personal counseling and I participated in his personal growth groups. The hatred, anger, resentment, and sense of inferiority throughout the years of being raised in a single-parent family were washed away by the tears, self-disclosure, and self-affirmation. Experiencing total unconditional positive self-regard and forgiveness helped me to reconcile with my father. I decided that I was not going to stay a "victim" of my parents' marital breakdown. I could transform the childhood pain into the energy of love and compassion for others in need. I firmly believe that "there is no suffering that the soul cannot benefit from."

(continued)

(continued)

I worked as a community social worker in a low-income neighborhood for seven years after my graduation. Domestic violence, mental health problems, marital conflicts, teenage pregnancy, and gang fights were everyday events in the slum. Children were trapped in the culture of poverty, where they found no exit. As a community worker, I organized youth into volunteer teams, mobilized the residents to form a neighborhood watch, and empowered them to form their own organization for mutual help and support. I also felt empowered through working with my clients and witnessing their successes in improving their community.

After my doctoral studies, I decided to focus on advocating for chronic patients and children, for their welfare. My husband's profession as an oncologist contributed to my interest in working with cancer patients and their families. Through working with them, I realized how stressed patients can be, not only from their physical illness but also from the psychosocial and spiritual adaptations caused by their illness. Mr. S.K. Choi, leader of the New Voice Club (larynx cancer survivors' group), who was actively involved in the formation of the Alliance of Patients' Mutual Help Organizations, shared with me his view: "It is God's gift that I am put into the position to be involved in the patients' mutual help movement in Hong Kong." He recalled his frustration at not being able to speak after his surgery. He hid at home and threw temper tantrums at his wife for many years until he was nominated to join a voice training program in Japan that was sponsored by a Japanese larynegectomee organization. He was deeply impressed by how dedicated the Japanese survivors were in the promotion of voice training and community acceptance of survivors of larynx cancer. After his return to Hong Kong, he devoted all of his time to the patients' self-help movement.

There were exceptional cancer patients who taught me *qigong*, *taiji*, breathing exercises, massage, meditation, special diet, and other things that worked for them. I become curious about what TCM philosophies and practices could contribute to health promotion.

In working with children on welfare, I found that most of them had lost their fathers through accidents, suicide, illness, imprisonment, mental illness, gambling, or divorce. Their mothers were mostly sick, weak, or had little education, could not find work to support the family, and thus had to live on public welfare. When the mothers shared their painful stories, many of them collapsed in tears. Despite their pain, many of them lived with dignity, kept a tidy home, and provided well for their children. I helped them to retell the stories of their resilience and growth through their suffering. Many of them became peer counselors to help other women on welfare.

My mother suffered from frozen shoulder. The pain was devastating and she could not sleep. She had tried different treatments by a number of specialists but nothing helped. I took my mother to an acupuncturist who also taught her *qigong*. Her pain was finally under control. I realized that there are traditional wisdoms and practices that I knew very little about. Subsequently, I learned several types of *taiji* and *qigong* from various masters and attended classes on Reiki, acupuncture, and massage.

(continued)

(continued)

There are Eastern wisdoms and philosophies about life that are not easily found in Western therapies. I went to acupuncture classes and became interested in simplifying techniques that therapists can use in day-to-day counseling.

From then on, instead of focusing on problems, I focused on strengths. Instead of complaining and blaming, I learned to take deep breaths and count blessings. Instead of staying hurt in times of bad moods, I meditate. Great masters such as Thich Nhat Hanh, David Spiegel, Robert Neimeyer, and Jon Kuber-Zinn visit Hong Kong occasionally and run retreats and classes for us. There is so much wisdom in life that we do not know. I wish I could share the skills and values of Integrative Body–Mind–Spirit Social Work with more professionals and serve our clients and families more effectively.

Integrative Body–Mind–Spirit
Social Work

A Theoretical and Practice Framework of Integrative Body–Mind–Spirit Social Work

The Philosophical Underpinnings of Integrative Body–Mind–Spirit Social Work: Holistic Wellness and the Beauty of Harmony

Integrative Body–Mind–Spirit Social Work attempts to expand beyond existing social work practice models and integrate a more holistic orientation based on Eastern philosophies and therapeutic techniques in order to create effective, positive, and transformative changes in individuals and families. A core philosophical position undertaken by Integrative Social Work is its holistic orientation, which emphasizes the body–mind–spirit connection with the larger environment. The emphasis is on a "both-and" perspective that views the client as a whole person with strengths and resources.

A highly differentiated service system is a sign of advancement of our modern technology-oriented society, in which specialization based on scientific knowledge and expertise is promoted and valued. Although we certainly benefit from this setup, such a system can easily lend itself to compartmentalization and disconnection when little awareness or understanding is paid to the whole. Such disconnection can happen at the individual level (such as the use of psychotropic medications without consideration of age, gender, unique individual physiology, psychological impact, and developmental characteristics) and at the systems level (institutions that focus on care versus control, education versus treatment, or empowerment versus patronization). When this happens, well-intended, but disjointed, helping efforts can become barriers for client change.

The following scenario is familiar to many social work practitioners and certainly familiar to the first author when she codeveloped and evaluated Integrative Family and Systems Treatment (I-FAST) for home-based populations (Lee et al., 2009; Lee, Greene, Solovey, Grove, & Fraser, in press):

The Smith family received intensive home-based treatment from a local mental health agency, primarily because of severe emotional and behavioral problems in their 11-year-old girl, Tracy. Tracy stayed with her mother, Ruth (27 years old), and her 5-year-old brother, Tony. Ruth moved back home and stayed with her mother primarily because she was at risk of losing her children if she failed to provide a stable home environment for them. Ruth did not finish high school, got involved with drugs and alcohol as a teenager, and was pregnant at the age of 16. She worked odd jobs to support herself and did not have a stable employment history. Different boyfriends whom Ruth had lived with physically and sexually abused Tracy. Tracy was diagnosed with posttraumatic stress disorder and intermittent explosive disorder. In addition, she washed her hands compulsively and was obsessed with the presence of an unnamed monster that lurked near her day and night. Tracy did poorly in school and had severe temper tantrums when she could not get her way. She did not have friends because she was aggressive with peers. Tracy was on seven medications, receiving play therapy from an outpatient child therapist, under the attention of the school guidance counselor, and regularly seeing an educational psychologist and a psychiatrist. The family had a case manager from Children's Services, an intensive home-based case manager from the local mental health agency, as well as an outpatient therapist who provided family therapy to the Smith family. In addition, Ruth was court ordered to attend a parenting group as part of the case plan.

Despite the hectic treatment schedule the family had to stick to, Tracy did not get better. Tracy had trouble adjusting to the numerous medications that were prescribed to her for various diagnoses. She had been on Thorazine (sedative) Depakote, Topamax and Trileptal (mood stabilizers), and Haldol and Seroquel (antipsychotic medications). She complained of drowsiness, dry mouth, rapid heartbeat, muscle spasms, stiffness, tremors, and so on. Drug holidays and different medications, including Cogentin (to offset potential side effects of Haldol, including stiffness and tremors), were used to control the side effects of psychotropic medications. The family was confused by the treatment orientations and approaches of different helping professionals. The case manager from Children's Services was suspicious of the mother's ability to protect the children and was inclined to remove Tracy and Tony from the home. The psychiatrist shared concerns regarding the consistency of the mother in administering medications and monitoring Tracy's emotional problems. The goal of their intervention was safety, not changes in how Ruth dealt with Tracy's problems. In addition, the preferred approach was to have the child settled by outside forces, such as medication and removal, and not by the family. The family therapist, however, perceived the punitive and patronizing external control by Children's Services and the psychiatrist as barriers to the family's control of their out-of-control child. Her focus of treatment was about utilizing strengths of the family and changing the

(continued)

(continued)

family's interactional pattern so that the mother was empowered to help Tracy regain control over her problems. Tracy's individual therapist, who provided play therapy sessions for Tracy, was doubtful of Ruth's ability to provide a "secure base" for Tracy to process her earlier trauma. Ruth participated in a parenting group that used a solution-focused approach to empower parents to find small changes and utilize their existing resources to become better parents. Despite the hopelessly confusing messages from the diverse, but well-intentioned, helping professionals, the family was still struggling to get better and to stay a whole family.

CONTEMPORARY KNOWLEDGE BASE OF A HOLISTIC ORIENTATION

While a holistic orientation is not yet mainstream in social work, therapy, and human services, the notion of mind–body connectedness has long been described by influential figures in history. Freud noted that the mind could influence the body, which could lie completely outside our conscious awareness sometimes (Freud, 1961). Carl Jung also documented that the spiritual core exists in our psyches and strives to find meaning and balance in our lives (Jung, Adler, & Hull, 1977; Jung & Wolfgang, 1955). Even Gustav Fechner, the founder of experimental modern psychology, wrote a book titled *Life after Death* and proposed that man lives on earth not once, but three times, in a deeply spiritual way (Fechner, 1906). The term "holism"—that the whole is more than the sum of the individual parts—was first used by South African philosopher Jan Christian Smuts in 1925 to counteract the trend of fragmenting and reducing living systems to atomistic units in biology and science (Shannon, 2002). Holism constitutes an important philosophical foundation of the Integral movement in medical health care (Shannon, 2002) and Integral Psychology (Wilber, 2000). There are contemporary knowledge and thoughts that also support the shift to a more holistic and integral approach in health care and psychology.

A Systems Perspective

General systems theory was first proposed by Lugwig von Bertalanffy, an Austrian-born biologist, to identify universal principles that can be applied to general systems in nature (Bertalanffy, 1968). Gregory Bateson, an anthropologist, introduced the use of a systems perspective to study human systems when he started working at Mental Research Institute in the 1950s. A systems perspective is fundamental to family systems theory, which forms the basis for most contemporary family treatment and therapy approaches (Chibucos & Leite, 2005). Basic concepts of a systems perspective include the following:

(1) feedback, which describes the process of regulation and control of the system through the operation of positive and negative feedback
(2) recursiveness, which denotes the mutual interaction and influence among different components in a system. The concept of recursiveness also implies reciprocal causality versus linear causality and that all systems are self-regulating
(3) connectionism, which refers to the interrelatedness of all parts of a system and that everything is connected
(4) morphostasis and morphogensis, which contribute to stability and change in systems (Bateson, 1972; Becvar & Becvar, 2003; Keeney & Thomas, 1986).

Quantum theory further expands the study of general systems theory to the study of second-order cybernetics. Second-order cybernetics challenges the assumption of the existence of an independent, objective reality and recognizes the influence of the observer on the observed phenomena. Fundamental concepts include self-reference (whatever we see reflect our personal qualities), organization closure (autonomy of a system), autopoiesis (the process of self-generation and self-organization), structural determinism (the system determines the range of structural variations acceptable without loss of identity), and structural coupling (the system responds to changing context within a range determined by the structure of the respective system). In essence, second-order cybernetics postulates that understanding is possible only from the perspective of the subject who is doing the questioning, describing, or explaining and that there are multiple realities (Becvar & Becvar, 2003).

A systems perspective brings forth the following views of change in human systems:

1. Wholeness: The whole is more than the sum of individual parts.
2. Interrelatedness and connectedness: Change in one part of a system leads to change in other parts of the system.
3. Change is constant.
4. A strengths-based perspective: Feedback processes are self-corrective and regulating for the functional survival of the system.
5. Participation: Understanding is possible only from the perspective of the subject who is doing the questioning, describing, or explaining.
6. The existence of multiverses that are experienced, lived, and interpreted by the involved individuals.

Quantum Theory

Albert Einstein postulated that $E = mc^2$, implying that energy and matter are merely different forms of the same thing (that is, all matters can be waves and particles). This is an important revolution in modern scientific thought. Phenomena in the physical world are more connected than people have traditionally assumed. David Bohm, a quantum physicist who studies, among other subjects, holography and the principles of holograms, elaborates on the proposition of "wholeness:"

> Relativity and, even more important, quantum mechanics have strongly suggested . . . that the world cannot be analyzed into separate and independently existing parts. Moreover, each part somehow involves all the others: contains them or enfolds them. The fact suggests that the sphere of ordinary material life and sphere of mystical experiences have a shared order and that this will allow a fruitful relationship between them
>
> (Wilber, 1985, p. 44)

These ideas have exerted an important influence in the study of consciousness and human behaviors. David Bohm, together with John Briggs and David Peat, continues to explore the implications of quantum mechanics and chaos theory on creativity, change, and human life (Bohm, 1998; Bohm & Peat, 2000; Briggs & Peat, 1999). Alwyn Scott, an applied mathematician (1996, 2000), convincingly suggested that nonlinear science implies that consciousness is more dynamic, interconnected, and nondeterminant than conventional functionalist approaches believe. Stuart Hameroff and Roger Penrose apply aspects of quantum theory and propose the "Orch OR" model for consciousness (Orchestrated Objective Reduction). While explaining that the model is beyond the scope of the current discussion, they essentially propose that conscious thought and understanding is a self-organizing and nonalgorithmic process, which is neither deterministic nor random (Hameroff, 1998; Hameroff & Penrose, 1996; Penrose, 1997, 1994; Penrose & Hameroff, 1995). The development in science provides an important impetus for social work and other helping professionals to revisit our assumptions of a linear, disconnected view of consciousness, human behaviors, experiences, and change (Hameroff, Kaszniak, & Scott, 1996; Velmans, 2000).

Integral Psychology: Ken Wilber

Ken Wilber, who is at the forefront of Integral Psychology, attempts to include insights, knowledge, and scientific evidence from major schools of thoughts (e.g., cognitive science, neuropsychology, psychotherapy, psychiatry, quantum approaches) and diverse ancient thought traditions ranging from premodern, modern, and postmodern sources to formulate a multiverse, constructive, contextual knowledge base for understanding human consciousness and development (Wilber, 2000). Using the two dimensions of "the individual versus the collective" and "the interior versus the exterior," he came up with four quadrants in which evolution can take place: Evolution can be (1) individual and interior (forms of consciousness), (2) collective and interior (forms of cultural life), (3) individual and exterior (physical forms), and (4) collective and exterior (social forms). Wilber proposes that each quadrant is a part of the whole (Wilber & Walsh, 2000). Focusing on any one of them at any specific domains or levels will only lead to "partial truths." Integration means the recognition of all quadrants as mutually supporting, which need to be simultaneously explored, apprehended, and confirmed. Thus, Integral Psychology takes an "all level, all quadrant" approach to the study of human development (Wilber, 2000, Wilber & Walsh, 1996).

One major contribution of Ken Wilber's thought is his recognition of the "shadow" that people are usually not aware of or do not recognize (Wilber, 2001). For instance, he suggests that the enduring truths of premodern insights include the ideas of levels or dimensions of reality and consciousness, reaching from matter to body to mind to soul and spirit, with the spirit fully and equally present at all of these levels. The "shadow" of these insights was the use of these conceptions in a rigidly hierarchical fashion to justify the oppression of people in ancient traditional societies. Likewise, modernity provides us the knowledge and tools for "differentiation" but also leads to "dissociation" (the shadow of scientific materialism). Postmodernity recognizes interpretation and meaning as an intrinsic fabric of the universe. Such a recognition allows postmodern knowledge to be inclusive and multiverse, although it can also fall into extreme relativism where there is "no within, no deep, just the surface, a flatland holism." (Wilber, 2000, pp.169–170, 192). A truly holistic/integral method of knowing ensures that the important differentiations of modernity are fully integrated and equally honors the phenomenal, social, and scientific accounts of the evolution of human consciousness (Wilber, 2000).

Cultural Traditions Relevant to a Holistic Orientation

While a systems perspective, quantum theory, and integral thought is more rooted in scholarly domains, a holistic orientation is inevitably influenced by many ancient traditions, philosophies, and practices, including, but not limited to, Ayurveda, Traditional Chinese Medicine (TCM), aromatherapy, and Native American medicine. Ayurveda, a Sanskrit word derived from the Sanskrit words "ayur" (life) and veda (knowledge), is an ancient healing tradition in India that goes back 5000 years (Brooks, 2002; Varma, 1995). It has its root in ancient Vedic literature and encompasses life, body, mind, and spirit. TCM also capitalizes on the holistic concept of body–mind–spirit connection and balance as the roots of health and illness (Lu, 1994; Wong, 1987). Acupuncture, which is based on TCM, is gaining increasing prominence in health care (Motl, 2002). Aromatherapy describes the art and science of using plant oils and herbs for health, well-being, and medical treatment (d'Angelo, 2002). It has its roots in India (Damian & Damian, 1995), China, Egypt, and the Middle East (Lyons & Petrucelli, 1987). Native American medicine, another holistic tradition, proposes that the person consists of four elements: spiritual, emotional, physical, and mental. Illnesses are caused by a person being out of balance (Lee Winter, 1996). All these ancient traditions have existed for thousands of years. While each has their unique features, beliefs, and practices, they all share in common a belief in the body–mind–spirit connection.

INTEGRATIVE BODY–MIND–SPIRIT SOCIAL WORK: A HOLISTIC PERSPECTIVE

Integrative Body–Mind–Spirit Social Work adopts a holistic perspective in treatment. Holistic social work treatment involves an orientation to the total context; attention to the relatedness between people, events, or objects; and a preference for explaining, predicting, and responding to events based on such relationships. Holistic approaches are dialectic and rely on experience-based knowledge rather than on abstract and rule-based logic. Consequently, there is an emphasis on change, recognition of contradiction, recognition of the need for multiple perspectives, and a search for the "middle way" between opposing propositions and perspectives (Nisbett, Peng, Choi, & Norenzayan, 2001). A holistic social work treatment perspective would not compartmentalize the person, the family, the systems, or the environment. Assessment and treatment would focus on collaboration among systems and utilization of client strengths.

While sharing the ideas and concepts suggested by systems perspective, the integral movement, and other cultural traditions that emphasize holism, the holistic orientation of Integrative Body–Mind–Spirit Social Work was particularly influenced by the Eastern philosophies of the yin–yang perspective, philosophical Daoism, and Buddhism. In addition, the practice of Integrative Social Work adopts relevant knowledge of TCM, whose development was strongly influenced by the yin–yang perspective. Prior to a detailed description of Integrative Body–Mind–Spirit Social Work, it will be beneficial to briefly describe these philosophies, for they informed the development of the conceptual framework of Integrative Body–Mind–Spirit Social Work Practice. A coherent conceptual framework for social work practice ensures the following: (1) A detailed description of the conceptual framework of I-BMSSW enables social work professionals to critically examine, question, validate, and revise the assumptions and values of the practice approach prior to adopting the approach in their practice, and (2) it provides a cognitive map for developing assessment and treatment techniques in the process of change. The following clarifications are necessary prior to the discussion:

1. The yin–yang perspective, Daoism, and Buddhism all consist of rich and diverse traditions with fascinating histories regarding their development. The discussion of these Eastern philosophies is framed in the context of their implications for social work practice with individual and families, and the discussions are neither intended to be comprehensive nor exhaustive. We have included a more detailed description of each philosophy in Appendix A for readers who are interested in learning more about these philosophies.

2. Integrative Social Work utilizes wisdoms from these Eastern philosophies to provide a framework for understanding human experience and facilitating client change in social work treatment. The approach was not developed based on either one or all of the philosophical traditions. Consequently, we neither claim nor attempt to integrate these philosophies; in the same manner, we neither claim nor attempt to integrate all Eastern and Western philosophical traditions.

3. Eastern philosophies and traditions are diverse. We have only included the yin–yang perspective, Daoism, and Buddhism in formulating Integrative Body–Mind–Spirit Social Work. However, this is in no way minimizing the importance of other philosophies or traditions. For instance, Confucianism significantly influences the development of eastern philosophies, values, and customs. While Integrative Social Work emphasizes collective existence and interrelationships between people, its development is less influenced by the philosophy of Confucianism than the yin–yang perspective, Daoism, and Buddhism. Likewise, Ayurvedic medicine is the oldest healing system in the East and was the root for Chinese and Tibetan medicine.

4. Traditionally, the yin–yang perspective, Daoism, and Buddhism have been treated both as philosophical orientations and as religious beliefs and practices. Our discussion focuses purely on these traditions as philosophies and not religions. Religious conversion does not have a place in the learning and practice of Integrative Social Work.

THE YIN–YANG PERSPECTIVE

The concepts of yin and yang have been described as fundamental to the Chinese view of the world. No one knows any historical details about the people who first formulated such ideas, nor do we have any ancient texts that set forth their ideas. However, there is general consensus that these ideas were developed among students of *The Book of Change* (*Yijing*, formerly known as *I Ching*). The yin–yang perspective can be perceived as a systems perspective described in ancient Chinese terminology. Based on the perception and long-term observation of nature, ancient Chinese scholars believed that all things in the world could be classified into two broad categories: yin and yang. Yin and yang are the two fundamental forces or building blocks of all things that define, make up, or are in life (Höchsmann, 2001; Wong, 1997). Yin is the dark principle, represented by darkness, softness, stillness, and receptive energy. It is frequently symbolized by the moon, night, winter, earth, and women. Yang is the light principle, represented by brightness, hardness, movement, and creative energy. It is oftentimes symbolized by the sun, day, summer, heaven, and men. Common examples of yin-yang pairs are the earth and sky, night and day, moon and sun, cold and heat, winter and summer, and women and men. There is a constant interplay between the yin and yang forces: for example, as the sun goes down, the moon rises, which brings an end to the day, but also the anticipation of a new day. It is important to recognize that although yin and yang are contrasting forces, they are also mutually facilitating and mutually repressing. In fact, both yin and yang originate from the same universal and nontransient force, the *Dao*, from which life originates and from which one can never be truly separated (Chan, 2000). As such, the dualistic holism conceptualization of the yin-yang perspective is embedded within a monistic and nondual conception of reality (Canda & Furman, 1999).

The classic yin–yang symbol further illustrates the dynamic interplay, intricate balance, complementarity, and inseparability of the diverse and contrasting life forces (Figure 1.1). The boundary between yin and yang is not a straight, rigid line. Instead, the boundary is moving and changing—it is depicted as a smooth and curving line. Also, no matter where you attempt to divide this circle in half, the divided section will always contain both yin and yang. There is always the presence of yin in the yang half and the presence of yang in the yin half, even if it is just a small dot. It represents balance,

FIGURE **1.1.** The yin–yang symbol.

mutuality, change, and interdependence. The inseparability of yin and yang is grounded in the belief that both the yin and yang forces originate from the *Dao*.

A yin–yang perspective suggests the following views of change and health:

1. Everything is connected. Because yin and yang originate from the same universal and nontransient force, the *Dao*, from which life originates and from which one can never truly be separated, they have an inseparable relationship and are connected in a fundamental way.
2. Relativism. Yin and yang are relative and not absolute concepts. The designation of something as yin or yang is always relative to, or in comparison with, some other things. Among a group of yin subjects, there can be elements that are considered relatively yang. For instance, the sun and daytime are considered yang in relation to the moon and the night. But within daytime, early morning is considered yin compared with noon.
3. Mutuality and interdependence. Yin and yang are mutually dependent. One cannot exist without the other, and they cannot flourish on their own. Their relationship is complementary and connected.
4. Change is constant. Yin and yang are dynamic forces that are changing and evolving at all times. The sun goes down and the moon rises. Hot summer yields to the cool autumn and cold winter before everything blooms again in the spring.
5. Dynamic equilibrium. Yin and yang are mutually facilitating as well as repressing. These are two contrasting forces that maintain a dynamic equilibrium together.
6. The centrality of balance and harmony. There is no value attached to any one attribute or characteristic. The criterion for well-being or health is not an overwhelming abundance of either yin or yang but a balance of the contrasting forces that exist in harmony with each other.
7. Attainment of balance can only happen in movement. Although a balance of contrasting forces in harmony with each other is central to the state of health or well-being, such a balance is not a static state but is accomplished in a process of dynamic movement.

Energetic and Restful

To illustrate these concepts, just think about the following examples that mostly describe daily experiences: After a day of energetic activities, we sleep or rest when we are tired. The energetic and restful states are inseparable and interdependent, as one cannot exist without the other. It is hard to imagine someone feeling "tired" if he or she sleeps well. We wake up and are on the go again (change is constant) before the cycle repeats itself. However, if someone is under great pressure and is constantly deprived of rest or sleep, he or she will eventually experience health problems (a system out of balance is in a state of disharmony). On the reverse, if a person suffers from major depression and sleeps most of the time, there will also be negative physiological and psychological consequences. Again, neither energetic nor restful is better than the other. Energy in excess or rest in excess is harmful to a person. It is well known that in the manic phase of bipolar disorder, the person suffers from energy in excess. The boundless upsurge of energy and activities is a clear example of an unbalanced emotional and physiological system that is in disharmony with the rest of the body.

In addition, the accomplishment of balance and harmony is not a static or end state but is attained in a process of dynamic movement. A good illustration would be riding a bicycle. One can maintain balance only when the bicycle is in motion. However, a bicycle is in motion only when a person maintains a dynamic balance between the contrasting forces of steering right or left. Similarly, movement created by a dynamic balance of diverse forces of life facilitates development and change in life.

In sum, a yin–yang perspective is fundamentally holistic because of the intricate connectedness between diverse forces and phenomena in the world and in our daily lives. It speaks to a view of change that emphasizes mutuality, complementarity, interdependence, and dynamic equilibrium. Such a perspective does not emphasize or value one quality, state, characteristic, or phenomenon over the other, because all forces are necessary for facilitating a beneficial process of change for healthy human existence. Also, the designation of forces as yin and yang is relative and defined by the context. Because of the nonabsolute nature of forces or phenomena, categorizing them as stable, permanent entities is unhelpful. The criterion for well-being or health is based on the concept of balance and harmony and can only be attained in a state of dynamic movement. This perspective speaks to a holistic, "both-and" orientation to change (Laird, 2001) and away from an "either-or" perspective.

DAOIST TEACHINGS

Daoism, previously known as Taoism, is an ancient Chinese philosophy that is primarily about how one can live a harmonious or true life. *Dao* literally means "the way." *The Book of Change, Yijing*, was a prime inspiration for Daoism. *Yijing* symbology, which contained the ancient sages' understanding of the world, provided useful metaphors for Daoist followers to explain and navigate life's subtle forces and processes (Kohn, 2000). Daoism consists of heterogeneous traditions (Kirkland, 2004; Oldstone-Moore, 2003; Kohn,

2001). Daoist teachings primarily originated in three texts: the *Daode-jing* (previously known as *Tao-te-ching*), *Zhuangzi* (previously known as *Chuang-tzu*), and *Neiyang* (previously known as *Nei-yeh*). The *Daodejing* and *Zhuangzi* were universally renowned as the primary texts of classical Daoism. The *Daodejing* is the most often translated book among the European Sino-logue, and it is estimated that 200 versions in different Western languages have been translated, the first Latin translation appearing before 1788 (Cheng, 1995). The focuses of these three texts are diverse and different, although all share the idea that one can live one's life wisely only if he or she learns how to live in accord with life's natural but unseen forces and subtle processes and not based on society's established ideals and concerns. The following is a brief description of each tradition. Please refer to Appendix A for a more detailed description of the teachings.

The *Daodejing*

The *Daodejing* is a collection of poetry and aphorisms that set forth the basic teachings of *Dao*. Laozi (formerly known as Lao Tzu), who lived in ancient China around 5 BCE, is believed to have written this text. The *Daodejing* describes a universal, nontransient force, the *Dao*, from which life originates and from which one can never truly be separated (Chan, 2000; Oldstone-Moore, 2003). There is unity amidst differences and diversity as *Dao* gives life to all things and brings them into harmony. The nature of the *Dao* is dynamic, interconnected, mutual, and relative. Consequently, making value judgments regarding the nature of any attribute has no place in Daoist teach-ings, as nothing is inherently good or bad. Being straight is not preferred to being crooked, because both states are connected in a constant process of change. Instead, maintaining a dynamic balance between contrasting forces is considered beneficial.

The *Daodejing* also revealed the transient, unreliable, but inevitable, nature of language, which primarily transmits and supports socially constructed stan-dards of all kinds (Chan, 2000). Because of the nature of dynamic revertism of the *Dao* and the transient nature of all earthly things as described by language, one should not be bound by socially constructed standards, such as moral or immoral, good or bad, existing or nonexisting, difficult or easy, etc., as these standards are relative and transient (Cheng, 1995). Instead, one should learn to perceive the unseen reality, which is the source of our life and our sustenance. By being in harmony with nature, the *Dao*, one can be freed from unnecessary competition, struggle, and confusion, and can better return to behaviors that are "natural" for us.

Daoism maintains a deep trust in the intelligence, inner wisdom, healing capacities, and goodness of human beings, and such a trust also extends to the nature and the cosmos. *Wu-wei*, an important teaching in the *Daodejing*, means nonaction or noninterference (Koening & Spano, 1998). When a person does not focus or force an act but practices *wu-wei*, she or he will be able to perceive reality and understand the world more holistically. Daoist teachings promote a simultaneous and unconscious knowledge that fosters spontaneity, respects instinct, intuition, and mystery (Watts, 1957). When living in harmony with the *Dao*, a person can relax and let go of his or her self-conscious and goal-driven work. He or she will be able to make decisions spontaneously based on experience and trust the mind and body to know what needs to be done.

The *Daodejing* proposed a life orientation that transcends the self, social standards, and the unreliable and perishable pursuits of wealth and objects. Instead, one should understand, attend to, and tune in to the *Dao* so that one can be in harmony with the natural forces of the universe and attain the ultimate peace and unity with the *Dao*. In addition, the *Daodejing* suggested a way for one to link with the *Dao* through meditative introspection.

Zhuangzi

Zhuangzi is a 33-chapter text that contains fascinating parables and stories. *Zhuangzi* advocates reverting to a boundless "heavenly mechanism" of life that is independent of the psycho-cultural constructs of good or bad (Höchsmann, 2001). The primary thesis is that life can never be fully predicted. If we just simply enjoy and adjust our life as it unfolds, our life can be pleasant and enjoyable. A "real person" simply abides and flows with the life processes rather than trying to manage, plan, and control life's events. "To see things from the light of Heaven, means to see things from the point of view that which transcends the finite, which is Dao" (*Zhuangzi*, Chi'I Wu Lun, in Chang, 1983). Such a person is in accord with the reality that is boundless and unending. Similar to the *Daodejing*, *Zhuangzi* emphasizes transcendence from worldly attachments and struggles. A person who understands "the way" transcends emotions and limitations (Fung, 1948). Consequently, the life orientation suggested by *Zhuangzi* transcends socially based constructs, such as good or bad, desirable or undesirable, and useful or useless. The ideal depicted in *Zhuangzi* has always appealed to many Eastern and Western readers. One does not really have to solve any problems. We simply have to see life as it truly is and allow life's surprises to unfold. *Zhuangzi*, unlike the *Daodejing*, does not concern itself with political or moral issues. It primarily contains a philosophical description of "truth and boundless living." *Zhuangzi* also does not provide any specific directions as to how one might attain the described ideal.

Neiyang

Neiyang literally means *inner cultivation*. Whereas *Zhuangzi* raises epistemological issues and the *Daodejing* raises moral and political issues, *Neiyang* is primarily concerned with biospiritual cultivation and offers advice and directions for guiding one to cultivate oneself (Kirkland, 2004; Oldstone-Moore, 2003). The teachings of *Neiyang* begin with the assumption of a powerful life reality called *qi*, or life energy. This life energy, *qi*, is present both within all things and all around them. It is fundamental to our living world as well as to each living being. In fact, *qi* forms a fundamental concept in TCM, including the practice of acupuncture. *Neiyang* recognizes the existence and the importance of an unseen life force that is generative in nature, operates within the world, and transcends things of diverse natures. Yet, the idea that different entities with their own distinct identities are filled with the same life force reinforces a holistic perspective of the world and the belief that all things are interconnected. To summarize succinctly, *Neiyang* proposed that the "heart-mind" is the center of an individual's existence. Our "heart-mind" oftentimes becomes confused as our thoughts and passions are intensified by diverse desires, such as wealth, status, and love. *Neiyang* suggested practices for a person to keep his or her heart–mind balanced and tranquil and to not be overwhelmed by excessive desires or emotions. If one can maintain a tranquil "heart-mind," one can naturally receive and retain healthy life energies and live a long, healthy, and pleasant life (Kirkland, 2004; Oldstone-Moore, 2003).

View of Change and Life Based on Daoist Teachings

Despite differences among different traditions of Daoism, they address the primary concern of how to live one's life wisely by learning how to live in accordance with life's natural forces and not on the transient basis of society's established ideals and concerns. Central to the teachings of Daoism is the belief in a constantly changing universe, a connection of all things to each other, an emphasis on relinquishing human efforts to control others and nature, and ways to be in harmony with the *Dao*. Daoism, among different traditions, suggests the following views regarding change and life:

1. A holistic, systemic cosmic view of nature. *Dao* is a force that gives life to all things and brings them into harmony. Therefore, there is unity amidst diversity and everything is connected.
2. Reality is constantly changing and in a state of becoming. *Dao* is constantly changing and evolving in a dynamic and complementary way.
3. The centrality of balance. Movement and change does not happen in a linear or "either-or" manner. Because of the connectedness

and complementarity of phenomena, maintaining a dynamic balance between any set of contrasting forces is necessary for movement and change. Such a view of change is consistent with a yin–yang perspective that recognizes the existence of contrasting, mutually interdependent, and complementary pairs of all phenomena. "If you want to become full, let yourself be empty. If you want to be reborn, let yourself die" (Mitchell, 1988, p. 22).

4. A trust in the innate wisdom, intelligence, and healing power of human beings, nature, and the cosmos. One should observe, appreciate, and be in harmony with the ways of nature instead of attempting to achieve self-conscious desires and goals, which are transient, illusory, and divisive. Virtue, as innate healing power, comes about when a person practices nonaction and is in harmony with the natural course of human life.

5. Unhelpful actions. Excessive emotions, desires, control, and planning is not helpful, as these are relative, transient, divisive, and not in alignment with natural forces. In addition, because there is no way a person can control the *Dao*, and consequently, control or plan his or her life, one should instead respect and follow nature's forces.

6. Transcendence of self, excess emotions, worldly desires, and social standards allow virtue (*de*) to come about and a person to be in harmony with the *Dao* and attain ultimate peace or a boundless life. One can do so by practicing nonaction *(wu-wei)* through meditative introspection, being mindful, as suggested by the *Daodejing*, or by practicing self-cultivation, as proposed by *Neiyang*.

In sum, Daoism advocates a simple, mindful life that is open to the natural unfolding of life. The ultimate objective is to attain human–nature integration. True freedom is not about how much power or resources one has. True freedom comes from within, through nurturing a clear, nonjudgmental heart that is open and receptive to the natural unfolding of life (Höchsmann, 2001). True knowledge is about knowing what one can know and what one cannot. Being bothered by what one cannot know is unnecessary. True living is living mindfully in the moment. By living fully in the moment, the transient and elusive desires for fame, wealth, and power are no longer relevant to living a full life (Chang, 1990).

BUDDHIST TEACHINGS

Buddhism is a philosophy that originated in ancient India. "Buddhism" literally means "the way of enlightenment," and "Buddha" means "enlightened person." Seeing life as full of suffering, Buddhism is primarily concerned about freeing people from such sufferings (Huston, 2003). Buddhism consists of diverse traditions, although all traditions are primarily based on the original teachings of the Buddha. When Buddhism gained popularity, it became institutionalized and ritualized. When Buddhism spread to China in approximately A.D. 400. and met Daoism, it led to an important revisit of the original purpose and focus of Buddhism. Zen Buddhism, a revitalized back-to-the-basics form of Buddhism, evolved from this tradition around A.D.600–A.D.700 It spread from China to Japan in the sixteenth century and then from Japan to the West in the beginning of the twentieth century. More recent Buddhist monks and philosophers, such as the Dalai Lama and Thich Nhat Hanh, influenced the discourse of spirituality in the Western world. Ideas like mindfulness practices, loving kindness, compassion, forgiveness, and nonattachment have become part of the discourse around spirituality and mental health interventions in social work practice (e.g., Ryan & Deci, 2000; Teasdale, Segal, & Williams, 2003; Teasdale et al., 2000).

The Buddha's teachings are a model of the elimination of suffering built on the Law of Dependent Origination, which he discovered while mediating under a bodhi tree just before attaining enlightenment (Sik, 2005a; Sik, 2005b). He perceived human existence and the endless process of cyclic existence as a long path of suffering (Bhikkhu Bodhi, 2000, p. 601). Through *bhikkhus* (careful attention), the Buddha was enlightened and realized that "when there is birth, aging-and-death comes to be; aging-and-death has birth as the condition" (Bhikkhu Bodhi, 2000, p. 601). What the Buddha noticed was that phenomena were conditional; that is, the coming of one phenomenon will bring about the next. This awareness of the dependent nature of the origination of all phenomena constitutes the theoretical foundation of all Buddhist teachings (Sik, 2005a; Sik, 2005b). The Law of Dependent Origination suggests the following nature and phenomena (Sik, 2005a):

- Impermanence: Phenomena are always changing, depending on the gestalt of cause and condition.
- "No-self": All phenomena are inherently empty in nature, because it is always a consequence of something else and therefore do not have an independent, distinguishable, or permanent "self." Such a view avoids emotional or sensory attachment because of the illusionary nature of reality.
- Phenomena exist interdependently and relatively, based on a "cause and effect" relationship: the Law of Karma.
- Middle path: The similar and different relationships between phenomena (such as the seed and the apple) promote a middle position that avoids the notion of duality, an either-or position, or a rigid attachment to the notions of "there definitely is" or "there definitely is not."

The Buddha observed that ignorance is the fuel of this cyclic existence and thus the root of suffering. Consequently, the key to eliminating suffering is to eliminate ignorance through the development of true knowledge and wisdom (Sik, 2005a). The Buddha perceives that thoughts and actions dictate a person's well-being and future. Deluded emotions, thoughts, and actions fueled by ignorance are the primary cause of suffering. The practice of mindfulness permits a person to stop ignorance and develop true knowledge, which liberates a person from suffering.

View of Human Change

The following succinctly summarizes the view of human change and life as espoused by Buddhist teachings:

- Life is constantly evolving depending on the cause and the condition of different phenomena.
- Sufferings can come from normal problems of living that are just an integral part of living (the "first dart" of suffering such as birth, aging, sickness, and death), or the mental reaction to the normal problems of living (the "second dart" of suffering).
- Interdependence of phenomena. Phenomena exist interdependently and relatively, based on a "cause and effect" relationship.
- The world is impermanent, and there is no distinguishable existence of an independent entity.
- Because of the impermanence of phenomena and nonexistence of an ultimate real "self," attachment to worldly emotions, desires, objects, and thoughts forms the basis of ignorance and only invites troubles and suffering. Nonattachment liberates a person from ignorance and suffering.

AN INTEGRATIVE VIEW OF CHANGE

The social work profession has traditionally been concerned with change. We have described ourselves as "change agents." Traditionally, social work treatment adopts a linear view of change, in that there is an implicit assumption of linearity between problems and solutions. If one can understand the cause of the problem, one will be able to use the specific therapeutic techniques, as suggested by an individual theory, to solve the problem and attain health. In addition, there are the assumptions that clients should take an active stance to control, master, and overcome their problems (Lee, 2005). Regardless of diverse social work treatment approaches, the reduction or elimination of clients' presented problems constitutes the primary treatment goal, and an individual's well-being, empowerment, and self-actualization also inform the ultimate concern of social work treatment.

The yin–yang perspective, Daoism, and Buddhist philosophies, however, provide a unique view of change and health that is different from the assumptions and practices of mainstream social work treatment. Such a view of change and health emphasizes mutuality, complementarity, and balance. Using the metaphor of yin–yang and the resulting focus on holistic dualism, the views of change and health as described by Eastern philosophies are different but complementary to the position adopted by conventional social work treatment. The views regarding change and health, as espoused by the yin–yang perspective, Daoism, and Buddhist philosophies inform the development of Integrative Social Work Practice. Also, the yin–yang perspective, Daoism, and Buddhist philosophies have diverse origins, traditions, and teachings. It is not our intention to attempt to integrate these diverse philosophical traditions. These philosophical traditions, however, do share a common concern regarding the nature of change and the way to live an authentic or satisfactory life.

Reality Is Constantly Changing and Evolving and Life Is Always in a State of Becoming

The Book of Change, which represented observations and wisdoms by ancient sages about the processes that operate in the ever-changing world, derived the concepts and symbology of the yin–yang perspective to describe the process of change in nature. The eight trigrams figuratively depict the constantly evolving movement of yin–yang forces. The ideas contained in *The Book of Change* influenced the later development of Daoist thinking. The central thesis of both the yin–yang perspective and Daoism is that reality is constantly, and naturally, changing, as well as evolving. There is no objective, fixed reality in a static state. Life is always in a state of becoming and is therefore a process, not an end state. Buddhist teachings also share a similar assumption regarding the changing nature of phenomena, although the philosophy supporting such a belief is different. The Law of Karma depicts phenomena as evolving as a result of "cause and conditions." Based on the Law of Dependent Origination, it is impossible to pinpoint any entity as truly independent on its own, because everything is a consequence of the cause and condition, which is evolving all the time. The emphasis on impermanence of worldly attachment reflects the belief regarding the changing nature of all phenomena. The view that reality is constantly changing and evolving has the following implications for social work treatment:

- A strengths perspective. Because change is constant, there will be movement and "ups and downs" in any problem patterns. Consequently, no matter how problematic a person or a situation is, there will always be movement or differences that signify strengths and resources.

- A developmental perspective of change and health: Because life is always in a process of becoming, there is no ideal state of health that can be attained, nor it is desirable. Instead, a developmental perspective of health that depicts a state of becoming better approximates the process of change.
- Movement, as created by the dynamic balance of diverse, contrasting forces, constitutes a necessary condition for change, growth, and development. As such, there is also no value judgment attached to phenomena, forces, or attributes, because they are all needed in the process of change.
- There is no objective static, independent reality that can be observed or assessed, because phenomena are changing and evolving all the time.

Monistic and Nondual Conception of Reality

One common thread that clearly cut across yin–yang perspective, Daoism, and Buddhism is the interdependence, mutuality, and ultimate unity of phenomena. While yin–yang perspective represents a dualistic perception of phenomena, it exists within a monistic and nondual conception of reality that recognizes the unity, complementarity, and interrelatedness of contrasting forces. Yin–yang talks about the dynamic equilibrium and mutual interdependence of yin and yang forces in that one cannot exist or flourish without the other. In fact, the seemingly contrasting yin and yang forces originate from the same universal force. Daoism speaks about *Dao* as the unifying force that gives life to all things and brings them to harmony. Because *Dao* is constantly changing and evolving in a dynamic and complementary way, everything in life is connected in a subtle manner to each other. The Law of Karma in Buddhist teaching perceives phenomena as existing interdependently and relatively, based on the "cause, condition, and effect" relationship. Despite diverse origins, all three philosophies point to a holistic perspective of phenomena and human change in that there is nothing that can be perceived as an independent entity that exists purely by itself and is not related to something else. In addition, there is no judgment placed on any attribute or phenomena as desirable or undesirable, because both contrasting forces are necessary to maintain a dynamic balance that keeps the system/phenomenon changing and evolving. A holistic perspective implies the following:

- The irrelevance of an "either-or" position or a polarized view, because diverse forces are complementary and needed in the process of change.
- Reality needs to be understood in relation to the whole pattern or the total context: A contextual understanding is necessary.

- Reality needs to be understood based on direct experience instead of abstract, isolated concepts or representations of reality.
- A phenomenon, system, or pattern loses meaning and balance if the phenomena are broken down or reduced to parts.

Centrality of a Dynamic Balance between Diverse, Contrasting Forces

As contained in the yin–yang perspective and Daoist teaching, phenomena are constantly changing and evolving following their natural way (or the *Dao*), by a dynamic balance of contrasting forces. A system becomes out of balance, or distorted, through the emphasis of one end of a continuum over the other (e.g., yin versus yang, good versus bad). Here, there is no value judgment attached to good or bad, yin or yang, because both seemingly opposite forces are in fact complementary and needed for a well-balanced system. A person, system, or phenomenon becomes out of balance once we locate a phenomenon at one end of the continuum without recognizing the complementary existence of the other forces. Consequently, the system ceases to be an ever-changing reality and becomes stagnant. From such a perspective, the criterion for health and well-being is not the possession of any one attribute, characteristic, or force. Instead, health, well-being, or goodness is defined by the presence of a dynamic balance between diverse forces. Buddhist teachings do not used the term "dynamic balance" but "middle path." Based on the Law of Dependent Origination, all phenomena share a "same and different relationship" because of their interrelatedness as part of a cause, condition, or effect. "Middle path" denotes a middle position or a balanced position that avoids the notion of duality, an "either-or" position, or a rigid attachment to any attribute, beliefs, or phenomena.

Transcendence of the Self and Letting Go of Worldly Attachments

Social work treatment usually assumes that an individual or a family should take an active stance to control, master, and overcome their problems and perceives the individual/family's well-being, empowerment, and/or self-actualization as major goals of social work treatment (Lee, 2005). The self, in the conception of social work treatment, represents one primary concern of the person and social work treatment (Lee, 2005). Both Daoism and Buddhism, however, propose different views of well-being that call for the transcendence of the self. Daoist teachings perceive that socially based standards and desires are transient and relative. Recognizing the limitation of human beings to control life and the transient nature of earthly desires, Daoism perceives that attempting to achieve self-conscious desires and goals is unhelpful. Instead, the transcendence of the self, excess emotions, worldly desires, and social standards allow a person to be mindful of his or her experiences rather than going after elusive standards or desires promoted by the dominant, social discourse of what should be. When a person is in harmony with the *Dao* and in touch with the inner wisdom and intelligence of nature, of which he or she is part, the person will attain ultimate peace and a boundless life. Coming from a different perspective, Buddhism also suggests the transcendence and nonattachment of the self. Based on the Buddha's teaching, because of the impermanence of phenomena and the nonexistence of an ultimate, real "self," attachment to worldly emotions, desires, objects, and thoughts forms the basis of ignorance and only invites troubles and sufferings. Transcendence of the self and nonattachment liberate a person from ignorance and bring an end to the cyclic existence of human suffering.

Some of the views regarding change and health suggested by the yin–yang perspective, Daoism, and Buddhism might seem familiar to social work professionals. For example, the primary thesis of a systems perspective consists of the constant nature of change and the interrelatedness of different systems (Bateson, 1979). Social work practice with families was heavily influenced by a systems perspective that recognized the importance of connectedness among diverse systems and a contextual understanding in working with families. The Integral movement (Wilber, 1985; Wilber, 2000) focuses on the ideas of "shadow," "partial truths," and on the importance of balance; these ideas well echo the focus on balance as espoused by a yin–yang perspective. Solution-focused brief therapy, influenced by social constructivism and a systems perspective, adopts a strengths perspective in facilitating positive changes in clients and families (Berg & Kelly, 2000; DeJong & Berg, 2007; Lee, 2007; Lee, Sebold, & Uken, 2003). Social constructivism (Gergen, 1999) provides a theoretical backbone for a strengths perspective (Saleebey, 1997), which represents a recent advent in social work practice in reaction to the deficits perspective. Social constructivism clearly recognizes the transient and relative nature of phenomena, the power and limitations of language, and the importance of experience as opposed to linear, abstract thinking.

There are both similarities with and differences between the views of change and health suggested by these Eastern philosophies and other social work treatment approaches. We do not view a polarization of these views of change with existing assumptions of change adopted by social work professionals as helpful or necessary. The important question is how these views can beneficially complement our current understanding and practice of social work treatment. Two major distinctive characteristics of these Eastern philosophies pertain to their emphasis on the centrality of balance and the inclusion of spirituality in their view of change and health. When the yin–yang perspective and Daoism describe reality as constantly changing and evolving, it moves beyond the current discourse of a systems perspective and focuses on the centrality of balance as the primary criterion of health. For instance, based on such a view, neither the strengths perspective nor the deficits perspective is better, or more valid, than the other in providing social work treatment. What counts for a beneficial treatment process is the manifestation of a dynamic balance of contrasting but interrelated perspectives in helping clients attain a holistic, contextual understanding of their situation. Based on that particular understanding, the client may engage in beneficial behaviors or actions to further the process of change. Such a view will not entertain the conception that problems represent bad things that need to be destroyed or solutions as good things that should be retained forever.

Although religion conversion does not have a place in our discussion of the yin–yang perspective, philosophical Daoism, and Buddhism as related to Integrative Social Work practice, these philosophies do bring spirituality into the discourse of social work treatment primarily through the recognition of the inseparability between human beings and the nature (as postulated by the yin–yang perspective and Daoism) and a transcendence of the self so that one can shift the focus from the "small self" to the "big self" (as suggested by Buddhism). By doing so, our innate virtue (*de*) and inherent qualities of loving kindness, compassion, joy, and nonattachment can be realized. Transformation of the self in order to be connected with a person's spirituality is clearly implied by these philosophies.

Assumptions of Integrative Body–Mind–Spirit Social Work Regarding Change

AN INTEGRATED VIEW OF PROBLEM FORMULATION AND CLIENT CHANGE

The assumptions, values, and practices of Integrative Social Work practice are influenced by ideas of the yin–yang perspective, philosophical Daoism, and Buddhism. However, Integrative Social Work neither claims to be developed based on nor representative of any one or all three philosophies. In addition, the practice of Integrative Social Work is built upon the accumulated knowledge and experience of mainstream social work practice developed under a humanistic and Judeo-Christian culture. The introduction of Eastern philosophies, however, serves as a balancing force to complement the current developments of social work practice with individuals and families.

Zeig and Gilligan (1990) suggested that most clinical practice approaches should have their own theory regarding problem causation, problem maintenance, and mechanisms to bring about beneficial changes in clients. Integrative Social Work practice exemplifies the following views regarding problem formulation, problem maintenance, and client change.

How People Get Engaged in Problems of Living

Problems as normal challenges of living

Murphy's Law is a gentle reminder that many things in our life can go wrong and that unpleasant surprises are just part of normal living. Both the yin–yang perspective and Daoism portray life (and reality) as a process of constant change in which we are always in a state of becoming. Regardless of how well a person tries to plan and control his or her life, there is no way that one can absolutely control the way life unfolds. Buddhist teachings depict life as consisting of inevitable sufferings that include, but are not limited to, birth, loss, aging, sickness, grief, and death. Such a view of problem causation, however, is not new to social work. The passage of life itself suggests a constantly recurring pattern of movement and change. Erik Erikson proposed the eight psychosocial stages of life to describe the normal conflicts and issues of individual development from infancy to old age (Erikson, 1963). Carter and McGoldrick (1998) wrote about developmental stages that families would normally go through. Birth, adolescence, marriage, children leaving home, and old age are all passages that are filled with accomplishments, challenges, and anguish. Finally, there is the ultimate challenge and disorder that death brings. Throughout our lives, there are crises and changes created by sickness, accidents, loss of work, loss of friends, environmental trauma, natural disasters—crises that disrupt our agenda and security and force us to revisit our carefully laid plans. A psychosocial perspective of crisis (Gilliland & James, 1997) fully acknowledges different types of crisis, including developmental crises (e.g., adolescence, getting married, empty nesting), situational crises, which can be human or natural disasters (e.g., unemployment, injuries, violence, wars, earthquakes), and existential crises (e.g., mid-life crisis, bereavement, suicide of loved ones). In their Life Model of Social Work Practice, Germain and Gitterman (1980) first developed the concept of "problems in living" and later renamed it "life stressors" (1996) to describe different challenges that clients and families encounter in the normal process of living. Life is humbling. Having problems and experiencing difficult situations are normal in everyday living.

Integrative Social Work shares with these social work theories and other practice theories, such as crisis intervention, solution-focused brief therapy, and strategic therapy, the view that problems and difficulties are just an integral part of living. Because of the assumption that life is ever changing and evolving, Integrative Social Work believes that problems will come and go. The more important questions, therefore, are how clients and families get stuck in their problem situations and how they can get out of them.

How Are Problems of Living Maintained?

A system out of balance

The yin–yang perspective and Daoism provide a uniquely Eastern view of how problems of living are maintained. Both the yin–yang perspective and

Daoism suggest a holistic perspective of viewing change in that they both recognize the complementarity and interrelatedness of contrasting forces in maintaining a dynamic balance of growth and movement. Contrary to most Western criteria of health or well-being that usually involve dualistic thinking and identify some characteristics or properties as good or healthy and the opposites as bad or unhealthy, the yin–yang perspective and Daoism perceive a dynamic balance of contrasting forces as central to the health and well-being of a system. There are no "good" or "bad" events, experiences, or happenings. They are just events or forces that exist side by side and complement each other in a dynamic process of change and development.

Suzanne is a highly regarded teacher at an elementary school and a responsible mother of two young children. She grew up in a middle-class family that taught her to be a responsible and decent person. She set high standards for herself, and sometimes, other friends tease her as a "perfectionist." She always meets deadlines, keeps the house clean, takes care of her two children, and her husband. Her 65-year-old father recently had a heart attack and just underwent bypass surgery. As a responsible daughter, she attempts to squeeze in the role of taking care of her aging father. Suzanne came in for treatment because she felt overwhelmed, anxious, and depressed. She had difficulty sleeping, was easily agitated, had increasing trouble keeping up with her responsibilities at school, and although her husband was supportive of her, she felt like she was increasingly distant and alienated from him, and she did not understand why.

Suzanne was an out-of-balance system. She obviously took "being responsible" and "taking care of family members" as "good" or "virtuous." The unspoken other end of the continuum, consisting of taking care of herself, was probably perceived as selfish, which is "bad." Although the position that Suzanne adopted is widely accepted as virtuous based on socially constructed standards, the consequences were not beneficial to her because, by being totally influenced by one end of the continuum without regard to her personal needs, her psychological and physiological systems were out of balance. The imbalance is likely to have happened in the following ways:

- Suzanne probably understood "being responsible" as a virtue, and consequently, "being responsible" was reduced to an isolated and absolute standard to be attained regardless of the circumstances.
- When "being responsible" is understood as a context-free, absolute standard, Suzanne became at risk of being oblivious to the total context, which also included her psychological and physical well-being.
- Once Suzanne defined herself based on a single-dimensional criterion and rejected the complementary existence of caretaking behaviors that represented the other side of "being responsible" (namely, behaviors that possibly range from taking care of oneself to being self-centered or selfish), those

behaviors became the "shadow" and were unrecognized. As a result, the dynamic balance between the forces and behaviors focused on taking care of others and those focused on taking care of herself was disrupted.

- As Suzanne had to be responsible at all times, there was no longer dynamic movement in the caretaking domain. The system ceased to be dynamic and responsive to current needs and demands, and so became stagnant and stuck.

An out-of-balance system inevitably becomes a stagnant system. An out-of-balance system is a symptom of the dominance of a single-dimensional aspect of any phenomenon, characteristic, behavior, perception, thought pattern, sensation, mood, and so on, in determining a person's reactions and behaviors. As postulated by systems perspective and cybernetic theories, feedback processes are inherently self-corrective and self-regulating mechanisms, which enable a person to sustain functionality (Keeney & Thomas, 1986). However, in order for a person to be self-corrective, there needs to be variations in input to activate the self-regulating abilities in the person (Becvar & Becvar, 2003). A simple analogy would be the functioning of a heating or air-conditioning system. The self-regulating mechanism of a heating or air-conditioning system will only be activated when the system detects changes in the room temperature. The system will remain inactive if there is no variation in the temperature or if the system failed to notice the change. Variations in the temperature as well as the ability of the system to detect the change constitute necessary inputs to the system to initiate the self-regulating or self-correcting feedback process. In human systems, people also need changes and variations in input as well as awareness of these changes and movements to activate the feedback process on which they can base their responses and behaviors.

In Suzanne's situation, "being responsible" became the single most important definitional characteristic in her social relationships. There was no variation in how she perceived what might be appropriate responses to others' requests and demands. As "being responsible" had become such an overbearing standard, she might not have been aware of her own needs, desires, or limits. Consequently, instead of making choices of behaviors that were consistent with her context and current needs, there was no longer flexibility in her behavioral pattern, as "being responsible" became a habitual or automatic response. Suzanne was probably not just acting on her own isolation. It is highly likely that the social milieu where Suzanne was situated also reinforced her ideals and the behavior of "being responsible." Suzanne's father, husband, children, and colleagues were included in the dance in which her "responsible" character was expected, rewarded, and reinforced. As there were no longer variations in how Suzanne responded to other people or how others responded to her behaviors, there were no variations in the input to the system that could activate a different feedback process around Suzanne's responses to environmental demands. Suzanne continued to behave in a habitual way that was harmful to her psychologically and physiologically. Consequently, Suzanne felt overwhelmed and could no longer bear the burden. She became stuck in her situation when the system became stagnant, without a natural flow of energy to maintain movement and balance (Ng, Chan, Ho, Wong and Ho, 2006).

Figures 2.1a and 2.1b are diagrammatic representations of common observable indicators of a balanced system and an out-of-balance system, based on clinical observation. Although it is important to describe observable indicators of a balanced and out-of-balance system for purposes of illustration, we are well aware of the danger of providing a dualistic description of what is desirable versus undesirable, as the polarization of any attributes or characteristics can lead to an out-of-balance condition. Any person will have

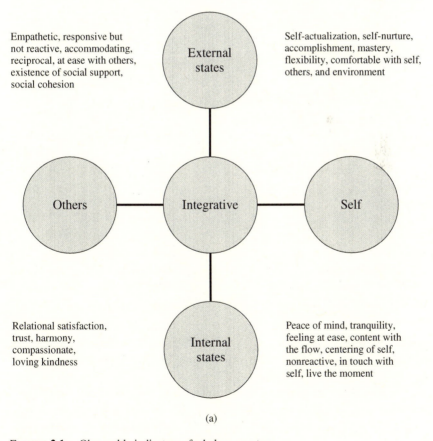

(a)

FIGURE **2.1a.** Observable indicators of a balance system.

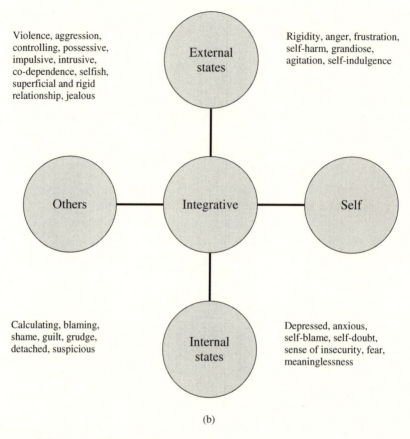

Violence, aggression, controlling, possessive, impulsive, intrusive, co-dependence, selfish, superficial and rigid relationship, jealous

Rigidity, anger, frustration, self-harm, grandiose, agitation, self-indulgence

Calculating, blaming, shame, guilt, grudge, detached, suspicious

Depressed, anxious, self-blame, self-doubt, sense of insecurity, fear, meaninglessness

(b)

FIGURE **2.1b.** An out-of-balance human system.

moments of anger or tranquility, or sadness or happiness. We observed, however, based on clinical experience, that a balanced system will manifest more of the indicators listed in Figure 2.1a whereas an unbalanced system will show more of the indicators described in Figure 2.1b. In other words, Figures 2.1a and 2.1b are intended to describe the outcomes of a balanced system and an out-of-balance system from a cross-sectional perspective. It does not describe the dynamic process in achieving this balancing act.

An out-of-balance system usually polarizes forces and becomes a disconnected system. Integrative Social Work believes in interconnectedness between the mind, body, and spirit, as well as the environment. Whenever there is an overemphasis of one end of the continuum of any phenomena, forces, attributes, or behaviors without recognizing the complementary existence of the other end, there will be a disconnection in that particular dimension, attribute, or pattern of human experience. Disconnection can take many forms and manifest in diverse problems (Ng, Chan, Chan et al., 2006).

It can happen across different domains of human experience, such as the disconnection among the body, mind, and spirit in a person. For instance, most mainstream social work practice approaches emphasize cognitive and behavioral domains but downplay the body process or spirituality of clients (Canda & Furman, 1999). Likewise, too much emphasis on the educational accomplishment of a child can result in an unbalanced development, with educational accomplishment disconnected from his or her other areas of development, such as social or physical development. Disconnection can happen at any level of our social existence when we locate one dimension without recognizing the complementary existence of the other parts. Disconnection can happen across different societal systems when one class or country exploits members of another class or country. Disconnection also happens between humans and nature when we ruthlessly exploit natural resources without realizing or respecting the interdependence between humans and nature.

In Suzanne's experience, the disconnection manifested itself in the following ways:

- When "being responsible" existed as an abstract, isolated ideal, the opposite end, taking care of herself and her self-interests were likely pushed over to become the "shadow" of "being responsible." Suzanne no longer perceived her responses to others' needs or requests as purely situationally informed responses based on current context, needs, and requests. Instead, her responses were increasingly dictated by the ideal of "being responsible" and became disconnected from her experience, which led to physical and psychological exhaustion.
- "Being responsible" was reduced to a separate domain, probably the moral domain, and consequently disconnected from her physiological domain, as well as other psychological and spiritual needs.
- The disconnection that happened within Suzanne also led to a disconnection in the social domain. Suzanne's relationship with her significant others was reduced to the role of "being responsible." When she was feeling exhausted and depressed, Suzanne did not feel connected to her father, husband, children, or colleagues. It is likely that the latter also felt disconnected to Suzanne, despite the fact that she was "being responsible" in fulfilling her roles.

What makes a system out of balance?

Some crucial questions asked by any curious reader would be, "What makes a system become out of balance?" "What makes people overemphasize an attribute, value, behavior, dimension, or aspect of a phenomenon to the extent that they lose sight of the complementary, interrelated, contrasting, and diverse forces of the other side of the phenomenon?" While there are probably no quick or finite answers to these questions, Integrative Social Work perceives that systems become unbalanced primarily because of an over-attachment intimately related to the inability of a person to be mindful and "live in the present." In addition, the system could become unbalanced as a result of the presence of unhelpful mental representations of problems of living as well as linear and reductionistic thinking that promotes fragmented or disconnected views of phenomena (Figure 2.2).

Over-attachment

Naked were we born and naked must we depart . . .
No matter what you may lose, be patient, for nothing belongs, it is only rented.
Gluckel of Hemeln, *Memories of Gluckel of Hameln* (1724)
(Schneider, 2000, p. 71)

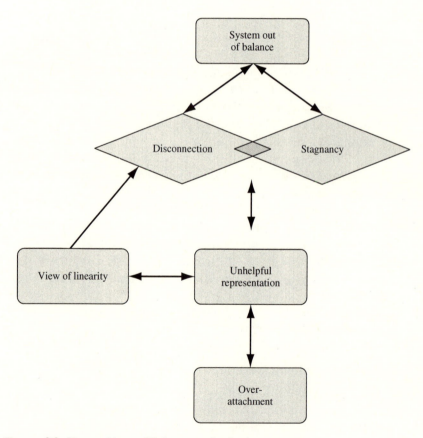

FIGURE **2.2.** How problems of living are maintained.

The yin–yang perspective describes reality as changing and evolving and life as in a state of becoming. Daoism focuses on the limitations of humans to control life and the transient nature of human desires and socially based standards. Buddhism exemplifies the impermanence of all phenomena, relationships, and even ourselves. Attachment to any phenomena, objects, desires, emotions, standards, ideals, or thoughts, without first realizing the transient nature of them is at best elusive, and at worst, forms the basis of suffering and problems. The concept of attachment is called *jizhou* in Chinese, which denotes holding on, rigid attachments, and fixation on desirable attributes, values, and behaviors as determined by the individual. Although we all have things that we like, values that we adhere to, and relationships that we treasure, *jizhou* can become a source of emotional frustrations when these desirable character, values, or relationships are not attainable or are changed. When a person rigidly attaches to a relationship, value, behavior, attribute, or habit, he or she has limited ability to adjust to the changes of everyday life.

Integrative Social Work is not interested in explaining why people form attachments. Many other psychological theories, such as psychodynamic theories, attachment theory, and self-psychology, have insightful and perceptive explanations of the process. Integrative Social Work also does not take a negative stance toward attachment. In fact, as suggested by attachment theory developed by John Bowlby (Bowlby, 1979, 1982), learning how to attach constitutes an important developmental process that human beings undertake since birth. The concern we have is that, when people form attachments to something without realizing or appreciating the contrasting forces of change and impermanence, the person or the system will run into increased risk of becoming unbalanced. Secure attachment can nurture flexible, positive, and independent individuals. Insecure attachment, however, usually results in an overemphasis of the object of attachment (material or immaterial), polarization of views, and ultimately, an imbalance in the system in which attention is focused on the isolated object of attachment to the detriment of the other complementary phenomena and forces.

Reduced ability to be mindful of the present.   When a person is attached to a relationship, a social standard, a value, or any entity, the object of attachment becomes an isolated but dominant desire for the person to pursue or possess. In this way, attachment is intimately related to an increased risk of a person's inability to be mindful of the present. Instead of attending to and being keenly aware of what happens in the current context *as it is* and regulating behaviors and responses based on the recognition of current needs, demands, and interests, the attention is directed toward the object of attachment. When the attached object is something established in the past, such as

We ran groups for clients and families who were dealing with bereavement issues and infertility problems. A core struggle for both client populations is the issue of loss, whether losing loved ones or losing the hope of having a child. The love for the deceased person or the desire to have a child is normal, although such desires can be problematic or dysfunctional to a person if he or she is over-attached to the desire and cannot accept the loss. We created three experiential games for our group members: (1) We had a treasure box with a small hole in the center, through which people could freely take the gifts from the box. However, the gifts were larger than the hole. We asked clients to use whatever means they had to take the gifts from the box. (2) We placed a balloon in a narrow-necked vase and asked clients to blow the balloon through the vase. Clients would tie the balloon. Then we asked clients to use whatever means they had to release the balloon from the vase. (3) We asked clients to stand next to a wall with the left hand and ankle touching the wall and try to raise their right leg (without holding onto any support). These impossible tasks helped clients to realize that, no matter how hard one tried, there were tasks that one cannot fulfill or accomplish. Life is not always within our control. We have to acknowledge and accept our own limitations.

a relationship, a habit, or a traditional value or practice, the person tends to live in the past and not in the present. People may experience grief or become depressed when they are attached to objects in the past. When people are attached to expectations and a sense of control, they may experience problems related to anxiety. When the objects of attachment are absolute or isolated ideals, behaviors, or standards, the responses or behaviors of the person could easily be disconnected from the total context, as that person is likely to attend to the attached standard, such as "being responsible" in Suzanne's situation. Suzanne did not accept or forgive herself or others in her frustrations, which might have been diminished by a sense of humor and a let-it-be attitude. The person may become rigid, uptight, and inflexible, unable to address life challenges at hand and may become strangled by his or her own emotions and frustrations.

Unhelpful representation of problems of living.   'When explaining how people develop emotional disturbances and problems, cognitive therapy suggests that cognition influences emotions and behavior and that the individual responds to the cognitive representation of an event rather than to the event itself (Beck, 1995; Beck, Rush, Shaw, & Emery, 1979). Interestingly, the Buddha expressed a similar view of problem causation thousands of years ago. The Buddha differentiated between two types of suffering as the two darts of suffering (Bhikkhu Bodhi, 2000, p. 1263). When a person experiences a problem of living, for instance, children leaving home or getting sick, he or she will experience the feelings of pain, as determined by the nature of the problem.

The original experience constitutes the first type of suffering, which is fundamental to any problem of living and will come and go as the event unfolds and changes. However, the person is not only affected by the first type of suffering—the person "worries and grieves, he laments, beats his chest, weeps and is distraught" (Bhikkhu Bodhi, 2000, p. 1263). This person experiences both types of suffering arising from the primary bodily sensation and the secondary mental feelings. Instead of being mindful of the current experience, which can also include painful feelings in the body, like when one is sick, the person is trapped by the unhelpful mental representation of getting sick. When that happens, the person no longer just lives in the present and is affected by current events; he or she also responds to his or her mental representation of being sick, which can include a polarized view of "I'm unhealthy," "I won't live long," or "I have a poor life." Attachment to these unhelpful mental representations forbids the person to realize or appreciate the dynamic balance of health and sickness as complementary forces of our physical well-being. The system is no longer in balance when a person responds not only to the problems of living as it is but also to his or her mental representation of these experiences.

Robert suffered from ankylosing spondylitis. The joints in his body and spinal cord ached badly almost all day. Robert was depressed, bitter, angry, and suicidal. The disease resulted in emotional turmoil. The two darts of suffering were in action. Alex suffered from the same problem. His joints also ached almost 24 hr a day. However, Alex volunteered in his church and spent time taking care of small animals. He endured the pain and found great meaning in his life by serving other people in need. The first dart of bodily pain was unavoidable, but the second dart of suffering was not.

A linear and reductionistic mode of knowing.   Greek civilization constitutes the foundation of European and post-Columbian American civilization. One profound characteristic of the Greeks was their sense of curiosity about the world and the presumption that it could be understood by the discovery of rules (Lloyd, 1991; Toulmin & Goodfield, 1961). Consequently, the Western system of thought promotes a way of knowing by categorizing objects and events and generating rules about them for purposes of systematic description, prediction, and explanation (Cromer, 1993; Toulmin & Goodfield, 1961). Phenomena or objects were understood as individuals or particulars that "had properties" (Hansen, 1983, p. 80), were observable, and could be understood independently of their context (Nakamura, 1964/1985). The resulting philosophy of scientificism, rationalism, and individualism promoted a way of understanding in which phenomena are broken down into the smallest possible parts to be studied for precise understanding, prediction, and control. In addition, they emphasized linear thinking, which implicates cause-and-effect relationships among different domains and variables in explaining human behavior and resolving human problems. Although such patterns of thinking facilitate and lead to tremendous knowledge and techno-logical development, they also promote a disconnected and fragmented view of the world when used to understand of problems of living and ways to address them. For instance, the recent exponential growth of the pharmaco-logical industry is at least partly related to a biomedical understanding of not just health problems but also mental health, emotional, and behavioral prob-lems in children and adults. Using a pill to treat attention deficit/hyperactivity disorder (ADHD) without examining the impact of parenting practices, fam-ily, or school environment represents a disconnected view of problem solving. Not only is the development of the social work profession and its knowledge base for practice inevitably a product of the system of thought that character-izes the civilization it originates, but the ways clients experience, perceive, and address problems of living are also culturally embedded (Lee, M. Y., 1996). The linear and reductionistic mode of knowing characterized by a Western way of thinking has definitely contributed to significant technologi-cal advances in the West. Such a way of thinking, however, also easily leads to a disconnected and fragmented view of problems of living as well as ways to solve them.

In sum, Integrative Social Work views that problem of livings will come and go; they are part of the natural, developmental, and continuous process of life. A more useful question for treatment is how problems are maintained and how beneficial changes can be initiated. Integrative Social Work postu-lates that people are stuck in problems of living when there is a polarized view of things or an overemphasis of one end of a continuum of any phenomena, forces, attributes, or behaviors without recognizing the complementary exis-tence of the other end as necessary in the process of change. In other words, problems of living are maintained as a result of a disrupted balance between diverse forces in the person or between the person and his or her social system, which leads to a stagnant state of disconnection and disharmony. Integra-tive Social Work also assumes a holistic perspective in understanding human problems of living and supports the interconnectedness among diverse sys-tems, phenomena, and forces. The reduction of any attribute to an isolated, context-free ideal, behavior, or pattern, separated from the total context, will result in the disconnectedness and imbalance of the system. The system then becomes rigid and stagnant because there is no longer variation in input to activate the self-regulating abilities of individuals and families through the feedback processes in response to current needs and situation. In place of dynamic movement and change in the system, disconnection and imbalance in individuals and families usually manifest in the form of symptoms and problems.

Client Change

Integrative Body–Mind–Spirit Social Work is primarily concerned with the following questions pertaining to client change: (1) How can treatment create a context that initiates movement in a stagnant system? (2) How can treatment create a context that enhances the client's awareness of movement in a stagnant system? (3) How can treatment create a context that facilitates a dynamic balance in the system? Integrative Social Work uses the language of "balance" and "transformation." Balance describes the beneficial and complementary coexistence of diverse forces or parts of a phenomenon or system that work together to facilitate movement and change. Transformation speaks to a developmental and growth perspective of change. Integrative Social Work views change as constant and ongoing. The important question is how clients and families can benefit from the change process and how people are being transformed when going through the different life stages and challenges of living.

Integrative Social Work makes the following assumptions regarding change mechanisms.

Change is the rule rather than the exception

Integrative Social Work perceives that life is naturally and constantly changing and evolving. There is no objective or static state that can be described as ideal, desirable, or healthy. Life is always in a state of becoming and is, therefore, a process. As such, the question is not so much about how to create changes in clients and families. Instead, the crucial therapeutic task should be to create a context that can facilitate and allow the natural unfolding of the dynamic balance of diverse and complementary forces that keeps the person or the system changing and evolving.

Movement, as created by a dynamic balance of diverse forces of life, facilitates development and change in life

> If we had no winter, the spring would not be so pleasant:
> If we did not sometimes taste adversity,
> Prosperity would not be so welcome.
>
> Anne Bradstreet (c.1612–1672) *Thirty-Three Meditations*, 14.
> (Schneider, 2000, p. 71)

Integrative Social Work perceives that the accomplishment of balance and harmony in a person is not a static or end state but is attained through a process of dynamic movement. A simple analogy would be that a person can only maintain balance when the bicycle is in motion. However, a bicycle is in motion only when a person maintains a dynamic balance between the contrasting forces of steering right or left. In other words, movement, as created by the dynamic balance of diverse, contrasting forces, constitutes a necessary condition for change, growth, and development. The important therapeutic challenges, however, are the following: (1) How can treatment create a context that facilitates dynamic and ongoing movements in a system? (2) How we can enhance the ability of individuals and families to recognize, attend to, and be aware of these movements either within the person or in the larger environment?

Mindfulness: live in the moment

While reality is constantly evolving, people have to be able to attend to, notice, and be aware of movements both within and outside in order for the balancing act to occur. What is noticed becomes reality, and what is unnoticed does not exist (Lee et al., 2003). Mindfulness denotes a quality of consciousness that is characterized by enhanced attention to, and awareness of, current experience or present reality *as it is* (Brown & Ryan, 2003). Mindfulness, by enhancing one's awareness of and ability to attend to the moment-to-moment experience, allows a person to recognize movements and changes in the self and external environment, regulate behaviors, and make adjustment based on current needs and interests, instead of being trapped by past experiences, future desires, or isolated, rigid standards.

A man was chased by a tiger. He was very scared and ran to a cliff. There was a lion at the bottom of the cliff waiting for him. As the tiger approached, the man jumped. He ended up hanging onto a branch of a small tree at the cliff. As he was greatly relieved, he found a rat biting the branch and the branch was going to break. What could he do? He focused on the branch that he was holding and suddenly realized that it was a cherry tree blossomed with red cherries. He ate the cherries and fell asleep. When he woke up, he was still hanging onto the small tree. The tiger jumped down the cliff and died; the lion left and the rat ran away.

The tiger represents past worries, the lion symbolizes anxieties for the future, and the rat stands for everyday problems. The most important of all, however, are the cherries, which are the joy of life that one should never miss.

Accept and go with the flow

The truth that many people never understand until it is too late is that the more you try to avoid suffering the more you suffer.

Thomas Merton, *Love and Living* (1979) (Schneider, 2000, p. 76)

Integrative Social Work recognizes the complementarity and interrelatedness of different forces, events, and experiences in life as playing different roles in facilitating a dynamic balance of growth and movement. As such, there will be pleasant and unpleasant feelings, events, or happenings, but not in the sense of "good" or "bad" in relation to the process of change, development, and growth. Instead of fighting against, ameliorating, or getting rid of certain feelings, behaviors, or experiences, Integrative Social Work assumes that it will be more helpful for the person to notice, recognize, embrace, and accept those feelings or experiences. There are moments in life when we will suffer. The ability to endure and accept pain will facilitate the natural unfolding of the process of change. When one is mindful, he or she is perceptive, receptive, and open to internal and external stimuli without making value judgments. The state of consciousness is perceptual and nonevaluative (Brown & Ryan, 2003). Individuals observe and describe their feelings and reactions without applying positive or negative judgments or seeking immediate relief. The ability to attend to moment-to-moment experiences and emotions, even distressing ones, and accept them for what they are enables people to be open and receptive to naturally occurring changes, as well as allowing the contrasting and complementary forces in the person or the system to attain a dynamic balance that will lead to growth, development, and change. For example, instead of fighting against certain negative emotions, such as anxiety, the person will just accept them. The complementary force of anxiety—a calmer feeling—will naturally unfold itself, as one can never be anxious all the time. The ability to not fight and accept the anxious feeling facilitates the unfolding of a calmer feeling as a natural flow in our emotional contour. When a person can comfortably experience both anxiety and calmness, he or she will have an increased ability to regulate his or her emotion.

Healing from within

> To confront a person with his own shadow is to show him his own light
> Carl Jung (Schneider, 2000, p. 117).

Consistent with a systems perspective, Integrative Social Work assumes the presence of self-regulating or self-corrective abilities in individuals and families for a beneficial existence. As such, this approach recognizes the inherent healing abilities of individuals and is based on a strengths perspective. Instead of focusing on eliminating the problems, we believe that it is more helpful to develop and utilize strengths and resources in individuals and their environment so that they have increased abilities to address whatever problems they have in life.

Utilizing strengths. Integrative Social Work shares with other solution-focused and strengths-based approaches in that we believe that because change is constant, there will be movement and "ups and downs" in any problem patterns. Consequently, no matter how problematic a person or a situation is, there will always be movement or differences that signify strengths or resources (de Shazer, 1991; Lee et al., 2003). The challenge is for us to create a therapeutic context for individuals to be mindful of their present experiences, accept distressful experiences, attend to and be aware of those times of strengths and resources, make adjustments based on these recognitions, and allow the strengths and healing power to unfold in a developmental process.

Stay simple.   Integrative Social Work assumes that a human system self-regulates for the benefit of its existence. Staying simple is consistent with a "minimalist" approach to treatment. Effective treatment should emphasize making a small shift that will allow the person to utilize his or her innate abilities and forces to regain movement and balance. Drastic intervention, without full recognition of the person's total context, will only serve to further disrupt the dynamic balance and aggravate disconnectedness. A minimalist approach to treatment is also suggested by prominent theorists and professionals at the Mental Research Institute, such as Gregory Bateson (1972), Watzlawick, Weakland, and Fisch (1974). Based on a systems perspective, they are concerned about introducing any change that may disturb a person's equilibrium in unpredictable ways as a result of reiterating feedback. Intervention should stay simple so that clients can be convinced that change is possible, and within their reach and understanding. Clients and families are empowered when they are the masters of their own life. We also believe that small change is more possible, manageable, and consumes less energy (Lee et al., 2003). Clients are usually encouraged when they experience successes, even small ones.

Compassion

> No act of kindness, no matter how small, is ever wasted
> Aesop (550 BCE) "The Lion and the Mouse."

Intimately related to the assumption regarding healing from within is the belief in the healing power of compassion. The Eastern belief of karma, cause, and consequence, can be empowering. Kind and generous actions will always be recognized, one way or another. In the flow of life events and experiences, a positive action under kind intentions will naturally lead to other beneficial consequences. Compassion, altruistic behavior, unselfish love, forgiveness, and loving kindness are keys to happiness (Ricard, 2006). When a person is filled with a mean mind and calculating thoughts, he or she is bound to be unhappy. The bondage of hatred, anger, jealousy, as well as thoughts of retaliation and revenge can be mental toxins that poison the physical and mental well-being of individuals. Compassion, through altruistic action to eliminate suffering of other people, is the best medicine for anger and rage. The negative thoughts arising from discontent can be directed to positive, altruistic behavior and compassionate action. By sending love and blessings to oneself and others, individuals can relinquish destructive desires by relating to higher goals of love and inner peace. By involvement in acts of compassion and loving kindness, the heart of individuals can be cleansed and their souls freed. Volunteer participation in helping needy and underprivileged persons based on respect and humility can yield fruits of bliss and wisdom. Dedication to serve can be a transforming experience for people who experience loss and grief. Compassion is a key to this discovery process (Schneider & Zimmerman, 2006).

Jonathan was severely abused by his father when he was a child. He developed a strong sense of insecurity and had nightmares until he became an adult. He refused to see his father for 20 years. When he was at last persuaded to see his father, his father was on his death bed, the morning before he died. Jonathan found a stranger who was skinny and frail. His father said that he was sorry for what he had done and Jonathan forgave his father. His nightmares stopped. The inner power of love and forgiveness is the greatest source of healing from within. By forgiving his father, Jonathan also set himself free from the bondage of hatred and hurt. He freed himself from his past wounds through expressing his love for his dying father. The reconciliation was a beautiful healing experience that washed away thirty years of pain.

A holistic perspective of social work treatment

Integrative Social Work recognizes the interdependence, mutuality, complementarity, and interrelatedness of contrasting forces and phenomena. It promotes a holistic perspective in understanding human experience and change, in that there is nothing that can be perceived as an independent entity that exists purely by itself and is not related to something else. In addition, there is no judgment put on any attributes or phenomena as desirable or undesirable, because diverse forces and phenomena are necessary to maintain a dynamic balance that keeps the system changing and evolving. Within a person, the domains of behavior, thought, feeling, sensation, value, morality, meaning, intuition, spirituality, body, and functioning are all interrelated in a connected web and are never viewed as separate domains of the human experience. Similarly, the self, others, family, community, workplace, social environment, economic environment, political environment, global environment, nature, and cosmos are all mutually related and influence each other.

A focus on body–mind–spirit connections.   Integrative Social Work assumes the dynamic balance of and interrelationship among mind, body, and spirit as fundamental to health, mental health, and the well-being of individuals. The physical body (sensation, energy, physical strength, body functioning, physiological responses, etc.), the mind (cognition, perception, mood, affection, problem-solving ability, memory, willpower, etc.), and spirituality (meaning, life goals, morality, values, commitment and fulfillment, relationship with higher being and cosmos) overlap and are intimately related to each other. Assessment and treatment should fully acknowledge the interrelatedness of and mutual influences among these domains.

Systems collaboration.   Systems collaboration is an integral part of Integrative Social Work. In addition to body–mind–spirit connectedness, an individual system is constantly in interaction with family systems, social systems, environment systems, and service systems. Similarly, individuals or families are oftentimes served by different agencies and their representatives, e.g., mental health, social services, juvenile courts, schools, psychiatric hospitals, and so on (Lee, Greene, Solovey, Fraser, & Grove, in press). Collaboration among these systems is fundamental to successful outcomes, as a holistic perspective recognizes mutuality and interconnectedness of diverse systems in providing resources and support, as well as working together to create a context for change in individuals and families.

Multidimensional treatment orientation.   A holistic perspective requires a multidimensional treatment orientation that recognizes contributions of different domains, forces, or systems in facilitating dynamic flow for the benefit of change and development. The treatment will entail assessment of and intervention into the three levels of the mind, body, and spirit of the individual in the context of his or her family, broader social environment, and beyond, as appropriate. It is important to recognize that a holistic perspective does not mean that social work professionals have to conduct assessments or intervene at all levels. Such an ambitious goal is unrealistic at best and unhelpful at worst. In addition, change can be initiated at any part of the system. As everything is connected, change in one part of the system will be passed on to other parts of the system. Integrative Social Work, therefore, does not assume that treatment needs to happen at all levels of human experience. However, it does not exclude any domains as an appropriate target of assessment and intervention, and, in doing so, takes a holistic perspective in understanding and treating individuals and families.

SMART: Strength-focused, Meaning-oriented Approach to Resilience and Transformation

> Although the world is very full of suffering, it is full also of the overcoming of it.
> Helen Keller, *Optimism* (1903) (Schneider, 2000, p. 75)

To put the above assumptions together, the team developed the Integrative Body–Mind–Spirit model in 1993, through working with cancer patients, divorced women, bereaved persons, and grieving children. Through the development of the Integrative Body–Mind–Spirit Social Work and continuous research with diverse client populations for ten years, the SMART principles of practice were articulated (Ng, Chan, Chan et al., 2006). The SMART practice principles signify Strength-focused and Meaning-oriented Approach to Resilience and Transformation. Such a practice principle has been successfully adopted for treatment with cancer patients, chronic patients, divorced women, and couples with infertility problems. The SMART principles should be viewed as dynamic and evolving practice guidelines. Its development primarily serves as a balancing force to complement the current developments of social work practice with individuals and families and, therefore, should never be viewed as ultimate solutions or miracle practice guideline that stay true forever. The SMART principles attempt to address the following characteristics of social work treatment that may have contributed to an imbalance in our treatment orientation with individuals and families:

- Deficits perspective: A focus on presenting problems, deficits, and what people are lacking in assessment and treatment
- Underlying assumptions of disconnectedness in domains of human experiences including downplaying the role of spirituality in human experience
- A "fighter" mentality toward problems and the emphasis of treatment on symptom reduction and removal
- A focus on external and expert intervention

Strength-focused: The SMART model helps clients and families notice, attend to, and be aware of the times that movement in themselves is indicated by strengths and accomplishments. Effective social workers have to be genuinely committed to assess strengths and available resources in clients, families, and their social systems. The process of working with strengths involves: (1) actively assessing strengths; (2) naming strengths that are observable in clients' personality, expression, coping, and thriving; (3) articulating these strengths and sharing them with the client or family; (4) reinforcing by giving positive recognition, appreciation, and by prescribing exercises to further cultivate the strengths; and (5) consolidating strengths within an individual, as well as in the family and broader social system.

Meaning-oriented: The ability to find meaning out of problems of living involves a process of searching for meaning, articulation, and reconstruction of meaning. Such a meaning-making process creates a context for individuals to first begin by

(continued)

(continued)

narrating their own perception of the cause and consequences of events, relationships between events, and people in the situation, historical and broader cultural-socio-political contexts, and ultimately, the relationship between personal experiences and their life values, aspirations, and/or spirituality. The meaning-making process attempts to integrate spirituality as part of the regular discourse in treatment. A coherent narrative of personal experience is conducive to a more integrative sense of self.

Affirmation: Affirmation and appreciation of one's ability and strengths in dealing with problems of living is consistent with a strengths perspective. Affirmation is a cognitive and spiritual process for individuals and families to connect with, accept, and appreciate their experiences, pleasant or unpleasant ones, as part of their life journey. Affirmation utilizes self-dialogues, affirmation stories, autobiographies, and self-appreciation as channels for change, which also consolidate commitment to change.

Resilience: Resilience acknowledges and utilizes healing abilities that exists within individuals and families, as opposed to reliance on expert and external assistance. Resilience describes a quality and capacity for individuals and families to lie low during stormy days, and to rebound after difficult times or adversities in life.

Transformation: Transformation reflects a developmental perspective of life. Life is in a constant process of becoming and therefore there is no ideal state that can, or should, be attained. The diverse problems of living associated with the passage of life allow individuals to learn, grow, and be transformed. When individuals recognize problems of living as the window for transformation, they not only grow out of the problems, but they turn curses into blessings and convert crises into opportunities. Individuals and families do not just regain previous levels of functioning after their experience with problems of living, including trauma and loss, but they can be transformed with renewed values of life, a new sense of purpose, broadened vision, and enhanced emotional capacity for self and others.

A developmental and transformative perspective of treatment

Treatment goals based on Integrative Social Work are not about symptom reduction or problem eradication. Integrative Social Work does not endorse a "combat" attitude about problems of living. Problems of living are just normal passages of life that could become disguised opportunities for change, growth, and transformation. By connecting with suffering and pain, one can gain access to new spiritual resources in healing (Wright, 2005). By utilizing strengths, appreciating life, making meaning, and reconnecting with their resilience and inner healing abilities, Integrative Social Work creates a transformative context for individuals and families going through problems of living.

Assumptions of Integrative Social Work Regarding Problems

- How people get engaged in problems of living?
  - Problems as normal challenges of living
- How are problems of living maintained?
  - A system out of balance
    - Stagnation
    - Polarization and disconnectedness
- What make a system out of balance?
  - Over-attachment
  - Reduced ability to be mindful of the present
  - Unhelpful representation of problems of living
  - A linear and reductionistic mode of knowing

Assumptions of Integrative Social Work Regarding Client Change

- Change is constant
  - Movement facilitates development and change
  - Live in the moment
  - Accept and go with the flow
- Healing from within
  - Utilizing strengths
  - Staying simple
- Compassion
- A holistic perspective of treatment
  - A focus on the body–mind–spirit connections
  - Systems collaboration
  - Multidimensional treatment orientation
- A developmental and transformative perspective of treatment

Elements of Integrative Body–Mind–Spirit Social Work

3

Systemic Assessment: Everything Is Connected

Assessment has always played an important role in social work treatment. Conventional social work assessment with individuals and families usually focuses on understanding the history of the problem, risk factors contributing to the onset and maintenance of the problem, the effect of the problem on the self and others, and current symptoms, dysfunctions, and deficits. A comprehensive assessment of the problem is thought to help clients and families understand the reasons for their problem, which will help them gain insight into it, leading to beneficial behavioral changes and the elimination of the problem. Consequently, the key tasks of a problem-based approach to assessment are (1) taking a detailed history of the presenting problem, (2) classifying the problem or making a diagnosis, (3) coming up with a case formulation of the identified problem, and (4) agreeing on a treatment plan with the clients to solve the problem.

A problem-based approach to social work assessment does have a number of advantages. The more notable ones are: (1) It directly and explicitly acknowledges the primary concerns of the client. This is particularly true in a managed care environment where cost effectiveness and accountability become an everyday reality of social work practice with individuals and families. (2) The linear, step-by-step, assessment process is logical and rational, making it easier to understand and to be explained to the stakeholders.

(3) When problems are clearly defined, it is easier to have specific, measurable indicators of treatment outcomes. Such clarity is important from both a clinical and an administrative perspective. In addition, as a result of the advent of the evidence-based practice movement in social work, such clarity increases the credibility of social work treatment among other mental health professionals by providing empirical evidence of effectiveness of treatment.

A closer examination of the characteristics of problem-based assessment reveals the influence of a positivist paradigm that underlies its practices. A positivist paradigm emphasizes objective, rational, and linear thinking that implicates cause and effect relationships in explaining phenomena and solving problems (Katz, 1985). An accurate assessment of a detailed understanding of the history of the problem and how is it connected to the current symptoms is assumed to inform treatment choices, and therefore, is intimately related to successful treatment. Insight and identification of the problem are the first step, if not the road, to positive changes in clients. If helping professionals can precisely (or microscopically) study a particular presenting problem, such as depression or marital discord, and discover the fundamental principles or rules governing their behaviors, they will be able to accurately understand, predict, and treat the problem in clients and families.

A more fundamental assumption of a positivist paradigm is that the problem to be studied or treated exists independently as an objective entity outside the person who is making the observation, assessment, or providing treatment. In other words, we can, for instance, study depressed people as an independent entity and discover unifying patterns or traits that characterize this particular group of people. Such a belief underlies the importance of making clinical diagnosis; such a diagnosis will inform professionals of the common characteristics of different types of problem, which then serves as a valid basis for determining treatment. Another implicit consequence of a positivist paradigm is the expert position assumed by therapists. The therapist assumes the role of the expert, who possesses domain-specific professional knowledge that allows him or her to conduct an assessment of the client or family, who inadvertently takes a more passive "patient" role in the assessment process.

In sum, a problem-based assessment approach assumes that there is a direct relationship between the solution and the problem. The solution is to "eradicate" the problem by developing insight into the problem, taking responsibility for the problem, and learning new ways to handle the problem at hand. The therapist assumes the role of an expert, who assesses the causes of the problem and derives a treatment plan that helps clients and families develop better alternatives to handle their problems.

THE SHADOW OF A PROBLEM-BASED APPROACH TO SOCIAL WORK ASSESSMENT

Conventional problem-based assessment has definitely made significant contributions to the understanding of and effective treatment of many problems. However, we have concerns about the implications of a problem-based assessment for different reasons.

Problem Talk as Sustaining a Problem Reality

Because of the emphasis on understanding the history, the roots, and the dynamics of the problem, social work professionals and clients are required to spend an enormous amount of time and energy discussing the presenting problem. In addition, an important component of problem-based assessment is coming up with a diagnosis of the presenting problem. The *Diagnostic and Statistical Manual of Mental Disorders IV (DSM-IV)* provides a comprehensive problem classification system for helping professionals from diverse disciplines in the assessment process. The *DSM-IV* has made significant contributions in advancing social work assessment and treatment. Such a diagnostic system helps the professional, and perhaps the client, to draw on established knowledge about the particular presenting problem and to develop an understanding of the etiology, course, and prognosis of the problem, which bears significant implications for treatment. However, the "shadow" of such a diagnostic system pertains to its inevitable focus on symptoms and problems, and therefore, its inherent deficit perspective.

We are concerned about the impact of a problem-based assessment and of making diagnoses on clients and families, because of our concern about the role of language in sustaining reality (Lee et al., 2003; Saleebey, 1997). Language is the medium through which personal meaning and understanding is expressed and socially constructed by persons in conversation (de Shazer, 1991, 1994). As language is inherently powerful in creating and maintaining conceptual realities, extended pathology or problem-talk in assessment may have the unintended consequence of sustaining a problem framework and distracting the clients' and professionals' attention from developing solutions (Miller, 1997). We are especially reserved concerning using language and diagnoses that label clients' problems as stable or unchanging (Berg & Miller, 1992; de Shazer, 1994), because pathologizing clients' claims of their problems and drilling into the "deep" causes of their problems may serve to further disempower the client through self-fulfilling prophecy (Lee et al., 2003). In other words, diagnosis may bring about labeling effects that may have negative impacts on the clients, as well as restrict the vision of the helping professionals to within the pathological perspective only.

The case of Bonnie: depression precipitated by diagnosing

Bonnie was a 34-year-old woman. She started suffering from muscle pain and stiffness of joints at several locations, at the age of 21. She had received medical care at a teaching hospital and had undergone numerous physical examinations by physicians of various departments. Nevertheless, the exact etiology and diagnosis remained unclear. Interestingly, the pursuit for a diagnosis kept her going energetically for years. The same might also be true for the healthcare professionals involved. About five years after onset, a physician in the Department of Rheumatology came up with an ingenious diagnosis—fibromyalgia syndrome (FMS). That sounded like an end to the uncertainty. However, the optimism was soon proved to be over-simplistic. As Bonnie was looking for information on FMS on the Web, she found that FMS was a "newly invented" diagnosis with unclear etiology. It informed her little about either treatment or prognosis. Finding it so hard to accept that a diagnosis could be so illusive, Bonnie felt desperate and very disappointed. Early optimism was replaced by depression.

The case of David: good "insight" into a problem can be a problem in itself

David was a 50-year-old man. He reported to have been suffering from "bus phobia" for 10 years. He could develop panic-like symptoms easily when riding on a bus. Adopting a positive stance, he faced the problem proactively, sought professional help, kept taking the bus as frequently as possible, and tried hard to control or eliminate the symptoms. He fully agreed to mental health professionals' view that his problem was primarily anxiety. He was keen to learn whatever anxiety management techniques were introduced to him. In conventional mental health practice, he was seen as a "good" client—having good insight and motivation. However, such good "insight" was indeed the key problem in this case—he somehow had developed an obsession for complete symptom elimination. Further anxiety management intervention would only reinforce such obsession. The effective intervention turned out to be most paradoxical: regaining control by letting go of absolute control. By making him able to see having anxiety symptoms come and go as normal and able to downplay the psychiatric label, a single session resolved the 10-year problem.

The therapist saw David in a live clinical training session together with 20 graduate students who were mostly social workers and healthcare professionals. To understand precisely what happened to David, the therapist directed the group to simulate a scenario in which David was riding on a bus. David chose a window-side seat in the bus for a more airy feeling. The therapist kept track of David's responses as the students boarded the simulated bus. In contrast to the therapist's expectations, David's arousal increased only slightly, even when the "bus" got really crowded. He said, "I am not anxious because they all know my problems."

(continued)

(continued)

The therapist responded, "You mean if they didn't know, you would be anxious?"
David said, "Yes."

The therapist further asked, "Are you worried that others may know that you are anxious?" Along this line, the therapist helped him understand that he was anxious about being anxious, and anxious that others might otherwise know and then think negatively of him. He assumed total responsibility for controlling and even eliminating all symptoms. Therefore, the issue was not just anxiety management, as suggested by the conventional diagnostic framework. It was about letting go of the diagnosis and anxiety management. Instead, the cure for his anxiety was anchored in reassurance and self-confirmation.

Missing the Person in the Context

The development of a diagnostic system to assess mental health problems is built upon the assumptions that there is a direct relationship between the solution and the problem. Accurate assessment—a detailed understanding of the history of the problem and how it is connected to the current symptoms—can inform treatment choices and therefore is intimately related to successful treatment. In addition, we can study different problems as independent entities and discover unifying patterns or traits that characterize a particular group of people who have the same diagnosis. Such a belief underlies the importance of making clinical diagnoses; such diagnoses will inform professionals of the common characteristics of people who have a particular diagnosis, which can serve as a valid basis for determining treatment.

Not to minimize the significant contribution of a diagnostic system for helping professionals to systematically understand and assess the diverse presenting problems of clients and families, but a problem-based assessment approach may run the danger of neglecting the whole person, the context, and the mind–body connection. For instance, when an adult is diagnosed as schizophrenic or a child as one with ADHD, people tend to selectively focus on the displayed symptoms. However, a person is much more than the diagnosis. In our experience, we find that the immediate presentation of the individual, his or her intentions, situational variables, and resources are the most important factors in determining the capacity to make changes (Lee et al., 2003). These "surface" issues are far more important to us than a problem-based, diagnostic, complex assessment in determining what will be helpful. Each individual presents features that are relevant at the moment but tend to change as they begin to define the situation differently, learn, and change (Lee et al., 2003). Professionals can miss these "windows of change" when the sole focus is on the client's presenting problem or the diagnosis. For some clients, the presenting problem may be a legitimate reason to seek help or attention, but it is not the core problem. If the intervention focuses on the presenting problem, the therapist may be colluding with and reinforcing the client's avoidance of the core problem.

The case of Cathy: obsessive-compulsive disorder versus problems of living

Cathy was an 11-year-old girl. Over the past year, her behavior of washing her hands incessantly worried her parents and teachers. Her hands were dry and her skin cracked. She wanted to make sure that her hands were absolutely clean, with no germs. The features neatly met the diagnostic criteria for obsessive-compulsive disorder. Such a diagnosis would have suggested a treatment regime focusing on reducing the compulsive behavior, say, by a behavioral therapy method—exposure and response prevention. For Cathy, the context of her compulsive behavior was important. The behavior developed a year ago when she lost her best friend, whose death was somehow related to a complicated case of pneumonia, which first started as flu. She somehow related the sudden death of her friend to her not washing her hands often, which resulted in the flu and later, pneumonia. For her case, unresolved grief and an unhelpful cognitive frame were more relevant than a psychiatric diagnosis of obsessive-compulsive disorder. After intervention that addressed issues in Cathy's current life context, the compulsive behavior remitted spontaneously.

Diagnoses can be influenced by nontreatment related issues that include, but are not limited to, insurance reimbursement requirements, accountability, benefits, power, status, and politics. The process of diagnosing can serve purposes other than deriving treatment plans. Therapy ends at diagnosing is a common phenomenon in health and mental health practices nowadays. Oftentimes, it fulfills professional procedural requirements and administrative accountability. Diagnoses can also be related to medical benefits or sick leave from work or school. The ability to make diagnoses may be seen as a symbol of professional superiority. As such, the motivations behind seeking a diagnosis by the service users and making a diagnosis by the service providers can serve purposes other than the original goals of formulating a treatment plan. These underlying motivations can be barriers to treatment and recovery.

While acknowledging the potential contributions of a problem-based approach to assessment, Integrative Body–Mind–Spirit Social Work is well aware of the potential problems associated with a conventional approach to assessment that puts the social work professionals as the expert and views the client's problem as symptoms that can be assessed or diagnosed objectively. Instead, Integrative Body–Mind–Spirit Social Work utilizes an assessment framework that is strengths based and systemic oriented.

ELEMENTS OF ASSESSMENT IN INTEGRATIVE BODY–MIND–SPIRIT SOCIAL WORK

The essential elements of assessment in Integrative Body–Mind–Spirit Social Work are systemic and strengths based. Emphasizing a holistic understanding of the person, Integrative Body–Mind–Spirit Social Work adopts a systemic approach in assessment (Chan, Ho, & Chow, 2001; Chan, Ng, Ho, & Chow, 2006; Ng & Chan 2005; Ng, Chan, Chan et al., 2006). Whereas the conventional mental and functional disorder classification systems focus on looking for clusters of symptoms, we emphasize a careful examination of the underpinning system imbalance. Moreover, we emphasize assessing and eliciting the strengths of the clients.

Systemic Assessment

When systems are interconnected, the presenting problem is only one of the many phenomena that are indicative of system imbalance. Assessment and diagnosing based solely on the presenting problem is bound to only offer a partial view of the picture. Alternative diagnoses may be made if the focus is shifted to another cluster of symptoms. This is exactly why there is extensive overlapping between many common mental and functional disorders, such as depression, anxiety, chronic fatigue syndrome, and irritable bowel syndrome. Some researchers have proposed a single, inclusive syndrome naming so as to avoid the problem of excessive overlapping among diagnoses (Barreiro & James, 2005). We propose to go beyond the symptoms and look at the underpinning system imbalance. That can be an even more satisfactory solution in conceptualization and clinical applicability.

Systemic assessment concerns the body, mind, and spirit domains and the connectedness among them. Although issues may be revealed one by one, an important goal in systemic assessment is to reveal the connections among those three domains. Doing so can bring about a holistic perspective—the intrapersonal systems, as well as the person in the environment. In systemic assessment, we pay special attention to two notions: "balance" and "dynamic flow." Balance concerns the snapshot composition of the system at a specific time, whereas dynamic flow concerns the interchanges among all components.

Balance

We draw heavily upon the Yin–Yang Theory in our systemic assessment. The Yin–Yang Theory is an ancient Eastern systems theory that has important unique features that supplement current understanding (Cai, 1995). The yin–yang concept sounds deliberately vague for good reasons. It provides a neutral language that does not impose positive or negative values on the observed phenomena. The primary concern is not about maximizing "positives" or minimizing "negatives." "Positives," if excessive, are bound to be harmful; whereas "negatives" always have a functional side that is indispensable. For example, many people, including helping professionals, tend to view anger as a negative emotion, which is based on a dualistic view. The function of anger is often overlooked. The lack of anger or repression of anger can lead to mental health problems. Freud described depression as "anger turning inward" (Freud, 1923/1961). Chinese medicine describes it as "stagnation syndrome" (Ng, Chan, Ho et al., 2006). The key concern is balance, which is a healthy mix of "positives" and "negatives" that mutually regulate each other.

Based on a yin–yang framework, there are four basic scenarios of imbalance (Ng, 2003). To make the abstract concept comprehensible, the cautious–adventurous pair is used as an example through out the explanation. Cautious and adventurous are neutral qualities that are neither absolutely good nor bad. They are natural and necessary to every person. From a yin–yang perspective, being cautious is yin, and being adventurous is yang. With appropriate balance between them, they compliment and regulate each other so that the person can be prudent, rational, but not indecisive, calculative, or obsessive; and can be creative, innovative, but not impulsive or reactive.

Figure 3.1 graphically illustrates the four basic scenarios of yin–yang imbalance. The following is a more in-depth discussion of each of the states.

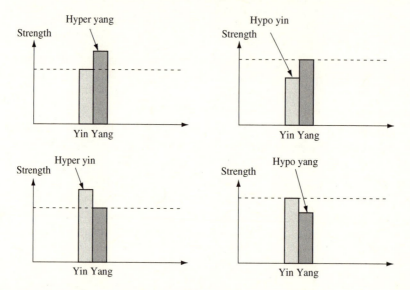

FIGURE 3.1. The four basic yin–yang imbalance scenarios.
Note: The horizontal line represents a reference level of yin and yang. Theoretically, such a reference line does not exist, because yin–yang is an infinitely relative concept. In clinical practice, such a reference line does exist, because all human systems are calibrated to function within a certain level of capabilities.

Hyper yin: yin is excessive.   In the cautious–adventurous pair, cautious is yin and adventurous is yang. The two qualities regulate each other. If we are overly cautious, we may be preoccupied in thinking about every detail and become indecisive and inefficient. It also represses our adventurous side. This is often observed in persons in anxious and obsessive states or in clients with diagnoses of panic disorder, anxiety disorder, or obsessive-compulsive disorder (Figure 3.2).

Hyper yang: yang is excessive.   Using the cautious–adventurous pair as an illustration again, being overly adventurous makes a person impulsive, reactive, and inconsistent. It represses our cautious side. This behavior is often observed in persons in a hypomanic or manic state or in clients with diagnoses of hyperactive disorders or intermittent explosive disorder.

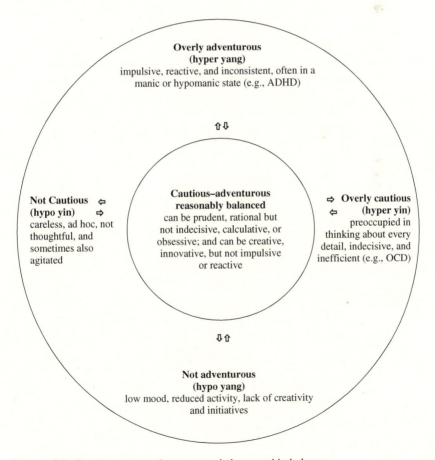

FIGURE 3.2. Cautious versus adventurous—balance and imbalances.

Hypo yin: yin is deficient. Using the same illustration again, the person is not cautious enough, though he or she is not particularly adventurous. The behavioral manifestations can be similar to a hyper yang condition, that is, impulsive, reactive, and inconsistent. However, manic features, such as elevated mood, grandiose, and hyperactive behavior, are absent. Instead, the person appears more careless, ad hoc, absentminded, and sometimes also agitated.

Hypo yang: yang is deficient. This time, the person is not adventurous enough. The behavioral manifestations can be similar to a hyper yin condition, that is, preoccupation with details, indecisive, and inefficient. However, depression features are also common, such as lowered mood and reduced activity, resulting in lack of creativity and initiatives.

It must be noted that these four basic imbalance scenarios are for illustration only. The key to assessment pertains to understanding how yin and yang forces in a system mutually regulate each other to strive for balance. The cited scenarios are far from exhaustive because there are many more possible yin–yang imbalance combinations, for example, hypo yin hyper yang, hypo yin hypo yang, and so on. Moreover, there is no "gold standard" to determine what the normal, hyper or hypo levels are. Yin and yang are relative concepts and must always be considered in pairs. At the end of the day, it is the client who must determine his or her own optimal balance.

Dynamic flow

Balance can be seen as a snapshot of the existing gestalt. Add in a time component, however, and balance becomes dynamic and ever-evolving instead of static. There are constant flows among the components of the body, and such dynamic interflows are essential for maintaining a healthy living system. Borrowing from ideas in Chinese medicine, there are two basic unhealthy states in the dynamic flow of energy: stagnant and hyperactive.

Stagnant: energy not flowing freely. When the system is stagnant, the flow of energy is weakened. There are two further subtypes of this condition:

Low Energy Level: The weakened flow is a result of a lowered energy level. A good example is a depressive episode. Many people describe the experience using the metaphor of being helplessly stuck in a dark pit without sufficient energy to get out.

Blockage: The weakened flow is a result of obstruction in the energy pathways. Considering the lack of communication flow between couples, the reason may not necessarily be lack of energy. It can be due to prejudices and unpleasant past experiences, which create a communication blockage between them. As such, even though sufficient energy is around, flow, that is, communication in this situation, can hardly take place.

Hyperactive: rapid flow of energy.   The flow of energy among diverse subsystems or components is at such an overwhelmingly high speed that it pushes the system to its limit. Again, there are two further subtypes:

High Energy Level: The overly active flow is a result of elevation in energy level. For example, a person who is extremely excited for particular career achievements or successes may enter into an elevated mood state. However, it is common for highly successful people to make premature decisions and engage in impulsive actions because they are overconfident.

Disinhibition: The overly active flow is a result of a lack of proper regulation. Disinhibition is common in both extremely low and extremely high mood states. In extremely low mood states, a person may give up self-inhibition altogether, whereas in extremely high mood states, a person can be so grandiose and self-important that he or she fails to exercise any self-inhibition. Both scenarios can potentially lead to actions that may harm the person and others.

The problems with balance and dynamic flow often coexist and reinforce each other, forming a vicious cycle and preventing the normal self-regulating properties of the system from functioning. These abstract ideas may be better illustrated by the case below.

The case of Mary: transient high blood pressure and hyper yang

Mary was a 45-year-old woman working as a cleaner in a big company. Her presenting problem was a sudden upsurge of blood pressure during the past two days, triggered by a heated quarrel with a coworker at work 2 days back, and she was worried about it. She was also preoccupied with anger and hatred. According to the Yin–Yang Theory, the nature of anger and hatred is yang. Yang needs to be regulated by yin, and vice versa, but excessive yang can hurt yin. Because of weakened yin, the excessive yang was even more disinhibited. The imbalance became self-progressing and led to a hyper yang state, which became stagnant and failed to synthesize and flow back to yin. Meanwhile, yin continued to be consumed to synthesize and support the hyper yang, which, if prolonged, could be overconsumed and eventually weaken the yin. To regain balance, the intervention had to reduce the yang and nourish the yin. Therefore, after Mary received a brief psychoeducation on the mind–body connection concept, the therapist taught Mary simple *taiji* breathing and body work and practiced with her. The slow body movements helped Mary calm down almost instantly, as yin was nourished. After that, some practical dietary advice was given, that is, avoiding food that is hot or yang in nature. Last, but not least, the psychosocial aspect of the event was explored with Mary. Reviewing the incident, she saw that the escalation of the quarrel could have been avoided if either one of them had been less reactive. It was a matter of communication and emotion regulation, not of who was right or wrong—in fact, neither was either right or wrong. Subsequently, Mary took the initiative of apologizing to her colleague for her rudeness and emotional outburst. Her colleague also apologized for her explosive reactions, and they became amicable coworkers again. Her blood pressure returned to normal the following day, and the progress was well maintained subsequently.

Strengths-Based Assessment

In addition to a systemic orientation to assessment, two primary assumptions in Integrative Body–Mind–Spirit Social Work are the beliefs that a client's strengths should be identified and mobilized and that clients have innate healing abilities. Clients and families are usually preoccupied with problems when they seek treatment. Metaphorically, the preoccupation with problems may become a nutshell, shielding all resources inside and making them inaccessible to the person. The concept can be illustrated graphically in Figure 3.3.

Strengths-based assessment is somewhat like creating "cracks" in the shell so that the person can access his or her latent resources, perhaps bit by bit initially. However, as more and more "cracks" appear, clients and families

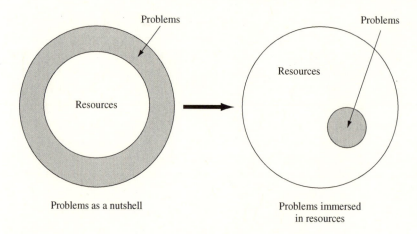

FIGURE **3.3.** "Problems as a nutshell" to "problems embraced by resources."

become more aware of and connect with their strengths and resources. Meanwhile, the stubborn nutshell will start to disintegrate. Eventually, the person will have an opportunity to reorganize a new formulation of his or her condition. For some situations, the problems may be eradicated. Many other problems and challenges in life such as getting old, physical fragility, past childhood abuse may not be "solved." Nonetheless, these problems can be embraced by the clients' strengths and resources. Many psychological and interrelationship problems are fundamentally ones of living that occur naturally when we go through our life journey. The important thing is that the person has strengths to successfully address the problems and a sense of harmony.

A focus on strengths

We explore and acknowledge problems that bring clients and families to treatment. However, we do not spend too much time focused on the problem. Instead, we use the following indicators to let us know when the problem-talk has served its purposes: (1) when the discussion regarding the problem does not offer any more new information for assessment or understanding purposes, and (2) when the clients or families engage in a repetitive recitation of the problems. We believe that problem-talk can sustain a problem reality because of the power of language and self-fulfilling prophecy (de Shazer, 1994; Lee et al., 2003). The more the clients think about their problems, the more they become consumed by and involved in them. Integrative Body–Mind–Spirit Social Work also takes a fundamentally different view of the problem. Instead of viewing problems as negative and troubling, we perceive that problems are indicative of the person or family system's efforts to regain balance.

Identifying personal strengths

Recognizing the power of language in creating and sustaining reality, we are more interested in exploring with clients the times when they were well, resourceful, or able to handle the problem in a more satisfactory manner. Such a practice is influenced by solution-focused and strengths-based approaches (Berg & Kelly, 2000; Lee et al., 2003). We usually do so by asking clients to describe in great detail the times and context when they did not have the problem or were able to address it effectively. Such a therapeutic process helps raise clients' awareness of moments when they were well, capable, and resourceful. "What is noticed becomes reality and what is unnoticed does not exist" (Lee et al., 2003, p. 32). We routinely ask clients and families early on in treatment the following questions:

- What are some of your recent successes?
- What are the achievements that you are most proud of having accomplished?

- For what kinds of things do people compliment you?
- What would others say about the strengths in your family?
- Have you ever made an important change in your life that was difficult to make?
- When was the last time that you successfully broke a habit that was hard to break?
- What is working better for you now?
- What things are you doing that contribute to your life becoming better?
- What little things are you doing that make life a little better?
- How do you keep focused on what you have to do to make things better?

Exploring the "strengths" and potential "contributions" of the problem

Clients and families usually come in with a negative view of their presenting problems or even themselves. It is common for clients and families to have the following descriptions: "I am bound to fail," "Nothing is going to help," "I have tried everything I can and nothing has helped." Integrative Body–Mind–Spirit Social Work holds a different view of the problems, which results in our effort to explore with clients and families the "hidden" strengths of their problem situation. Based on a yin–yang perspective, Integrative Body–Mind–Spirit Social Work assumes that movement created by the dynamic balance of diverse, contrasting forces constitutes a necessary condition for change, growth, and development. From our perspective, problems are in fact indicative of an out-of-balance system that recognizes a force at one end of the continuum without recognizing the complementary existence of the other forces. Consequently, the system ceases to be a dynamic and changing reality but instead becomes stagnant. In addition, when clients and families are in an out-of-balance state, they usually focus on the problematic side of their lives and context. As such, we attempt not to attach value judgments to the presenting problems or problematic situations, because diverse forces are needed in the process of change. In fact, presenting problems experienced by clients or families are likely to be complementary forces or processes in an effort to assist the system in restoring balance.

Consequently, a primary therapeutic focus is helping clients be aware of and appreciative of the "shadow" of their problems, as well as embrace the problem as part of the process of change and growth. In one of our groups with cancer patients, we routinely engage clients in a body scanning exercise and ask them to identify the part of their body that has unpleasant, uncomfortable, or even painful feelings. We then ask clients to have a dialogue with that particular part of their body, asking questions such as, "What does your breast lump (in the case of a breast cancer patient) try to share with you?" "What is

Nora, 75, a widow living alone, often complained about heart problems. When she felt irregular heartbeats, she would call her only son, who was an engineer in a computer company in another town. Her son would immediately come back home and take her to see her physician. She would stay with her son in his house and spend time with her grandson before she went back to her own home the next day. The frequency of Nora's heart problems increased, and Nora's son became very exhausted. Nora enjoyed spending time with her grandson, but her son responded only when she had heart problems. He had never taken the initiative to invite Nora to stay at his place. Her heart problem provided a legitimate and acceptable reason for her to feel cared for and receive attention. During therapy, the therapist helped Nora and her son explore the meaning and the "strengths" of the problem. They realized that the incidents of irregular heartbeat allowed them to have more time together, although in a painful and hectic way. Nora and her son discussed a regular schedule for Nora to stay with her son for a weekend once every 2 weeks. From then on, there was a dramatic decrease in the frequency of Nora's heart problem. Nora and her son had more fun times together. She was healthier and her son much less exhausted.

the message?" We help clients to have a detailed dialogue with their problems. Oftentimes, clients will, at first, come up with negative messages, but it is not surprising when they also share with us other discoveries such as, "my cancer is asking me to take better care of myself and not just bury myself in work."

- When was the last time that you realized that the problem was helpful to you (or your family)?
- If your problem has a voice, what do you think it is trying to share or communicate with you?
- How might the problem be helpful to you (or your family)?
- If we could get rid of the problem, what might be some aspect of it that you might want to retain?

Consistent with strengths-based treatment approaches such as solution-focused brief therapy, Integrative Body–Mind–Spirit Social Work puts great emphasis on helping clients and families notice and reconnect with their strengths and resources. However, we also create a therapeutic context for people to be aware of and appreciate the "shadow" and the "hidden strengths" of their problem situations. The recognition and acceptance of diverse forces in the person or the environment will activate a feedback process that allows for the natural movement and dynamic balance of the system to be restored.

Cat Claw Syndrome: Assessment or Intervention?

Johnson was a 12-year-old boy in grade seven. He had had sporadic attacks of acute muscle spasms in hands, legs, and tongue since the age of six. Over time, he and his parents gave the problem a vivid name: "cat claw syndrome." Johnson and his parents attended the first session, during which all three were told to report and reflect on the onset and subsequent development of the problem and deliberate on the possible causes. Toward the end of the "assessment," Johnson said that the spasm was a way of escaping from difficult situations. In his words, he said, "It is just like a small insect abandoning its shell in order to get out of the scene." The insight emerged because of expanded awareness. With that, the presenting problem was resolved almost instantly. The parents knew how to respond if the "cat claw syndrome" recurred, and they discussed and agreed on ways to help Johnson develop a stronger character that could withstand tough situations. This case illustrates the idea that assessment can facilitate reflection, awareness, and insight. In this sense, it was extremely powerful and therapeutic.

Assessment as an Ongoing Process

Although we discuss assessment and intervention as separate processes, we must emphasize that the two are in fact inseparable in Integrative Body–Mind–Spirit Social Work. They are presented sequentially here just for the sake of clarity and ease of explanation. Because system equilibrium is dynamic rather than static, assessment has to be a continuous process. During the course of intervention, the system may fluctuate wildly and therefore require closer monitoring. In Integrative Body–Mind–Spirit Social Work, assessment and intervention are embedded in each other. Their relationship is neither sequential nor linear. In practice, the assessment process can be extremely therapeutic, and therapeutic intervention can also be diagnostic and enlightening.

TASKS AND THE PROCESS OF ASSESSMENT

Integrative Body–Mind–Spirit Social Work views the assessment process as a continuous and ongoing one that is characterized by a process of expanding and reconnecting. Clients and families come in, afflicted by the particular problems in their life. We do not take an expert position in the assessment process. We believe that clients and families are experts of their own lives and the center of change efforts. They self-assess the nature and extent of their problems as well as what they can do to make the situation better for themselves or others. They are the assessors of their own problems, aspirations, and solutions (Lee et al., 2003). The role of a therapist is that of a facilitator.

We collaboratively work with clients and families in a process that helps them expand their awareness and perspective of their life situation. Although it is important to acknowledge and understand the presenting problem, which is often a specific concern, we also facilitate clients in exploring the body–mind–spirit domains, as situated in their broader environment. We emphasize the utilization of clients' strengths early in the intervention, and we focus on small things and accomplishments, such as not giving up and taking the initiative to seek help. We highlight the strengths of clients early on in the treatment process and continue to do so throughout the helping process. As assessment continues, we help the client see how the various aspects revealed are connected. Most importantly, we facilitate clients in rewording their presenting problems into positively stated goals; we help them to focus on what they can do, or are already doing, to make the situation better, instead of focusing on what has gone wrong. Figure 3.4 elucidates our conceptualization of the assessment process.

We conceive the key therapeutic tasks of the initial phase of Integrative Body–Mind–Spirit Social Work as the following: (1) making initial contacts, (2) developing a collaborative therapeutic relationship, (3) understanding the problems and assessing lethality, (4) accessing and appreciating

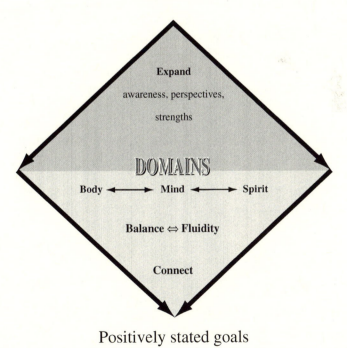

Positively stated goals

FIGURE **3.4.** Systemic assessment: a process of expanding awareness and making connections.

clients' strengths, (5) expanding awareness and perspectives, (6) facilitating body–mind–spirit connection, (7) assessing the person in the environment, (8) assessing balance and dynamic flow, and (9) assessing goals.

Making Initial Contacts

We view being connected with the client as a prerequisite for any successful treatment. We are working with a person, not on a set of problems, and the person is more than the presenting problems. Consequently, we are interested in knowing the clients as unique beings instead of people with particular presenting problems. Adopting a strengths-based approach, the therapist acknowledges the client's primary concerns, as well as strengths and efforts in coping with the problems, and helps clients to feel hopeful. The principle is normalizing the presenting problem and avoiding labels or diagnoses as much as possible.

Normalization is a useful technique often employed in the Integrative Body–Mind–Spirit Social Work during the initial treatment sessions. It does not downplay or dismiss the client's problems of concern. While acknowledging the problems, normalization sees them as part of a universal process of becoming, and highlights the client's strength and resilience in surviving. Many problems can be seen as normal responses of normal people to unexpected situations. Normalization is a form of empathy that also enables assessment to be more complete, that is, client's strengths can be revealed as well. Normalizing the experience of seeking treatment is another important strategy.

We believe that the way we treat clients and families when they first come for treatment sends them a powerful message about the way we perceive them and the fact that they have problems. Integrative Body–Mind–Spirit Social Work attempts to send them a message that is consistent with our view of problems as a normal part of living. We normalize clients' help-seeking experience by making sure that they feel comfortable with and welcome by the treatment facility. We do so by (1) taking the clients and families around the treatment facility, showing them the rooms, sharing with them the vision and mission of the facility, which is, in our situation, the cross-fertilization of Western and Eastern philosophy and therapeutic techniques in creating effective, positive, and transformative changes in individuals and families; and (2) offering or making a cup of tea or coffee for the clients so that they feel more at home. The simple act of walking into the pantry and making a cup of tea or coffee is a symbolic and empowering gesture that signifies a person-to-person interaction. The treatment facility is no longer an intimidating or a dehumanizing institution for people with problems.

On the wall of the clinic, there is calligraphy by Thich Nhat Hanh that says, "Be happy, enjoy the present moment." The therapist will describe to the client how the great Zen Master Thich Nhat Hanh promotes the idea of peace, tranquility, and appreciation of every moment in life. On a bench in a counseling room, there is a beautiful boat made by a cancer patient, Elaine. The therapist will point to the boat that was made of beads to describe Elaine's experience. Elaine shared with us that, when she was diagnosed with breast cancer, it was as if she had been thrown into the sea. She was shocked, anxious, and almost drowned in her own fears and tears. After learning how other cancer patients were transformed through finding meaning in their suffering, Elaine joined a cancer support group, learned more about alternative methods to help herself, and became a peer counselor to help other newly diagnosed patients. She found her new life by climbing onto the boat. On the boat, she could appreciate the beauty of the sea.

These posters on the wall and the stories of individuals relax the client as well as plant in their minds the idea that having problems in everyday living is normal and fine. It can personalize the experience of seeking help. Clients can recover from their symptoms and may even be able to grow out of their help-seeking experience.

Developing a Collaborative Therapeutic Relationship

While a diagnostic-based assessment emphasizes objectivity and the expert position of the therapist, a strengths-based assessment emphasizes collaboration with clients and families in the assessment process. Integrative Body–Mind–Spirit Social Work views the therapist–client dyad as a facilitator–participant relationship. The therapist's role is an expert in facilitating change, while the client's role is an expert on his or her life. This role differentiation should be consistently emphasized even from the first session. Applying this persistently can help the client believe and accept that he or she is an expert on his or her own life. This is extremely empowering and can facilitate a growing sense of mastery, not only over the problem but also over one's life at large. Ultimately, it is the life of the client, and the major decisions of life have to be made by him or her.

The ability to feel the feelings of clients and to give accurate empathetic responses is instrumental to developing a collaborative therapeutic relationship. Competence in joining and relational skills such as active listening, summarizing, and reframing are indispensable. We relate to the client as a person and not just as a client with a diagnosis or presenting problems. We also expect and allow ourselves to behave more like a real person instead of a distant professional or expert. We do not believe that our involving attitude will negatively affect the assessment process. Our clinical experience indicates that such an approach can actually help bring out more from the client.

Self-disclosure is another area used comparatively more in Integrative Body–Mind–Spirit Social Work. Conventional assessment involves asking clients to self-disclose according to a certain format, and during the process, therapists should adopt a relatively detached, objective stance. We are in favor of an involved and collaborative approach. As clients disclose very personal experiences, we often respond with appropriate self-disclosure as bounded by our ethics (see Chapter 15 for a detailed discussion). For instance, in live clinical training sessions, we adopt a transparent and open approach in which trainees are housed in the same room with clients, rather than hiding and observing "subjects" or "patients" behind a one-way mirror. We adopt the procedures of a reflecting team (White & Epston, 1990) and encourage trainees not to analyze and give "expert" opinions but engage in dialogues of personal views and experiences that give rise to multiple voices. Our experience suggests that the multiple voices of therapists' and trainees' reflection are oftentimes more powerful than expert opinion and advice. The connection with clients is much stronger, and thus there will be less resistance or defensive reaction. It definitely helps foster a collaborative therapeutic relationship.

Although collaborative and more personable, Integrative Body–Mind–Spirit Social Work does not downplay the importance of appropriate professional relationships and/or boundaries. Instead, we strongly believe that these are important principles for social work professionals.

Understanding the Problems and Assessing Lethality

Integrative Body–Mind–Spirit Social Work conceptualizes presenting problems as normal problems of living and part of the process of becoming. Life gives people many surprises, some excruciating, some disappointing, and others devastating. The primary goal of Integrative Body–Mind–Spirit Social Work is not about getting rid of the problems. Most problems, particularly those that have happened in the past (such as childhood sexual abuse, car accidents, parental divorce and aftermath turbulence), or those pertaining to developmental changes (fragile health conditions associated with aging) just cannot be eradicated. Although some problems may not be easily resolved, clients and families still have choices in how they address the problem. Integrative Body–Mind–Spirit Social Work focuses on solving solvable problems in some situations (e.g., communication problems between couples or parent–child, and performance anxiety). At other times, it can be about problem appreciation or letting go. The ultimate goal, however, is growth and transformation.

We explore and acknowledge problems that bring clients and families to treatment. Active listening to the presenting problems is necessary, and is

considered extremely helpful in engaging clients and families in a therapeutic process of change. It is important that the client feels listened to and
understood. We also collect information regarding the history of the problem,
factors contributing to problem maintenance, the effect of the problem on the
client and others, and current symptoms. However, we do not spend more
time on understanding the problem situation than needed. We use the following indicators to let us know when the focus on understanding the problem
has served its purposes: (1) when the discussion regarding the problem does
not offer any new information for assessment or understanding purposes, and
(2) when the clients or families engage in repetitive recitation of the problems. These are signals that tell us to shift from focusing on problems to other
beneficial therapeutic processes that will help create change for clients and
families.

Although Integrative Body–Mind–Spirit Social Work is not interested in
making pathological diagnoses, it is important to pay attention to and assess
lethality. Our practice is bounded by the professional Code of Ethics National
Association of Social Workers (NASW, 1999). The bottom line is that protection of personal safety should always be given top priority. Should there be any
hint of self-harm or harming others, the risk must be assessed accordingly. If
there are clues of psychiatric symptoms, such as firmly held, abnormal beliefs
and hearing unreal voices, the client's mental state should be examined.

Because this book targets readers who have already had foundation training
in clinical practice, family therapy, or counseling; risk-assessment techniques
and mental state examinations will not be repeated here. Readers may refer to
psychotherapy, psychiatry, counseling, or clinical social work textbooks for
further information. Nevertheless, we must reiterate that therapists must be
competent in identifying, assessing, and managing risk. For example, in working with clients with suicidal risk, therapists must be sensitive to the clues of
suicide, which can be verbal, behavioral, or emotional, and therefore should
conduct clinical interviews assessing the risk level. Listening to the precipi-
tating event is often a helpful strategy in engaging the client in the therapeutic
process. While listening to the story, attention should be paid to the perception and coping patterns of the client. Dichotomy, perfectionism, rigidity, and
overgeneralization of thought are associated with increased self-harm risk.
If a client has recently deliberately attempted self-harm, the incident must
be inquired into, especially on the motivation and means (lethality) of self-
harm, and if there was prevention against discovery. Since hopelessness and
helplessness are strong clinical predictors of suicide, a client's view of self,
the world, and the future should be inquired into. Last, but not least, it is
important to inquire about suicidal ideations and plans of the client. All these
inquiries are important whenever one is working with a client with self-harm
risk, regardless of the therapeutic approach.

In addition to the conventional risk and mental state assessments, we often include another assessment—assessing the "strengths" of the problem, that is, the role of the problem from a systemic perspective. Oftentimes, presenting problems do have self-protection functions and are important for survival in the face of adversity. For example, depression may help a person conserve his or her energy, and externalized aggression may help someone avoid facing internal weaknesses or pain. As the problems are being dealt with, the protective functions will also be modified, typically weakened. If the weakening of these protective functions is quicker than the restoration of healthy systemic balance, it may lead to acute intensified frustration, and even physical risk to oneself or the others. For instance, it is well known that the initial period coming out of depression carries an elevated risk of suicide. The important implication here is that assessment of risk is a continuous process throughout intervention while vigorous restructuring and rebalancing are taking place.

Assessing and Appreciating Clients' Strengths

Integrative Body–Mind–Spirit Social Work utilizes clients' strengths early on in the assessment process. Presenting problems are, oftentimes, problems of normal living and part of the process of becoming. We adopt a stance of curiosity to learn from the client how he or she keeps surviving, functioning, performing, or even enjoying difficult times. No matter how desperate or vulnerable the client is, he or she must have strengths and resilience. Human systems have an amazing ability to self-regulate and heal, as long as healthy energy flow is not totally blocked. Soliciting the client's strengths early on can help lay a foundation for embarking on the self-healing process.

Being strengths-based, Integrative Body–Mind–Spirit Social Work is not interested in coming up with a diagnosis on the "abnormal" aspects. On the contrary, we routinely normalize the problems from the developmental and person-in-context perspectives. As mentioned earlier in the chapter, we assess clients' personal strengths and resources, past successes, and assets in the environment. We put great emphasis on helping clients and families notice and reconnect with their strengths and resources. Instead of viewing the presenting problems as negative and something to be gotten rid of, presenting problems experienced by clients or families are likely to be complementary forces or processes in an effort to assist the system in restoring balance. Integrative Body–Mind–Spirit Social Work provides a therapeutic context for clients and families to assess the "strengths" of the problem and to be aware of and appreciate the "shadow" and the "hidden strengths" of their problem situations. The recognition and acceptance of diverse forces in the person or the environment will activate a feedback process that allows the system to restore balance.

To help clients and families see their problems from a different perspective, instead of a diagnosis, we oftentimes use metaphors to describe and name clients' problems as based on their descriptions, such as "Oh, you were like a cactus in the desert!" or "You were like bird flying with only one wing!" An appropriate and helpful metaphor can deeply touch clients and families and help strengthen the therapeutic relationship. It makes the therapeutic contacts more humane and brings life and energy to the counseling room. More importantly, it creates space for imagination, so that hope and strengths may start coming out of a stuck condition. After all, the goal of assessment in Integrative Body–Mind–Spirit Social Work is to connect various perspectives of the problems to strengths, no matter how weak the connection. Through identifying the strengths explicitly, the strengths can be groomed further. Enhancing the existing strengths is usually easier than reverting to the weaknesses.

The case of Bonnie and Jack: an animal trainer and her obedient lion

Bonnie is the 34-year-old woman suffering from the fibromyalgia syndrome mentioned earlier in this chapter. In the first few years, she was frustrated at having no diagnosis. After being given a diagnosis, she was equally frustrated, if not more so, because of the vagueness and emptiness of the diagnosis. She entered into depression, and she was not only disappointed, sad, and fearful, but also angry and hostile. And the only outlet for her anger was her husband, Jack, a big guy with a muscular build, somewhat like a lion. In contrast to his strong appearance, Jack had a submissive character. He was a diligent delivery worker, and his hobby was small pet animals, on which he spent most of his leisure time. Bonnie wanted Jack to be much more sensitive and concerned about her emotional needs. Repeatedly feeling disappointed, she often beat Jack up (not to an extent that substantial physical injuries were inflicted) to release pent-up emotions. Jack always behaved like an obedient lion in front of his master and simply surrendered to the physical punishment. As the therapist was listening to Bonnie's story, a vivid scene of a lion trainer popped up in his mind. He shared it with Bonnie, and her facial expression suggested that she was deeply touched—there was laughter, tears, and helplessness. If a good picture is worth a thousand words, so is a good metaphor. It helped deepen the therapist's connection with Bonnie.

Instead of diagnosing and classifying problems, such as depression or domestic violence; or pathological theorizing, such as "periodic outburst of violence is a result of guilt and repressed anger," the therapist simply adopted a stance of curiosity and was keen to learn how they got along over the years. The approach revealed the other side of the story. Punishment is only one aspect of the relationship between an animal trainer and a lion. After all, the relationship is built on love and mutual concern. If we focus on problems, we may mistake the problem for the whole. If we look for strengths, there will be no shortage of them.

Utilizing clients' strength is a continuous process throughout assessment and intervention. In subsequent work with Bonnie, many more of her strengths were revealed, including being intelligent, conscientious, proactive, sensitive, and conversant. Assured of her merits, she felt that she might be a good companion to Jack in his hobby of small pet animals. She succeeded. The trainer–lion pair became a loving couple who shared their love of small animals. Although it sounds somewhat silly, the important point is that it is their marriage and their lives.

Expanding Awareness and Perspectives

Acknowledging the client's concerns is the first task in the assessment process. There are two levels of acknowledgment: firstly acknowledging the client's situation, and secondly, helping the client acknowledge his or her own cognitive, emotional, and behavioral responses. The conventional counseling and psychotherapy treatment relies heavily on verbal conversation. This may not be entirely satisfactory, in particular when working with clients who are not comfortable with articulating deeper feelings verbally or who are so acutely distressed that normal verbal expression abilities can hardly be drawn upon. Integrative Body–Mind–Spirit Social Work incorporates and routinely uses a wide range of nonverbal intervention techniques in the first session. These simple techniques can facilitate the client in becoming grounded rapidly and attain an expanded awareness of the mind and body. Such awareness is instrumental for further inquiry of the mind–body connection.

The case of Dorothy: expanding understanding of emotions

Dorothy came for help because of the frustration arising from her husband's extramarital affairs. She described how angry she was, her sense of betrayal, jealousy, and hurt. She gave details of conversations, which were not very helpful. Instead of staying in a conventional assessment, the therapist engaged her in body movement exercises. The therapist asked her to vent her emotions on a big exercise ball, as if this ball could feel and hear her. She screamed, hit, kicked, and squeezed the ball, and let out her mixed emotions. "This is unfair! I hate you! Why do you do this to me?. . ." There were many tears on her face. Behind her aggression, Dorothy was actually saying "I love you. I don't want to lose you. You mean a lot to me." The therapist asked her to take a few slow, deep breaths, and sit on the ball as if she were her husband. Through reversing the role, Dorothy further understood the relational aspects of her emotions and behaviors.

(continued)

(continued)

The therapist helped Dorothy articulate her mixed bag of emotions—anger, a sense of betrayal, loss of trust, a sense of insecurity, fear of abandonment, jealousy, hatred, and confusion. The love–hate possessiveness coupled with strong destructive thoughts of revenge and divorce were indeed strangling and suffocating. If the therapist had continued with the conventional assessment, Dorothy would only have stayed mentally preoccupied with and ruminating about the event, which was unhelpful to the therapist and unbeneficial to the client. We utilized body movement to get around the mental fixation, so as to expand her awareness and perspectives. That helped assessment, as well as provided alternate entry points for intervention.

We utilize a number of simple exercises to help expand awareness and perspectives. The most commonly used are meditation and body scan.

Meditation

In stillness and nonaction, one can be more aware of the body, mind, and the surroundings—breathing, heartbeat, emotions, thoughts, desires, noise, temperature, air flow, smell, light, and so on. To prepare a client for a more calm, relaxed, and open session, simple breathing and meditation exercises for 5–10 min are usually very helpful. Before the exercises, the therapist provides a brief explanation. Then, the client is asked to sit comfortably, with eyes closed, and focus on observing his or her breathing. Whenever the concentration is hijacked by thoughts popping up, he or she needs to gently refocus on observing breathing. After meditation, a short debriefing, when a client is helped to share his or her brief meditation experience, can follow. This can often be naturally connected to the primary concern of the client.

In Dorothy's case, she was asked to acknowledge her thoughts and emotions as they came. She was also taught to couple her breathing with a peaceful and safe scene. Dorothy responded very positively, as she had been using such techniques to help herself relax since childhood. She described three scenes in which she could find comfort and freedom: first, riding on a horse and racing through a big meadow; second, sitting in a waterfall with cool water droplets washing away all of her worries; and third, lying on the sofa at Grandma's, who was totally loving and forgave unconditionally. Thus, Dorothy could fully be herself at Grandma's farmhouse in the village.

Body scan

Body scan is another technique that is often routinely used in the assessment session, typically after acknowledging the client's concerns. The client is guided to be in a meditation-like state and to pay attention to different body parts, one by one, slowly trying to be aware of bodily sensations, whether they are comfortable or uncomfortable, subtle or profound. The usual practice is either going from toes to head, or from head to toes. The "scanning process" takes between 5 and 10 min to complete. Afterwards, the client may be asked to put down marks on a sketch of the human body where discomfort is noticed. The client is then helped to share the discomforts and explore the possible connections with psychosocial factors. The discussion naturally opens up the mind–body connection notion.

In Dorothy's case, the therapist asked about the somatic response when she thought about her husband's extramarital affairs. She could vividly described a sense of pain in her heart, the numbness of her hands and feet, a dull headache, and a sense of emptiness, as if her soul had left her body and her physical body had become hollow. The expanded awareness helped free her from the mental entanglement. She began to listen to signals from her body and attempted to take better care of it. It opened up useful perspectives for subsequent intervention.

We are often amazed while using these simple techniques with our clients. Disconnection and incongruence between the mind and body is indeed more common than most people think. Clients often report, "Oh, I was not aware of that!", "Oh, this is the first time that I have noticed the sensation!", or "Oh, I had not thought of the connection between the two!" In prolonged difficult situations, the cognition and emotion domains are often preoccupied with problem solving. They may stretch their body to the limit with only limited awareness. Acknowledging the signals of the body is an important step in coming to a complete acknowledgment of our physical and mental strengths and limitations and the strengths and limitations of the problem and the context. This can trigger useful discussion instrumental to the next task—connecting the body, mind, and spirit.

Facilitating the Body–Mind–Spirit Connection

Building upon the experiences from the previous tasks, more dynamic work on the body, mind, and spirit may follow. In Integrative Body–Mind–Spirit Social Work, assessment and treatment are inseparable. Through expanding awareness, clients get in touch with more aspects of themselves, including the wounds—both visible and hidden—whether in the body, mind, or spirit. Believing that the client is the best assessor, we often ask him or her to rate the overall degree of distress in relation to the key issues brought up. For instance, solution-focused brief therapy routinely uses the scaling question to engage clients in the self-assessment process (Berg, 1994; de Shazer, 1991). The scale was originally used by Howard Volpe in his work on desensitization in the late 1950s and has been subsequently adopted by different therapeutic approaches, such as solution-focused brief therapy and cognitive-behavioral approaches.

We ask the client to respond on a scale of 0–10, in which 0 means no distress, and 10 means extremely distressed. This self-assessment process is not just for the sake of assessment. It aims to enhance awareness and integration.

We frequently enact simple self-healing exercises with the client. The goal here is to enhance the body–mind–spirit connection and channel innate energy for self-healing purposes. By carefully observing responses, we can get a better idea of the client's state of distress, as well as a better idea of the state of the client's strengths. As such, many treatment techniques mentioned in the following chapters pertaining to treatment can also be used in the first session and during assessment. To avoid duplication, we introduce a few of them here for illustration.

Healing Hands

The client is instructed to put his or her hand on the part of body that hurts. The hand gently touches and massages the body part. Also, the client focuses his or her attention as much as possible, to attempt to communicate with the body part. The client is then guided to acknowledge the stress withstood by the body part, appreciate it, and be grateful. This simple activity can legitimize and nurture self-love. The client is then helped to explore the connection between somatic discomforts and psychosocial distresses. A simple exercise like this can help client appreciate the mind–body connection.

Physical movement

Many clients are stuck in a problem situation when they come for therapy. Bypassing the verbal and cognitive venues, sometimes it is helpful to engage the client in bodily movement as a way to metaphorically release body rigidity and allow for a sense of control. Pent-up energy and emotions can be vented. Depending on what the clients feel more comfortable with, we can encourage the client to just jump or walk vigorously for a short while. The moderate physical movement may help to ease the body and mind and allow the client to express the pent-up problem. Another exercise is the "rapid shoulder movement." This exercise involves shaking the shoulders backwards quickly for about a minute. It symbolizes throwing away unnecessary burdens and attachments. The therapist can help clients to be aware of situations, persons, or thoughts that he or she should let go. The symbolic meaning associated with the exercise may open space for a discussion about spirituality issues. What are the attachments? What may be let go?

Self-affirmation

Problem solving is not merely a task. It is very much about hope and faith, especially when the problem is difficult to solve, or simply unsolvable. In addition to cognitive ability, we need strength from the domain of spirituality.

To achieve this, we encourage clients to explore sources of affirmation, inspiration, and hope by asking them to come up with statements that are affirming and inspiring for them. These statements can be "I deserve love even though I have been deeply hurt in relationships." "I love myself and will live well despite all these difficulties around me" and so on. Clients may need some coaching initially. As they make the statements more comfortably later on, we can tell that some progress has taken place. Further discussion of the client's spiritual beliefs and mental health status can follow.

Returning to Dorothy, with a better awareness of the mind–body connection, she was taught simple hands-on healing techniques so that she could help herself be better grounded. Dorothy was asked to rub her hands hard until they were warm, then put over her heart and liver, rub the skin, and gently pat on the body, so as to remove the sense of being hollow, by imagining a light of love and nurturing radiating through her palms into her body. Dorothy tried the method and felt empowered because she did something to help herself physically and emotionally.

Dorothy had always trusted her husband. She adored him and was dedicated to staying with him the rest of her life. Growing up in a loving family with parents who were intimately attached to each other, Dorothy had always believed in a total dedication to the marital bond. Her husband was her sense of ultimate meaning, because she did not practice any religious faith. Confronted with the risk of losing her husband, Dorothy almost collapsed, for her meaning for life had shattered. When asked about her belief system on love and marriage, Dorothy shared her recent experience of listening to a self-help tape on the sources of suffering—greed and attachment being two key sources of suffering. The discussion naturally entered the domain of spirituality.

Assessing Persons in Their Environment

Person-in-environment constitutes another important area of assessment. It is a dynamic and dialectical concept that moves beyond a linear analysis of the relationship between the client and his or her environment. More importantly, it involves seeing how the client is viewed and treated by the environment, how he or she reacts to others, and how others react to the client. This is a psychological process at the meta-cognition and the meta-relational level (Ho, Chan, & Zhang, 2001). An environment is multilevel and multidimensional. The more important social systems include the family, the extended family, school or work, peers, and other social, cultural, religious, or spiritual engagements. Although Integrative Body–Mind–Spirit Social Work does not advocate a mechanical approach that reviews all the key systems routinely in performing assessments, the therapist should be alert to the significance of these systems. The therapist should selectively explore the relevant systems with the client.

Adopting a dynamic systemic perspective, we not only look at how the environment is influencing the client, but we also look at how the environment is influenced while influencing the client. From a strengths-based perspective, we are interested in understanding the interface between the client and the broader system and the purposes served by the interface. Furthermore, we should be aware of the interactions among various systems. For example, a married person is involved in the nuclear family system, extended family system, friends, job, and so on. These holons are embedded in the broader socio-cultural-political-economic system. A change in the interaction between the person and one of the systems (e.g., unemployment) will induce changes in all other interactions.

Although the notions of "illness behavior," "maintaining factors," and "secondary gains" are popular among mental health practitioners in conducting assessments and making diagnoses (Gelder, Gath, Mayou, & Cowen, 1996), these concepts imply pathological meanings. Integrative Body–Mind–Spirit Social Work adopts a developmental stance and understands the problematic behavior patterns as unsuccessful attempted solutions in the process of becoming, which result in an unbalanced system. Consequently, instead of labeling environmental factors as "problem-maintaining factors," it is more fruitful to understand dynamic patterns and how the person-in-environment strives for a transitional balance that helps survival. Such an attitude recognizes the "hidden function" of the problem context, acknowledges the client's survival efforts, and therefore is more likely to successfully engage the client in the process of change.

Assessing Balance and Dynamic Flow

The notions of balance and dynamic flow provide a framework for understanding the client or family from a systemic perspective. Although these are fairly abstract concepts, they are, in fact, fairly easy to apply in social work practice with individuals and families. First, yin and yang are relative concepts, and the Yin–Yang Theory makes sense only when we are considering a pair of related but dialectical concepts. In order to apply the framework of balance and dynamic flow, we must firstly identify a pair of core issues that concern the client. In working with a client, we usually develop awareness of a key issue first, for example, "anxiety." The next step is to discover and reflect on the related and opposite issue that concerns the client. For example, it could be "calmness." As such, "anxiety–calmness" forms a yin–yang pair that may fit into the framework of balance and dynamic flow for further analysis. We may reflect on which is overabundant (hyper) and which is inadequate (hypo). We can also reflect on how frequent and to what extent the two switch between each other (flow). An important principle is that we must strive to understand the issues from a systemic perspective. Oversimplistic good–bad labeling and value judgments must be avoided.

The case of David: meaningfulness versus meaninglessness

David was a bright young man with an educational background in business management. However, despite his committed attitude, he had made no career advancement four years after receiving his MBA from a prestigious university. Worse still, he could not stay in any job for long, typically less than a year, and usually resigned. While listening to David's story, the notion that he "must do meaningful things" appeared strongly and repeatedly. The therapist reflected on his understanding of David and became aware of another highly relevant notion—the notion that he "must not do meaningless things."

Meaningfulness–meaninglessness becomes the yin–yang pair of concern in the David's case. In choosing and starting a new job, David typically focuses more on the meaningfulness (yang aspect) of the job. That was the honeymoon period, during which he performed and enjoyed his work. After the honeymoon period, his excitement and dedication subsided, and he began to perceive his job as meaningless (yin aspect). The beginning of a new job may be seen as a hypo yin (meaninglessness) and hyper yang (meaningfulness) state. Such an out-of-balance state is bound to be unsustainable. With the nourishment of yin (the "meaningless" side of the job), a hyper yang will eventually diminish. However, doing "meaningless" things is indeed most natural and necessary. David viewed small talk, taking breaks after lunch, and even negotiation tactics with colleagues as meaningless. We all know that we need to do these "meaningless" things in order to support our pursuit for the "meaningful" things.

A few months into a new job, David would start feeling exhausted and querying the meaningfulness of the job. While the notion of "meaningfulness" was shrinking, the notion of meaninglessness grew steadily. When meaninglessness reached a certain level, David would experience a sudden, rapid change of balance, and meaningfulness would rapidly transform into meaninglessness. After that, the job was seen as totally meaningless. The balance became a hyper yin (meaninglessness) hypo yang (meaningfulness) state.

David would then resign and go for a quiet retreat for a few weeks. During the break, he would reflect on and reduce his preoccupation with meaninglessness and gradually nurture his meaningfulness energy. He was successful, and every time he would become reenergized, leave the retreat, and is ready for another meaningful adventure. Of course, this was exactly the seed of the problem for the next cycle.

The therapist shared with David his understanding of this pattern by using the framework of balance and flow. David felt greatly inspired and enlightened, and we discussed a suitable balance for him in subsequent contacts.

Since the concepts we use for assessing balance and dynamic flow are new to most social work practitioners, we summarize the key steps below for easy memorization:

Step 1: What is the key notion of concern? (e.g., I must do meaningful things.)

Step 2: What is the yin–yang pair? (e.g., meaningfulness versus meaninglessness)

Step 3: What is the dialectical aspect of the phenomenon? (e.g. I must not do meaningless things.)

Step 4: What are the relative intensities of the two notions, that is, examining yin–yang balance?

Step 5: What is the flow between the two notions (e.g. rigid/fluid, consistent/inconsistent, or gentle/vibrant)?

Assessing Goals

Goals for change that are determined by clients have an important and pervasive impact on the therapeutic process (Elliot & Church, 2002; Foster & Mash, 1999). A major challenge encountered by most clients in social work treatment is that they know when they have a problem, but they do not know when the problem has been successfully addressed. When this happens, clients may be in treatment for a long time, because there are no clear indicators of health and wellness. Goal setting becomes crucial in successful treatment because it gauges clients' progress toward beneficial solutions to their problems (Maple, 1998). When goals are defined as a major focus of treatment, accountability for changing one's behavior can be effectively achieved (Lee, Uken, & Sebold, 2007). The use of goals shifts the focus of attention away from what cannot be done to what can be accomplished; it moves clients away from blaming others or themselves and holds them accountable for developing a better, different future. Goals also increase the client's awareness of his or her choices and offer an opportunity to play an active role in the treatment (Lee et al., 2003). Consequently, clients' goals influence how they orient to treatment, participate in the process, and evaluate the effectiveness of the treatment efforts (Elliot & Church, 2002).

When the therapist and the client engage in a facilitator–participant relationship, Integrative Body–Mind–Spirit Social Work emphasizes that treatment goals must be determined by the client. The therapist should routinely ask the client what he or she wants to get out of the treatment process and invite clients and families to imagine how they would like to be different. According to traditional Chinese wisdom, there are always opportunities in crises. The client is asked to explore opportunities in personal growth, as well as growth opportunities for his or her significant others. Because assessment is a continuous process, the goals are subjected to the client's continuous self-assessment. We routinely facilitate clients in reviewing their progress in achieving self-determined goals identified in the previous sessions. While acknowledging the problems, we also focus on helping clients see their strengths and resources in pursuing the goals.

SUMMARY

Assessment in Integrative Body–Mind–Spirit Social Work is characterized by being systemic oriented and strengths based. We use the framework of balance and dynamic flow in understanding the dynamic equilibrium of clients and families from a systemic perspective. We emphasize assessing a client's strengths and help him or her recognize the "hidden strengths and messages" of the problems early on in treatment. Integrative Body–Mind–Spirit Social Work views the assessment process as one of expanding and reconnecting. Primary beginning tasks of assessment involve helping clients and families expand their awareness and perspectives regarding their problem situation. This is achieved through multi-modal activities involving the body, mind, and spiritual domains. With expanded awareness, therapists begin the process of helping clients to connect their body, mind, and spirit together, with the purpose of helping clients and families reconnect with their inner and environmental strengths and resources. Adopting a person-in-environment perspective and systemic orientation in assessment, we use the framework of balance and dynamic flow in understanding the dynamic equilibrium of a client both within the person and between the person and the broader environmental context. A useful assessment process should lead to clients and families that are more able to self-assess their situation and develop clear and specific goals that will bring beneficial changes to their life.

It is fundamental that the therapeutic relationship is collaborative and client centered. The relationship is one of facilitator–participant, in which the client is seen as the expert on his or her own life and the best person to assess his or her aspirations and goals, whereas the social work professionals assume the role of facilitators who collaborate with clients and families in the process of change.

Formulating a Treatment Plan: A Multidimensional Approach

THE INTEGRATIVE BODY–MIND–SPIRIT HEALING WHEEL

Integrative Body–Mind–Spirit Social Work uses the metaphor of a "healing wheel" to describe a multidimensional orientation in treatment. The conceptual framework of a multidimensional treatment orientation is based on our clinical experiences as well as assumptions about the multidimensional and interconnected nature of human beings, problem contexts, and reality. We affirm the body–mind–spirit connection within an individual and the person-in-environment perspective in providing treatment. The healing wheel idea is graphically illustrated in Figure 4.1.

Spirituality, life values, culture, and personal meaning provide a foundation for the mind and body, the other functions revolving around mind and body in a dynamic and vibrant way. We use the metaphor of a spinning wheel to represent the dynamic movement of the system. It is conceptualized as somewhat like a body–mind wheel spinning on top of a base, spiritual health. If the spiritual foundation is fragile or distorted, the body/mind wheel on top can hardly revolve properly or stably. The facilitation of spiritual growth is therefore a key component in Integrative Body–Mind–Spirit Social Work.

In addition, the body–mind wheel has to keep revolving steadily in order to maintain a dynamic balance on the spiritual foundation. The body–mind

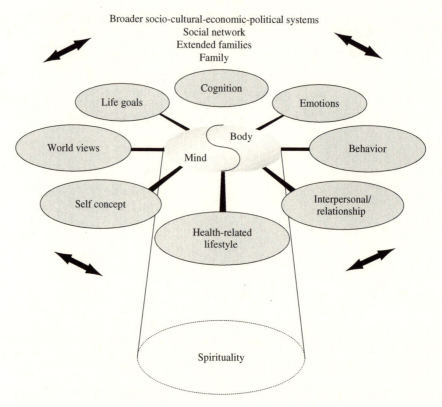

FIGURE **4.1.** The Integrative Body–Mind–Spirit healing wheel.

wheel has an amazing self-balancing ability that can weather diverse changes and challenges in life. However, if the body–mind wheel spins too slowly or stops spinning, it will fall off. If it spins at extremely high speeds, it will overwhelm and eventually damage the whole system. The equilibrium is a dynamic equilibrium that demands fluid interactions and interflows among the various components inside. Building on a person-in-environment perspective, the system is constantly interacting with the external broader socio-cultural-economic-political environment. More importantly, the system has the amazing power of being able to constantly self-adjust and balance in response to internal and external changes. Although the system may look delicate, it is very robust.

When the body–mind wheel fails to revolve properly or stably, it is an indication of disequilibrium and unbalance in the system. Such a state will ultimately be manifested in diverse health and mental health problems. The disequilibrium can be related to problems in balance and dynamic flow. The treatment goal is for the person to strive for or regain an adaptive balance by easing blockages, regulating disinhibitions, and modulating any hyper or hypo state downward or upward respectively. These concepts have been introduced in earlier chapters. The following case example can further illustrate the ideas more clearly and vividly.

The Case of Julie: Strong but Vulnerable

Julie, aged 34, was in the process of a turbulent divorce. To avoid endless conflicts with her ex-husband, she moved out of the matrimonial home with her three children, aged between 12 and 20. She had a strong character. In face of such great difficulty, she had become even stronger—much stronger than she had ever been. She managed to set up a new home quickly and settle down with the three children. She found a job in a home for elderly people, and, she pursued vocational training in personal care for elderly people. She kept up with her hobby—dancing—kept going to church and maintaining her social life as normal as possible. She was keen to prove that she was strong, and was living a life no worse, if not better, than before. However, such "outer strength" was not complimented by corresponding "inner strength" and was therefore not well grounded. Deep in her heart, she was fragile and weak, but these attributes were very much suppressed and denied. The cost was steep, because she denied her needs for emotional and tangible support from others. Pursuing strength rendered the slightest setbacks intolerable, and thus she was highly irritable and volatile. Family relationships suffered, as witnessed by increased conflicts between Julie and her youngest son, often over his studies. She and her ex-husband had an adversarial fight over the ownership of the matrimonial home, which, in fact, was not worth much. The irrational fight was clearly heading toward a lose-lose ending, but both parties were still bitterly fighting with each other. Julie was highly vulnerable and was at the edge of "losing her mind." Suffering from stubborn insomnia and headaches, she felt as if her head were about to explode. Julie was physically and psychologically exhausted, very close to the point of total collapse.

The healing wheel provides a useful framework to understand the experience of Julie. Fueled by the burning desire to be strong, Julie's body–mind wheel was spinning at exceptionally high speed. However, there was not a strong spiritual foundation to support the wheel. Imbalance was radical—being strong (yang) was not balanced with being weak (yin); being firm (yang) was not balanced with being flexible (yin); and being hard in facing the problem directly (yang) was not balanced with being soft in allowing one to have a safe haven (yin). Using the yin–yang framework, each pair of opposite attributes was at an imbalanced state, with hyper yang and hypo yin. As the condition continued, yin was further overconsumed and weakened. A damaged yin could not regulate yang effectively. Consequently, a hyper yang without yin's regulation could be extremely unpredictable and volatile. The self-balancing and healing capability of the system was lost due to the imbalance. The disequilibrium led to a range of physical and psychological problems, such as insomnia, headache, irritability, and emotional volatility. At the end of the day, the root of fragility was related to the spiritual foundation. Divorce entirely shattered Julie's worldview and her view of herself. She badly needed new meanings and identities, which were yet to be discovered.

To restore the equilibrium and the system's self-healing capability, a key treatment goal for Julie was to nourish yin, that is, the soft and tender side, and to reestablish a spiritual foundation. The discussion on the dialectic pair—being strong versus being weak—enlightened her. Being strong and being weak do not necessarily reject each other, but they can also compliment each other. Being weak can be a form of being strong at a higher level. For instance, confessing weaknesses requires a lot of inner strength, and forgiveness requires not only strength but also wisdom. Along this line of thought, Julie tried to tone down her "being strong" stance. That helped her become more in touch with her other aspects. Also, Julie tried to allow herself to be "weak," and she began to recognize and nurture the needs of her "weaker" side. She found a new equilibrium point between being strong and being weak. Hardness could be complimented by softness. Having more inner strength and being spiritually grounded, she could relate to her ex-husband again. They later came up with a voluntary agreement about the divorce. She also found a new balance point in relating with children, relatives, and friends. She found her new life.

FORMULATING A USEFUL TREATMENT PLAN

A treatment plan, if put together well, provides a useful map with clear indicators to help clients and helping professionals accomplish positive changes. In Integrative Body–Mind–Spirit Social Work, the first task in formulating a useful treatment plan is to select the most relevant and helpful entry point that will quickly produce desirable changes in clients. We understand that it is our ethical responsibility to help clients make positive changes as quickly as possible.

Multiple Entry Points for Treatment

In Integrative Body–Mind–Spirit Social Work, there can be multiple entry points when starting to work with a new client (Chan, Ho et al., 2001; Chan et al., 2006; Ng & Chan, 2005). For example, the entry points can be cognitive, emotional, behavioral, interpersonal, physical, environmental, and so on. The approach is strategic in the sense that it can be extremely flexible and highly individualized. The aim is to connect with the client through a therapeutic task that is relevant to him or her and can produce positive effects quickly. Having encouraging experiences during treatment will make the client more ready to work with the therapist in other dimensions of life and living.

Although the selection of a helpful and useful entry point is an art, there is a systematic way of approaching it. Here are the key steps:

1. Firstly, at the macro level, the therapist should pay attention to and get a feeling about the balance and dynamic flow of the client. Is the balance too yin or too yang? Is the flow too turbulent or too stagnant? These ideas provide a general direction for the intervention.
2. Secondly, Integrative Body–Mind–Spirit Social Work emphasizes the spontaneity, immediacy, and relevance of a treatment plan to clients. The best entry point is preferably an issue mentioned by the client during the session.
3. After identifying the issue, we may choose to approach it through the body, mind, or spiritual domains, as well as the family and broader social systems, or a combination of them.

More information on the common entry points and techniques we use is given in a later part of the chapter. Before that, let us consider two case examples so as to have a better idea of the framework first. In Julie's case, she was obviously hyper yang, with turbulent energy flow in the beginning of the intervention process. Her preoccupation was with being strong and not showing any signs of weakness. The preoccupation prevented her from accessing other natural needs, whether they were bodily, psychosocial, or spiritual. We chose the body and spiritual domains as the entry point, and picked breathing and meditation as the initial techniques. Our reasons for making such a choice were:

- At a hyper yang and turbulent energy flow state, the technique should be more yin, that is, more quiet, calming, and soothing.
- The issue of concern, that is, Julie's preoccupation, was primarily in the cognitive domain. Intervening at the cognitive domain ran the risk of further cognitive entanglement. From our clinical experience, it is much quicker to intervene through the body in such a situation.
- Breathing and meditation were chosen as the intervening techniques because they were consistent with the above line of thinking. Breathing is a fundamental sign too often forgotten. A few deep, slow breaths help us to

focus our attention on existential sensations and bypass mental entangle-ment. In a meditative state, we practice nonreactivity and observe our inner self. The "mind channel" was deliberately not chosen so as to avoid further entanglement with the existing mental preoccupation and rumination.

The approach proved to be extremely effectively and efficient. Julie was able to slow down and calm down substantially, and was relieved from her state of mental entanglement. She was more aware of different aspects of her body, mind, and spirit. She could hear her inner voice: "I need to slow down, I can and should be weak in some situations, I need to love myself..." and so on. Such enhanced awareness provided a helpful anchor for further therapeutic work.

Let us consider another client who was in a different state of imbalance. Peter was a retired teacher living with his wife, Nancy, who was also retired. Their children were grown up and had moved away. Peter suffered from a mild stroke a few months ago, resulting in weakness in his right arm and right leg, but physical recovery was satisfactory: He could walk stably without aid, and could cope adequately in daily living. However, Nancy's reaction greatly bothered him. Despite Nancy's concern about Peter, she was covertly jealous of Peter because he received most of the attention and care from their children. She became overinvolved in "caring for" Peter. Starting as early as 4:00 a.m., Nancy started delivering all sorts of "goodies" to Peter, such as massage, physical exercise, food, drinks, health snacks, walks, entertainment, and so on. Quite often, Nancy was in a mixed emotional state (love, jealousy, worry, fear, etc.) and was at the edge of losing self-control. Many of these "goodies" were mental and physical torture for Peter.

Peter had a very gentle and tolerant character. He loved and cared about Nancy. He understood Nancy's emotional and behavioral reactions, and adopted a patient, accommodating stance. For Nancy's protection, he kept everything within himself and did not disclose the problem to his children. However, he was already stretched to the limit.

Peter attended the first session on his own. He appeared to be down, spoke slowly, and spoke little. He did not gesture or move much. Nevertheless, the therapist could easily observe and feel his pain and emotional turmoil. There was an obvious obstruction of his free expression. He also shared that he felt as if his chest was obstructed and he could not breathe smoothly. Using the "talk approach" at this point may not be helpful because of his depressed state and physical complaints. Other entry points had to be considered.

Using the framework of systemic assessment and focusing on the concepts of balance and dynamic flow, Peter was at a hypo yang and hyper yin balance, with stagnated energy flow, as reflected by his depressed mood and repres-sion in emotional expression. A key issue of concern here was obstruction, in both communication and the body. The body domain was selected as the entry point. Firstly, the "five sound technique" (see Chapter 6 for details) was used. Peter was asked to take a deep breath and then make a sound as loud and long as possible. The feeling of ventilation and exhaustion was extremely refreshing and revitalizing to him. Secondly, the therapist engaged Peter in rapid jumping (see Chapter 3 for details). His body was loosened and energized. The rationale for choosing these techniques were the following: (1) These activities addressed the system imbalance. They helped lift the energy level and flow. (2) They were highly relevant to the felt needs of the body, that is, feeling obstructed in the chest. The effects were quick and effective. Peter felt a sense of decongestion, emotionally and somatically. He was helped to share the experience with these two exercises. The therapist discussed the body–mind connection phenomenon with Peter. This process enabled the therapist to join with the client and set the groundwork for further treatment.

Table 4–1 provides examples of strategies and options in selecting entry points. Because Integrative Body–Mind–Spirit Social Work emphasizes

TABLE **4–1.** Strategies and Options in Selecting Treatment Entry Points

EXAMPLE OF CLIENT'S CONDITION	Selecting Entry Points	
	STRATEGIES	EXAMPLE OF TECHNIQUES
A) Low energy level and stagnant flow (hypo yang, hyper yin)	Increase energy and activity level (nurture yang, contain yin)	
Sadness, hopelessness, depressed	Nurturing love for both self and others	Loving kindness meditation, imagery, affirmation, praying, body movements, healing hand, self-massage, nutritious drink or food, snacks
Self-disapproval, low self-esteem	Divert attention to strength	Self-affirmation, life review, meaning reconstruction, body movements
Worry, contemplation	Detach from thinking, activate other senses	Body movements, mindfulness training, live the moment
Over-attachment, fear of loss	Let go and move on	Accept impermanence, nonattached appreciation
Lack of motivation, meaning/direction of life	Identify internal calling	Life review, death–life deliberation, reconstruct concepts of self and world

TABLE **4–1.** *(continued)*

EXAMPLE OF CLIENT'S CONDITION	Selecting Entry Points	
	STRATEGIES	EXAMPLE OF TECHNIQUES
B) High energy level and disinhibited flow (hyper yang, hypo yin)	Slow down and decrease activity level (nurture yin, contain yang)	
Craving for something, feeling needs unmet, increasing discontent	Learn to count blessings	Mindfulness training, appreciation of life, live the moment
Hatred, anger, impulsive, violence	Expand awareness of emotions, channel energy into constructive activities	Body movements, use of sound, expressive art, letter writing, loving kindness, and forgiveness
Indulgence in getting something	Appreciate inaction	Discussion of life and death, mindfulness practice
Anxious, agitated, impulsive	Promote self-discipline, appreciate stillness	Meditation, mindfulness training, live the movement
Elevated mood, self-important, self-centered	Nurture loving kindness and compassion	Loving kindness meditation, death–life deliberation, recognize impermanence

spontaneity, immediacy, and relevance, the table does not aim to be exhaustive. Many of the techniques mentioned are described in detail in the following chapters on treatment.

The Role of Spirituality in Formulating a Treatment Plan

Facilitating spiritual growth is of paramount importance in Integrative Body–Mind–Spirit Social Work. Getting in touch with the spiritual dimension oftentimes helps clients set priorities and make decisions regarding desirable changes and tasks to be accomplished (Culliford, 2002; McSherry, 2000; Richards & Bergin, 1997). Such awareness constitutes the basis for formulating a useful treatment plan. A useful starting point for helping clients to explore their spirituality is expanding their awareness regarding personal existence. Through meditation, other mindfulness practices (such as mindful eating and walking), and simple body–mind exercises, the client can develop a closer relationship with him or herself as well as the social and natural environment (These therapeutic techniques are introduced in Chapters 5 through 8). With deeper existential insight, the client is ready to venture further when exploring spirituality issues. Also, the spiritual foundation gets stronger and is ready for the body–mind wheel to take changes and challenges.

Revisiting the meaning of life is a useful strategy for exploring spirituality. It is enlightening to discuss dialectic pairs, such as successes versus failures; happiness versus suffering; living versus dying and death; and detachment versus attachment. Deliberating conflicting concepts related to life can help the client loosen his or her existing rigid paradigm, gain new perspectives, and explore potential and viable equilibrium points. Julie's experience provides a good illustration; the discussion about "being strong" versus "being weak" helped her gain insight about her problems and embark on search for a new equilibrium point.

FORMULATING A TREATMENT PLAN: PROCESS ISSUES

Formulating a useful treatment plan requires attention not only to the content but also to the process. The following are pertinent issues that we have found important during the process of formulating a treatment plan with clients and families.

Client-Centered

During the process of formulating a treatment plan, the client has to agree on both short-term and long-term treatment goals. In Integrative Body–Mind–Spirit Social Work, the client is seen as the expert on his or her life. He or she should determine the scope and pace for the process of change. Integrative Body–Mind–Spirit Social Work maintains that clients remain the center of change and that social work practitioners are facilitators of the change process. Findings from empirical studies affirm such a collaborative orientation. Goal agreement between the client and the therapist is important for the client's success in treatment (Busseri & Tyler, 2004; Long, 2001). Conversely, negative treatment outcomes in decreased client satisfaction, treatment incompliance, and premature termination are associated with incongruity of goal content between the client and the therapist (Goin, Yamamoto, & Silverman, 1965), or the client's request is ignored or overruled (Lazare, Eisenthal, & Wasserman, 1975).

Specific and Doable

A useful treatment plan is one that can guide the process of change. It should provide detailed and specific information about steps that the client can take to accomplish positive changes. Such a practice orientation is influenced by solution-focused brief therapy. Primary characteristics of a useful treatment plan include the following (Lee et al., 2003):

- The treatment plan is manageable and doable. A lofty plan usually sets clients up for failure, as they may have neither a clear idea of, nor the ability to accomplish, the many intermediate steps that may lie in between.
- The plan should contain goals and tasks that can be initiated and maintained by the client and should not be dependent on the initiation of someone or something else. People have more control over what they can do, and they can change themselves but not others.
- The plan should be stated as specific as possible in behavioral terms, so that the client has a clear direction and a "behavioral map" to guide goal-oriented behaviors.
- The plan should contain goals and tasks that are stated in a positive form so that the client has a clear idea about what he or she will be doing versus what he or she won't be doing. "Not doing" something does not keep the client focused on goal attainment.
- The plan should be stated in a process form, because the process is indicative of specific steps and tasks, but the end goal is not.

Focus on Strengths

It is worthwhile emphasizing again that the Integrative Body–Mind–Spirit Social Work adopts a strengths-focused stance and aims to foster growth and transformation. The focus is on what people can do well versus what they are lacking (Berg, 1994). The primary purpose is to reconnect clients with their unused or underused resources and strengths (Lee et al., 2003). Therefore, the treatment contract should fully reflect these core values. It is fine for the clients to have goals about being "less anxious." However, it is important to include goals about becoming and staying "calm." Moreover, it is important to make positive meanings out of "being anxious and worry." Pain and suffering can be blessings in disguise.

An Ongoing Process of Becoming

The treatment plan is never a static entity. In practice, it keeps evolving as the client evolves. Goals are added, removed, and modified continuously. The presenting problem is simply a part of normal living and becoming. Assessment and treatment go side by side. No assessment can be purely evaluative. Assessment is inevitably intervening and therapeutic in a sense, whereas treatment always brings about new insight, hence new information for assessment. As such, assessment and treatment formulation and implementation form a dynamic, interactive, and ongoing process. After all, the client is the center of his or her own process of evolution or, sometimes, transformation.

AFTERWORD

Is transformation a golden moment of enlightenment? Or is it a continuous process of relentless learning and practicing? This has been a heated debate in Zen Buddhism for many centuries. It is plausible to conclude that both are true. As individuals can be very different, overgeneralization is usually not helpful. Transformation may appear more like a quantum leap to some people. Nevertheless, a moment of enlightenment can rarely be complete. As there is no limit in spirituality, expanding transcendental awareness can go on forever.

Although the process of becoming is a lifelong journey, there has to be an end to treatment. In many psycho-pathological models, the length of treatment may be prescribed fairly specifically upon completion of assessment and diagnosing. In Integrative Body–Mind–Spirit Social Work, however, the length of time the client and therapist work together is not specified explicitly. Because it is a process of rebalancing, transforming, and becoming, it is primarily up to the client to decide when it is helpful for the therapist to join him or her, and when to terminate treatment. In to our experience, most cases require fewer than 10 sessions. The client and therapist collaboratively make the decision for when to end treatment. When the client feels largely rebalanced and grounded, and self-healing capabilities are restored, he or she will naturally show readiness for being on his or her own again in the journey of becoming.

The end of treatment signifies the beginning of a new phase of becoming for the client. The therapist's key tasks are, firstly, to appreciate the opportunity to become part of the client's process of change; secondly, to review with the client the learning, growth, and transformation gained from the process; and last, but not least, to send wholehearted blessings for the client to embark on the next phase of journey of life. In a sense, the treatment continues beyond the ending, as the process of becoming continues. It is common to hear clients reporting their continued growth and transformation even after the termination of the case. Every ending is a new beginning, and vice versa. After all, life is an ongoing process of becoming.

As a brief summary, the roadmap and key stages of Integrative Body–Mind–Spirit Social Work are summarized in Table 4–2. It must be noted that a stage model is used for simplicity of presentation only. In Integrative Body–Mind–Spirit Social Work, assessment and intervention are embedded in each other and form a spiral process, as do the four "stages."

TABLE **4–2.** Roadmap of Integrative Body–Mind–Spirit Social Work

STAGES OF CHANGE	THERAPEUTIC MOVES
1. Building relationships	• Forming collaborative facilitator–participant relationship • Strength-oriented, acknowledgment, normalization, and de-stigmatization • Unconditional positive regards
2. Expanding awareness	• Articulation and emotional expression • Meditation, body scan • In touch with one's body, mind, and spirit
3. Connecting	• Body–mind–spirit connection within the family and broader social systems • Understanding "strengths" of problems or symptoms • Systemic perspective: balance and flow of various systems and subsystems
4. Making shifts	• Self-acceptance • Acceptance of ambiguity, letting go of control • Regaining balance and fluidity

SUMMARY

The chapter introduces the multidimensional treatment approach of Integrative Body–Mind–Spirit Social Work. The healing wheel conceptualizes spirituality as a base for the body–mind wheel to revolve steadily on top of it. Building a solid spiritual foundation is seen as the ultimate goal of treatment. To intervene in the dynamic equilibrium of the body–mind wheel, a multiple entry points approach is advocated. Integrative Body–Mind–Spirit Social Work emphasizes spontaneity, immediacy, and relevance in formulating treatment goals. It is unnecessary to restrict ourselves to "talk therapy." Intervening in the body, mind, or spirit domains flexibly and appropriately can bring about quicker and better changes. Intervention should be client centered, specific, doable, and strengths focused. Last, but not least, change is seen as an ongoing process of becoming. The ending of treatment signifies the beginning of a new phase of becoming.

5

The Power of the Mind: Moving Beyond Cognition and Problem Resolution

Social work practice traditionally recognizes the human mind as a key component that plays a pivotal role in problem formation and influences human behaviors as well as human changes. The interpretation of the human mind, however, is constantly changing and evolving, as facilitated, or constrained, by the values and available knowledge at the time regarding human behaviors and the change process (Donzelot, 1979; Johnson & Sandage, 1999; Lee, M. Y., 1996). Prior to the 1950s, social work practice with individuals was predominantly influenced by psychodynamic theories that originated from the work of Sigmund Freud (1923/1961). Psychoanalytic theory, as developed by Freud, emphasizes a belief in the power of the unconscious mind, biological impulses, and other internal processes of a person to determine behaviors (Freud, 1936). Treatment focuses on assisting individuals to get in touch with their unconscious mind and work through deep-seated intrapsychic struggles through analysis.

Building upon Freudian psychoanalytic theory, but refining and modifying its concepts, ego psychology (Goldstein, 1995; Hartmann, 1939), object relations theory (Mahler, 1968), and self-psychology (Kohut, 1971, 1977) developed. Together, these theories form the contemporary psychodynamic base of clinical social work. Of these theories, ego psychology has exerted substantial influence on clinical social work practice. The work *Ego Psychology and*

Social Work Practice by Goldstein (1995) is a well-cited example. Different from psychoanalytic theory, which focuses on the unconscious, instinctual, and irrational aspects of human mind and personality, these approaches draw attention to the more rational, autonomous, and problem-solving capacities of the mind. Treatment focuses on enhancing individuals' abilities to adapt to the environment and to gain mastery by utilizing ego-supportive and ego-modifying techniques. The focus of treatment shifts from the unconscious mind to the rational and autonomous mind.

Starting from the 1950s, the predominance of psychodynamic thinking in clinical social work practice was increasingly replaced by a growing acceptance of theoretical plurality. Existentialism and humanism arose as a third force in psychotherapy. These approaches are characterized by a positive view of human nature and the perception of self-actualization as the ultimate goal of therapy (Frankl, 1967; Lantz, 1993; Rogers, 1965). The approaches also focus on assisting individuals to be more in touch with their feelings and to reflect on themselves, others, and their situations, in a search for personal meaning and self-actualization. They also form the basis of insight-oriented, reflective, and expressive forms of social work practice that enhance the clients' self-awareness and understanding as a way to promote positive changes in their lives. The focus is not so much on the rational and autonomous mind but rather on the meaning-searching and meaning-making aspects of the mind.

Current social work practice with individuals, however, is heavily influenced by cognitive approaches that emerged in the late 1950s and 1960s. The book entitled *A Rational Approach to Social Casework*, by Harold Werner (1965), represents an early classical example of applying a cognitive approach to clinical social work practice. The focus of cognitive approaches is the accessible conscious mind, which can be perceived as a reaction to the psychoanalytic approach that focuses on the inaccessible unconscious mind. It is also a legacy of a body–mind dualistic thinking, which originated from Descartes' view of the existence of two distinct domains: the thinking mind and the feeling body. Despite recognizing interrelationships between an individual's cognition, feelings, and behaviors, cognitive approaches explicitly support the primacy of cognitive processes over emotional and behavioral processes in constructing problems and instigating changes. The mind is treated as a distinct entity and an independent focus of treatment. Cognitive-based social work practice approaches also adhere to a narrow view of the mind as a mind that thinks and converses rationally (Beck, 1995; Beck et al., 1979; Ellis, 1996; Meichenbaum, 1977, 1995). In fact, cognitive-based social work does not use the word "mind" but instead chooses to use the language of cognition, which represents the functions, processes, and characteristics of the rational mind, which focuses on information processing, cognitive appraisal, attribution, decision making, problem solving, and so on. The works by prominent theorists such as Aaron Beck (Beck, 1976; Beck et al., 1979) and Albert

Ellis (Ellis, 1996; Ellis & Dryden, 1987) have exerted an enormous influence on social work practice with families and individuals from the past several decades to the present day.

Social work practice with families, however, is heavily influenced by a systems perspective (Bateson, 1972, 1979). A systems perspective constitutes the fundamental theoretical framework for the practice of structural family therapy (Minuchin & Fishman, 1981) and strategic approaches (Haley, 1990; Watzlawick et al., 1974). These approaches view families as interlocking human systems and individual pathology as only a manifestation of a problematic family structure that promotes or supports problem behaviours in individuals. Treatment focuses on creating beneficial changes in the family structure by expanding perspectives, reframing, creating a relational context by restructuring (structural approach) or paradoxical interventions (strategic approaches). The treatment focus is still on the conscious mind, with the addition of behavioral changes in how family members relate to each other.

A brief review of the historical development of social work practice with individuals and families reveals that the power of the mind, as utilized by social work practice, has continuously evolved over time, from a focus on the unconscious mind to the meaning-making mind and to the current emphasis on the conscious, rational, and autonomous mind, as exemplified by diverse cognitive-based approaches and systems-based approaches. The focus of reflective-expressive approaches or action-oriented treatment orientations in social work practice is on insight development (existential and humanistic approaches, self-psychology, ego psychology), identification of the cause of the problem to solve the problem, cognitive restructuring (e.g., task-centered, problem-solving, or cognitive-behavioral approaches), discovering the solution-building process by the conscious and rational mind (e.g., solution-focused approaches), family restructuring, or pattern changes (family therapy).

A HOLISTIC VIEW OF MIND: THE CONCEPTUALIZATION OF THE "MIND" IN AN EASTERN CONTEXT

Integrative Body–Mind–Spirit Social Work is inevitably a part of the evolving trajectory of how social work practice understands and utilizes the human mind in the process of change. We recognize the usefulness and contributions of existing cognitive-based interventions and utilize these approaches to bring about positive changes in clients and families. However, we bring in additional perspectives, influenced by Eastern philosophies and practices, to help clients formulate new and expanded perspectives and awareness in the process of change.

The conceptualization of the "mind" in an Eastern context encompasses a holistic view. The Chinese word *xin* denotes the concept of a "mind." In addition to the rational mind that people needs in problem solving, the Eastern mind also emphasizes the heart, which is more related to passion, care, concern, compassion, willpower, values, meaning, and so on. Table 5–1 summarizes the conceptualization of the Eastern mind, which includes the cognitive mind, emotive mind, and spiritual mind. The delineation of mind into the three domains of cognition, emotion, and spirituality is primarily for analytical and illustrative purposes. The mind is actually viewed as an entity with diverse and connected characteristics and functions.

Influenced by Eastern philosophies, Integrative Body–Mind–Spirit Social Work understands the power of the mind as follows: (1) The power of the mind not only lies in its instrumental functions and processes of rational decision making and problem solving, but the mind is also, in itself, a source of discipline and healing. (2) A holistic view of the human mind should include the cognitive, affective, and spiritual dimensions, as all three dimensions are interconnected. (3) The human mind is also interconnected with body processes.

TABLE 5–1. An Eastern Perspective of the Mind

THE MIND	COGNITIVE MIND/THINKING	EMOTIVE MIND/AFFECT	SPIRITUAL MIND/SOUL
Components of the mind	• Information processing • Recognition, perception, and memory • Cognitive appraisal, attribution, reasoning, understanding • Analysis, critical examination, weighing of alternatives, selection of options, decision making • Problem solving by forming mental maps of pathways and coping with complex tree of decision points	• Emotions and mood state • Affect, care and concern • Compassion and altruism • Capacity to handle frustration • Willpower and determination, perseverance and endurance • Self-concept and confidence	• Values and belief systems • Sense of purpose and meaning in life • Insights and intuition • Aspiration • Acceptance of unpredictability and vulnerabilities in life • Wisdom in nonattachment • Awakening and hope

THE POWER OF THE MIND

Conventional social work practice views the human mind as primarily represented by one's thinking or cognitive processes, which include information processing, appraisal, attribution, decision making, problem solving, and so on. A Western perspective of the mind focuses on what the mind can do and accomplish in relation to tasks, challenges, and problems experienced by an individual. Defining problems and setting goals are routine processes in social work treatment, regardless of the particular approach to which the practitioner adheres. Social work treatment is usually more interested in the functions and processes that a rational and conscious mind can achieve instrumentally.

Eastern philosophies and practices, influenced by Buddhism, share not only similarities but also differences with the Western view of cognition. Buddhism also assumes cognitive primacy over behavior. For instance, in the *Dhammapada Sutta*, the Buddha perceives that a person's thoughts and actions are the cause and conditions that will shape his or her future:

> Mind is the forerunner to all things. It directs and makes them. If someone speaks and acts with a deluded mind, suffering will follow him, as the wheels follow the footsteps of the animal that draws the cart.
>
> Mind is the forerunner to all things. It directs and makes them. If someone speaks and acts with a pure mind, happiness will follow him, as the shadow follows the body.
> *(Dhammapada Sutta)*

The major difference, however, lies in how Eastern practices focus on the human mind as a source of discipline and healing through meditation. The mind not only serves instrumental functions but also becomes the subject of interest in and of itself.

Meditation is a set of practices that have been around for more than 4,000 years, with roots in Buddhism, Ayurveda, and other contemplative traditions. Through meditation, one cultivates the ability to create a mindful existence, knowing the state of the mind and body at all times. Broadly speaking, mindfulness is characterized by two qualities that are related to two distinctive intentions associated with meditation practice. One intention is to expand awareness of the moment-to-moment existence in a nonjudgmental and nonattached manner. Nyanaponika Thera (1972) describes mindfulness as "the clear and single-minded awareness of what actually happens to us and in us at the successive moments of perception" (p. 5). Jon Kabat-Zinn describes mindfulness as the intentional cultivation of nonjudgmental moment-to-moment awareness (Kabat-Zinn, 1990). Mindfulness, in essence, describes a quality of consciousness that is characterized by enhanced attention to and awareness of the current experience or present reality *as it is*. When one is mindful, he or she is receptive (as opposed to reflexive, when the conscious attention is focused on particular cognitive operations) and open to internal and external stimuli. The state of consciousness is perceptual and nonevaluative (Brown & Ryan, 2003).

The other intention of meditation, however, is to encounter life and the world with an attitude of love and compassion. Loving kindness and compassion constitute two of the "Four Divine Abodes" which, together with sympathetic joy and equanimity, are the four cardinal virtues of Buddhism. From the Buddhist perspective, it is said that cultivating compassion for oneself and others treats many diseases. In Buddhist meditation, the means to bring someone back in touch with himself or herself is to cultivate compassion. The focus of loving kindness and compassion is about an egoless and unconditional love to self and others. It all starts with practicing love toward the self as an example of a sensitive being. Through cultivating compassion, one learns to be kind, trusting, sincere, and respectful to oneself and to give genuine love and care to oneself. Only then can an individual extend the same compassion and love to others.

In sum, an Eastern perspective suggests that one will need to nurture two fundamental qualities of the mind—moment-to-moment mindfulness, which is awareness in an open, receptive, and nonevaluative way, and an attitude of loving kindness and compassion—in order to allow our inner potential to fully unfold and to initiate self-healing powers that are integral to the mind (Schmidt, 2004).

The Benefits of Being Mindful

Being mindful has a unique place in the Buddha's teachings. The Buddha himself attained enlightenment and development of knowledge and wisdom by observing and learning by paying careful attention—mindfulness practices. In essence, the Buddha perceived deluded emotions, thoughts, and actions fueled by "ignorance" as the primary cause of suffering. The practice of mindfulness permits a person to develop clarity of the mind and attain true vision, knowledge, and wisdom, which can lead to the cessation of "greed," "hatred," and "craving," which liberates a person from suffering (for details, please refer to Chapter 1 and Appendix A). Buddhist teachings have their own religious reasons for the benefits of meditation and mindfulness practices, but recent advances in our understanding of meditation suggest that these practices also have far-reaching physiological and psychological benefits.

Early studies in the 1970s (Benson, 1975; Benson, Berry, & Carol, 1974; Lazar et al., 2000) found that meditation was a stress-reducing phenomenon that brought about "the relaxation response" by inducing favorable brain waves and lowering the physiological and biochemical byproducts of stress, leading to a lowered respiration rate, a decreased heart rate, and lowered blood pressure. Other studies also indicate that meditation is associated with reduced serum cortisol levels, increased total serum protein levels, lowered systolic and diastolic blood pressure levels, and reduced pulse rates (Sudsuang, Chentanez, & Veluvan, 1991). Meditation does not lead solely to relaxation. It also increases alertness and trains the mind to concentrate.

There is also empirical evidence regarding the effectiveness of meditation and mindfulness practices on diverse health and mental health problems. The mindfulness-based stress reduction program developed by Kabat-Zinn was shown to be effective in reducing anxiety (Carmody & Baer, 2007; Kabat-Zinn et al., 1992;) and pain (Kabat-Zinn, Lipworth, & Burney, 1985). Meditation and mindfulness practices were associated with significant positive outcomes in hospital inpatients (Reibel, Greeson, Brainard, & Rosenzweig, 2001); patients with hypertension (Schneider et al., 2005); cancer patients (Brown & Ryan, 2003; Chan et al., 2006; Speca, Carlson, Goodey, & Angen, 2000); clients with borderline personality disorders (Linehan, Cochran, & Kehrer, 2001); depressive disorders (Teasdale et al., 2000); community populations (Williams, Kolar, Reger, & Pearson, 2001); and student populations (Astin, 1997; Shapiro, Schwartz, & Bonner, 1998). More recently, Marlatt and his colleagues have developed a mindfulness-based relapse prevention (MBRP) approach in treating substance use problems (Marlatt, 2002; Marlatt et al., 2004; Witkiewitz, Marlatt, & Walker, 2005; Zgierska, Rabago, Zuelsdorff, Coe, & Miller, in press). Mindfulness meditation, a meta-cognitive skill learned through meditation practice, has been shown to help clients develop the coping skill of nonreaction to a cognitive urge through the "act of inaction," being in the moment, observing, and accepting, without analyzing, judging, or reacting (Marlatt, 2002). Such compelling evidence has contributed to a growing movement within mainstream science to fund further research in this area. Five centers dedicated to research on the body–mind aspects of disease have thus far been established by the National Institute of Health.

The benefits of being mindful on mental health outcomes have to be perceived in the context of many people failing to live in the present and instead being trapped by past problems or future anxieties. Many troubled individuals and families seek treatment because they are stuck in problem situations. Instead of being aware of, recognizing, or effectively responding to current demands of life, challenges and issues, people who get stuck in problem situations can be: (1) consumed by negative thoughts and emotions, absorbed in past problems or future anxieties; (2) preoccupied with problem-elicited emotions, concerns, and negative consequences, which distract people from fully attending to and effectively responding to the present demands; (3) conditioned to problem-based emotional, cognitive, and/or physiological responses to the point they compulsively, reactively, and/or automatically react to current sensations or stimuli that symbolize or resemble aspects of the problem without being aware of, nor attending to, what actually happened in their current life reality. The mindless quality of consciousness, as commonly experienced by clients and families, often serves as a negative feedback loop that continuously maintains the problem behaviors or situations.

Fiona was born out of wedlock. She could hardly see her father and felt ashamed to disclose the name of her father, as he was a celebrity. Her mother committed suicide when she was 11 years old, and she was sent to study abroad. Despite being a highly talented young woman, Fiona felt that she would follow in her mother's footsteps and kill herself one day. She felt that she did not deserve to be loved. She tried very hard to do well in school but broke down before her high school examinations. She was diagnosed with depression, and then lived in the shadow of this diagnosis for 10 years. She was convinced that her fate was destined and that there was no way she could get out of her depression.

Learning to be mindful plays a key role in facilitating informed and self-endorsed behavioral and emotional regulation, which, in turn, is related to well-being enhancement (Ryan & Deci, 2000). Theories on self-regulation have long recognized the importance of self-awareness and attention in maintaining and enhancing psychological and behavioral functioning. As postulated by systems perspectives and cybernetic theories, feedback processes are inherently self-corrective and self-regulating mechanisms that enable the system to sustain itself in a functional way. However, in order for a system to be self-corrective, there need to be variations in input to activate the self-regulating abilities of the system (Becvar & Becvar, 2003). In human beings, attention to internal and external stimuli constitutes input for a person to initiate the self-regulating feedback processes. As such, attention has been described as key to the communication and control processes that underlie the regulation of behavior (Carver & Scheier, 1981). A core problem with many clients is that problem-based emotional, cognitive, and behavioral responses become the dominant inputs that initiate feedback processes, which continually reinforce the presenting problems. This pattern of reinforcement explains why many clients get stuck in their problem situations and tend to live in the past rather than in the present moment.

Being mindful of the present fundamentally disrupts the negative feedback process that reinforces the problem patterns experienced by clients and families. Mindfulness practices help clients to learn to observe and to describe their feelings and reactions without applying positive or negative judgments or seeking immediate relief. Increased ability to attend to and be aware of the internal and external stimuli of the present moment leads to varied input that will activate a different feedback process in clients that is more responsive to current needs and demands. In other words, the ability to observe, be openly aware of, and attend to emotions, even distressing ones, and accept them for what they are increases clients' capacities to begin to develop psychological resources that allow them to increase the self-regulation of their emotions in a beneficial way (Linehan, 1993; Martin, 1997).

Learning to be mindful also helps clients to make choices that are responsive to their needs and well-being. Self-determination theory, as developed by Ryan and Deci (2000), posits that open awareness is needed in facilitating choices of behaviors that are consistent with one's needs, values, and interests (Deci & Ryan, 1980). Enhancing one's awareness facilitates the shifting of attention to cues for basic needs, making one more likely to regulate behaviors to fulfill individual needs congruent to his or her well-being, instead of being trapped by past problems or future worries. Similarly, mindfulness practices help clients to cultivate a quality of consciousness that is characterized by "living in the moment" and focusing on the present experience, as opposed to habitual or automatic functioning. Such practices also help clients to reduce negative thoughts and emotions. Meditation practices help people to accept thoughts as they are and "let them go," instead of reacting to them, and thus they have increased abilities to disengage from automatic thoughts, habits, and unhealthy behavior patterns.

Gary was a shy but highly intelligent engineer. He grew up in a loving family with caring parents and two older sisters. He obtained an international award in a professional competition. Gary should find no reason why he was depressed and anxious all the time. Still, inside he felt like he did not deserve to be loved and successful. Despite his impressive professional accomplishments, he felt inadequate, lonely, and frightened. He was greatly bothered by a machinelike rumbling sound in his head followed by a severe headache. The sound was so disturbing that Gary felt that his head was going to explode. He was also scared by his frequent crying spells.

Upon the suggestion of his therapist, he joined a mindfulness stress reduction program and practiced the daily exercises of observing his body sensations, feelings, and thoughts and allowing them to come and go. He learned to develop a healthy sense of detachment to negative thoughts and emotions by observing them and letting them go. After 3 months of practice, Gary became more comfortable with himself and willing to accept himself as who he is. He became a happier person, and he was freed from the noises in his racing mind. He said that even if the noise came back again, it would not bother him anymore.

In addition, being mindful of the present brings clarity and vividness to current experiences. Wilber (2000) suggests that, by bringing awareness to experiences that have been alienated, ignored, or distorted, "hidden objects" are converted into "conscious objects" that can be differentiated from, transcended, and integrated into the self. The "tunnel vision" that we see in many clients deprives them of opportunities to process past experiences and embrace new ones. Open awareness of current experiences and sensations constitutes the first step for clients to develop the ability to verbalize in their own language, their body sensation, experiences, emotions, thoughts, and observations, which creates the capacity to generate internal representation of one's reality. Such a process allows clients to decenter and gain emotional distance from the problem so they can observe the experience from different perspectives (van der Kolk, 2002). The vivid awareness of current experiences, undistorted by past perceptions, will enhance clients' abilities to engage in new experiences, feelings, relationships, learning, ventures, and perspectives, which is crucial for them to live a satisfactory life (Herman, 1992).

Being mindful to restore balance

Integrative Body–Mind–Spirit Social Work assumes that change is constant. Problems are maintained primarily because a person or a family system becomes out-of-balance and ceases to be dynamic and responsive to current needs and demands and becomes stagnant and stuck (Ng et al., 2006). While reality is constantly evolving, people have to be able to attend to, notice, and be aware of these movements both within and outside in order for the balancing act to occur. In other words, being mindful of the present constitutes an important first step for a person to be aware of the current reality so that he or she can self-activate appropriate responses to effectively address current tasks and demands. It is interesting how the Buddha describes similar processes using a different language. According to the Buddha's teaching, mindful practices allow one to develop vision, knowledge, and wisdom. "Vision" emphasizes a person's ability to be aware of and recognize objects that he or she might not have been aware of before. Based on Buddhist teachings, the four primary foci of mindfulness practices are (1) the body, (2) feelings, (3) consciousness, and (4) dharma. The focus is on the person, because we are usually attending to objects in the outside world instead of in our inside world. Vision undistorted by delusion or illusion leads to awareness, recognition, and information, which constitute the foundation of true knowledge. The knowledge is of the workings and functions of events and phenomena in our life and the world. True knowledge fosters wisdom in a person to differentiate, sort out confusion, and make beneficial decisions.

A common treatment goal, regardless of the social work treatment approach, is to assist clients in staying focused, being attentive, and developing competence to successfully address issues and challenges of day-to-day living, as well as to make meaningful interpersonal connections. Learning to live in the present, instead of focusing on negative thoughts or emotions, through meditation, although not yet a mainstream therapeutic approach, constitutes an important process in facilitating the clients' development of psychological resources fundamental to a satisfactory life.

Deborah was a 30-year-old high school teacher. She was shopping around to find solutions to tackle her severe mood swings, uncontrolled crying spells, and anger. She found the world unjust and was discontented with life. She had poor relationships with her parents and was under constant pressure from her job as a high school teacher. She was anxious and self-conscious, with a strong sense of self-denial. She was referred to us by a psychiatrist who felt that Deborah needed to find ways to address her mood, in addition to antidepressant medication.

Deborah described herself as unhappy and depressed since an accident that happened when she was 7 years old. Her uncle dropped a knife on her forehead that left a one-inch-long scar. She was angry with her uncle, despite it being an accident, and she could not forgive her parents, who only asked her to keep her hair long to cover the scar and said that it was not a big deal. She could not trust other people and felt anxious all the time. She did not have a relationship, as she believed that she looked ugly and that nobody would ever go out with her. She always wore long hair and did not like partying, as she felt that people would make fun of her because of her scar. She would become extremely self-conscious and anxious whenever people looked at her. Deborah repeatedly said to herself that she hated her uncle and parents, so she did not forgive them for 23 years. She convinced herself that the scar ruined her life.

Deborah lived in the shadow of the past instead of realizing that she was an accomplished adult and teacher. The therapist first introduced Deborah to practice breathing meditation and then to loving kindness and compassion meditation. Breathing meditation helped Deborah to be aware of the present and stay calm (as opposed to ruminating about the past), while loving kindness and compassion meditation taught Deborah empathy skills in terms of sensitivity to her own affect and sensitivity to others' affects and development of compassion and love for herself. Deborah still struggled with negative emotions about her past. However, Deborah was more able to observe and accept her feelings without analyzing, judging, or reacting to them and "live in the moment." She also learned to love herself and appreciate what she had instead of what was missing in her life. When she became less self-conscious, she began to enjoy social gatherings with other teachers at the school and recently considered having a new hairstyle.

Being Mindful: How

In the *Satipathanna Sutta* (The Discourse on the Four Foundations of Mindfulness), the Buddha set forth the fundamental principles of practicing mindfulness as, "A monk dwells contemplating the body in the body, ardent, clearly comprehending and mindful, overcoming covetousness and grief in the world." "Dwell contemplating" implies that the person should be at ease and comfortable with the objects of his or her mindfulness. "Body in the body" means that when contemplating the body (or emotions, thoughts, etc), the person should stay mindful in the moment and without judgment. "Ardent" represents the diligent and enthusiastic attitude with which one should practice mindfulness in order to keep the mind focused and not distracted. "Clear comprehending" is related to the development of knowledge and wisdom. Besides developing concentration, mindfulness practices focus on the development of awareness and comprehension of the nature and characteristics of the object of mindfulness, which will facilitate the development of vision, knowledge, and wisdom.

Different types of meditative practice, differing in the object of focus, developed based on the Buddha's teachings: (1) Concentration, in which attention is focused on a single, specific object (e.g., Transcendental Meditation), (2) Mindfulness, in which attention is focused on the mind or background perception (e.g., Zen meditation or Vipassana meditation), and (3) a combination of the two, in which both single-point concentration and mindfulness are used. Tibetan meditation techniques, for instance, have often combined single-point concentration and mindfulness to get desired effects. There are different ways to meditate using these different foci. Mindfulness techniques may bring one's attention to one's breathing and then scan the body. Concentration techniques may focus on a mantra or sound. Other forms of meditation, which are a combination of these techniques, may involve focusing on one's breathing and then contemplating a concept such as love or compassion.

Skills and Techniques When Working with the Mind

Although Integrative Body–Mind–Spirit Social Work fully recognizes the benefits of being mindful of one's health and mental health, we do not attempt to teach clients any particular style of meditation under specific religious roots. After all, social work has its distinguishable purposes and boundaries. We have, however, adapted meditative procedures for diverse therapeutic ends that help clients to enhance positive thoughts and reduce negative thoughts associated with anxiety, worry, and stress. These techniques and skills can be flexibly adapted to accomplish diverse therapeutic purposes, such as helping clients to reconnect with or anchor in their strengths and resources, or helping clients to reduce negative emotions.

Empty the mind: the art of not knowing

Clients usually come in with their minds filled with attachments, preconceived ideas, and assumptions that are taken for granted. This is almost a "necessary evil," as we do live with a frame of reference or working model through which we understand everyday occurrences. The shadow of our frames of reference is that, oftentimes, we live in the past instead of the present, and we judge others and ourselves. We often share the following story with our clients and families to accentuate the importance of emptying our minds and adopting a "not knowing" attitude.

A knowledgeable university professor comes to an old Zen master, eager for his teachings. The Zen master offers him tea and pours the tea into the cup until it overflows. As the professor politely expresses his dismay at the overflowing cup, the Zen master keeps on pouring: "A mind that is already full cannot take in anything new," the master explains. "Like the cup, you are full of opinions and preconceptions." In order to find happiness, he teaches his disciple, he must first empty his cup (Epstein, 1998).

Being mindful of the present: practicing breathing

Sit comfortably either in a chair, with your hands lying softly on your lap, or sit cross-legged on a cushion on the floor, and be sure your spine is vertical. The eyes may be open but the gaze should be downward, and the tongue should rest on the roof of the mouth. To break the chain of distractions and thoughts that arise, take a deep breath into your nostrils and bring it down below the navel, and then simply breathe out. This action centers you within your body. Then simply follow your breath in and out, not making any effort to interfere and change the speed of your breathing. Just let your mind observe your breath.

Affirming the positives: appreciating beauty

Actively look out for pleasant experiences throughout the day. When there is a positive event, smile and take three deep breaths to deeply ingrain the positive energy into yourself. Being aware of and appreciating what they have help clients and families to stay positive and hopeful.

Loving kindness meditation: empathy and blessings for self and others

Assume the same sitting position as for the breathing meditation and bring your attention to your breath. Observe the flow of your breath for a moment or two. First, begin by directing loving kindness to yourself. Allow the heartfelt radiance of loving kindness to fill your being as you recite each phrase of this meditation slowly and with deep feeling: "May I be happy and peaceful . . ." and so forth. Next, visualize a person for whom you feel love, respect, and gratitude. Radiate heartfelt loving kindness to this person reciting each phrase of the meditation slowly with deep feeling: "May you be happy and peaceful . . ." and so forth. Next, visualize a person toward whom you feel neutral or indifferent. This may be a stranger or an acquaintance, someone for whom you have no particular feeling for or against. Extending loving kindness to those for whom one feels indifferent develops the ability of the heart to love all beings without exception. Radiate heartfelt loving kindness to this person reciting each phrase of the meditation slowly with deep feeling: "May you be happy and peaceful . . ." and so forth. Finally, radiate loving kindness to all living beings throughout all realms of existence: "May you be happy and peaceful . . ." and so forth.

Compassion meditation: empathy and healing for others

Sit quietly, calm your mind, and center yourself. Imagine in front of you as clearly as possible, someone you care for. Although this may be more challenging, you may also imagine someone you feel indifferent toward. Open yourself to this person's suffering. Allow yourself to feel connected with him or her, aware of his or her difficulties, pain, and distress. Then, as you feel your heart opening in compassion toward that person, imagine all his or her suffering coming out in black smoke. Now visualize breathing in the smoke, seeing it dissolve. As you breathe out, imagine you are sending out the radiance of loving kindness, compassion, peace, happiness, and well-being to this person. Send out any feelings that encourage healing, relaxation, and openness. Continue this giving and receiving with each breath. At the end of the meditation, generate a firm inner conviction that this person has been freed from suffering and is filled with peace, happiness, and well-being.

Integrative Body–Mind–Spirit Social Work recognizes not only the power of our rational mind to develop insights, solve problems, and find solutions, but it also recognizes that the mind itself is a source of discipline and healing. By training our minds to be mindful and nurturing an attitude of loving kindness and compassion, we can allow the power of the mind to fully unfold and to initiate the self-healing powers integral to our mind.

Flora discovered that John, her husband, had developed a relationship with her best friend, Joan. She was angry and disgusted. John deeply regretted the brief affair, which he was determined to discontinue. However, he maintained his friendship with Joan, and Flora found it unacceptable. She was in constant fights with her husband, and she could no longer enjoy moments of intimacy with John, which the couple found frustrating. During treatment, the therapist helped Flora to pay attention to positives in her marriage. The therapist asked Flora to find one positive thing in her relationship with John each day, and to do the breathing exercise while enjoying the moment. Flora realized that her husband was regretful about the affair and was able to discontinue it. He was financially responsible, he was caring, and he was willing to tolerate her

(continued)

(continued)

outbursts of temper. Affirming the positives gradually helped Flora to come to terms with the affair. She accepted that her husband had made a mistake and was regretful about it. Flora was able to reaffirm her love for John and her commitment to the marriage. She chose to nourish the relationship rather than be consumed by anger. When Flora began to count her blessings, her moods became more stable, and she was able to enjoy moments of intimacy with John.

Exercises to Enhance Positive Emotions

1. Breathing in Energy of Love: Imagine that the air that you breathe is a continuous flow of unconditional love and self-acceptance. Mindfully, breathe this positive energy in deeply, so that it fills every cell of your body. Take in with every breath a sense of joy, peace, and tranquility. Breathe in through the nose and count to four (around 4 s). Breathe out through the mouth and count to six (around 6 s). Take ten deep breaths with this imagery of breathing in a light of love at least three times a day.

2. Mirror Work: Look into the mirror in the morning, smile, and tell yourself, "I love you," and follow that with any relevant and energizing messages for the day. These messages can be, "I am going to have a wonderful and meaningful day," "I am going to bring joy to others and be a peacemaker," or even "I am going to be blessed and surrounded with positive energy today." Give yourself an affirming blessing.

3. Developing Appreciation: Observe small environmental cues that are pleasant and positive. People will have different perspectives and ideas. Examples of these cues could be a clear blue sky on a sunny day, cool and refreshing raindrops on a rainy day, a smile on a baby, and so on. Keep a log of three positive events each day. Every time you think of something that you appreciate, put your hands together (or any other ritual that represents spirituality for you) and affirm to yourself that you are very grateful for the blessings.

4. Spiritual Camera: Imagine that you have a camera in your heart. Take photos of beautiful scenery and capture genuine smiles everywhere you go. Stop for a second to clip and frame a particular scene of the environment or people that you have found inspiring or energizing.

A HOLISTIC VIEW OF MIND: TRANSFORMATION AND SPIRITUALITY

While recognizing the power of the mind as a source of discipline and healing, Integrative Body–Mind–Spirit Social Work continues to build upon and utilize existing cognitive-based and emotive-based techniques in treatment. We routinely use paraphrasing, restating (fundamental interviewing techniques that speak to our conscious minds), journaling, reframing, identifying cognition distortions, evaluating beliefs and assumptions, cognitive restructuring (cognitive techniques), narratives, restoring, metaphor, rituals, meaning making, and meaning reconstruction (constructivist perspectives) in the treatment process. We fully recognize the importance of emotion in the process of change. A holistic and expanded view of the mind that moves beyond a rational mind, however, implies that social work interventions should focus on the cognitive, emotive, and spiritual dimensions in a connected manner. What also makes Integrative Body–Mind–Spirit Social Work different from some other treatment approaches is our belief in a developmental perspective of problems, our view that problems provide a context for transformative changes, our view that these processes are embedded in the spirituality of individuals, and our willingness to provide a therapeutic context in which clients can be in touch with their values, life goals, and spirituality.

Characterized treatment processes of our approach include (1) normalizing problems, (2) viewing problems as a context for transformative experiences, (3) expanding choices, and (4) reconnecting with the spiritual mind.

Normalizing Problems of Living

Clients and families coming into treatment oftentimes experience self-pity, shame, guilt, and frustration because of their problem situation. They usually blame themselves or others for the problem. "Why me?" is probably one of the most common questions asked by our clients and families. Normalization seeks to help clients and families to move beyond these negative emotions and thoughts and to nourish hopefulness in them. When problems are described as normal issues of wear and tear—problems of a developmental nature—clients will find it easier to admit their personal secrets or inadequacies, which they may have previously found too stigmatizing or shameful to acknowledge. Once the shame and blame are removed, new windows of opportunity for change are possible. Integrative Body–Mind–Spirit Social Work normalizes the process of seeking treatment through emotion validation, naming the presenting problems as developmental challenges or normal problems of living, and creating a "community of others."

Emotional validation

Integrative Body–Mind–Spirit Social Work echoes most therapeutic approaches and views emotional validation as a first step to establish rapport and a useful therapeutic alliance with clients and families. Literature has repeatedly described the important role of therapeutic alliance in facilitating positive outcomes in clients and families (Asay & Lambert, 1999). Clients,

oftentimes, are consumed by negative emotions fueled by a blaming attitude when seeking treatment. They may blame themselves, others, or both for
the problem situation. Bordin referred to the affective aspects of therapeutic
alliance as bonds (Bordin, 1979), which include, but are not limited to, trust,
respect, positive regard, acceptance, and caring (Johnson, Wright, & Ketring,
2002). The therapist is challenged to see beyond the problem situation and
to genuinely accept the client, appreciate his or her strengths, and actively
cultivate a nurturing environment of acceptance and respect regardless of the
problems he or she has.

Naming of the problem as normal problems of living or developmental challenges

While not underestimating the importance of mental health diagnoses in
assessment and understanding clients' problems, Integrative Body–Mind–
Spirit Social Work does not view diagnoses as particularly helpful for
clients in the process of change. Integrative Body–Mind–Spirit Social Work
views all phenomena, including problem scenarios, as in a constant process of change and, therefore, evolving. In addition, the language of mental
health diagnoses, such as obsessive-compulsive disorder, depression, anxiety,
and so on, may sustain a problem reality because of the deficits perspective implicated by the use of such language (de Shazer, 1994; Lee et al.,
2003). Consistent with our view that change is constant and that presenting problems are normal problems of living, Integrative Body–Mind–Spirit
Social Work prefers to use language that normalizes problems by reframing the particular challenges as normal problems of living or developmental issues. By doing so, the social work professionals, the client, and the
family can work together as a team to address a normal developmental
challenge.

Creating a community of others: I am not the only one

The existence of a "community of others" (Lax, 1996) who experience similar
problems fundamentally alters the nature of a client's perception and experience of the problem. Knowing that other people share similar experiences and
that others have come up with solutions to resolve similar problems of living
is likely to induce hope in clients and families (Lee et al., 2003; Yalom, 1995).
Recent literature has also emphasized the importance of hope in positive
outcomes (Snyder, Cheavens, & Michael, 1999; Snyder, Ilardi, Michael, &
Cheavens, 2000; Snyder & Taylor, 2000). When people are able to think of
pathways to goals and pursue them, they tend to have positive emotions and a
sense of hope.

A Teenager With Obsessive-Compulsive Self-Examination of Her Teeth:
Grief Reaction Versus Mental Health Disorder

Doris, a teenaged girl, was referred to counseling by her dentist, for she tore her lips
by opening her mouth widely to examine her teeth in a mirror in the bathroom for 2–
3 hr every day. Doris's grandfather was admitted to hospital for toothache but died soon
after his admission, and Doris was very attached to her grandfather. She was concerned
that poor dental conditions could take away her life and the lives of her family members. She began to spend hours examining and brushing her teeth to the extent that she
did not have time to finish her homework. She also insisted on examining her family
members' teeth every day. Whenever she saw a tiny mark on her teeth, she would be
very worried and would go consult a dentist. While one could easily label Doris' behavior as symptoms of obsessive-compulsive disorder, the therapist reframed her problem
as a normal reaction to the death of her beloved grandfather, which had also raised
her awareness of the importance of dental hygiene. Her grief over her grandfather's
death was turned into a concern for other family members' dental health. Because of
this loss, she wanted to become a dentist when she grew up. The therapist described
her obsessive-compulsive traits as perfectionist traits that could be converted into an
ability to attend to details. Thus, she was taught behavioral methods to help her focus
on school work and to distract herself when there was an impulse to examine her teeth.
Her conditions improved after the first session, and the family was greatly relieved, as
Doris was neither "crazy" nor mentally ill.

Integrative Body–Mind–Spirit Social Work views the creation of a "community of others" as one important component of the normalization process.
We routinely utilize groups, which are "communities of others" in which
members can share with and learn from each other, in the treatment process. We find it extremely valuable for group members to observe and share
their search for solutions among themselves. Many participants feel a sense
of relief because they have found people "in the same boat." They can also
constantly evaluate the relevance of others' experiences to their own lives
and learn from each other's successes and failures. When conducting individual sessions, we routinely impart relevant information about prevalence and
treatment successes pertaining to clients' problems. We share research findings, statistics, and relevant information with clients and families to show that
they are not the only ones troubled by the particular problem and that their
problems are just normal reactions under normal circumstances by normal
people. This invisible "community of others" helps to normalize the client's
problems and induce hope.

A final word of caution, however, is that professionals should be fully aware
of the difference between normalizing clients' problems and minimizing

Jack suffered from early ejaculation. His wife, Joan, became easily irritable and hostile to Jack, who became depressed as his wife was distancing herself from him emotionally and sexually. Jack was referred to a treatment group. The therapist provided information on the high prevalence of various forms of sexual dysfunction among couples, and Jack was greatly relieved that he was not the only one. It was actually consoling for Jack to find other men who suffered from more severe sexual problems. He was not the worst case. A survivor served as the peer counselor, and Jack was greatly encouraged and felt that the situation could improve.

their experiences as unimportant. Therapists need to fully recognize and acknowledge a client's distress, pain, and suffering.

Growing Pains: Problems as Contexts for Transformative Experiences

A developmental perspective views presenting problems as developmental challenges or normal problems of living and views problems as opportunities for growth or windows for change. Problems constitute contrasting forces necessary for a dynamic balance to keep the system changing and evolving, which further denotes the values of problems in the process of change and growth. When we accidentally put our hand too close to a hot stove, the heat and pain will start our reflex actions, which will help us to stay away from the danger. Pain is a bodily defense signal that serves protective functions. Fever is a consequence of the body's defense system fighting inflammation. Pain and fever, although unwelcome sensations, are necessary forces in our bodily systems to restore healthy functioning. Clients and families come in with a wide array of different problems, and Integrative Body–Mind–Spirit Social Work perceives clients' problems as signals of an out-of-balance system that is attempting to regain a healthy balance. Once clients and families become aware of the protective functions of pain and problems, they can develop a sense of appreciation for how important such signals are and make changes accordingly.

The following are brief case examples that illustrate how Integrative Body–Mind–Spirit Social Work turns problems into a context for transformative experiences. Clients are taught how to communicate with their bodies and minds, so that warning signs of pain and suffering can be detected and appropriate action be taken.

Externalizing the problem: the case of Lindsey

When people are emotionally in pain, many may adopt high-risk behaviors as an escape from their distress. Many sexual abuse survivors abuse illegal substances and alcohol to temporarily escape from their personal pain, despite the fact that their solution possibly puts them in deeper trouble. Lindsey was a sexual abuse survivor with a diagnosis of posttraumatic stress disorder. She is currently in a residential treatment facility for women who have substance use problems.

Instead of solely focusing on the substance use problems, the therapist first taught Lindsey simple breathing techniques to center and focus. The therapist asked Lindsey to externalize the problem and imagine her substance use problem as something outside and describe what it looked like. After struggling a while, she described her problem as a black hole that constantly tried to drag her into itself. The hole was deep and empty. She felt empty and powerless. After initially helping Lindsey to externalize the substance use problem and explore its psychosocial and spiritual meaning for Lindsey, the therapist created a context for Lindsey to realize the plausible messages that her substance use problem may have been trying to communicate to her. Instead of condemning the substance use problem as all-negative, which oftentimes was interpreted as a reflection of the Lindsey's unworthy character, the therapist helped Lindsey to explore the meaning of the problem for her. "How has your drinking been helpful to you and in what ways?" "What has been taken away from you because of your drinking?" Lindsey realized that her drinking has helped her to cope with her shame, her anger, and her sadness, although she also suffered from all the negative consequences of drinking and substance use. The problem was no longer a pure devil but a part of her that attempted to speak loudly enough to be heard, although in a destructive way. The treatment focused on clarifying her personal goals and increasing her personal power to fight the temptation of being dragged into the black hole. By externalizing the problem, Lindsey was no longer the problem but a detached individual who was determined to live a life free of substance use. By realizing the "message" of her substance use problem, Lindsey was able to accept herself without condemning herself as a worthless and shameless addict.

Embracing and accepting the problems: The case of Jack

Jack was a 57-year-old man who broke his leg when he crashed his car into a tree after drinking and driving. He was admitted to hospital and had to stay in a wheelchair for two months. Jack started to drink after his wife died of a heart attack two years ago. He was depressed and lost his meaning in life. After his admission to the hospital, he came in contact with other patients who were either paralyzed or stayed in a coma after severe car accidents. With the help of the therapist in the hospital, Jack admitted that he had actually wanted to kill himself through serious drinking and drunk driving as a form of grief expression. By owning his problem, he felt that the accident was a warning sign that he could ruin his own life by maintaining his grief in such destructive manner. His deceased wife would be sorry to find him hurting himself after her death. Jack made a decision to try to live an active life and communicate with his deceased wife through talking to her photos. As he adopted a positive attitude in his rehabilitation, he became a delight in the rehabilitation ward. Jack started dating a nurse whom he had met in the hospital, his rehabilitation process was smooth, and the accident became a turning point in his life.

Appreciation: the case of George

George was a retired high school principal. He had a stroke after his first month of retirement. He was in a coma for 2 months, and the doctor thought that his chance of recovery was minimal. Because he was Christian, his friends came to his bedside to pray for him. They saw him shaking his head during his coma. Every time they mentioned to him of getting well to take care of his wife, George moved as if he agreed. His students and his friends visited and talked to him despite the fact that he was in a coma.

When George regained consciousness, he shared that he had been in a long, dark tunnel walking toward a light. He saw a deceased uncle waving to him and asking him to join him. George did not like this uncle and shook his head. He felt that he had to turn back to see his friends and family. He told himself that he could not die and that there were duties that he had to fulfill before he could report for duty in heaven.

In the hospital, George found that there were others who had had a stroke at the age of 36, 40, 44, and 50. He was lucky to have retired, been financially secure, and have children who were all grown up. George could count his blessings and convert them into a strong motivation to heal. After active rehabilitation, George became the chairperson of a stroke patients' self-help group. He went to elderly groups in the community and hospital wards to encourage healthy lifestyles among the elderly population.

By encouraging clients to count their blessings, available resources, and support, a therapist can move clients from dismay, self-pity, a sense of loss, and frustration into a state of appreciation.

Expanding Choices

While providing a therapeutic context for clients to normalize their problems and take a transformative view of problems, it is important to help clients appreciate that they have a choice: the choice to become a victim or a survivor, the choice to stay in resentment or to move on, the choice to focus on past wounds or to take losses as opportunity for growth. Thinking that they have no way of getting out of a bad fate, many people get stuck in negativities and are filled with bitterness. Once they realize that they can look at life differently, their sense of control can also be greatly enhanced.

The case of Michelle: a bitter divorced single mother for 18 years

Michelle married her boyfriend against the wishes of her parents. After the birth of her daughter, her boyfriend started to abuse her and her daughter. Michelle returned to her parents' home, but she was treated scornfully by her siblings and parents. She had no choice but to stay with her parents, as her income would not allow her to rent a place by herself. Michelle isolated herself and lived as a victim of this failed marriage for 18 years. Her daughter was 19 years old and very attached to the mother. As the mother was depressed, the girl was also very unhappy, withdrawn, and underweight. After participation in an empowerment group for divorced women, Michelle came to the realization that she could not change the reality of her failed marriage but she could be the master of her own life. She decided to enjoy every day and focus on creative, happy moments for her daughter as well. Her daughter gained ten pounds in 2 months, and her daughter's boss described her as a much more cheerful person. Michelle's decision to look at her life differently not only freed herself but also her daughter.

Reconnect with the spiritual mind

> If you wish to travel far and fast, travel light. Take off all your envies, jealousies, unforgiveness, selfishness, and fears.
>
> Glenn Clark

Social work practice largely separated spirituality and values from the other domains of the human experience and avoided the associated discourse until quite recently. Such an orientation at least partly accounts for our emphasis on the rational mind, but not on the spiritual mind, in treatment. As a profession, social work chooses to build its professional knowledge upon scientific traditions and divorces itself from spirituality and values primarily because of its alignment with positivism, scientificism, and rationalism, which represent the privileged knowledge paradigm esteemed by professionals and academia. Spirituality and value discussions are excluded from the discourse of social work treatment for reasons such as social work, as a profession, should be objective and value free, the concept of spirituality is too vague and unscientific, and so on. There are also concerns about intruding on the private domain of clients, as spirituality primarily addresses ideas of the religious, supernatural, or private experience that should not be brought into the public domain of social work agencies.

While recognizing these dilemmas, Integrative Body–Mind–Spirit Social Work also acknowledges that values and spirituality are integral and inseparable parts of human experience. Not addressing these issues does not mean that they do not exist. We neither shy away from helping clients to explore and revisit the relevance of their religion, spirituality, and values in their everyday lives, nor do we shy away from helping clients to explore how spirituality interfaces with their problem experiences (refer to Chapters 8 and 9 for a detailed discussion of Integrative Body–Mind–Spirit Social Work practice and spirituality). We specifically view putting values into action and the cultivation of compassion and altruism as helpful in the process of change.

Cultivating compassion: promoting of altruism and benevolence

Compassion is an empathic understanding and ability to feel for the self and others. Compassion is an awareness, emotion, skill, and value. Compassion is similar to empathy and can be seen as consisting of three different aspects: (1) sensitivity to one's own affect, (2) sensitivity to another's affect, and (3) development of empathy for oneself and others. By focusing on cultivating compassion upon themselves, clients learn to love themselves for who they are. Compassion for oneself is a first step for people to cultivate compassion for others instead of judging and condemning them. Compassion cultivates one's ability to be in touch with oneself, as well as suffering and pain. It is a genuine concern and a true humility to the disadvantaged and humble. Compassion for themselves helps clients to move beyond self-pity to embrace their strengths and accept themselves for who they are.

Cultivation of Values in Action

Peterson and Park (2004) describe ethical and benevolent practice as Values in Action (VIA). The values to be put into action are characteristics such as wisdom, knowledge, courage, love, justice, temperance, transcendence, and so on. It is, however, imperative to respect individual differences in what people appreciate in themselves. Individuals have a greater ability to endure hardships and persevere through difficult moments in life when they are reconnected with their values and their spirituality. Instead of being value neutral, we explore with clients and families their values and encourage them to put the identified values into action, if appropriate. We ask them, "What are some of the things that you have done that greatly energized you? What happened at that time? What made the experience so different and energizing? What values underlie these actions? What do you anticipate will happen when you engage in these activities or behaviors again? Is there anything that you can think of right now that will help you to reconnect with those values?"

Karen was married to her high school classmate and sweetheart Kevin, who took up biochemical science as his career. While Kevin was doing his undergraduate, graduate, and doctoral studies, Karen was busy taking care of the three young children and financially supporting the family through working in a supermarket. After 10 years, Kevin finally finished his education and was rewarded with a highly paid position in China. Karen moved to China with her children and stayed there for 4 years. Then, she moved back to the United States, for the couple decided that it would be better for their children to receive a high school and university education in the United States. The couple maintained a long-distance commuting arrangement for four years before Karen found out that Kevin was cohabitating with a young female colleague in China. Karen was mad and sad, but mostly mad. She felt that she had spent 18 years and devoted her whole life to supporting her family and Kevin. She went to China, visited the company, and vented her anger and frustration in front of Kevin and his staff team. She felt humiliated and was at a great loss. Kevin told her squarely that she was no longer attractive to him and that he wanted a divorce. However, he assured her that he would be financially responsible for the family and sent Karen back to the United States. When Karen reached home, she attempted suicide by overdosing on sleeping pills. Recently, Karen had a big fight with Kevin. She took a vase and hit him on the head. Kevin was wounded and sent to a hospital and Karen was taken by the police. The court ordered Karen to attend an anger management group before she could move back home to stay with her children while Kevin left for China.

The therapist helped Karen accept the fact that a divorce may be the best way out for her, Kevin, and the children. Karen realized that her destructive tendencies to herself and Kevin were so strong that it was as if she was possessed. She was overwhelmed by hatred, and everyone around her was scared. In the anger management class, Karen saw drug addicts, a 20-year-old unwed mother who abused her own four children, gamblers, and compulsive shoppers as well as people with mental illnesses. Her problems were trivial compared with those of others. Karen decided that she could be doing something to help others in trouble. The therapist helped Karen to draw a wish list of what she wanted to do in life. Karen wanted to regain her compassion and help other people, to let go of her husband, and develop her own career as a helping professional. She went back to the college and later received a nursing degree. After 6 years of hard work, she was hired by a nursing home, where she devoted her energy to serve the needy.

Putting values in action translates compassion for others into altruistic and benevolent behaviors. We have had clients who decided to help deprived populations such as the elderly, people with disabilities, and children in developing countries. Others advocate for local or global issues such as environmental protection, sustainability, community development, and policy advocacy for disadvantaged populations. As Collins (1982, pp. 193–194) described in his study of altruism, "The rationale for action...provides neither for simple self-interest nor for self-denying altruism. The attitude to all 'individualities,' whether past and future 'selves,' past, future, or contemporary 'others' is the same—loving-kindness, compassion, sympathetic joy, and equanimity..."

A holistic view of the mind implies not just an expanded spectrum of interventions to work with clients and families but also a different orientation toward utilizing the mind in the process of change. We focus on the clients' spiritual mind as much as their rational mind in an effort to restore balance to the system. The following is an example of how Integrative Body–Mind–Spirit Social Work takes a holistic perspective and utilized the power of the mind to provide help to adolescents and people with chronic diseases during the 2003 SARS epidemic in Hong Kong.

1. Emphasizing growth through pain. Instead of focusing on the loss that is brought on by crisis and trauma, personal strengths and gains are explored throughout the sessions. Although caution must be exercised to ensure that clients do not feel coerced or alienated, it is therapeutic for clients to be immersed in a positive environment where they can briefly put aside the victim label that they are accustomed to and concentrate on opportunities for growth and learning.

   Mrs B was diagnosed with SARS. She was put into an isolation ward in April 2003. Mrs B was very scared and used her mobile phone to communicate with her therapist. During the conversation, her therapist reminded Mrs B to watch for personal growth and transformation and to find ways to cope with her breathing difficulties. As a result of this simple reminder to look out for growth, Mrs B gained greater strength in withstanding her hospitalisation and her days in intensive care.

2. Teaching the body–mind–spirit connection. The relationship between spiritual well-being, mood, and body immunity is discussed with clients. When clients know that they can improve their mood by taking care of their physical needs and when they know how to do so using physical movements, breathing practices, or massage, this sense of mastery can greatly boost their mental strength. Knowing that there can be things that one can do to help oneself is empowering.

   Mr C lost his job during SARS, for he worked in a hotel. He was depressed and at a loss as to what to do. As residents in Hong Kong were encouraged to go hiking and to engage in outdoor activities during the SARS period, he regained a sense of pride, confidence, and self-esteem by taking his daughter to country parks and teaching her exercises to strengthen her lungs. He regarded this period of unemployment as a special holiday that allowed him to spend time with his family and viewed the loss of income as a lesson on how to live a simple life.

(continued)

(continued)

3. Developing an appreciation for nature. Being too absorbed in their own miseries, clients are often reluctant to turn their attention to other areas of life. By appealing to the beauty of nature, clients are encouraged to appreciate their own life and appreciate people whom they love. We often start with the innocuous—birds in the sky and fish in the ocean—and proceed to nature and the universe. We help clients develop the habit of appreciating the small things in life, which slowly but steadily pulls clients away from their indulgence in pain.

> Mr D, a teenager, developed SARS when he volunteered to help relocate an infected housing estate, Amoy Gardens (more than 200 residents of this housing estate were infected with SARS). He was very frustrated because he failed a public examination and lost his physical strength. Homebound, he learned gardening at home. The new life of the small plants helped him to regain his appreciation of life and living.

4. Facilitating cognitive reappraisal. New perspectives can be developed through reflective discussions and sharing. By recalling significant life events, participants are reminded of their previous goals and dreams, their resilient experiences in facing other crises, and their past achievements, in an attempt to foster a sense of confidence in their capacity of dealing with their present trauma. The positive psychology techniques of downward comparison, positive illusions, and learned optimism are used to facilitate cognitive reappraisal and the reconstruction of a new worldview (Taylor, Kemeny, Reed, Bower, & Gruenewald, 2000).

5. Nourishing social support. Effective interpersonal communication and the pleasant experience of networking can often nourish an individual's whole-person development and especially enhances one's resilience in difficult times. In a group environment, participants experience a sense of acceptance and connectedness with other group members. They are also encouraged to appreciate support from loved ones and to strengthen their social network with family members and friends. Mutual help among survivors with the same problems is an effective mechanism to sustain morale and the energy that is needed for change.

6. Promoting the compassionate helper principle. Clients are encouraged to learn from their traumatic experiences through being compassionate both to themselves and to other people. By sharing their knowledge and experiences in coping with traumatic events, clients are urged to consolidate their experiences and to become sensitive to other people's needs. Being able to be helpful to others as peer counsellors can be very empowering. Selfless devotion to volunteering can move clients out of self-pity and onto a path of recovery.

Integrative Body–Mind–Spirit Social Work adapted these strategies in the intervention program through the use of writing (articles, lectures, books, and personal journals), expressive art (drawings, pictures, photos, and body movement), and multimedia materials (video, audiotapes, and CDs). Knowledge is delivered by showing

(continued)

(continued)

videotapes of outstanding role models and by distributing reading material such as poems, research findings, and personal testimonials. Throughout the intervention sessions, participants are encouraged to express their physical, mental, and spiritual needs, as well as experiences of growth and transformation.

Engaging in altruistic practices also brings benefits to individual well-being. Goleman and Gurin (1993) state that hope and psycho–spiritual values are central to coping with health problems. Thurman (1998) also described how an "inner revolution" from benefiting oneself to benefiting others can assist in the development of true happiness. By focusing on giving alms and selfless dedication to service to others, individuals can be fulfilled.

A word of caution, however: The cultivation of compassion or values-in-action is a choice made by clients and should never be imposed or coached by social work professionals. Over the years, what we have seen is that, when spirituality becomes a legitimate discourse in treatment and clients have permission to connect with their values, aspirations, and spirituality in treatment, many clients make compassionate choices that ultimately benefit themselves and others.

EMOTIVE MIND: ADDRESSING NEGATIVE EMOTIONS

A discussion of the power of the mind that does not address emotions certainly misses the importance of the emotive mind and the intimate connection between mind and emotion. When they seek treatment, clients are oftentimes consumed by negative emotions, whether toward themselves or significant others in their lives. Negative emotions, especially intense emotions, are known to constrict one's ability to think rationally and make beneficial decisions. That is probably one of the reasons why addressing emotions became such an important component in psychotherapy, regardless of the orientation of different approaches. Influenced by Buddhist philosophy and Traditional Chinese Medicine (TCM), Integrative Body–Mind–Spirit Social Work offers additional insights in addressing negative emotions.

The Interconnectedness of Emotions

According to the Five Elements Theory in TCM, the emotions of anger, fear, guilt, grief, blame, hostility, joy, etc are interconnected. In fact, the expressed emotion is often connected with deeper emotions, and these emotions also have a counteracting effect on each other. For instance, based on the TCM perspective on emotions, anger is generated by fear. When clients come in very angry, it would be beneficial for the therapist to first help the client explore the deep fear behind the articulated anger. The therapist should ask, "What is the fear behind the anger? What is it that you have the greatest fear of losing? Are there previous experiences of loss that hurt enormously?"

Through the study of Eastern philosophies and Chinese medicine, Pachuta (1989) concludes that:

> Anger is mothered by fear and controlled by grief. Hence, whenever you are angry, it would be useful to ask, 'What am I afraid of? What am I sad about?' . . . Since anger is generated by fear, it follows that the most violent anger is indicative of the greatest fear . . . The emotion under guilt is fear, the fear of retribution . . . Fear is controlled by empathy . . . The antidote for grief is love and joy. Joy prevents and cures depression . . . Anger is the antidote for sympathy . . . Grief is the antidote for and controller of anger
>
> (Pachuta, 1989, pp. 84–85).

Helping clients to be aware of the deeper emotions that generate the expressed emotions makes room for clients and therapists to address the negative emotions.

The Power of Love

Hippocrates said, "Where there is love for mankind, there is love for the art of healing" (Sheikh, Kunzendorf, & Sheikh, 1989, p. 484). According to body–mind psychology, love is the ultimate solution to all emotional problems (Pachuta, 1989). Such thinking is consistent with the TCM perspective on emotions, that the emotion of joy counteracts sadness and grief, which generates fear and anger. In other words, besides exploring what motivates anger, it is helpful to enable clients to appreciate that there are other emotions, such as loving kindness, that can help prevent anger. By converting energy used for anger into energy for benevolence, clients can perhaps adopt an empathetic sentiment to be actively engaged in activities and actions to help other disadvantaged individuals and groups.

During treatment, when the client is full of anger, frustration, fear, or negative emotions, we can coach the client to breathe in positive love energy (preferably through the nose) and breathe out (preferably through the mouth) negative energies by emptying the lungs through breathing out eight times. It is important to ask client to breathe in joyful positive energy through the nose and blow out dark and negative emotions through the mouth.

BODY AND MIND AS INSEPARABLE

To Integrative Body–Mind–Spirit Social Work, the mind is powerful not only because of its inherent healing abilities. The power of the mind has to be appreciated from a holistic point of view, in which the mind and body are inseparable. Integrative Body–Mind–Spirit Social Work believes that the way we think affects our bodily functions as much as our body processes influence our mind. As such, meditation practices will have repercussions on our body, just as the state of our bodies will influence the state of our minds. One important implication for social work treatment pertains to the utilization of these processes to make shifts that lead to positive changes in clients and families.

Making Shifts

A primary therapeutic process for any treatment approach is making useful shifts that will allow the family or client to shift from the problem-oriented direction to a beneficial direction that will lead to positive outcomes. For example, cognitive therapy provides a context for clients to identify, reevaluate and dispute their cognitive distortions prior to cognitive restructuring (Beck, 1995). Narrative therapy utilizes unique outcomes as an opportunity to allow clients to make a shift from problem-saturated stories to reauthoring new stories that are aligned with their localized experiences (White & Epston, 1990). Solution-focused brief therapy uses the miracle question to help clients depart from problem-talk and engage in solution-talk that allows them to envision a future without problems, which is another significant shift-making procedure (Berg, 1994; DeJong & Berg, 2002; Lee et al., 2003). Although making shifts has played a pivotal role in successful treatment and positive outcomes, many conventional treatment approaches confine the process of making beneficial shifts primarily to the cognitive or the verbal domains. We routinely assist clients and families in coming up with different problem-solving strategies and coping methods and encourage them to practice newly learned ways of thinking, knowledge, and so on. Integrative Body–Mind–Spirit Social Work, by recognizing the mind and the body as mutually embedded and by recognizing that the human mind encompasses the rational, emotive, and spiritual dimensions, offers practitioners and clients many more choices to make useful shifts in the therapeutic process.

From Problems to Connectedness: The Case of Wendy

Wendy was in the therapist's office primarily because her 15-year-old adolescent girl, Jody, was in residential treatment. Jody did not attend school, engaged in multiple sexual relationships, and used drugs and alcohol. Wendy was a bitter, divorced single mother. During the divorce process, she also lost her house to her husband, who was a habitual gambler. She was depressed and angry but also blamed herself for these events. A loving couple adopted Wendy when she was very young. However, she also went through turbulent teenage years, which resulted in her leaving home when she was only 16. She did not reconnect with her adoptive parents even when they passed away. Wendy felt extremely guilty about not being with her adoptive parents during their last years. She felt that what she was going through now was punishment for being ungrateful to them. Wendy cried histrionically when recounting the story. Wendy's rational mind was filled with anguish, guilt, sadness, anger, and frustration. She saw no way out of her troubles, which felt heavy, over-whelming, and insolvable at that time. Further laboring on Wendy's rational mind would have been unhelpful at that point, as there were few resources that she could use as leverage points.

The therapist, instead of asking her to identify, evaluate, and dispute her cognitive distortions (as suggested by cognitive-behavioral therapy,) or asking miracle questions (as suggested by solution-focused brief therapy,) decided that a shift was crucial at this point for Wendy to engage in a facilitative treat-ment process. The therapist suggested that Wendy engage in the following activities:

1. Breathing meditation: Take a few deep breaths and then just focus paying attention to her breathing.
2. Recall moments when Jody was a baby and very attached to Wendy: She described many occasions when she and Jody were loving to each other, such as when Jody was a baby, when Wendy took Jody to a park, when Jody went to preschool, and so on. They had many fun times together. The loving energy from the natural bond between mother and daughter was awakened.
3. Visualize herself as a big tree that can provide shade to others: Wendy was asked to visualize a big tree that could provide shade, shelter, and a place for children to play. Trees are nourished by air, water, and some nutrients from the soil. Wendy was taught to take deep breaths and to inhale love and energy from the universe to enable her to grow into this big tree, so that she could provide shelter to Jody unconditionally.
4. Seeing herself when she was Jody's age: Wendy recalled that she was equally rebellious when she was Jody's age. Teenagers normally do not conform to parental instructions. By normalizing Jody's behav-ior, Wendy's guilt of being disloyal was taken away. Wendy could accept Jody's unruly behavior and appreciate the importance of being an unconditionally loving mother to Jody.

The breathing and visualizing exercises provided diverse entry points for Wendy to access her strengths and resources when she became too immersed in the language of problems, guilt, and helplessness. Wendy was visibly calmer after the breathing exercise. The breathing exercise provided a different and complementary "technology" in treatment: Instead of directly addressing and focusing on the "content" of the problem, it allowed her to "discipline" her mind—to change her relationship to her thoughts—without directly focusing on the problems (Marlatt et al., 2004). By helping Wendy to attend to the present and stay physiologically calm, the breathing exercise allowed for a different treatment entry point when Wendy's mind was filled with anguish and negative thoughts. The dissipation of intense negative emotions through breathing allowed Wendy to engage in visualization exercises that focused on positives and strengths, which in turn facilitated Wendy to regain constructive energy and mentally make room for her to beneficially take steps to address challenges in her personal life.

Wendy still has to work with her depression, relational, and family problems. However, a holistic perspective of body–mind connectedness does permit therapists and clients to utilize diverse domains of a client's experiences to initiate and make useful shifts in the treatment process.

A FINAL WORD

Despite technological advances and knowledge development, the human mind is still a mystery to be solved. The fields of neurobiology, neurophysiology, and neuroscience are discovering new grounds and redefining what we know about the human mind and consciousness (Hameroff, Kaszniak, & Scott, 1996; Wilber, 2000). The way we understand and interpret the nature, characteristics, and functions of our minds inevitably affects how we utilize the power of the mind in social work treatment. Of course, influenced by our understanding and knowledge of the power of the mind, treatment orientations will evolve and change. Conventional social work practice approaches with individuals and families, as influenced by the Western analytical thought system, are mostly cognitive based, focusing on the conscious and rational mind as the primary agent for positive changes. Integrative Body–Mind–Spirit Social Work, as influenced by Eastern philosophies and practices, brings in an additional perspective to understand and conceptualize the power of the mind. The practice of meditation suggests that the mind is a subject of discipline and a source of healing, if people can be mindful of their existence. The cultivation of loving kindness and compassion through meditation and a focus on the spiritual mind legitimizes the discourse about values and spirituality in social work treatment. A holistic view of the mind also redefines the nature of the mind to include its emotive and spiritual aspects, in addition to the rational mind. Such an expanded view of the mind allows social work professionals and clients to have more leverage points to make beneficial shifts in the treatment process. We no longer have to rely solely on language or verbal communication and the rational mind to help clients and families create transformative changes in their lives.

6

Nurturing the Body for Balance and Tranquility

SOMATIZATION OR "PSYCHOLOGICALIZATION?"

Psychosomatization and somatization are concepts widely used by mental health practitioners (Gelder et al., 1996; Goldberg, Benjamin, & Creed, 1994). The core idea is that somatic problems are psychogenic, and therefore, the focus of intervention should be psychosocial or behavioral. The importance of the "felt body" is grossly undermined. There is a belief that attending to somatic problems will diffuse the effectiveness of psycho-behavioral interventions. Excessive and unnecessary examination and treatment of somatic discomforts can be a maintaining factor because of the possible secondary gains for the client.

From the clients' perspective, however, the somatic discomforts are just too real. Psychosomatic and somatization theories dismiss signals from the body and sometimes discredit clients as being weak, manipulative, and even hysterical. Some dissatisfied clients consult mental health professionals for their suffering from "over-psychologicalization," that is, having a strong tendency to attribute everything to psychological explanations.

Which is correct, somatization or psychologicalization? From Integrative Body–Mind–Spirit Social Work's perspective, focusing on the body–mind connectedness is more beneficial (Chan, Ho et al., 2001; Chan et al., 2006).

Any assumption of a linear, causal relationship is dualistic and oversimplistic. The interaction between the body and mind is interactive and circular. It is like the chicken-or-egg question. There is no way to differentiate between the cause and consequence. The more desirable and effective approach is to deal with the body and mind simultaneously.

ACKNOWLEDGE AND UTILIZE THE "FELT BODY"

Integrative Body–Mind–Spirit Social Work adopts a proactive attitude in working with the client in relation to his or her "felt body." If the client discusses the felt body spontaneously, his or her subjective feelings and views about the somatic discomforts will be fully acknowledged. If the client does not touch upon the felt body spontaneously, the therapist often takes the initiative to enquire about it. For example, it is common to do a body-scan practice with the client in the first session. The objective is to enable the client to get in touch with the body and then explore the possibility of a body–mind connection.

Very often, bodily problems are a warning signal as well as a protective mechanism. Despite the strength of the signals, many people are so detached from their own bodies that they have surprisingly limited awareness of what is going on in their bodies. People are usually surprised when they start noticing how hard their body has been trying to cope with stress. Paying attention to our bodies is a beneficial way to start self-healing.

EXPANDING AWARENESS OF THE BODY

"I think; therefore I am" is a well-known saying in the West and in many Eastern communities. Some people regard thinking as the most important component of human existence, and some even equate it to total existence. The importance of cognition is particularly emphasized. The cognitive process and outcome are the focus. When people are eating, they may be using their cognitive ability to analyze, judge, and grade the food, environment, and services. Other senses maybe neglected. Some people only eat "automatically"; they are, in fact, absorbed in reading, surfing the Internet, watching television, or doing something else. After the meal, they are not really aware of the food they consumed. What if the meal were our whole lives? If we are absorbed by our preoccupations all the time and are not in touch with our senses, we may end up not having really lived. To be in touch with the senses of our body is crucial for us to live a full life (Ng, 2003; Ng & Chan, 2005).

The Case of Theresa: Being Too Strong

Theresa, aged 40, unexpectedly lost her husband a year ago. Her husband died of a cardiovascular accident, a stroke. There had been no warning signs and no opportunity to communicate any last words. He was at work at the time of the stroke, and he passed away shortly after being admitted to the hospital. Subsequently, Theresa entered into a severe depression. She reduced her existence to the minimum—like a body without a soul, hanging around at home.

About half a year later, she felt so weak as if she was about to die. At the lowest point, she realized that she could not carry on this way. Encouraged by close friends, she pushed herself hard to go out and keep fully occupied—attending church services regularly, taking classes for interest, meeting friends, and even dating. At the behavioral level, she appeared to have succeeded and have come out of the depression. However, that was not consistent with what she really felt. She was still deeply trapped in sadness and preoccupied with mourning for her husband. Meanwhile, guilt was growing fast—she felt disloyal to her deceased husband and sorry for being an inadequate mother to her 12-year-old daughter. Nevertheless, she had already developed a dependence on going out, which provided tranquilizing effects for her to temporarily escape from her emotional turmoil.

At the rational level, Theresa believed that being active and going out as much as possible was good for her. It could help her overcome her depression. Apparently, she succeeded, as she no longer fit the textbook criteria for depression. She thought she should be on the right track, but she was feeling that something was seriously wrong. Incidentally, her menstruation stopped shortly after "getting out of depression." That puzzled her because her menstruation was more or less normal even during the most depressed period. She consulted her family physician, but no abnormalities were detected.

After "coming out of depression" and living an extraordinarily active life for half a year, she sought mental health consultation. She could not articulate what went wrong. The stopping of her menstruation continued to puzzle her much. That turned out to be a good entry point for the therapist to gain a deeper understanding of her situation. The somatic sign was a strong signal that Theresa was exploiting herself and pushing herself to a state of disequilibrium. She had swung from a hypo yang to a hyper yang state, and it was damaging the yin. The stopping of her menstruation was a warning signal as well as a protective measure to conserve yin. Theresa's hyper yang behavior was not grounded in inner strength. Using the Integrative Body–Mind–Spirit healing wheel framework, the spiritual foundation was extremely fragile, but the body–mind wheel was spinning at full speed. By discussing the possible body–mind connections suggested by stop of menstruation, Theresa gained insight into her disequilibrium. She slowed down and took time to reconstruct new meaning for her life.

Coming back to our senses sounds deceptively easy. Apparently, it is something natural and spontaneous and therefore should not be an issue at all. As a matter of fact, however, many people find it difficult, if not impossible. Those living a busy life even find it alien. Why is that so? Perhaps we human beings are too clever, but at a cost—we are overly preoccupied by our cognitive self. Being clever is not necessarily being wise. We have much to learn from our pets, like dogs, although their intelligence is probably inferior to ours. Can we be as excited and happy every time we greet a family member coming back home?

To resume the discussion on using our natural senses: The theory is simple, but the key point is persistent and regular practice and application in daily life. Practice is the means of expanding our awareness of the body, environment, and life, which is the goal. There are many different forms of practice, for example, sitting meditation, walking meditation, mindful eating, *taiji*, *qigong*, and yoga. Although they differ in form, they share common beliefs and assumptions. The key principle is doing one thing at a time, slowly, mindfully, and with total concentration. The focus is living in the moment. One should not be too bothered about the results, gains, or losses. Awareness of the various senses of the whole body should be expanded as far as possible. Being appreciative is helpful in the process. Maintaining concentration is difficult because automatic thoughts come in from time to time. In cognitive therapy, the client is helped to examine the automatic thoughts and challenged to see if these thoughts are irrational or dysfunctional (Beck, 1995; Beck et al., 1979). In meditative mindfulness practices, the person only needs to make note of the thoughts and then gently bring his or her concentration back. "Fighting" with the automatic thoughts is not advised. The person becomes a third person, objectively observing his or her own thoughts, which can be coming in or going out, from a detached position. In Zen Buddhism terminology, such a practice is called "inner observation" (內觀). Such detachment can often help the person see the negative thoughts as more trivial and less disturbing. Becoming nonreactive is one of the key goals. With consistent practice over an extended time, the person can gain deeper insight into the nature of the disturbing thoughts, into him or herself, the world, and the relationship among all these.

Some practical mindfulness practices that can help us expand our awareness of the body and existence are discussed below.

Meditation

The dictionary meaning of the word "meditate" is "to think seriously about something" (Carver & Wallace, 1995, p. 565). This is just the opposite of the original Eastern concept of meditation. Newer dictionaries such as the *Canadian Oxford Dictionary* (2000) give as the first meaning, "to exercise the mind in (esp. religious) contemplation," which is closer to the Eastern concept of meditation. Meditation is about concentration, experiencing, appreciating, and awareness. Thinking is, in fact, a barrier to entering a meditative state. Meditation comes in many forms. The most basic and common form is sitting meditation. The classic sitting form is the famous "double lotus sitting posture" on the floor, usually with a small cushion. For clinical practice, however, that can be too elaborate and too difficult for clients. The double lotus sitting position demands considerable flexibility and strength in the lower limbs. It is advisable to start by sitting in a chair, preferably in a more upright position, or, still better, with the body away from the back of the chair. That is good enough for a beginner to experience sitting meditation. It is easier to concentrate with the eyes closed, though this is not always necessary. The key principles of mindfulness practice mentioned above apply here. If the practice is facilitated during a session, it cannot be too long due to time constraints; between five and ten minutes should be enough. If the client is to continue practicing at home, he or she should practice once or twice a day, about half an hour each time. Spending too much time on meditation, say, over 2 hr per day, is not advisable. The ultimate objective is to bring an enhanced capacity of awareness to daily life. Meditation practice is a means to an end.

Some clients find it hard to sit down, be still, and "do nothing" for even a few minutes. If this is the case, walking meditation can be a good alternative. A good way of doing this is in casual, comfortable dress, barefoot, and in a nice, quiet outdoor environment. As the person is walking slowly, he or she should concentrate on sensing every minor movement of his or her body, as well as the interaction between the body and environment, that is., the ground, wind, light, insects, smells, etc. Other principles of mindfulness practices mentioned earlier also apply. It is possible to do this with the client during a therapy session, perhaps in a big, quiet room or outside space. Again, because of time constraints, it is advisable to limit the practice to 10 min or less. If the person is motivated to carry on practicing, he or she may do it for longer alone, perhaps once or twice a day, for about half an hour every time.

Utilizing the Body to Address Emotions

Oftentimes, clients have difficulty handling or regulating their emotions, primarily negative ones. The following is a detailed description of how Integrative Body–Mind–Spirit Social Work utilizes body processes to address emotions.

Rebecca was a lady in her late thirties. When she first came to the therapist's office, she talked with a soft and weak voice and seemed afraid of looking directly at the therapist. She did not clearly express what she wanted. She gave the therapist the impression that she was a timid, little girl instead of a woman in her late thirties. After building rapport, she shared with the therapist that she was thinking about changing careers but was not certain about what she could do. She hoped the therapist could help her develop self-confidence so that she could take charge of her life.

In the first few sessions, the therapist helped Rebecca to explore and clarify what she wanted. She wanted to make some changes in her life, but she was afraid of the uncertainty that would go with the change. She realized that she was stuck because she was used to staying with the familiar and not taking risks. Rebecca also discovered that she had made herself psychologically dependent on others, her father in particular. This dependence had developed into a pattern so that she always relied on others to make decisions for her. Though there was an inner voice calling her to meet a new challenge and attempt a new job, she dared not, as her father did not support the idea.

During the fifth session, the therapist revisited the treatment goal with Rebecca and tried to help her to make a choice for herself regarding her pattern of being dependent on others. The therapist said, "You told me that your goal is to take charge of your life. Now you realize that you have developed a pattern of being dependent on others. What are you going to do with this pattern? Do you want to keep it, or change it?" Rebecca promptly responded that she did not want to keep the old pattern, but having been used to relying on others for so many years, she felt uncertain of what she could do if she was on her own. She said, "I have not yet figured out how to make a change. In my conscious mind, I am aware that I choose to stay with the familiar, to stay in the comfort zone. I tend to rely on others. However, the current pattern is most comfortable to me. I don't know how I can survive without relying on others' support."

It came to the therapist's mind that utilizing the conscious mind alone would not help Rebecca in moving further ahead. The therapist decided to intervene using the experiential approach, utilizing not only the mind but also the body. The therapist said, "Having heard what you have just said, I have developed a picture in my mind. Would you like me to share it with you?" With Rebecca's consent, the therapist created the picture by putting a hula hoop on the floor around her to represent her comfort zone. Rebecca was asked to kneel down. The therapist then put many cushions around the hula hoop so that Rebecca was surrounded and protected by the cushions. When asked by the therapist how well the scenario created represented her current psychological state, Rebecca said, "Yes. I was just hiding myself like this. It was quite safe." The therapist went on asking Rebecca how her body felt in such a position.

She said, "Actually it's not very comfortable. People may not be able to see me . . . I am very small . . . I don't want to be like this."

"So what do you want?" asked the therapist.

After thinking for a while, Rebecca said, still in a weak voice, "I want to stand up."

The therapist said to her, "How can you do that? As long as you continue to stay in your comfort zone and relying on others, you cannot stand on your own feet."

Rebecca said, in a louder voice, "I really don't want to be like this. I want to stand up. I have to rely on myself." At that moment, Rebecca stood up. She had made a new choice. The therapist continued to utilize both the body and the mind to consolidate the change: "If you were to rely on yourself and take charge of your life, how would you be different? What would your whole body be like? . . . Take a deep breath. You may close your eyes. Try to get in touch with your life force . . . (Rebecca closed her eyes and focused on her breathing.) What would your posture and body position be like? . . . If you wish, allow yourself to move. Allow yourself to stand anywhere, in any position that you think fits . . . Make yourself comfortable, assume a posture in which you feel you are grounded and firm. . . . Allow your body to use its own way to express yourself. . . . Give yourself permission, give yourself freedom, be in whatever way fits you . . . " Moving her hands, body, and feet slowly, Rebecca finally stepped out of the hula hoop and stood upright. She took a deep breath and smiled.

When Rebecca opened her eyes, the therapist asked her what she experienced in the exercise. She said in a calm voice that she had set herself free. She said that she had made a choice to stand up and not to be dependent on others. When asked about the meaning of standing up, Rebecca said, "Standing up means that I am competent. It means that I have internal strength and resources." The therapist then asked Rebecca to list the strengths and resources she found in herself.

When Rebecca shared with the therapist the resources she had, she realized that all those resources were with her, but she had not utilized them in the past. Hiding all her resources, she could only experience a sense of incompetence and insecurity. She smiled, and in a firmer and louder voice, she said, "I believe I am competent. I am able to take charge of my future life. I have many resources. I can be self-reliant. I can be responsible for my own life."

The therapist continued to anchor the positive changes experienced by Rebecca. "You are now able to take charge of yourself. How does your body feel?" asked the therapist.

"I feel calm and relaxed, I feel connected with myself and my resources," answered Rebecca. The therapist asked, "What is your body like when you are taking charge of and connecting with yourself?"

Standing straight yet relaxed, Rebecca took a deep breath and said, "I stand up firm and feel grounded. I believe I can lead my life in ways I desire." The therapist invited Rebecca to take another deep breath and get in touch with the feeling she was experiencing at the moment. "In which part of your body do you feel in touch with your personal resources? You may put your hand over the body part where you can feel your resources." Rebecca put her hands over her chest and smiled. She said that she could feel the resources in her heart. She also said that, at the moment, she realized that she was no longer the dependent little girl. She was in touch with her mature and independent self. When asked what she meant by "be her own self," Rebecca said, "I am Rebecca. I have many gifted talents. I am competent, I am curious, I am loveable. I appreciate myself."

Before the session ended, the therapist invited Rebecca to meditate. "I invite you to visualize yourself taking all the resources with you when you step out of this counseling room. Give yourself a lot of appreciation for what you have done for yourself today. Appreciate yourself for having made a new choice for yourself. Also appreciate all your resources: your gifts and talents, your competence, your curiosity, and your love . . . May they be with you as you venture into a new journey in your life."

When Rebecca returned home that evening, she talked to her father about her plan of changing careers. In the next session, she reported that she no longer felt afraid of her father when she expressed herself. She believed that she had been transformed.

Body Scan

This technique was introduced in Chapter 3. The therapist guides the client in a meditation-like state and has the client pay attention systematically to the different parts of the body, say, from head to toes or vice versa. As the attention moves along the body, the client practices expanding his or her awareness of various bodily sensations, such as heat, cold, pain, tenderness, tension, movement, pressure, etc. Other principles of meditation also apply here, such as total concentration, gratefulness, and a nonfighting attitude toward automatic thoughts. After "scanning" the whole body slowly, the client is then helped to share his or her experiences and explore the mind–body connection. For example, a client experiencing tight shoulders may report feeling extra burdens and responsibilities. A client having indigestion may identify many worries and fears. A client feeling weakness in the lower limbs may discuss living in fear and uncertainty. It should be noted that the mind–body connection is very individualized. Although there are various theories suggesting the pattern of these ties, it is important to note that differences between individuals can be vast. It is always wiser to help the client in exploring the body–mind link him or herself.

Healing Hands

This is a good, logical exercise to follow the body scan. The exercise aims to promote mind–body connection and integration (Chan, 2001). The therapist has the client rub both palms quickly for about 10 s so that they become warm. The palms are then put onto a location of the body that requires attention and healing. The client is told to pay attention to the location and try to communicate with it. The aim of this exercise is to love ourselves. The client is guided to acknowledge how hard his or her body is coping, be grateful for it, and pledge to take care of it. The same process is then repeated on another location of the body that requires attention.

UTILIZE BODY PROCESS IN TREATMENT PROCESS

Body process work involves simple, but intriguing, exercises that can be used in both individual and group treatment. The exercises are related to the basic senses and functions of our body, such as breathing, hearing, tasting, touching, and moving.

Ethical Concerns

Because using treatment techniques involving body process work is nonconventional, there are important ethical issues that will need to be thoughtfully considered. Chapter 15 provides a detailed discussion on ethical issues pertaining to Integrative Body–Mind–Spirit Social Work. The described body process activities are designed for therapeutic and treatment purposes and can be safely utilized in the treatment process. However, it is imperative for social work professionals to develop competence in these activities prior to using them in treatment. In addition, these activities are meant for therapeutic purposes and not for curing physical symptoms. For any specific medical, physical, or psychiatric conditions, it is very important for social work professionals to fully respect the professional boundaries and refer the client for appropriate medical and psychiatric evaluation and treatment.

Ethical considerations regarding body process activities primarily exist at two levels: (1) ethics relating to the selection of body process activities, and (2) ethics relating to the implementation of body process activities. Integrative Body–Mind–Spirit Social Work only selects body process activities that are effective at treating clients, are safe, nonintrusive, can be self-administered to empower clients, and are simple, easy, and quick to learn. Transferability to one's daily life is an important consideration in selecting the exercises. Exercises should preferably be simple and safe and bring about pleasant results quickly. These exercises can help increase the chance that the client will incorporate them into daily life.

Because all clients are unique and different, social work professionals and therapists must assess individual receptivity to the activities. For instance, safety is a key concern and must be accorded careful consideration whenever adopting any body-nurturing strategies in working with a client. The physical condition of the client needs to be taken into account. For example, clients who are not steady on their feet may not be suited to many of the exercises described in this chapter. Mental condition is another important factor to consider. If a client has active psychotic symptoms such as delusion and auditory hallucination, it is not advisable to let the client enter a meditative state. When the therapist is uncertain about the appropriateness of an activity for a particular client, do not introduce the activity in the section.

When implementing body-nurturing activities, the therapist must thoroughly introduce the activities, explain the benefits and potential consequences, seek consent, teach the activities, and carefully observe clients' reactions when engaging them in a particular body process activity. The principle of voluntary participation must be respected. Explanations of every intervention should be given and the client's understanding should be checked. Some exercises may seem to be connected to a certain religion to some clients. If clients feel uncomfortable with the exercises for religious reasons, their worries should be recognized and discussed thoroughly. The exercises should never be imposed on the clients.

The possibility of harassment should also be noted. Because of ethical concerns about physical touch, Integrative Body–Mind–Spirit Social Work prefers body process activities that can be self-administered by clients. For any exercises involving physical touch, clear explanations and prior agreement by the client are necessary. Body parts that are socially considered "private" must be respected. Because the concept of what is "private" varies across cultures, cultural sensitivity is absolutely essential. Moreover, the concept of what is "private" also differs among individuals. Obtaining clients' consent is absolutely necessary prior to any bodily intervention.

In Integrative Body–Mind–Spirit Social Work, the process can be rather dynamic and interactive. Very often, a range of body–mind–spirit interventions is employed in the treatment session. The best strategy for addressing ethical concerns is maintaining open and effective communication between the therapist and the client. A deep respect for clients' choice, an empowering stance, and collaborative therapeutic relationship help toward this goal.

Breathing

Breathing is a vital sign of life, although most people are not aware of it. Helping clients to focus and be aware of their breathing brings them back in touch with their senses and makes them mindful of the present. Similar to the way the heart beats, the lungs breathe automatically and continuously around the clock. Unlike the heart, which is totally regulated by involuntary muscles, breathing can be regulated by our will when we wish to do so. Interestingly, through regulating our breathing rate, we can regulate our heart indirectly. Breathing slowly and deeply is a quick and effective way to moderate the rate at which the heart beats. In many ancient religions, attending to, and regulating, breathing is an important basic training in relaxation (Chan, 2001).

Breathing exercises can take many forms in a therapeutic session. Breathing meditation, mentioned earlier in the chapter, can be one form. Slow and deep breathing for about five breaths is even simpler, and it is probably the simplest and quickest way for a person to calm down and contain emotional disturbances, agitation, and nervousness. More importantly, it gives the person a sense of mastery.

Qigong can also be considered a form breathing exercise, though it usually also includes the components of body movement and imagery (Ng, 2003). If movement is a part of the *qigong* practice, it is called "moving *qigong*." Otherwise, it is called "still *qigong*." Some clients are so distressed and agitated that they may find it hard to practice breathing while sitting in a chair. In such situations, it helps a great deal by incorporating some body movements along with the breathing exercises. The movement can simply be moving the hands up and down rhythmically, synchronized with breathing in and out. If the client does not have significant physical limitations, the movement can be extended to include stretching the body. That can maximize the relaxation effect. When the hands are moving up, they are extended over the head so as to flex the spine backward. When the hands are moving forward and then down, they are lowered toward the toes as far as possible, and the knees are kept straight. This stretches the spine in the opposite direction. In a clinical session, doing this sort of slow breathing and body movement five to ten times is sufficient for the client to experience a mood change. It does not need to be overly elaborate.

Sound

In conventional counseling and psychotherapy, we primarily use sound with literal or verbal meaning—voice. In Integrative Body–Mind–Spirit Social Work, we use sound in a more general sense and cover a wider spectrum of sounds. Paying attention to sound (not words) helps us to return to our senses in a different way. It can be the ringing of a bell, the blowing of wind, rainfall hitting a window, birds singing, an airplane passing over, and so on. The sound can be intentionally made by the therapist or the client during the session. Hearing is an important, natural sense. However, as we are socialized, we become highly selective and even restrictive with our hearing, that is, paying attention only to sounds with "valuable information" and filtering those without. We miss a lot of the richness in the world of sound.

Listening to the ringing of a small metal bell is an interesting exercise. When we pay attention to it, putting aside our value judgments and filters, we can let the sound enter our bodies and touch our souls. We are in the sound, and the sound is inside us. The sound is not just heard but is also seen and felt. The awareness of resonance and the sound fading away can be extremely rich. Although using a small bell is good and convenient, it may seem a bit religious to some people. Using a handy musical instrument is an alternative, perhaps a small percussion instrument such as a triangle or glockenspiel. Asking the client to bring along his or her favorite music records to the counseling session is often helpful. Sometimes, the music can help the client express mixed, delicate feelings much more vividly. That can spark a much deeper and more insightful discussion. Sometimes, the music selected by the client is for counteracting his or her troubled state of being. That may inspire new possibilities in self-help. For instance, if a client finds it helpful to listen to happy songs to lift his or her mood, the client may experiment with other happy gestures, such as joyful facial expressions, dancing, and reciting positive statements. The important thing is that the therapist should avoid being interpretative when listening to the client's music. Instead, the therapist should help the client to explore and share the underlying meanings about him or herself.

Taste

To some people, eating is often something instrumental. Throughout the process of eating, they are preoccupied with something else, such as reading, responding to e-mail, watching television, etc. As life becomes busier, "instrumental eating" is the norm, whereas "mindful eating" is a luxury. How often do you fully enjoy the process of having a meal? If your answer is every day, you should be congratulated. For some people, this is a distant memory.

Mindful eating is a simple, effective exercise that helps us come back to our senses—taste, touch, smell, sight, etc. We have experimented with various types of food, including vegetables, fruits, and biscuits, but plain rice is our favorite. It is familiar to the people in the Asia because they have rice virtually every day. Because rice plays a complementary role in a meal, it attracts very little attention. The taste is often subtle because it is often masked by other, tasty dishes. As a result, many people forget the delicate taste, smell, and texture of rice. This is exactly why using plain rice in mindful eating exercises for Asian people can be inspiring. When designing the exercise, therapists should utilize culturally appropriate food, such as bread or dried grapes, to be used in the mindful eating exercise as people from different cultures have diverse eating habits.

Using mindful eating with rice as a group activity, the therapist puts a spoonful of warm rice in the palms of each participant. The participants are asked to regard the spoonful of rice as something they have never seen before. They need to know about this "new" food. They should not put the spoonful of rice into the mouth immediately. Instead, they should look at it, touch it, smell it, feel its heat, weight, texture, and so on. Then, they may proceed with putting the spoonful of rice into the mouth and must be mindful of every minor step of the chewing and swallowing process, for example, movement of the tongue and jaw, secretion of saliva, contraction of the throat muscles, and so on. Rice has an amazingly rich texture and taste that is often not noticed in a meal. A mindful eating exercise with rice is often a surprising experience to the participants. The most common reaction is, "Oh, I have missed out so much on the sweet taste of rice!"

Depressed people often prefer richer tastes. Perhaps that is one reason why chocolate is popular among people who are down and unhappy. People in depression often over-inhibit themselves and are consequently deprived of many normal sensual experiences. Using rich-tasting foods a client likes can be a good entry point to help him or her come back to his or her senses. We also often use extreme tastes, for example, strong bitter tea and very sour lemon sweets, with our clients. The experience is amazingly powerful and inspiring. The client typically feels really awful at the beginning and wants to give up and spit out the food. As the client persists, he or she will experience very subtle, delicate, and nice changes in taste and texture. The experience is beyond the description of words but is often described as bittersweet or soursweet. This is a good analogy to life—the saying, "no pain no gain" is quite often true. This tasting exercise can open up a discussion on exploring the meaning of sufferings.

Tea Drinking

Tea ceremonies are popular with Chinese and Japanese people. The process has many elaborate and complicated rituals that take time to learn and master. However, if we understand the rationale behind them, we can do away with most rituals and develop our own simplified form of mindful tea drinking.

Similar to designing mindful eating exercises, the therapist should be culturally sensitive to the drinking habits of clients and use appropriate beverages (such as coffee) in the process.

Mindful tea drinking is described for illustration purposes. The key principles of mindful tea drinking are concentration, appreciation, and gratefulness (Ng, 2003). With this spirit, the process of preparing tea and drinking tea can be highly flexible and individualized. To make tea, you may flexibly follow these steps:

1. Some basic items are needed: an airtight container for tea leaves, a tablespoon, a small electric kettle, a small teapot, a cup about the same size as the teapot (called the "fair cup" in Chinese), four to eight small teacups, a large plate, and a towel. Figure 6.1 shows a tea set for this purpose.
2. Arrange the small teapot, the fair cup, and the small teacups on the plate.
3. Boil water in the electric kettle.
4. Put one tablespoon of tea leaves into the small teapot.
5. Pour freshly boiled water into the small teapot.
6. Close the lid and let the tea steep for about 1 min.
7. Pour all the freshly brewed tea into the "fair cup." It is called the "fair cup" because it ensures that the tea is mixed well and that its richness will be evenly distributed in the small teacups.
8. Open the lid of the teapot to let the steam out and the tea leaves cool down. This step is important because, in the Tea ceremony, the tea brewing and tasting procedures are usually repeated three to five times. The color, texture, and aroma will change delicately after each brew. A key point of the tea ceremony is to be aware of these changes as far as possible. If the lid of the teapot is not opened after each brewing, the steam and heat trapped inside the pot will cook the tea leaves and waste them.
9. Evenly distribute the fresh tea into the small teacups.
10. Enjoy the tea slowly, with all the senses—sight, smell, taste, touch, hearing.
11. The tea brewing and tasting process is usually repeated three to five times, depending on the strength of the tea leaves being used. For example, Iron Buddha is a favorite with tea lovers. It can be good for around five rounds of tea brewing.

Tea drinking can be a therapeutic activity in an individual or group session. It can also be incorporated into the daily lives of clients. It helps remind us

FIGURE **6.1.** Mindful tea drinking.

to come back to our senses and resume and expand our awareness. It can be practiced at home and in the workplace.

Other Senses

So far, this chapter has described the use of sound and taste in clinical work. There are other senses like smell, sight, and touch, which have not been discussed yet. Regarding these other senses, there are some very sophisticated therapies, such as aromatherapy and various multisensory stimulation techniques. In Integrative Body–Mind–Spirit Social Work, these elaborative therapies are not used. Instead, in meditation and mindfulness practice, we simply guide the client to expand awareness and return to all the senses as far as possible. The objective is to enhance the ability to live in the moment and transfer it to everyday life. All forms of therapy or practice are just means to the ends. The skill is more important than skill transfer is.

Having said the above, we are not against other sensual stimulation therapies. On the contrary, we often encourage our clients to try out these therapies if they are interested in any of them. We often hear good feedback from our clients. Common subjective benefits reported by clients include better sleep, more energy, and less anxiety.

Acupressure

Before discussing acupressure as a body-nurturing activity, it is important to note that acupressure is based on the meridian and acupuncture theory of Traditional Chinese medicine (TCM), which has been practiced for over 2,000 years (Cai, 1995; Ng, 2003). While TCM is a sophisticated and complex field and practice that requires years of study to master the skills clinically, acupressure is a simplified form that can be safely administered by people with no training in TCM or simply self-administered. Because of its nonintrusive nature as well as simplicity in terms of learning, acupressure has been widely practiced by people to address physical or psychological discomforts. However, it is important to recognize that many presenting symptoms can be manifestations of specific medical or psychiatric conditions. Integrative Body–Mind–Spirit Social Work routinely conducts mental status examinations and refers clients to appropriate professionals to rule out any medical and psychiatric conditions. Acupressure complements conventional treatment as it empowers clients to engage in body-nurturing activities in the process of healing.

Acupressure is based on the meridian and acupuncture theory. The meridian network comprises twelve major channels, eight special channels, and numerous smaller channels covering virtually every part of the body, inside and out. The network connects the body and makes it an integrated whole. An acupuncture point is a point on either a major or a special channel that is close to the skin surface and has a high concentration of *qi* and blood flowing. There are more than 300 acupuncture points all over the body. The flowing of *qi* and blood in the meridian network can be regulated by manipulating selected acupuncture points through various means, such as needle acupuncture, moxibustion, and physical manipulation. The treatment objective is to restore systemic equilibrium and hence self-healing capacity.

While Integrative Body–Mind–Spirit Social Work is nonproblem-focused, acupressure, as practiced in TCM, aims at symptom relief. Even so, acupressure is incorporated in Integrative Body–Mind–Spirit Social Work as a self-administrated health practice that can empower self-efficacy and mastery and as a practice that activates and utilizes clients' innate healing abilities. Acupressure as used in IBMSSW is highly simplified so that it can be learned and mastered in a few minutes. For practical and safety reasons, only 10 points are selected for use in Integrative Body–Mind–Spirit Social Work. They are all on the head and limbs so as to minimize potential harassment issues. As these points have been extensively used in TCM for over 2,000 years, their therapeutic properties are well understood and documented. Table 6–1 summarizes the location and function of these ten points (Liu, 1987). Figure 6.2 further illustrates the locations of the points in photos.

TABLE **6–1.** The Ten Useful Acupressure Points

ACUPUNCTURE POINT	LOCATION	FUNCTION	MANUAL MANIPULATION METHOD
renzhong (人中)(6.2e)	At the longitudinal groove of the skin below the nose and above the upper lip, 1/3 of the way down from the nose toward the upper lip	Helps relieve dizziness and regain control from emotional confusion	Press hard with tip of the thumb or index finger for 1 min. There will be a mild sensation of pain.
baihui (百會)(6.2a)	On the median line of the head, at the top of the head just between the ears	Helps relieve dizziness, blurred vision, and headache	Rub it in circular motion with palm heel for 1 min. There will be a warm sensation.
lieque (列缺)(6.2c)	At the radial border of the forearm, about 1.5 inches above the wrist	Helps relieve headache, stiff neck, cough, sore throat, and skin hypersensitivity	Press hard with the tip of the thumb of the opposite hand for 1 min. Repeat on the other arm.
*hegu (合谷)(6.2b)	On the back of the hand, between the first and second metacarpal bone, at the middle of the second metacarpal bone on the radial side	Helps relieve headache, redness and swollen eyes, sore throat, cough, and abdominal distention	Press hard with the tip of the thumb of the opposite hand for 1 min. Repeat on the other hand.
neiguan (內關)(6.2d)	On the palm side of the forearm, two inches above the wrist and in the middle of the two central tendons	Helps relieve palpitations, vomiting, hiccups, stomachache, and insomnia.	Rub in circular motion with a thumb for 1 min. Repeat on the other arm.
zhigou (支沟)(6.2i)	On the outer side of the forearm, three inches above the wrist and in the middle of the ulna and radius	Helps relieve constipation, acute loss of voice and tinnitus	Rub it in circular motion with the thumb for 1 min. Repeat on the other arm.

TABLE **6–1.** (*continued*)

ACUPUNCTURE POINT	LOCATION	FUNCTION	MANUAL MANIPULATION METHOD
zusanli (足三里)(6.2j)	On the anterior exterior side of the shank, three inches below the lower edge of the knee bone, one finger-breadth (of the middle finger) from the anterior border of the tibia	Helps relieve pain and discomfort of stomach and abdomen, nausea, vomiting, diarrhea, constipation, and sensation of fullness in chest.	Press hard with the tip of the thumb of the opposite hand for 1 min. Repeat it on the other leg.
sanyinjiao (三陰交) (6.2f)	Three inches above the tip of the medial malleolus (the projected point on the inner side of the ankle), on the posterior margin of the inner side of the tibia	Helps relieve abdominal distention, diarrhea, irregular menstruation, and pain or numbness of lower limb	Press hard with the tip of the thumb of the opposite hand for 1 min. Repeat on the other limb.
taichong (太衝)(6.2g)	In the excavation posterior to the space of the first metatarsal bone on the back of the foot	Helps relieve headache, vertigo, tinnitus, and irregular menstruation	Press hard with the tip of the thumb of the opposite hand for 1 min. Repeat on the other foot.
yongquan (湧泉)(6.2h)	On the foot, on the connecting line of the web between the second and third toes and the heel, 1/3 of the way from the toes	Helps relieve dizziness, headache, blurred vision, insomnia, sore throat, and difficulty with urination	Rub in a circular motion with the thumb for 1 min. Repeat on the other foot.

*Note: Hegu and *sanyinjiao* can induce labor and therefore should *not* be used with pregnant clients.

Using these acupressure points is simple. The first thing is to identify the needs of the client. Is it for relieving a certain symptom or discomfort? Or is it to enhance general well-being? With reference to the needs, one or more acupressure points on the list may be selected. The physical manipulation is performed simply by using the thumb, index finger, or heel of the palm to press or rub each selected point for about a minute. Detailed instructions for physical manipulation are given in Table 6–1. If the point is on a limb, it is

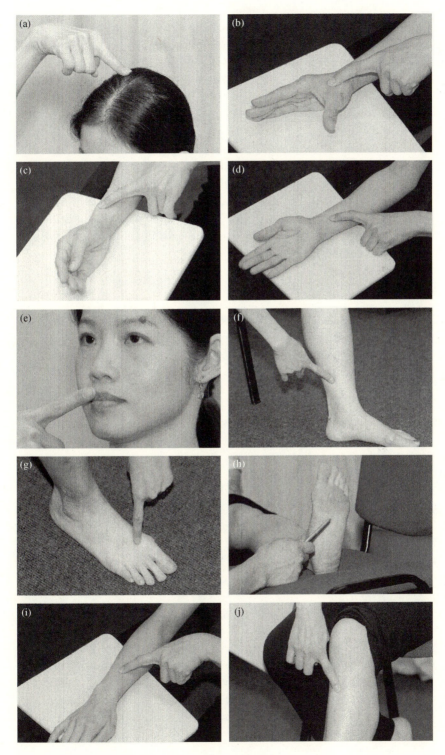

FIGURE **6.2.** Locating the ten useful acupressure points.

more effective to manipulate the points on both sides, one after another. For symptom control, the technique is applied whenever the symptom appears. It will take only a few minutes to know if the technique helps. If not, the client should then look for other responses. To enhance general well-being, the recommendation is to practice once or twice daily.

Here are examples of conditions often encountered in clinical practice. For dizziness, try *renzhong* and *baihui*; for migraine, try *lieque* and *hegu*; for sore throat, try *lieque*, *hegu*, and *yongquan*; for palpitation, try *neiguan*; for nausea, try *zusanli*; for constipation, try *zhigou*; for digestive problems and abdominal discomfort, try *zusanli* and *sanyinjiao*; for premenstrual discomfort, try *sanyinjiao* and *taichong*; and for sleep disturbances, try *yongquan*. The effectiveness of acupressure does vary from case to case. However, the important thing is for the client to gain a sense of mastery through self-administering simple acupressure techniques.

Light Massage

Therapeutic massage adopted by Integrative Body–Mind–Spirit Social Work is also based on the meridian and acupuncture theories of TCM. Instead of focusing on manipulating the tiny acupuncture points, it focuses on manipulating the channels, muscles, and joints (Cai, 1995; Ng, 2003; Shen & Yan, 2004). Although the approach is different, the ultimate objective is the same, that is., restoring systemic equilibrium and self-healing capacity through body process work. Therapeutic massage should be done by professionals, as it involves strenuous physical manipulations that can lead to injuries when not properly administered.

Like acupressure, light massage intends to be administered by people with no training in Chinese medicine or therapeutic massage. It is often self-administered. The design of light massage exercises is often loosely based on the meridian and acupuncture theories. Four popular exercises are selected and introduced below. They are simple, safe, effective, and fun. The following are several useful and simple light massage exercises for clients.

Head tapping

Head tapping is a self-administered technique. According to the meridian and acupuncture theories, different parts of the head correspond to different organs, systems, and functions. For example, the forehead above the hairline is associated with the digestive and reproductive systems; the back of the head is associated with vision; the lateral part is associated with the mobility of the opposite side of the body; and for a person who is right-hand dominant, the left side of the brain locates the language center; it is the reverse for a person who is left-hand dominant. For head tapping, because the objective is to

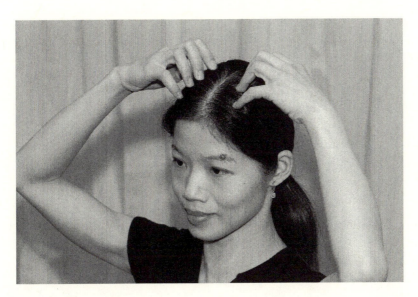

FIGURE **6.3.** Head tapping.

enhance general well-being, the approach is simply tapping all over the surface of the head, by using all 10 fingertips. Using the wrists as the pivot points, both palms touch the head quickly, with the fingertips hitting the surface of the head briskly. Practicing for 2 to 5 min is sufficient to feel refreshed, like clearing the mind (Figure 6.3).

Shoulder massage

The muscles around our shoulders take a lot of stress in daily life. This is especially true for people who work in offices or use computers and mothers with young children. In a treatment session, shoulder massage is best conducted for couples or as a group activity in which members form a queue or circle. Family members can also learn to do it for each other. The client's consent to engage in this activity is absolutely necessary because of the involvement of body touch. Chapter 15 includes a detailed discussion on the ethical practice of Integrative Body–Mind–Spirit Social Work. A person sits up straight in a chair while the partner stands behind and massages the shoulders of the seated person (see Figure 6.4). The basic forms of physical manipulation are (Shen & Yan, 2004):

a. Pushing: The manipulator pushes on the client's body along a straight path with the thumb, "sword-fingers" (i.e., the index and middle fingers), palm heel, fist, or elbow.

b. Pressing: The manipulator presses on the client's body with the tips of the thumbs, palm heel, or elbow. Pressing may be done with single hand or with the hands interlaced to strengthen the pressing force.

c. Circular rubbing: The manipulator rubs the client's body in a circular motion with fingers or palm.

d. Pinching: The manipulator holds the client's skin and some subcutaneous tissues and pulls them up with the thumb and other fingers.

e. Grasping: This is similar to pinching, but in grasping, not only the skin and subcutaneous tissue are held but the muscles as well. Then the tissue slips out of the fingers. The stimulation is stronger than pinching.

In a session, doing shoulder massage for 3 to 5 min is enough to reap the benefits. The pair then switch roles and practice the massage for another

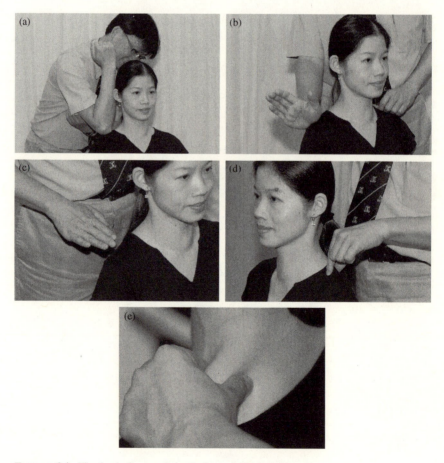

FIGURE **6.4.** Five basic forms of physical manipulation.

round. The clients can be motivated to introduce this mutual massage activity to the family. In a home setting, each shoulder massage may last between 5 and 10 min. The practice is a good opportunity for intimate contact and demonstration of mutual care and concern. Sometimes, more meaning can be expressed through nonverbal behavior.

Back tapping

Meridian and acupuncture theories of TCM postulate that a number of acupuncture points are associated with key organs and systems and that they are clustered at the back of the body. Massaging the back regularly helps maintain and enhance a person's well-being. This is the reason why professional body massage focuses so much on the back.

In Integrative Body–Mind–Spirit Social Work, we use a simple form of massage—back tapping. Again, the practice is best conducted for couples or as a group activity in which members consent to engage in this exercise with each other. A person stands upright, while the partner stands behind him or her and faces the back of the person. The partner closes his or her fingers and forms the palm in the shape of a bowl. He or she uses the two palms to tap rapidly the two sides of the back of the person in front, going up and down between the shoulders and hips (Figure 6.5). Similar to the shoulder massage, back tapping for 3 to 5 min is sufficient. The pair then switch roles and practice the massage for another round. Clients can be motivated to introduce this mutual massage activity to their families. In a home setting, the person being

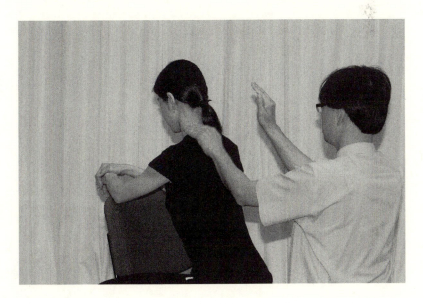

FIGURE **6.5.** Back tapping.

massaged may choose to lie face down on the bed. A light massage may last between 5 and 10 min.

Whole body tapping (拍打功)

Whole body tapping is a self-administered activity. The idea of this exercise is to tap the whole body with both palms, following the flow of the major meridians. Unlike back tapping, whole body tapping does not require a partner (see Figure 6.6). The steps are:

1. Get ready: Stand up straight with the feet two-shoulder widths apart. Put the right palm on top of the left shoulder, and lift the left arm horizontally on the left side with the palm facing up.
2. Tapping the left arm: Tap the inside of the left arm, from shoulder to hand, using the right palm; turn the left palm down so that the dorsal side of the left arm is now facing up, and then tap the dorsal side of the left arm, from hand to shoulder, using the right palm.
3. Tapping the head: Tap the left, top, then right side of the head using the right palm. At the same time, the left palm follows through and taps the left, top, and right side of the head.
4. Tapping the right arm: Lift the right arm so that it stretches straight horizontally on the right side, the palm facing up. Tap the inside of the right arm, from shoulder to hand, using the left palm; turn the right palm down so that the dorsal side of the right arm is now facing up, and then tap the dorsal side of the right arm, from hand to shoulder, using the left palm.
5. Tapping the head: The left palm taps the right, top, and then left side of the head. The right palm follows. Both palms tap the head simultaneously: lateral, back, top, front, and face.
6. Tapping the neck: Turn the head up. Tap the front part of neck with both palms.
7. Tapping the front of the body: Both palms rapidly tap all the way down the front part of the body, from chest to abdomen and to hips.
8. Tapping the front of the legs: Keep the legs straight while bending down. Tap the front part of the left and right legs using the left and right palms, respectively, from hip to the lowest reachable point. (Note: The lowest reachable point varies a lot among individuals. The important thing is not to exceed our own limit.)
9. Tapping the back of the legs: Tap the back part of the left and right legs using the left and right palms, respectively. While the palm is going up from the lowest reachable point, the body should straighten up.

10. Tapping the kidney posterior region: The palm continues to tap upward until reaching the back at approximately the level of the left and right kidneys. Keep tapping the area about 20 times.

This whole body tapping exercise takes only a few minutes to complete once. It is extremely refreshing, and with the big tapping noise, it is great fun, especially in a group setting. Doing two to three rounds are about right in a clinical session.

FIGURE **6.6.** Whole body tapping.

FIGURE **6.6.** (*continued*)

Body Movement

TCM has long recognized the value of physical exercise in the enhancement of health. A few traditions characterize the health exercises of the Chinese (Ng, 2003). Firstly, imagery is often incorporated. For example, body movements mimic certain animals such as a dragon, cat, monkey, or snake; or mimic things in nature such as the wind, clouds, or plants. Therefore, a high level of mental concentration is required. Secondly, breathing is often part of the exercise. Oftentimes, the exercises require one to consciously regulate the rhythm of breathing during the exercise. Thirdly, slow movements, and even stillness,

FIGURE **6.6.** (*continued*)

are common in many Chinese health exercises. This makes Chinese physical exercises look deceptively easy. In fact, they demand a higher level of "inner strength" that includes muscle strength, endurance, concentration, and emotional stability (Cheng & Macfarlane, 2001).

Taiji

Taiji is a good representative of traditional Chinese health exercises. It was developed as a form of martial arts, or kung fu in Chinese. Although most forms of kung fu emphasize speed and strength, *taiji* emphasizes slowness

FIGURE **6.6.** (*continued*)

and softness. Because a high level of mental concentration is required during practice, *taiji* is more than a physical exercise; it is a good mind–body exercise. *Taiji* has been extensively studied in Chinese and non-Chinese communities and has been found to be beneficial to both physical and mental health. Because *taiji* is often practiced in groups, it can also provide a social network for the participants.

However, there are a number of limitations with *taiji*. Firstly, it is not as easy as it appears to be. People who have mobility problems or are too frail will have difficulty practicing. Secondly, *taiji* requires good three-dimensional spatial sense. People with a weak sense of direction will have great difficulty with *taiji*.

To address these limitations and make *taiji* suitable to a wider audience, efforts have been made in developing simplified *taiji*. Whereas classical *taiji* may have over 100 forms, the simplified versions have fewer than 20 forms. Moreover, only easy movements are included. Simplified *taiji* is especially welcome in day centers and residential homes for the elderly. However, simplification is not achieved without cost. The most significant is that simplified *taiji* has lost much of the spirit of real *taiji*. For people with an adequate physique and a spatial sense, classical *taiji* is still preferred.

Qigong

Qigong has an even longer history than *taiji* and can be traced to over 2,000 years ago. It can be seen as a mind–body exercise blending breathing, body postures or movement, and imagery together (Cai, 1995; Ng, 2003). If there is only holding one position but no movement, it is called "still *qigong*." Conversely, it is called "moving *qigong*" if there is movement. In *taiji*, there can be over 100 forms of movement. In *qigong*, there are fewer forms of movement, typically fewer than ten. There can be only one form of movement or position throughout the practice, which lasts for about 30–60 min. The absence of variety implies that an even higher level of concentration and endurance is required.

A key advantage of *qigong* over *taiji* is that it is less demanding on the physical and spatial sense of the participant. Because there are few forms of body position or movement, it is also less demanding on one's ability to memorize. Having said that, *qigong* also has a number of significant limitations. Firstly, it can be boring for some people, as the positions or movements are repetitive. It can be difficult to keep the participants motivated. Secondly, the cardiovascular loading of most types of *qigong* is not sufficient. As such, *qigong* is better supplemented by another physical exercise that can provide more strenuous cardiovascular training.

Stretching

Many clients are emotionally tense, and as a result, their body is also tense. Stretching the body systematically can quickly ease both body and mind. It is quick because addressing the big, major joints is already sufficient for psychosocial intervention purposes. Going over every single small joint is unnecessary.

The neck and shoulders are important sites to pay attention to, as they take a lot of stress throughout the day. For the neck, simple slow left-right and up-down stretching, five times in each direction, is good enough. Caution must be taken, for rotating the head in circles with the neck as the pivot is not advisable, as it may hurt the joint.

For the shoulder joints, slow, large-range rotations can "defrost" a "frozen shoulder." A good sequence for shoulder rotations is forward ten times (i.e., same as the rotation of the butterfly stroke, but only the shoulders rotate; arms and hands are kept down), backward rotation ten times, forward rotation ten times, and finally backward rotation ten times again, for a total of forty rotations.

Training the strength and flexibility of the spine is instrumental to maintaining one's health. Yoga especially shares this view point, as witnessed

FIGURE **6.7.** Three flexes nine bows.

FIGURE **6.7.** (*continued*)

by its incorporation of extensive spine training in its practice. A simple traditional Chinese stretching exercise called "Three Flexes Nine Bows" (三仰九叩) can achieve this purpose nicely (Figure 6.7). The sequence of the body movements is:

1. Get ready: Assume an upright, standing posture. Feet are shoulder-width apart. Arms should be kept straight, with hands on top of each other in front of the abdomen.
2. The first flex: Very slowly, swing the arms up, over the top of the head, and then lean backwards, flexing the body backwards. At the

FIGURE **6.7.** (*continued*)

extreme backward position, hold the posture for a few seconds. (Note: The extreme position varies greatly among individuals. It is important to caution the participants not to force themselves to exceed their limits.)

3. First four bows: Relax and slowly get up from the extreme backwards position. Keeping the legs straight, slowly lower the hands toward the floor, between the two feet, and lean forward, bending the body over. At the extreme low position, hold the posture for a few seconds. (Note: Again, the extreme low position varies greatly among individuals. Do not try to exceed the limits.) Then, relax, and lift the hands up to knee

F<small>IGURE</small> **6.7.** (*continued*)

level, rotate to the left and sink slowly toward the left foot. At the extreme low position, hold the posture for a few seconds. Then relax and lift the hands up to knee level again, rotate to the right, and lower them slowly toward the right foot. At the extreme low position, hold the posture for a few seconds. Then relax and lift the hands up to knee level, rotate back to the center, and bend slowly toward the floor between the feet. At the extreme low position, hold the posture for a few seconds.

4. The second flex: Relax and then repeat step 2. This is the second time of flexing backward.

5. Second four bows: Relax and then repeat step 3. This becomes the second four bows bending forward.
6. The third flex: Relax and repeat step 2. This becomes the third and the last flexing backward.
7. The ninth bow: Relax and follow step 3 in doing the first bow bending forward toward the middle.
8. The closing form: Turn the palms up. While standing upright, slowly take in a deep breath. Meanwhile, bend the elbows and lift the palms slowly up to chest level. Then bring the feet together, palms facing down. While slowly lowering the palms, breathe out. Relax and rest the hands naturally on both sides of the body. Remain in this standing position for about a minute. Pay attention to the gradual relaxation of various parts of the body, and be aware of the surrounding environment, sound, light, wind, warmth, etc.

The "Three Flexes Nine Bows" exercise takes only a few minutes to complete. The effect is quick and refreshing. Many of our clients incorporate it as part of their routine morning exercise. Some also do it before going to bed because it quickly helps relax the body and mind. It is especially suitable for those whose bodies are tensed and rigid while sleeping.

One-second techniques

The one-second techniques were developed by Cecilia L.W. Chan and her associates during their extensive work with cancer patients (Chan, 2001). Many of the techniques were, in fact, learned from the patients and therefore have been tried and tested. The techniques were adapted from a wide range of popular physical exercises and practices originating from *qigong* or *taiji* in Hong Kong and China. Chan and her associates further simplified them and put them into clinical practice. These techniques are so easy to learn that they are called one-second techniques. They involve moving or massaging the hands, nose, ears, eyes, mouth, feet, and body.

Therapists can use these techniques in both individual and group sessions. They can teach clients one or two techniques each time and can ask them to practice daily between sessions. None of the techniques requires special equipment or venues. They can be conveniently practiced at home or in the office.

The one-second techniques can be easily learned by viewing video-recorded demonstrations. A complete set of the videos can be accessed at http://cbh.hku.hk, the Web site of the Centre on Behavioral Health, The University of Hong Kong.

SUMMARY

Emphasizing the body–mind connection and the significance of the felt body, this chapter introduces practical methods for nurturing the body that can be incorporated into clinical practice. There are two broad categories of these bodily activities: (1) expanding awareness of the body, and (2) utilizing body process in the treatment process. A range of strategies and methods has been introduced, including meditation, body scan, healing hands, breathing, activities related to sound and taste, tea drinking, acupressure, light massage, and body movement. The methods suggested are by no means exhaustive. In addition, different cultures have culturally based practices, wisdom, and perceptions regarding what are beneficial body-nurturing activities (Lee, 1996, 2003). For instance, exercises (perhaps in gyms), gardening, and jogging are common body-related activities esteemed by many people in North America. Swimming is more common for people who live in tropical and subtropical regions and close to the oceans. Onsen experiences are highly valued by Japanese because of the geological characteristics of Japan. Finnish enjoy spas immensely. Learners of Integrative Body–Mind–Spirit Social Work are encouraged to use culturally appropriate and sensitive knowledge and practices in adopting the described techniques and creatively developing body process activities in their social work practice, with thoughtful attention to their unique socio-cultural milieu.

7

From the Body to the Mind and Spirit

Holistic health is the result of a balanced and integrated body, mind, and spirit. As the body functions as a system, change in one of the components affects the others. Traditional social work and counseling approaches emphasize working through the mind; the body component is less emphasized. This chapter intends to place importance on working on and through the body in order to illustrate how work on the body, mind, and spirit can be linked together.

THE IMPORTANCE OF WORKING ON AND THROUGH THE BODY

The body is the primary receiver of external stimuli. We experience the world through our kinesthetic senses—the sense of moving in space, bodily position, sense of body mass, transfer of weight, movement of muscles, tendons, and joints—as well as our sensory system—taste, smell, hearing, vision, and touch. From those physical sensations, we constitute our view of the external world and thus our existence in this world. Freud proposed that the first experience of a "sense of self" comes from bodily sensations (Freud, 1923/1961). Piaget talked about the sensorimotor system with which children interact with the environment. The sensorimotor stage begins at birth and extends through the first two years of life. Children at this stage use their senses and motor capabilities, rather than cognitive or verbal abilities, to construct their own understanding of the world (Hoffman et al., 1994). Psychodynamic theorists also emphasize the impact of early experiences on the development of a person's personality and social relationship, for example, Freud's psychosexual theory, which emphasizes early sexual experience, and Erikson's psychosocial theory, which pays more attention to conflict resolutions between needs and social demands. Despite the many schools in psychology holding different points of views, there is a general acceptance of the influence of early development on the establishment of the concept of a self, differentiation between the self and others, sense of intimacy, relationship between reality and fantasy, and so on. The major concern here is that most of those early experiences are kinesthetically recorded, or unconsciously retained, rather than consciously remembered or verbalized. Therefore, working on the body may help access such information and further the therapist's understanding of the whole person.

Due to the fast-acting sensory components responsible for receiving external stimuli and the high-speed neural pathways responsible for transmitting signals, bodily experience is also the first and foremost experience of a person. Reactions in the body usually occur before the participation of cognition and verbalization. Research evidence shows that the amygdale system in the brain, which prepares the body's immediate responses—flight, fright, or freeze in life-threatening circumstances—is not conscious (Le Doux, 1998). Stress-induced immediate responses, which include changes of brain chemistry and the secretion of neurotransmitters and hormones, may lead to somatic imprints which are difficult to erase in the person who experienced them (Rothschild, 2000). Furthermore, recurrent and intrusive flashback memory commonly associated with persons who have experienced trauma or threatening conditions is usually kinesthetic—visual, auditory, vestibular, olfactory, or tactile—rather then verbal (van der Kolk, 1994). Therefore, approaching or accessing those experiences using a verbal or cognitive approach may not be effective. Body-oriented approaches may be more appropriate in dealing with those unconscious and nonverbal experiences.

Working on the body can also help access a person's life history, as our sensorimotor systems, for example, muscle, skin, nerves, and sensory receptors, have memory. Sensorimotor memory remembers sensory inputs, such as another person's skin temperature, texture, or shape, long after physical contact. This type of memory can be extremely pleasant, as in the case of hugging an intimate friend, or completely horrible, as in the case of being physically or sexually abused. According to the theory of neurocognitive memory, sensorimotor information contributes to the generation of "implicit memory," which operates from birth and is usually unconscious and nondeclarative (Hovdestad & Kristiansen, 1996; Reber, 1993). Skills, habits, and conditional emotional responses such as fear are in this category. Explicit memory, in contrast, is conscious and declarative. It involves conceptual, factual, and verbal processing and starts functioning from about age three, when cognitive and verbal abilities start to develop. Thus, implicit memory stored in the body can be difficult to verbalize or even address. Working on the body can access those memories and may help understand the background of many psychological or behavioral problems, which may be caused by events in early childhood or stored deep in the unconscious level.

THERAPEUTIC PROCESS

Neurocognitive research has showed that implicit memory is processed through the amygdale in the brain, which bypasses cognitive process (Hovdestad & Kristiansen, 1996; Schacter, 1987). Working on the body, which involves mainly the sensorimotor system, is not the same as working on the mind, because body responses are immediate and unconscious. The therapist has to be fully aware of the subtle changes happening moment to moment in the client and has to keep the eyes, mind, as well as the heart open, ready to make instant adjustment. Since we are working on the whole person, we have to use the whole of ourselves as well.

Focusing on the Process Rather Than the Outcome

> Letting go of attachment to outcome, tolerating chaos, staying with it, suspending right–wrong judgments, paying more attention to the inner feeling than the outer appearance, and cultivating the qualities of acceptance and patience, of practice and discipline
>
> (Halprin, 1998, p. 92).

Body-oriented therapeutic work focuses on the process rather than the outcome. By actively taking action and paying attention to inner feelings, a mind-oriented person may discover alternative ways to perceive and interpret things encountered. It is imperative for the therapist to have nonjudgmental attitude during the process and give space for the client to explore the new experience.

The case of Kyle

Kyle is a highly organized and efficient man. He works very hard and is a very successful person. He described himself as a problem solving machine as he keeps finishing one task after another. He seems all right with his life. However, his wife and family members complain about his task-oriented approach, because it puts the whole family into a very stressful condition. Even when he is on vacation with his family, he never slows down but keeps rushing here and there.

In one session, the therapist asked Kyle to find a spot in the room, try to walk straight to the spot, and then take a curvy route to the same spot. The therapist asked him what he discovered after taking the two different approaches. He said that walking straight to the spot was more efficient and faster to reach the destination, whereas taking the curvy route took more time. However, he also found that when walking straight to the spot, he could only focus on the sport, while walking in curvy route, he could spend some time looking around and enjoying the process. Whether he could get to the spot became less important in the second approach.

We always help our clients set up goals, either short term, such as small daily tasks, or long term, such as life goals. Sometimes achieving those goals can be a burden, when failure or success are much concerned. As life itself is a process rather than just going from the beginning (birth) to the end (death), enjoying the process and trying to fully experience it become more meaningful than rushing toward the end.

Expanding Movement Repertoire so as to Enhance Coping Ability

Coping ability refers to the ability to deal with different difficult conditions. Some clients say that they cannot find a way out or cannot find a method to deal with their problems. In assisting our clients to face the problems and difficulties, we help them explore alternatives and options. In a body-oriented approach, through expanding the movement repertoire of an individual, we can help the client discover alternatives, thus increasing his or her flexibility and coping ability. Because body movement needs action rather than cognition, through giving opportunities for self-exploration, clients can learn about their limitations, strengths, and abilities.

The case of Bella

Bella had a specific movement preference. Whenever she moved, she moved symmetrically, using both sides of the body. In real life, she said that she tended to use the same approach in dealing with different people and problems. Sometimes it worked, but sometimes it did not. When it did not work, she felt frustrated but would keep trying to use the same approach. She could not tolerate changing the method because she felt unsafe doing so. People around her said that she was too stubborn.

Several sessions were spent on expanding Bella's movement repertoire. Activities included, for example, moving different sides of the body separately, in different directions and types of movement. After that, Bella started to have fewer restrictions on her movement choices. She could move with a single side of the body, with both sides, or with different sides moving in different directions. She started to enjoy exploring alternative ways to move rather than just using her previous approach. After several sessions, she told the therapist that she had become more open to change, braver, and less stubborn than before.

In helping our clients improve their coping abilities, a body-oriented approach allows them to use themselves and explore alternatives in their own ways. The aim is to stimulate our clients to discover different options within their abilities in the process, instead of telling them what to do. As we cannot always be a lifelong helper for our clients, facilitating them to find out their inner resources as well as enhancing their coping abilities become most important.

From Physical to Psychological Blockage

Body movement reflects and affects psychological status. Emotions and feelings are usually associated with bodily experiences. Unpleasant memories stored in specific body parts induce uneasy feelings within that specific spot, which sometimes expand to the whole person. Liljan Espenak (Espenak, 1981), one of the pioneers in the field of Dance/Movement Therapy, indicated this psychomotor connection in her book:

> Every motor action of the body relates to some change in feeling or interest, influencing expenditure of energy and the timing of the action . . .But, where an individual suffers from a number of blockages, ambivalences, inner confusions, and restraints; the various psychological mechanisms involved will impair the free flow of the emotional dynamism. For example, some children in the vicissitudes of their growth find that holding their breath makes them more insensitive to unpleasant sensations and feelings. They pull in their bellies and immobilize their diaphragms to reduce anxiety; they deaden their bodies to avoid the feeling of pain or anxiety. In this defense, they avoid pain, but they also deaden themselves to all feeling, including happiness and joy
> (Espenak, 1981, p. 21).

When the experience is too painful, it is our natural response to suppress the sensation or feeling and stop the specific body part from sensing or moving, either consciously or unconsciously. In this case, psychological blockage manifests itself in the form of physical blockage (Espenak, 1981, p. 21).

The case of Penny

Penny told the therapist that her arms were always cold and she could not lift them above her head. They spent time working on her arm movement. Penny's body was actually very flexible, as she practiced yoga and never had any physical injuries. It was strange, then, that the range of movement in her arms and shoulders was very limited but all her other joints were quite flexible.

They tried different ways to move the arms and finally held hands together. Her arms were weak and not as strong as they ought to be for an adult. While

Penny and the therapist were moving their arms and hands together, they suddenly got into a pulling and pushing action. She stopped for a while and told the therapist that some faces had appeared in her mind. She felt annoyed and angry; she wanted them to go away from her life. The therapist asked if she could try to push them out symbolically by pushing her hands. She started to push forcefully and aggressively.

Penny's hands became very warm after she calmed down from her aggressive pushing actions. She told the therapist that she understood how helpless she had been in the struggle with the annoying people around her. She wanted, but never had the courage, to try to get out of the situation. A lot of anger was suppressed and locked inside. After expressing the struggle and the stored anger, she was released and relaxed. She also learned that she could have the courage to face and deal with the problem directly rather than just avoiding it.

Psychological blockage is magnified on the body level, either consciously or unconsciously. When a blockage consists of intense emotions, such as anger or hatred, tremendous energy can be stored underneath. In some cases, the person may know about the stored power or the potential danger of exposing the energy. The only way to prevent an explosion is to suppress oneself from expressing that energy. In that case, psychological blockage will lead to physical blockage. Releasing the blockages and letting the energy flow will benefit the whole person.

From Kinesthetic Awareness to Psychological Understanding

Body movement assists cognitive understanding of abstract concepts. It is always easier to capture the concept of size by physically drawing big or small circles with the hands. When body action is translated into emotions, it helps our clients understand the affect and meaning behind the movement and gradually build up a sense of interconnectedness between mind and body. For instance, doing a flying movement or jumping produces a sense of freedom and release; stamping hard with the feet shows energy and sometimes expresses anger. Kinesthetic awareness and symbolic expression can be used to help understand abstract psychological and spiritual meaning.

The case of Suzi and Mandy

In a group therapy session, the members were asked to work on their own personal space and to explore their inner space. After working for a while, Suzi, who is a cancer patient and always be the last one to move, told the therapist that it was the first time she knew about personal space and learned that she could also have her own inner space. In all her life, she kept focusing on other people: As the eldest daughter, she took care of her whole family before she got married. After getting married, she spent all her time and effort taking care of her husband and daughters. She never left time and space to herself, not to mention self-care. "That's why I went to see a doctor long after I felt something wrong in my body. I did not leave myself any time and space. I used all my time to take care of my family," she said, "but now, I know that I have my own space too. I will take care of myself more."

Another group member, Mandy, said that she found her personal space and thus she respected more others' personal space. She was upset before, because her son and husband always complained about her being too controlling—she thought she was just caring and showing concern for them. She understood that everyone needs space, and she knew how to get along with them comfortably.

By linking body movement to psychological and spiritual meaning, our clients can always discover something meaningful and relevant to their experiences. This process of articulation is important, as it gives therapeutic meaning to a body movement, thereby linking up the sessions and everyday life.

From Physical Movement to Life Attitudes

Because clients need to use their bodies rather than just sitting, talking, or thinking, therapeutic sessions using body movement encourage the active participation and commitment of the clients. Once they start to use themselves, which can be as little as just moving a finger, they start to participate in the process.

The case of Joan

Joan was diagnosed with depression and had severe sleeping problems, but no progress could be observed after several talk therapy sessions. She told the therapist that she understood how important it was to do something to help herself, but she never had the energy to do so. The therapists asked Joan to mimic her movements. At the beginning, Joan did not move at all, but after a while, she started to move her fingers and her head, following the music. For several sessions, they kept working on rhythmic body movement. She moved from fingers to palms, arms, and finally the whole body. One day, she suddenly told the therapist that she exercised every day and could sleep well—she no longer needed sleeping pills!

As body–mind–spirit functions as a system, change in one affects the change in the others. We believe that, once our clients "move" out for the first step in the therapeutic process, they start to engage in the process of self-help. The more the body parts are involved, the more the clients participate in the work. The cultivation of this attitude—active participation, motivation, and enthusiasm for life—helps them find the way out; it is the ultimate goal of almost all kinds of therapies and interventions.

From the Body to Spirit: Embodied Transcendence

Body awareness and endurance has long been an essential part of religious and spiritual practices. Self-awareness through meditation and retreat, or going through pain and suffering beyond one's limit, serves as the bridge to spiritual transformation. In clinical practice, we also observe clients who have experienced trauma and crisis but are able to develop spiritual insights after the experience, regardless of the course of their recovery. In all cases, sensing through the body, thinking through the mind, and feeling through the heart open the ground for spiritual transformation.

The case of Grace

At the end of a group session, the therapist asked the participants to close their eyes to better focus on their own bodies. As the clients sensed the contact between the floor and their bare feet, the therapist asked them to feel the connection between the ground and their bodies and gradually extend such connection to the Earth and the Universe. After the process, one group member, Grace, talked about the experience of becoming very small in the sense that she understood that she was just a tiny little piece of the Cosmos. She said that, after getting this image in mind, when she looked back at her own problems and troubles, she could view them from a higher level, and they became much smaller and less important.

For some people, they might feel the transcendental life energy through dance and movement. Trudi Schoop, another pioneer of Dance/Movement Therapy, explained this connection in her writing:

> Individuals dance within their lifespan here, in their time, in their space, using their individual energies. They feel the security of a floor supporting their moving feet. They feel the muscles of their body stretching and contracting. They feel their strong heart beating, sending blood coursing through their veins. They experience space in all its aspects as their body leaps, sinks, whirls, opens, closes. The rhythmic stamping of their feet in a folk dance, however, is the eternal stamp of man. The muscles that respond to their dance-needs are those that swung the ape through the jungle branches. The energy that carries them through a difficult bit of choreography is the same that mobilized the bodies of the cave man. The lungs that regulate their breathing are but refinements of those acquired by the first sea-creatures who ventured onto the land. The heart of the dinosaur still beats in man's breasts
>
> (Schoop & Mitchell, 1994, p. 44).

With this sense of embodied transcendence, we feel the connection between individual and nature, human beings and the Cosmos. The exploration of this transpersonal connection is important in clinical practice, as it help our clients to look at their problems and difficulties in a distant fashion, rather than getting very close to them and being trapped inside.

BODY–MIND–SPIRIT CONNECTION

In the past decades, research studies in the fields of psychoneuroimmunology and psychoendocrinology have revealed the connection between psychological health and physical health, with special regard to the connection of the nervous system, immune system, and endocrine system (Moody, 2006; Pert, Dreher, & Ruff, 1998; Sephton & Spiegel, 2003; Tosevski & Milovancevic, 2006; van Middendorp, Geenen, Sorbi, van Doornen, & Bijlsma, 2005; Vitetta, Anton, Cortizo, & Sali, 2006). This gives both biological and molecular connections among mind, emotion, and body, and thus supports their reciprocal interactions. In many cases, although medicine and drugs can be used to manipulate physiological responses, they are disease specific and not preventive, and the effect depends on the individual's condition and response. There is no medicine that can guarantee long-term health and longevity. Based on the interconnection between mind, body, and spirit, keeping these three aspects healthy and in balance will help maintain total well-being. Thus, body work, positive attitude, and spiritual experience are of equal importance and need to be addressed equally.

SUMMARY

The body provides channels for intrapersonal, interpersonal, and transpersonal communication. It gives form and structure for feelings and emotions, opens us to transcendent energy, and thus gives us a sense of passionate aliveness. In holistic health practice, working on the body is an indispensable part through which the mind and spirit can also be assessed. This chapter states several important issues in addressing the mind and spirit through the body, and how body work leads to psychological changes and, in some cases, helps develop spiritual insights. There is no universal step-by-step protocol for this approach, because every individual and every case is unique. The entire process is cocreated by the therapist and the client. Throughout the process, the therapist has to interact with the clients and be ready for immediate changes and adjustments. Because the whole person is addressed in this approach, the personal integrity and sensitivity of the therapist are of utmost importance.

8

Spiritual Growth and Transformation: Expanding Life's Horizons

SPIRITUALITY AND SOCIAL WORK PRACTICE

Despite the fact that the social work profession was developed by pioneers who had strong spiritual motivations for services, the social work profession continues to downplay spirituality as an integral part of social work practice. As a profession, social work chose to build its professional base upon scientific and humanistic traditions and divorced from spirituality. However, spirituality is a necessary component of an ordinary, even of a secular, life. Problems like domestic violence, burnout in the workplace, gambling addiction, substance abuse, and so on are related to a sense of inner emptiness, meaninglessness, and the absence of compassion and love in individuals and families. These are more or less spiritual problems. In fact, alcoholism has been described as a futile search for spirituality. In a review by Hodge (Hodge, 2001a), spirituality was found to be a significant variable in recovery from divorce, homelessness, sexual assault, and substance abuse. Studies in a healthcare setting also found that spiritual resources foster meaning and a sense of life affirmation and personal growth in cancer patients at different stages (Gall & Cornblat, 2002; Parry, 2003) and that daily spiritual experiences may mitigate physical, cognitive, and emotional burnout (Holland & Neimeyer, 2005). Of even greater significance, over half of therapists who

Richard, a 28-year-old, worked as a management trainee in a large corporation after graduation. Two years later, he changed his career to creative advertising work, in spite of the disapproval of his father. After working in the new firm for some time, he was unexpectedly laid off by his employer. Since then, he has experienced depression and ruminations of self-defeating thoughts. He suffered from insomnia, was very agitated, smoked heavily, and became an alcoholic.

Richard's parents had very high expectations of him. Likewise, Richard had high expectations of himself. He was concerned about how others looked at him. He liked to compare his own performance with that of others. When he found he was not as successful as his friends and colleagues, he became unhappy. The incident of being laid off was devastating to his self-esteem.

Richard sought treatment to get rid of the self-defeating thoughts and regain self-confidence. Instead of focusing on his self-defeating thoughts, the therapist explored with Richard what he wanted and what he valued in his life. The therapist guided Richard to visualize himself in a happy state with self-confidence. He recalled moments when he felt joyful and content. After the exercise, he was asked to make a list of personal qualities that he valued and appreciated. In doing so, Richard was able to get in touch with his internal resources and his spirituality. He experienced a more peaceful mind. In later sessions, the therapist explored with Richard how his family and personal experiences shaped his concept of "self" and his present coping. Going on a spiritual journey and exploring his core values, aspirations, meaning, and purpose in life, Richard gained a new perspective on his issues and his "self." He realized that, in the past, he looked for outside validation. He focused on getting rid of the self-defeating thoughts to solve his problem. The more he wanted to control his mind, the more he found out how little control he had over it. With treatment, Richard learned and practiced meditation. He found that, by focusing on his breathing and calmly observing his mind, the self-defeating thoughts became less disturbing to him. He realized that the thoughts would come and go. He no longer cared about how others perceived him. He realized that his value did not depend on performance and achievement. He was able to value his own self and became aware of what he was passionate about and what he wanted to be as a person. Later, Richard reported that he not only improved his mood but was also successful in quitting smoking, abstaining from drinking excessive alcohol, and building up the habit of regular exercise.

This is an example of how Integrative Body-Mind–Spirit Social Work utilizes spirituality and brings forth change in the body and the mind of a person. Applying the concept of a healing wheel, spirituality was chosen as an entry point in Richard's case. Through inviting him to a therapeutic dialogue that identified and addressed issues of values and beliefs and engaged him in a process of meaning making and self-discovery, the self-defeating thoughts withered gradually. As Richard began to value his own "self" and to discover what he really wanted for his life, he had no problems taking positive action, which resulted in better physical and psychological well-being.

participated in National Association of Social Workers (NASW) national survey said that they do not shy away from discussing spirituality in the treatment process (Canda & Furman, 1999). The resurgence of interest in spirituality (Canda & Furman, 1999) is not unique only in the field of social work. An increasing awareness of spirituality in clinical practice is also evident in the fields of counseling, psychotherapy, and nursing (McSherry, 2000; Richards & Bergin, 1997; Sherman, 2001).

Integrative Body–Mind–Spirit Social Work uses the metaphor of a healing wheel to describe its conceptual framework (see Chapter 4). Spirituality forms the foundation of the healing wheel, on which a body–mind wheel spins. Integrative Body–Mind–Spirit Social Work believes that spirituality is the foundation for the healthy and dynamic functioning of the body–mind system, which connects to and interacts with different domains of human existence. The facilitation of spiritual growth in individuals and families is therefore a key component in Integrative Social Work.

WHAT IS SPIRITUALITY?

Spirituality entails cognitive, philosophical, experiential, emotional, and behavioral aspects. In the context of Integrative Social Work, spirituality is defined in a broad sense that includes religious as well as the nonreligious idiosyncratic beliefs and values of individual clients that constitute a source of personal aspiration to them. Recent literature shares a common view in distinguishing spirituality from religiosity (e.g., Anandarajah & Hight, 2001; Bullis, 1996; Carroll, 1998; Richards & Bergin, 1997). Religiosity usually refers to a set of organized institutionalized beliefs and behavior rules anchored in a particular religion. It is an expression of spirituality. In contrast, spirituality includes multidimensional parts of human experience (Chan et al., 2006). It is universal and more encompassing. Eastern conceptions of spirituality, with philosophical roots in Buddhism and Daoism, include the capacity to endure and even grow from suffering and pain, to embrace the present, to live in the moment, to integrate different parts of "self" into a harmonious whole, to deepen connection with humankind and the universe, and to strive for higher goals such as compassion and loving kindness (Chan, Ho et al., 2001; Dalai Lama & Cutler, 1998). This conception has been validated by a recent study on Chinese spirituality conducted in Hong Kong. It was found that spirituality comprises three distinct aspects: tranquility, resistance to disorientation, and resilience (Ng, Yau, Chan, Chan, & Ho, 2005). The definition of spirituality adopted by Integrative Body–Mind–Spirit Social Work is in line with this conceptualization, which is ecumenical and is applicable across different cultural and philosophical traditions.

TREATMENT GOALS AND PROCESS OF CHANGE UTILIZING SPIRITUAL STRATEGIES

Kearney (2000) refers to healing as the process of becoming psychologically and spiritually more integrated and whole. As therapists, we frequently hear stories of people who have been transformed by harrowing ordeals in life. People reported that they ultimately changed for the better after surviving serious illness, disasters, accidents, and life crises, such as the loss of a loved one, experience of abuse and violence, and the like. Even when there is no hope for a cure, as in the case of advanced disease, healing is always possible. One can become more fully alive and whole when in touch with one's own spirituality, as it addresses the deepest, most profound components of human existence. Spirituality is believed to be the heart of holistic care and the core of healing (Bullis, 1996; Canda & Furman, 1999; Wong, 1998). Recognition of the role of spirituality in social work treatment necessitates that the social work profession revisit our assumptions regarding the goals of treatment and the change process.

Enhancing Growth through Working with Problems

Integrative Body–Mind–Spirit Social Work offers more than the alleviation of symptoms; it aims to enhance the client's positive growth toward resilience and transformation. The therapist believes in a client's strength, provides the context within which the client taps into his or her inner power, utilizes innate wisdom about his or her own life, and searches for meaning. The therapist appreciates the inherent spiritual potential in every client as she or he accompanies and assists the client in this searching and discovering process and expects the client to determine what fits him or her in the growth process. The connection between the client and the therapist in the treatment process can be perceived as part of a spiritual journey with the client (Canda, 1998).

Accepting Pain Rather Than Eliminating Pain

Influenced by the medical model, mainstream social work practice advocates a stance of active control and mastery of one's own problems and environment (Siporin, 1983). People seek comprehension in the social world and tend to believe that people get what they deserve and deserve what they get (Janoff-Bulman, 1989). Although there are definitely aspects of life that require mastery and planning, other life events, such as incurable illness, death of loved ones, and crises like natural disasters, terrorist attacks, and accidents also remind us how little control we have over some other aspects of life. Pleasure and pain coexist.

Selina: Growing Through Pain and Suffering

Selina was diagnosed with system lupus erythematosus (SLE) at age 29. She had a close boyfriend and a job with promising prospects. The treatment brought about physical changes. She gained weight and her face became square due to the side effects of the drugs. She had to avoid outdoor activities, as sunshine could trigger complications of her SLE. As a young woman and an outdoor activity lover, Selina became very upset. She also lost her job, and even more tragic, her beloved boyfriend left her. She suffered from depression and was thinking about killing herself. She lived in embitterment, constantly asking, "why me?"

Selina joined our Integrative Body–Mind–Spirit group. In the group, she cried bitterly in most of the sessions. The turning point came when she found a model, another group participant with the same disease, who faced her losses squarely and who joked about her own pain. She also found the concepts of impermanence and letting go shared in the group particularly striking. Inspired by the Buddhist teaching on impermanence, she chose to live in the moment. Selina gradually recovered from her depression and started to appreciate things and people around her: nature, her family and friends, and even the illness experience. In reviewing her journey of surviving the illness she said, "It was a growth experience, but it was painful. I wish it hadn't happened, but I really grew spiritually... to me, being able to live is a blessing. To have connected with other people was a wonderful and spiritual experience to me." Selina later did volunteer work to offer care and support to the needy elderly in the community.

A systems perspective, which provides the theoretical framework for several important therapeutic approaches, such as strategic and solution-focused brief therapy, explicitly recognizes that change is constant. Buddhism takes a step further and emphasizes that suffering comes from ignorance of the true nature of life, which is inherently painful. The first noble truth of Buddhism is *Dukkha*, meaning that misfortune, dissatisfaction, and suffering are salient characteristics of human life (Davidson & Thomas, 2002; Gunaratana, 1991; Nhất Hạnh, 2002; Rubin, 1996; Sik, 2005b). Yet, pain will go away if people do not desire a pain-free state. It is the aversion of pain and the pursuit of and attachment to pleasure and comfort that brings the most suffering. According to Buddhist teachings, suffering can be eradicated. The acceptance of *Dukkha* (i.e., suffering as an inherent part of life) and the extinction of one's desires are the beginning of the road to personal freedom.

While fully recognizing the unpleasantness of pain and suffering, Integrative Body–Mind–Spirit Social Work utilizes the concept of letting go and nonattachment in the treatment process. Practicing nonattachment and letting go is to accept life events as they unfold and be at peace with whatever comes in life. There may still be pain and discomfort, but the person just lets it come and go. The opposite of letting go is holding on. When undesirable events come and people experience suffering, the suffering will go away sooner or later. However, if the person holds on to the victim role, negative emotions, such as hatred and resentment, or the desire to control, she or he will continue to suffer. Imagine a person with a clenched fist. As long as he keeps his fist clenched, he can only feel the tightness in his hand; the energy is stuck. If he is willing to uncurl his hand, he can reach out to touch and feel. He is freed. Letting go is the practice of acceptance and the realization that absolute control is illusionary. It opens up new space and new possibilities, which allow people to move on in life.

Reconstruct New Meaning

Extensive literature documents the important role played by meaning in promoting psychological and physical health in individuals. For example, cancer patients who reported a high degree of meaning in their lives were found to experience significantly more enjoyment and better quality of life than those who did not, despite having experienced different symptoms (Brady, Peterman, Fitchett, Mo, & Cella, 1999; Zebrack & Chesler, 2002). Even for cancer patients at an advanced stage, it was evident that spiritual meaning countered end-of-life despair (McClain, Rosenfeld, & Breitbart, 2003) and facilitated personal growth (Greenstein & Breitbart, 2000). Bower, Kemeny, Taylor, and Fahey (1998) found that men with HIV who could make sense of their experience showed less rapid declines in CD4 T-cell levels. Another study by Bower's team on bereaved women found that women who reported positive change in meaning-related goals had increased immunity (Bower, Kemeny, Taylor, & Fahey, 2003). Although the mechanism by which meaning promotes health is not yet clearly established empirically, studies in psychobiology suggest a connection between the body and mind (van der Kolk, 1994). We speculate that finding meaning in life may help channel life energy into creative activity and positive health habits, which in turn promote physical health and psychological well-being. By ascribing a new meaning to pain and suffering and by reconstructing one's meaning in life, one can achieve spiritual growth. By adopting an integrative approach with spiritual components in intervention, therapists can help clients to reconstruct meaning, search for purpose in life, and go beyond problem coping to self-transformation.

Joanna, 28 years old, described herself as passive, shy, and introverted. Her presenting problem was a lack of self-confidence and goals in life. She found her current job unsatisfying. She was struggling with what she really wanted and what she could do. Using a metaphor, she described herself as being trapped in a pot, having no idea how

(continued)

(continued)

to escape or where to go. In exploring with Joanna her resources and inner strengths, the therapist helped Joanna to realize that she had many strengths but she had not utilized them. They discovered that it had something to do with her family when she was young. Joanna's parents had never shown appreciation to her. Her parents had been critical of Joanna, which resulted in her developing a perception that she was inadequate. Whatever she did, she could never earn their praise. Her negative childhood experience partly explained why Joanna was not confident about herself. When the therapist helped Joanna to look into the meaning of her parents' critical attitude, Joanna realized that it was well-intended. They had been critical, as they believed that being harsh to children would help them to become better people. Joanna also found out that her father grew up with criticism, which had been a motivating force for him to work hard. His father had been motivated by the critical attitude of the adults around him and became successful in his career. To Joanna's father, being critical was a way to nurture children. Having found the meaning of her father's behavior, Joanna found that she could discard the belief that she was not good enough. She started to appreciate and integrate her own strength and resources, and her self-confidence came back. In addition, she developed a new relationship with her father.

In the later sessions, the therapist helped Joanna to search for her own purpose in life. Joanna was asked to think about a number of questions: What was her passion in life? What unique characteristics and strengths did she appreciate most in herself? What did she value most in her life? In what circumstances was she was most satisfied about herself? Joanna reported that she had never thought about those questions in the past, as her mind was occupied by the thought that she was never good enough. When she reconstructed new meaning about her self, she started to get in touch with her own spirituality. She got to know more about herself and her unique purpose in life.

Promoting Resilience and Affirming Inner Strength

Koening and Spano (1998) contend that virtue represents the internal power of an individual and that it is central to healing. Eastern philosophies promote the cultivation of virtues (Tu, 1979). In Chinese communities, many people derive meaning from striving to realize cultural virtues, such as endurance and resilience. The story of Grace is an inspiring example (see box).

The Case of Grace: A Model of Optimism and Resilience

Grace grew up in a poor Chinese family. She had had to work hard to help her family ever since she was small. Living in a community prevalently influenced by a Confucian culture, Grace valued hardship in her life. She found it an opportunity for self-cultivation. She always encouraged other people to be optimistic and shared with them her belief that suffering is the teacher of life. In middle age, she developed breast

(continued)

(continued)

cancer. She remained calm and peaceful throughout the course of the illness. She was actually happy to have cancer. She said, "See, I am now much more convincing when sharing with others my belief that hardships are blessings in disguise. I survived the cancer, the ordeals that came with the treatment, and am at peace with the threat of mortality. I can joke about my lost breast and laugh at my own death. I encourage and comfort other patients with cancer and people undergoing hardships. I am myself a model to them." Grace's optimistic attitude has inspired many people.

SPIRITUAL ASSESSMENT IN SOCIAL WORK PRACTICE WITH INDIVIDUALS AND FAMILIES

Chapter 3 discusses how Integrative Body–Mind–Spirit Social Work conducts systemic assessment of individuals and families. The focus is on system imbalance—how normal problems of living become a problem for the client and the extent of connectedness among different parts of a person and the environment. This chapter focuses on discussing spiritual assessment to mobilize clients' spiritual resources for therapeutic change and personal transcendence.

Common spiritual assessment approaches described in social work and healthcare literature include taking spiritual history (e.g., Anandarajah & Hight, 2001; Bullis, 1996) and using diagrammatic instruments such as spiritual genograms and spiritual maps (e.g., Hodge, 2001a, 2001b, 2005a, 2005b). Spiritual assessments adopted by Integrative Body–Mind–Spirit Social Work share a commonality with these approaches in aiming at discovering spiritual assets in clients. Integrative Social Work, however, adopts a more ecumenical orientation. Questions relating to experiences of religious affiliation and conversion, which are commonly asked in Western practice, are not of focus in Integrative Social Work. The aim of spiritual assessment in Integrative Body–Mind–Spirit Social Work is to assess people's inner strength and spiritual resources, whether religious or not. We adapt Canda and Furman's (1999) lifespan timeline assessment approach and combine it with narrative interview in assessing clients' spiritual development. We call it the autobiographical timeline interview (Leung & Chan, 2006a). This approach has the advantages of being universal and ecumenical and can be used in counseling people with diverse spiritual backgrounds.

Autobiographical Timeline Interview

Using an autobiographical timeline interview, therapists can understand a client's personal aspirations, values, and idiosyncratic meaning of different life experiences in the context of the client's overall life history. Instead of focusing on the problem or what religious label has been attached, it focuses on understanding the client as a whole person and how spirituality affects his or her life, attitude, and coping.

There are three major steps in utilizing the autobiographical timeline in doing spiritual assessment: (1) preparation and introduction, (2) life review through drawing and storytelling, and (3) and narrative interview.

Preparation and introduction

To prepare the client for a spiritual journey, it is important for the therapist to build rapport with the client and to explain how the exercise is going to take place. In doing spiritual assessment using the autobiographical timeline, the therapist starts with saying that she or he is interested in the client's life, in particular how the client experiences and copes with important life events, which are unique for each individual. The therapist then explains that she or he would like to hear the life story of the client in a special way, with an exercise, which serves as a review of the client's life. A worksheet with a horizontal timeline from birth to the present and a vertical dimension representing the subjective perception of the ups and downs of life is given to the client (Figure 8.1). The therapist then explains that the client is going to place the perception of her or his life visually on a temporal framework by drawing out the course of the life along the timeline, the peaks symbolizing ups in life and valleys the downs.

Life review through drawing and storytelling

To start with, the therapist asks the client where along the vertical dimension she or he was at birth. The client then delineates the course of his or her life from birth to the present along the timeline. The client is encouraged

FIGURE **8.1.** Worksheet for autobiographical timeline.

to delineate the lifeline freely, as it reflects the client's subjective perception and experience of his or her life. When there are turning points, the therapist asks questions to elicit information about significant events or experiences in the client's life, as any delineated peak or dip may represent important changes in a client's life that may bear important meaning to the client. The therapist should ask, "Was there any significant event going on in your life at this point?" Even clients who are not good at verbal communication find that the process of drawing facilitates storytelling.

Narrative interview

An interview process goes along with the drawing exercise. The purpose of the interview is threefold: to explore the client's perception of the impact of significant events on his or her own life, to facilitate sense making and meaning reconstruction, and to identify spiritual resources in a client's life. It is conducted in the context of an interpersonal dialogue that interfaces with the client's drawing and narrative. The box below lists commonly asked questions in an autobiographical timeline interview. The questions are intended to guide the client in reviewing how he or she overcame problems of living in the past, reviewing how the client relates past experiences to coping with the present problem, discovering aspects of his or her life that may have been of great importance to him or her, and bringing out core components of meaning and spirituality.

Commonly Asked Questions in an Autobiographical Timeline Interview

Questions for exploring the client's perception of the impacts of significant events:

- What happened at this turning point in your life?
- What impact did this peak experience (or dip experience) have on you at that time?
- How have you been changed by this experience? In what ways?
- Do these experiences still influence you at present?

Questions for facilitating sense making and meaning reconstruction:

- People attach different meanings to their significant life experiences. Looking back, how do you perceive this experience?
- Is there any change in the way you look at this experience now? In what ways have you made sense of this experience? What was the most valuable part of it?
- Was there any change in your core values or any shift in your aspirations or life perspective after the experience? What new meanings in your life, if any, have emerged from this experience?
- How has that experience made you a stronger/better/different person?

(continued)

(continued)

Questions for identifying spiritual resources in the client's life:

- What resources did you use to cope during this dip experience? What or who helped you to rebound?
- In what ways do those resources and abilities influence you now?
- What changed in your relationship with other people after this experience? With whom? In what aspect and how? How do you feel about this change?
- What changed in your relationship with God or the Universe? In what aspect and how? How do you feel about this change?
- How has this experience made a difference in the purpose of life or what matters most to you before and after the experience?

The story of Betty

Figure 8.2 is an example of a completed autobiographical timeline. Betty was a 65-year-old breast cancer survivor. She came to the therapist's office for an assessment of how she had been doing in her recovery from cancer. She had just completed all medical treatment procedures. The interview served to understand how the cancer experience had affected her life and whether psychosocial service was needed. To start with, the therapist asked Betty how she perceived her cancer experience. Betty said that she was depressed when she first received the bad news. At that time, she was planning to retire and expecting to enjoy life. However, she rebounded quickly from this emotional turmoil. She indicated in her autobiographical timeline that she experienced the high point of her life after the cancer experience. She described cancer

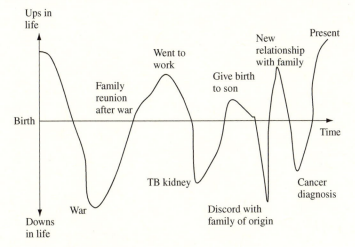

FIGURE **8.2.** Betty's autobiographical timeline.

as just one of the different challenges in life—not a particularly remarkable experience for her. While she delineated her lifeline, she described how she survived great hardships in her childhood, during which there was war. At that time, poverty was common; everyone had to work hard in order to survive. Life was fragile and people died from bomb attacks almost every day. Betty developed resilience, as adverse circumstances served as a fertile ground for cultivating the virtues of endurance and self-reliance.

Betty was also influenced by the Daoist teachings of living in harmony with the law of nature. "Following the will of heaven" and "accepting predestined life" were emergent themes in her narrative. She said, "Everyone has to die, in one way or the other. Getting cancer is just a natural process of life.... I believe that my life was given by heaven. If heaven tells me that this is the end of my life, I'll accept it." Betty had accepted her situation. Her belief helped her to cope with her illness.

When Betty told her story, "family" came up as another important theme. Betty derived the meaning of life from being able to contribute to the well-being of her family. Even when she had a tuberculosis infection in her lung as young adult, she still worked hard to earn money for the family. She realized that the will to continue serving her family became the source of her strength when coping with different life challenges.

Throughout the interview process, Betty appreciated her many inner strengths, including endurance, perseverance, self-reliance, selfless devotion to the family, and so on. She said that it was the first time that she had shared so much of her life with another person. There were different life circumstances that were very difficult but which she survived. She felt proud of herself. She felt energized, as the interview process helped her to integrate her own resources and to affirm her faith. She said that she was more convinced that she could face any upcoming challenges in her life in the future. She also expressed her gratitude to the therapist for listening and accompanying her during her life review journey.

This is a case of the patient coping well with her illness. Even so, she benefited from the process, as the assessment also served to help her integrate her resources. The process can be applied to people facing different issues. It is both a tool for spiritual assessment and a vehicle for mobilizing clients' spiritual resources for therapeutic change and personal transcendence.

Autobiographical Timeline as an Intervention

Unlike conventional social work approaches, which view assessment and treatment as distinct and separate processes, Integrative Body–Mind–Spirit Social Work believes that effective assessment is not a mere information-gathering process; it is a journey of co-exploration and co-construction with therapeutic effects. We engage clients in a process of narrating their own life story and meaning making during the assessment process. In addition to eliciting information for assessment, the process of creating the autobiographical timeline and life review is itself an intervention. It helps the client to articulate his or her own experiences and appreciate strengths and internal resources. It also fosters reappraisal of events and construction of new meaning from the experiences. Assessment and treatment, therefore, are not linear processes; they are circular processes. Effective assessment not only gives therapists valid information about clients' issues but also expands the clients' perspective, brings them new insight, and makes inaccessible spiritual resources more accessible. We discuss assessment and treatment as separate processes in our presentation, although they form an integrated process in practice. The following discussion introduces a number of intervention tools for enhancing spiritual growth in the treatment process.

SPIRITUAL INTERVENTIONS IN SOCIAL WORK PRACTICE

The purpose of spiritual intervention in Integrative Body–Mind–Spirit Social Work is to help clients to search for their idiosyncratic meaning and purpose in life, to enhance their ability to embrace pain and live in the moment, and to deepen connection with the authentic self and the transcendence. The commonly used spirituality-related tools in Integrative Body–Mind–Spirit Social Work include reauthoring life narrative, use of meditation and guided imagery, metaphors, rituals, and self-affirmation. Forgiveness, nonattachment, meaning reconstruction, self-discovery, loving kindness, and equanimity are also addressed in spiritual intervention.

Reauthoring Life Narrative: Meaning Reconstruction after Loss

In life transitions and trauma, the individual may experience different losses that may assault the individual's self-identity and disrupt the sense of continuity of who she or he was and whom she or he is to be (Fife, 1994). Integrative Body–Mind–Spirit Social Work utilizes spirituality to foster the development of a more coherent narrative of an individual's life in integrating loss experiences. We adapted Neimeyer's (2006) technique of writing "chapter titles" for an autobiography in helping clients to reauthor their life narrative. In doing the exercise, the therapist asks the client, "If you were going to write your autobiography, how would you describe and organize your life journey into different chapters?" The client is asked to formulate a title for each chapter and write the titles down on a sheet of paper. There is no need to write out the entire autobiography in the session. In this process, we engage clients in a reflective exercise in reorganizing their life stories.

Let us use Selina's case as an example again. Selina participated in an Integrative Body–Mind–Spirit group and was asked reauthor her life narrative. After a meditation exercise led by the therapist, participants were invited to contemplate writing an autobiography. In the process, Selina consciously examined her own life story. Her autobiography is about her life after getting SLE. She delineated her life after the illness into seven chapters: "The bad news," "Love in this world," "Knowing about the love I cherished only when it is gone," "Gratitude," "Living in the moment," "Facing life with a peaceful mind," and "Giving back." The therapist continued to ask her, "What is meaning of each chapter title? How did each part of the whole story affect you at that time and your later life?" These questions opened up the platform for Selina to narrate her life story. She said that the diagnosis of SLE and the resulting losses not only assaulted her identity as a capable, independent young woman but also disrupted her belief in a just, benevolent world. Thus, her life at that period was overwhelmed by "The bad news"— this became the title of the first chapter of her life after having the illness. However, Selina found that there were also gains in the loss. She found abundant love and support from her family and friends in those dark days. She titled this session of her life "Love in this world." Selina said that she then learned a lesson: In the past she did not realize that others loved her. However, when the love vanished, she got to know how much she had cherished it. This lesson formed a new chapter, and she titled it "Knowing about the love I cherished only when it was gone." The subsequent chapter was called "Gratitude." After she learned the lesson, Selina became grateful for whatever she possessed. The illness punctuated Selina's life story and changed her life perspective. She realized that nothing is permanent and chose to live in the moment, and thus she has a chapter titled "Living in the moment." She was able to be at peace with whatever came into her life, and she gave her present life the title "Facing life with a peaceful mind." She described the experience of surviving SLE as a growth experience. She titled the last chapter "Giving back" as she had committed herself to volunteer work helping people in need. Selina said that she gained energy, vitality, enthusiasm, and regained her self-esteem and identity through the process of helping and giving back.

Finally, the therapist asked Selina: "If you were to give a title to your self-narrative, what would it be?" Selina gave a beautiful title for her autobiography: "The Flowing Cloud." The cloud is impermanent, but the sky where the cloud rests is stable and eternal. The cloud is nothing but water, which will return to the earth and the sea to nurture thousands and thousands of nature's creations. The cloud is transitory in one sense and eternal in another sense.

Selina's metaphor of the cloud succinctly revealed the deep structure of the meaning of her changed reality and her reformulation of her "self."

Telling stories of life before illness (or other life crises) and afterward can be very revealing about the self, as it allows for a potential contrast to be made between what one was like before and after the event. The attainment of a coherent life narrative reconstructs meaning. We asked clients to formulate chapter titles of their autobiographies rather than writing the actual contents of the chapters or the entire autobiography. In Selina's example, just asking her to delineate her life into different chapters and to give each chapter a title elicited an extremely rich narrative. The process of telling a reauthored life narrative is a healing journey. This exercise can be used in individual sessions or in groups. The therapist may also ask the client to write the entire contents of a particular chapter as a homework assignment and share it in later sessions if that chapter's described experiences had a significant impact on the client.

Creative Visualization for Self-Discovery

Creative visualization is a form of meditation in which people visualize themselves living more desirable lives in the future and believe in their own creative potential to bring it about (Chandler, Holden, & Kolander, 1995). During creative visualization, an individual visualizes how she or he wants to live at a future time, for example, 10 years from the present. During the process, the therapist guides the participant in visualizing the self-doing things that the participant is passionate about. After the visualization, the participant is asked to write down the imagery and answer the following questions:

- What are the key values that are meaningful to me?
- What key roles do I play? What do they mean to me?
- What are my greatest moments of happiness and fulfillment?
- What am I motivated by, fascinated with, and passionate about?
- What legacy do I want to leave? How do I want to be remembered when I'm gone?

Visualization is a meaning-searching activity that helps individuals to discover their own unique qualities and identity—the values, roles, aspirations—and their unique purposes and enduring mission of life.

Forgiveness: Utilizing Color Imagery

The use of color as affirmations and visualization in the intervention process has been adopted by integrative practitioners (Milulas, 2002). According to the Indian healing system of Ayurveda, each color represents a source of energy: blue is for peace and detachment; white is for peace and purity, green is for harmony and balance (Mikulas, 2001). In Integrative Body–Mind–Spirit Social Work, color imagery is practiced to facilitate the psychological activity of forgiveness (Chan, 2001). For instance, the therapist can invite clients to visualize themselves surrounded by blue light and imagine the healing energy of blue light dissolves frustration and anger and sets the self free from past hurts. Such imagery may enhance feelings of acceptance and forgiveness and facilitates love, tenderness, and compassion within the person. The client may eventually bring in the color energy that she or he needs most of in the imagery. The client could then repeat this mental process on someone who needs to be forgiven. In the process, the client is guided to cast a blue light on someone who has hurt him or her. If the client is ready, we invite him or her to connect with the person again in the imagery, seeing both of them peaceful, happy, and free. The imagery then ends with the client appreciating the self.

Forgiveness: Blowing Away Hatred and Vengefulness through Breathing

For those who have difficulty practicing color imagery, breathing techniques can be used to foster forgiveness when practiced with guided imagery. The client is asked to sit quietly, close the eyes, and take a few deep breaths. The client is then invited to focus on and observe his or her own breathing and be in touch with the negative feelings, whether they be anger, hatred, vengefulness, or whatever. When breathing in, the client is asked to be in touch with the anger (or whatever feeling the client wants to let go). She or he is then asked to imagine blowing out the negative feelings in the next breath into a balloon. In every exhalation, the client imagines blowing out and letting go of more and more of the negative feelings. The balloon gets bigger and bigger in his or her visual imagery, until he or she feels all the negative feelings have been blown out. When the client is ready to forgive, he or she imagines letting go of the balloon and letting it float in the air. The client should recite silently, "Breathe in, I feel calmness inside me . . . Breathe out, all my negative feelings have been blown out and I now forgive." While continuing to focus on breathing, the client visualizes the image of the balloon fading away as it goes higher and higher into the sky. The client is asked to remain centered and send a message of love and appreciation to the self and to the person whom she or he forgave. This exercise can be practiced together with meditation on loving kindness, discussed below.

Meditation for Loving Kindness

Meditation can also be used to nurture loving kindness. Sit quietly, calm your mind, and center yourself. Imagine in front of you, as clearly as possible, someone you care for. Although this may be more challenging, you may also imagine someone you feel indifferent toward. Open yourself to this person's suffering. Allow yourself to feel connected with him or her, being aware of his or her difficulties, pain, and distress. Then, as you feel your heart opening in compassion toward that person, imagine all of his or her suffering coming out in black smoke. Now, visualize the smoke dissolve. As you breathe out, imagine you are radiating loving kindness, compassion, peace, happiness, and well-being to this person. Send out any feelings that encourage healing, relaxation, and openness. Continue this giving and receiving with each breath. At the end of the meditation, generate a firm inner conviction that this person has been freed from suffering and is filled with peace, happiness, and well-being.

Compassion Breathing

Bring your attention to your breath. Observe the flow of your breath for a moment or two. First, begin by directing loving kindness to yourself. Allow the heartfelt radiance of loving kindness to fill your entire being as you recite each phrase of this meditation slowly and with deep feeling: "May I be happy and peaceful...," "May I be forgiving and free...," "May I be wise and humble..." Next, visualize a person for whom you feel love, respect, and gratefulness. Radiate heartfelt loving kindness to this person, reciting each phrase of the meditation slowly, with deep feeling: "May you be happy and peaceful...," "May peace and happiness be with you always...," "May you be filled with blessing and love..." Next, visualize a person toward whom you feel neutral or indifferent. This may be a stranger or an acquaintance, someone whom you have no particular feeling for or against. Extending loving kindness to those one feels indifferent toward develops the ability to love all beings without exception. Radiate heartfelt loving kindness to this person, reciting each phrase of the meditation slowly: "May you be happy and peaceful...," "May kindness and compassion be shared," "May the universe be in harmony..." Finally, radiate loving kindness to all living beings throughout all realms of existence: "May you be happy and peaceful...," "May peace and happiness be with you always...," "May you be filled with blessing and love..." Alternatively, count to four while breathing in through the nose, and let the positive light fill the body. Then, count to eight while blowing out love and compassion to people who need the positive energy. Imagine a clear light cleansing your whole body and blow out that clear light to light up the world. It is empowering to be able to help others by sending them the energy of love and accommodation throughout the day.

Buddhism and Compassionate Behavior: The Four Immeasurables

Buddhism teaches that enlightenment comes only when the practitioner can live with the Four Bodhisattva's Immeasurables: (1) immeasurable loving kindness, (2) immeasurable compassion, (3) immeasurable appreciative joy, and (4) immeasurable equanimity. The important attitudes that form the basis for all altruistic actions are unselfish love, compassion for the weak and feeble, a positive appreciation of nature, uncalculating peace and joy, and caring for others.

The concept of loving kindness in Buddhism is wishing everyone, including oneself, others, friends, and enemies, to be happy. This love is unselfish and unconditional; it requires courage and acceptance (including unconditional self-acceptance). The opposite of loving kindness is to love only those we care about (conditional love) while wishing enemies to be unhappy, angry, and hurt by hatred. In order to attain this state of loving kindness, one needs to avoid both material and nonmaterial attachments.

The concept of compassion is wishing everyone, including oneself and others, to be free from suffering. Compassion happens when one feels sorry for someone in pain and feels an urge to help alleviate the pain. Compassion is not pity, which looks down upon the ones in pain and keeps at a distance. The sin of not being compassionate is wishing others to suffer or being involved in cruelty.

The definition of sympathetic joy is feeling happy for others' fortune and happiness. Sympathetic joy refers to the potential of bliss and happiness of all sentient beings, as they can all become Buddhas. Those who do not have sympathetic joy are hypocritical and jealous of others' achievements.

The state of equanimity is to not distinguish between friend, enemy, or stranger but to regard every sentient being as equal. It is a clear and tranquil state of mind—not being overpowered by any delusions, mental dullness, or agitation. Those who cannot attain equanimity are overwhelmed by indifference, apathy, anxiety, worry, stress, and paranoia. Equanimity is the basis for unconditional and altruistic love, compassion, and joy.

The aim of practicing the Four Immeasurables is to be able to love all sentient beings as oneself and to be able to accept and love one's enemy as oneself. To practice the Four Immeasurables, recite the following brief prayer every day:

May I/all sentient beings have happiness and its causes.
May I/all sentient beings be free of suffering and its causes.
May I/all sentient beings be filled with bliss and always be without suffering.
May I/all sentient beings be in equanimity, free of bias, attachment, and anger.

Meditation for Equanimity

To practice meditation for equanimity, breathe in while mentally saying the phrase, "not knowing" slowly, (around four seconds), breathe out while mentally saying "nonattachment" very slowly (around eight seconds). As suffering is linked to material possessions and attachments to relationships, the ultimate sense of freedom is to maintain a healthy sense of humility and willingness to let go. Breathing while focusing on a mantra, which can be a phrase or sound, can be a form of self-instruction. For example, the breathing mantra can be modified into breathing in "relaxation" and breathing out "freedom"; breathing in "joy" and breathing out "peace." The mantra can be co-constructed with the client according to his or her needs and preferences at that particular time. The same phrase can be thought while both breathing in and breathing out.

Meditation for Letting Go and Nonattachment

Integrative Body–Mind–Spirit Social Work teaches clients to practice "letting go" meditation. Below is an example of a meditation for facilitating letting go:

> I can let go of all my past;
> let go of experiences that upset me,
> let go of fear, unhappiness, and attachment to wants.
> I will fill my heart with peace and love.
> I am filled with happiness and bliss.
> I will offer my joy and love to others.
> I am filled with the joy of life and peace of mind, joy and love that I shall share.
> I dare to start anew, and let go of negative emotions.
> I shall let my love and forgiveness cure my sorrow and rage.
> I will value every relationship with love and appreciation.
>
> (Chan, 2001, p. 101)

Very often, the experiential strategy of visual imagery is powerful in facilitating letting go. For some people, the most difficult thing to let go of is another person or relationship. Meditation is also very effective in helping clients to untangle themselves from another person.

Letting-Go Rituals

In our Integrative Body–Mind–Spirit groups for bereaved individuals, we practice a "kite-flying" letting-go ritual in our last group session. We bring group members to an outing and invite them to write their blessings and unfinished business on a kite. Group members then fly the kites, with their words of love written on them, high into the sky. To symbolize letting go of emotional attachments to the deceased person, there is a kite-cutting ritual. Members

The Story of Linda: Letting Go of Emotional Attachment

Linda was a young woman who was terribly hurt by her husband's extramarital affair. Her husband had moved out and had been living with another woman for a year. Linda suffered from insomnia, depression, and loss of appetite. She cried almost every day for a year. In the session, she told the therapist that she wanted to let go of her husband. However, images of her husband with other women frequently popped up in her mind, which was very disturbing to her. Linda was emotionally attached to her husband.

The therapist invited Linda to practice visual imagery. She was asked to close her eyes and visualize herself with her husband. She said that she visualized herself standing apart from her husband but connected to him by many strings, which were all tangled together. The therapist asked her how she would like herself to be in the imagery. She said that she wanted to be free and wanted to move on with her life. The therapist asked whether she could visualize her internal resources (Linda had been helped to access and appreciate her own resources before doing this visualization). Linda said that she could see her resources in her imagery. She was then invited to take out a pair of scissors in the visualization and cut the strings one by one until she was free. During the process, she visualized her resources supporting her and giving her energy. In her visualization, she tied the loose ends of the strings into ribbons of love around herself on her dress. She also visualized the loose ends of the strings turning into a bowtie around her husband's neck. She saw the strings flying away from her and her husband. Both of them became happy and free.

Linda was then guided to do the blue color imagery (discussed previously). She let herself be surrounded by abundant love and compassion. She visualized her internal resources becoming shining stars of different colors surrounding her. With tears, she smiled. She was then invited to look at her husband again in her imagery and let the blue light shine on him also. Linda sent her husband love and forgiveness through this color imagery.

In the next counseling session, Linda reported she was more able to let go of her anger toward her husband. This was the first time that she could calmly discuss with him over the phone the arrangement for their divorce. She was more emotionally stable and secure after the phone conversation. Although Linda was still struggling with the anger and hurt, she had more energy to plan her new life, as she was more able to let go of the past.

would cut the string of the kites and set them free. This exercise helps the bereaved persons to let go of the attachments and provides an opportunity for them to send their love and blessings to their deceased family member. This ritual symbolizes the transition into a new phase of life in which the client lets go of the negative effect brought about by the loss and decides to move on. After the exercise, participants are invited to share their feelings. Some of them also share their wishes and future plans.

> The Story of the Monkey That Clenched Its Fist
>
> One day, while a monkey was wandering around in the forest searching for food, it saw a banana that had been placed inside a small cage on the ground. It stretched its fingers straight and put them through the bars into the cage. It grasped the banana and held it in its hand. When it wanted to withdraw its fist, which was holding the banana, its fist could not get through the bars. The space between the bars was just wide enough to allow its hand to pass through with fingers stretched straight but not for its fist and a banana to pass through. The monkey was locked outside the cage simply because it held onto the banana. It could not set itself free because it was unable to let go.

Use of Metaphors and Stories

Integrative Body–Mind–Spirit Social Work utilizes metaphors and stories to bring important therapeutic messages to clients. Some concepts, such as letting go, are difficult to grasp for many clients. Using metaphors and stories has the advantage of being accessible to the client's mind. Integrative Body–Mind–Spirit Social Work believes that human beings are proactive participants in their own experience (Mahoney, 1995). The use of metaphors or stories provides space for clients to make their own interpretations about the underlying messages carried by a metaphor. This fosters creative meaning making and proactive solution searching on the part of the client.

In our Integrative Body–Mind–Spirit groups for cancer patients, one of the themes is letting go. Instead of explaining the concept of letting go and its relevancy to problems of living, we present a story to group participants (see box).

In our experience, stories and metaphors are well received by clients. Symbolic messages carried over by a story or metaphor can be very effective in bringing insights and eliciting change. Inviting clients to give metaphors for their concerns is another commonly used strategy in Integrative Body–Mind–Spirit Social Work. By going beyond the conscious and logical expression of problems faced by the client, the use of metaphors facilitates exploration at a deeper level. Many clients articulate their issues more readily with the use of metaphors.

Remember Selina? She is the woman with SLE we mentioned at the beginning of this chapter. She attended an interview 10 years after she participated in our Integrative Body–Mind–Spirit group. During the interview, she was asked what helped her to recover from her depressive-suicidal state. She reported that it was the "the monkey that clenched its fist" story shared in the group session that liberated her. She became aware that she could choose to not hold on to the victim role. She decided to let go of her emotional attachments to her boyfriend and the influence, authority, status, and material rewards that came with her job. She made a decision to say goodbye to her past wounds, to steer her life into a new direction, and to lead a renewed life.

Anchoring Transformation after Life Transitions or Crises

Personal growth and transformation is evident in many people who survive crises or life transitions (Linley & Joseph, 2004; Neimeyer, 2002; Tedeschi, 1995). Very often, people construct new meaning in the aftermath of traumatic losses (Neimeyer, 2001). For example, in our breast cancer survivor treatment group, many participants found that they had developed a new perception of themselves after the experience. To help these women access their newly constructed meaning of themselves and anchor their transformation, we practiced meditation and asked these women to give a visual image of their transformed self (Leung & Chan, 2006b):

> Sit comfortably. If you are ready, close your eyes, relax, and take a deep breath... In your next breath, relax yourself further; notice how the air comes in and how it goes out through your nose... Relax and enjoy every breath you take in... In your next breath, visualize yourself with your cancer experience... As you vivify this experience, what form does it take? Take a few moments to find an image of who you are as a person now... You can use whatever image or metaphor fits... It can be anything: a living creature, animal, or plant, any object, or any picture that fits you... Or it can be a color... It can also be any sensation that comes to you... If you find that metaphor, please nod your head.

The clients were then invited to open their eyes and share their visual imagery or metaphors, and the therapist would ask the client to describe in detail the images or whatever came up as a metaphor. For example, one woman gave a metaphor of the self after the cancer experience as "a big tree, grounded, with a wide crown to provide shade for others," and she described herself as "a vulnerable clay bowl" before getting the cancer. The use of metaphors helps give a much richer and more vivid understanding of the client's change in the perception of him or herself.

For clients who are not verbally oriented or when the client is experiencing intense emotions the use of meditation is a good way to help the client center and be in touch with himself or herself and the issue.

MEDITATION AND SPIRITUAL INTERVENTIONS

There are different traditions of meditation practice, but they all attain healing through relaxing the body, creating mindful awareness, and directing attention toward the inner self. As discussed in different parts of this book, meditation is a commonly used strategy in Integrative Social Work. It can be used to prepare a client to relax and be centered at the beginning of a therapy session (see Chapter 3). It can be used to restore balance and develop positive emotions in an individual (see Chapter 5). Meditation can also be used before the end of each session to help clients anchor the learning and accomplishments made during the session. In our Integrative Body–Mind–Spirit groups, we invite clients to engage in guided imagery with content that matches the themes of the respective session, such as self-healing, love, forgiveness, letting go, altruism, and loving kindness.

In general, meditation practices can be divided into different phases: relaxation and connection, visualization, affirmation, appreciation, and conclusion.

1. Relaxation and Connection: As breathing connects the body and the mind (Nhất Hạnh, 1991), focusing on breathing is a good way to start meditation practice. Some traditions use sound, such as repeating a mantra (a phrase, word, or syllable) in meditation. The purpose is to make the body relax and to make the mind focus.

2. Visualization: When relaxed, the client is led to an image of a comfortable and secure place of peace and harmony, often a place of natural beauty such as a seashore, forest, riverside, etc. The place has to suit the client. Negative feelings and emotions are removed through visualization; for example, imagining blowing away worries into a balloon and letting it go. It can also be a beautiful waterfall with healing water that washes away stress and refreshes the body, mind, and soul. Clients are also invited to imagine breathing in fresh air and loving, healing energy from nature (Chan, 2001; Chan, Chan, & Lou, 2001; Chan, Lo, & Leung, 2000; Leung, 1997).

3. Affirmation and Appreciation: Affirmations are assertions that involve positive attitudes or thoughts, creativity, and energy. They have the power to impress upon the mind the need to accomplish positive tasks. They can erase old thought patterns and produce desirable changes in a client's life. Some clients may think that they are unworthy of happiness or of healthy lives or that they may have repeated to themselves how stupid and unworthy they are for years. Affirmations usually have a message of hope and renewal. Some examples of affirmations are, "Deep in the center of my being there is an infinite well of love and power . . . ," "Explore life; there's always something new to discover." We can also invite clients to appreciate their bodies and send love and compassion to their body parts and to nurture their own life force. We can invite clients to connect with others in their meditations by imagining themselves sending out loving kindness to other people (Chan, 2001; Leung, 1997).

4. Closure. A closure is used to help the client to return safely to the normal state of consciousness. It is usually done by bringing the awareness to physical sensations, such as hearing the music or noise in the room, feeling the body in contact with the chair, etc.

Applications of Meditation and Cautions

Meditation is not only used as an intervention during the session, but clients can also practice it on their own. Sometimes, the therapist can recommend meditation practice to the client as a homework assignment. Meditations like the one for loving kindness and the one for equanimity are suitable for daily practice. They can be recommended for practice before bedtime or just after waking up. Other meditative practices like forgiveness color imagery can be recommended for clients dealing with the issue of forgiveness. Then, the therapist can review with the client in the next therapy session the experience and effect of the practice. Deep breathing meditation can also be recommended to clients for dealing with different negative emotions. Recommendations pertaining to meditation as a homework assignment should be given according to the clinical judgment of the worker, who should continuously check with clients on their response to and the effectiveness of the practice.

However, there are cautions when using meditation in clinical practice. Protective measures have to be taken, as meditation can bring the client to an altered state of consciousness (Bullis, 1996). During the meditative processes, many images may be revealed to the practitioner, some comforting, some frightening. It is therefore important to prepare the client before doing the exercise. The worker should explain to the client what she or he is going to do and inform the client what to expect during the exercise. This not only serves to get the client's informed consent before participating in the exercise but also helps the client to get prepared for the experience. It is important to create a "holding" environment, because intense emotions may unfold. Therefore, ongoing checking of the client's mental state during the exercise is necessary. The worker can observe the client's respiration, eye movements, facial expressions, and body posture, which are indicators of the physical and mental state of the client. When the exercise is over and when the client has reentered a normal state of consciousness, a debriefing should be conducted. It serves as a safeguard to ensure that the client has safely returned to normal activities. It also allows participants to talk about their experiences. The therapist can solicit information on how the experience has affected the client and how the client can integrate the insight straight from the experience into his or her daily life. In Chapter 15, we discuss more fully the ethical considerations pertaining to the use of spiritually based interventions/activities in our practice.

WORKING WITH SPIRITUAL DIVERSITY

While Integrative Body–Mind–Spirit Social Work emphasizes the importance of utilizing spirituality in practice, it pays special attention to issues regarding respecting spiritual diversity. Integrative Body–Mind–Spirit Social Work utilizes nonsectarian interventions and activities. This approach enables transcultural applicability and easy adoption of these practices by clients with diverse religious and nonreligious spiritual backgrounds. Although many of the meditation techniques adopted by Integrative Body–Mind–Spirit Social Work are rooted in Buddhism, they are applied without using any religious language or any religious imagery attached. However, when religious or spiritual beliefs are sources of strength and resources for a client, these nonsectarian practices can be linked to specific religious versions of the practice if a client so desires. For example, for meditation on loving kindness, the image of God or Jesus can be introduced in the guided imagery for a client with a Christian background. Likewise the image of Guan Yin, the Bodhisattva of Compassion, can be introduced to a Buddhist client during a meditation practice. The therapist can also invite clients without any religion to think of a visual image that would bring peace of mind or a feeling of love. In general, spiritual interventions should be in line with therapeutic goals and the client's interest. The guiding principles of value clarity, respect, client centeredness, inclusiveness, and creativity suggested by Canda and Furman (1999) serve as a useful guide in working with clients with diverse spiritual backgrounds.

1. Value clarity: The worker needs to reflect on his or her own spiritual values and beliefs so that he or she can identify any possible presuppositions, biases, strength, or limitations that may be brought into the helping relationship and how these values and beliefs may have shaped his or her own practice approach.
2. Respect: Integrative Body–Mind–Spirit Social Work builds on clients' spiritual strengths and resources. Therefore, we see a client's religious or spiritual values and beliefs as part of the solution to his or her problem and do not challenge those values or beliefs. A client's spiritual values and perspectives need to be respected. It is imperative to avoid imposing the worker's own values or spiritual perspectives on the client.
3. Client centeredness and inclusiveness: Integrative Body–Mind–Spirit Social Work appreciates and honors clients' worldviews, aspirations, beliefs, and values. It is therefore important to be knowledgeable and respectful of the diverse religions/spiritual beliefs that clients may hold.
4. Creativity: It is imperative that spiritually based interventions and activities are practiced with creativity so that they can be adapted to suit

clients with different religious or spiritual traditions. The therapist has to tailor the spiritually based activity introduced here for specific purposes and spiritual beliefs that suit the client and the context.

SUMMARY

Integrative Body–Mind–Spirit Social Work believes that spirituality is the core of healing, and that it is necessary for the healthy functioning of the mind, body, and other domains of human existence. It forms the basis of the human life force that motivates individuals to undergo a dynamic process of self-transcendence toward a sense of wholeness. Spirituality is broader than religion. In the context of Integrative Social Work, spirituality refers to the idiosyncratic beliefs and values of individual clients that constitute a source of personal aspiration and sense of meaning. As such, spiritual intervention in Integrative Body–Mind–Spirit Social Work examines the core issues of human existence, regarding a sense of meaning, purpose, and mission, as well as the relationships with and the connectedness among oneself, others, nature, and the ultimate reality. It invites clients to a therapeutic dialogue that identifies their specific values and beliefs, addresses existential and transcendent issues in their life, and engages them in a process of meaning reconstruction that fosters the development of a more coherent narrative of their life experiences. Unlike conventional approaches that focus on mastery and control, Integrative Body–Mind–Spirit Social Work advocates embracing pain rather than eliminating pain, promoting resilience, affirming strength, and constructing new meaning in adversity. Utilizing spirituality in human existence therefore goes beyond solving the problems at hand but expands the clients' life horizon and brings the prospect of achieving personal growth and transformation. This brings us to the last chapter on self-transformation and personal growth, a topic that goes beyond the conventional goal of therapy but is of paramount importance in Integrative Body–Mind–Spirit Social Work.

9

Centering the Self: Personal Growth and Transformation

AN ONGOING PROCESS OF BECOMING

Throughout life there are challenges and changes created by life transitions, sickness, accidents, loss of loved ones, and other crises. Based on the assumption that life is a process of constant change and evolution, Integrative Body–Mind–Spirit Social Work sees therapy as part of this process of searching, discovering, and becoming that the client goes through in his or her life. Believing that problems will come and go, Integrative Body–Mind–Spirit Social Work does not consider problem resolution the ultimate goal of therapy. Rather, it aims to provide a therapeutic context for enhancing the self-healing and self-balancing abilities of individuals and families. Only when the self is well grounded can an individual maintain a sense of peace and personal integrity while facing life's unfolding challenges. Nurturing and rediscovering the "self" is therefore of paramount importance, not only for restoring the self-healing and rebalancing abilities of individuals but also for ongoing personal growth and becoming. In Integrative Body–Mind–Spirit Social Work, nurturing and rediscovering the "self" is more than enhancing self-awareness and self-actualization. It is about achieving and maintaining balance in the self–other dynamics in an individual's identity (Leung & Chan, 2006b) and connecting to a larger sense of self. This chapter describes an understanding of the "self" based on Eastern traditions and how it shapes the practice of social work.

THE EASTERN PERSPECTIVE ON "SELF" AND SELF-AWARENESS

Although both Western and Eastern practices emphasize the importance of the "self" and "self-awareness," the notion of the "self" in Western and Eastern psychology is different. There are also differences in the use of self-awareness in therapy.

Influenced by a culture that emphasizes a sense of personal agency (Nisbett et al., 2001), Western discourse on the self favors individualism and autonomy. The "self" is perceived as a unitary, autonomous, and independent entity that exists separately from the outside world. Self and not-self are clearly demarcated. This "individualistic self" is at the center and perceives the world, constantly exercising autonomy and striving for a sense of mastery. As such, the majority of mainstream social work practice with individuals aims at fostering ego strength in sense of control, self-efficacy, competence in social functioning, self-actualization, and self-esteem. Social work treatment based on Western systems of thought largely views self-awareness as a way for individuals to achieve personal insights and understanding that will allow them to better master, control, address, and overcome the problems at hand and achieve self-actualization.

The "Shadow" of an Individualistic and Forever Actualizing Self

Social work practice adopting an individualist view of self and a treatment paradigm that gives privilege to mastery, accomplishment, and self-actualization has certainly helped millions of people effect desirable changes in their lives. However, problems arise when mastery and control are regarded as the only desirable therapeutic ends. In fact, grasping for mastery and control sometimes brings more problems than solutions in many life situations. The case of incurable illness is just an example. Sudden death caused by accidents, natural disasters, and mass terrorist attacks remind us how little control we have over the world. Welwood (2000), a Buddhist psychologist, speaks about the problem of "self-fixation," a phenomenon of people being constrained by internal conflicts associated with chasing worldly status and clinging to things, feelings, and ideas. The ceaseless pursuit of an actualizing self and not letting go when life circumstances require is actually an attachment to an egoistic self. In Buddhist psychology, the egoistic self is but a mental creation of the mind and is ultimately unreal (Ramaswami & Sheikh, 1989). Holding on to the illusion of a permanent, individualist self is regarded as the source of suffering (Walsh, 1989). When an individual lives only in his or her own personal universe without appreciating the needs and existence of other beings, he or she becomes disconnected with others and the environment. An individual preoccupied with an egoistic self would be cut off from

FIGURE **9.1.** The self–other dynamics as represented by the yin–yang symbol.

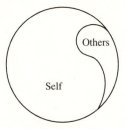

FIGURE **9.2.** A "self" overshadowed by individualism and egoism.

the intuitive knowing and spontaneous acting that arises from our authentic being (Welwood, 2000). Applying the yin–yang perspective, the self can be understood as a dynamic entity that is composed of a pair of opposite forces: egoism and selflessness. A healthily functioning self would be one that maintains a harmonious balance between pursuing self-interest and individuality and being inclusive and selfless. The "self" is thus constantly striving for a balance in a "self–other dynamic" (Leung & Chan, 2006b). Figure 9.1 is a graphic representation of the "self–other dynamics" with the yin–yang symbol. The two forces interact with each other, leading to a dynamic relationship and intricate balance between them. When the "self" is overshadowed by individualism and egoism, the intricate balance of the self–other dynamic is disrupted. The person becomes out of balance (Figure 9.2).

An Example of Self-Fixation: Clinging Onto Pain Causes More Pain

Benson was a young man in his early twenties. In his family, he could easily get what he wanted, as everybody had treated him like a little prince since he was small. After he married, his mother still looked after him, although Benson lived in another apartment with his wife, Irene. Irene found that Benson's mother intervened in their lives, for she came to their home every day. She discussed the issue with Benson, who responded by telling Irene that she would get used to it soon. Recently, Benson developed neck and shoulder pain. He complained that his mother bought a pillow that was too hard for

(continued)

(continued)

him. Irene accompanied him for physical treatment to every appointment and stayed home from work as long as possible to accompany Benson. She also took over all the housework so that Benson could take a rest. Benson was fully absorbed in his pain and did not appreciate the things that Irene did for him. He always complained to Irene how disturbing the pain was. Months passed, but Benson's neck pain did not improve. He became uninterested in all things in his daily life except examining his neck and spine day after day. He did not sleep well and was very angry with his mother for giving him a bad pillow. He convinced himself that the neck pain ruined his life and that he was not going to forgive his mother. He also believed that any intimate activity with Irene would make his physical condition worse. Consequently, he did not let Irene touch him: even holding hands and hugging was not allowed, not to mention more intimate interaction. Benson withdrew from all social activities, including those initiated by Irene. However, Benson disliked the fact that Irene went to meet her friends on her own, as he wanted to have Irene's company at home. Benson was totally absorbed in his pain, anger, and victim role. He was disconnected with others in the social world.

The "Shadow" of an Other-Centered Self

A "self" without individuality or one that is overly others-centered creates other problems. For such people, actions are not driven by an independent and autonomous mind but are delivered in accordance with perceptions of social requirements, obligations, and expectations. There is no place for individual needs, aspirations, intuitions, or spontaneity. The "self" is subdued and is out of balance (Figure 9.3). Spontaneous self-expression is restrained. People are disconnected from their authenticity.

FIGURE **9.3.** A "self" overshadowed by other-centeredness.

A Loving Daughter Who Lost Her "Self"

Helen was a 40-year-old single woman. She was depressed and had suicidal thoughts. She felt helpless and unable to bring happiness to the family, her mother in particular. Recently, her mother had been in constant conflict with her paternal grandmother, who was in her eighties. Helen wanted to be a peacemaker, but she found herself torn

(continued)

(continued)

between these two old ladies. Also, her younger brother developed a relationship with another woman after 3 years of marriage. Helen was the eldest daughter in the family and had been responsible for taking care of her younger brothers and sisters since she was young. Helen tried hard to convince her brother to leave the woman, but her efforts were in vain. The couple is now planning to divorce. In Helen's view, this shamed the family. She blamed herself for not able to help.

Helen was a loving daughter who devoted herself wholeheartedly to the family for many years. She quit school at the age of 13 and went to work to support her younger brothers and sisters' education. Helen's mother was a Buddhist who believed that ancestor worship by offspring following Buddhist rituals was very important and wanted her children to do so after her death. Being a filial daughter, Helen converted to Buddhism when she was 24 to satisfy her mother's expectations. Helen had several boyfriends in her twenties, but her mother found none of them met her expectations. To avoid discord with mother, Helen decided to remain single. All these years, she has put the interest of her parents and her family above her own. There was no place for her needs and aspirations. As Helen was middle-aged, she was lost and did not know how she was going to lead her life. She was exhausted, as she was never able to make everybody happy. She also found that she did not know much about herself—she did not even know what she wanted for her life.

When looking at the above two cases using the yin–yang perspective, we found that the "self" of both were out of balance in terms of the self–others dynamics. For Benson, the self was overshadowed. More so, the more he was focusing on his own pain (the self), the more difficult it was for him to connect with his wife (others). On the contrary, Helen's case is one with the self being subdued. The imbalance, whether it is overshadowed of self or others, was not contributive to the dynamic and healthy functioning of the individual.

Transcending Egoism and Connecting to a Larger Sense of "Self"

Contrary to individualistic discourse, Eastern perspectives view the boundary between the "self" and the "not-self" as fluid and moving. From a Buddhist perspective, nothing is isolated; everything is interdependent. There is ultimately no real boundary between "self" and "not-self." The "self" "not-self" dichotomy is regarded as an illusion created by the human mind and the result of attachment to the ego self. Zen Master Thich Nhat Hanh (2002) spoke inspirationally about the interconnected nature of things and human existence. He used the term "inter-being" to describe the intricate connectedness of all living creatures, reminding us that every living thing comes from the same mother Earth. All living things exchange air with the environment and with one another when they breathe. Breathing helps us realize our own inherent connectedness with the rest of life. We also share with each other the same water, as it is constantly changing its form from rain to river to sea to vapor to cloud in a ceaseless cycle. The earth, the rain, the minerals in the soil, the sunshine, the clouds, the rivers—everything coexists with us and with every living and nonliving thing in this world. According to Thich Nhat Hanh (1991), when an individual is able to discard the isolated, unitary, and autonomous conception of the self from the mind, she or he can experience the beautiful connections with others and the universe. This is a state of transcending consciousness (Ho, Peng, Lai, & Chan, 2001).

The notion of "self" in a Daoist perspective is also concerned with connecting the self to a larger being. The "self," according to Daoism, is one of the countless manifestations of the *Dao*, the law of nature. When the "self" is identified with the *Dao*, there is a "unity of heaven and human beings" (*tien-renheyi*), meaning that the self is connected, both within and outside. The ideal "self" is exemplified by the metaphor of water in the classic Daoist text, the *Daodejing*, as follows: "The perfect goodness is like water. Water approaches all things, instead of contending with them. It prefers to dwell where no one would like to stay; hence it comes close to the *Dao*. A man of perfect goodness chooses a low place to dwell, like water. He has a heart as deep as water" (Gu, 1995, p. 77). Water droplets seek to lie low and water vapor stays invisible, providing moisture and nourishment to the living creatures of the earth. The "self," in its authentic and harmonious state, should be well connected with the environment and be able to exhibit spontaneity, flexibility, and humility.

When individuals transcend their own egocentricity, they are able to appreciate the notions of "self-in-others" and "others-in-self" (Ho et al., 2001), or the essence of "inter-being" (Nhất Hạnh, 1991). They become aware that the realization of one's well-being is inextricably connected with the well-being of other beings in this universe. With this awareness, people can see things without personal judgment or prejudice. They simply see people and things exactly as they are in their natural states. There is virtually no place for the seeds of antagonism and arrogance to grow. This new understanding of things that comes with a transcended consciousness fosters a sense of equality and compassion. An individual sees humanity in him or herself and in others. Love and compassion flow out naturally.

Self-Awareness in an Eastern Perspective

This transcended consciousness is the essence of self-awareness in Eastern practice. Unlike the Western perspective that sees self-awareness as a way for individuals to achieve self-understanding for better mastery, control, and self-actualization, Eastern traditions view self-awareness as part of the process that allows an individual to overcome the illusion of a permanent, enduring self and to gain insights into the transcendent nature of things. With this self-awareness, an individual is able to free him or herself from indulging

The Case of Margaret: Transcending Egocentricity in Loss

Margaret was a 50-year-old woman. She grew up in a protected environment and, to some extent, was spoiled by her parents when she was young. She was always success- ful in getting what she wanted from her family. As an adult, she married a man who took good care of her and her whole family. To her, things were taken for granted. She was very dependent on her husband in almost every aspect of daily living. Her primary concern was about earning money and being self-sufficient. However, misfortune came unexpectedly. Her husband was suddenly diagnosed with liver cancer and passed away 10 days later. She was totally shocked and unprepared. She felt miserable and at loss.

In an interview with Margaret, the therapist listened to her story. The therapist guided Margaret to review her life and the significant events that had happened over her life. Meanings attached to different life events were explored and reviewed. In the process, Margaret realized that she has a worldview that life was predictable and ordered. Good things in life seemed to be a matter of course. She has been living a life in ways that was rather self-centered. The death of her husband represented the shattering of her fundamental assumptions about the world and a discontinuity in her life story. More so, the transition to widowhood was a disorganization of her sense of identity.

In subsequent interviews, the therapist helped Margaret into a process of rediscover- ing meaning. Margaret attributed her husband's death to God's will. She believed that it was an important message from God to remind her not to be self-centered. She also realized that what she possessed was not permanent, so she learnt to cherish what she already has. She started to reconstruct a worldview that can integrate the loss. She also began to think about what she could do to contribute herself.

The reconstructing of meaning and worldview seemed to help Margaret to relinquish the comfort and security that went along with an egoistic self, Margaret tried new things and reached out to help others. Later, she devoted herself to missionary work in her church. She visited elderly people and shared the teaching of God to people from different walks of life. She found herself changed internally; she was more inclusive and compassionate. She developed connections with others and God. Spiritually, she was more content. She said that she found her mission and inner peace that she greatly cherished.

in the egoistic self and the cravings that come with it, such as greed, hatred, desire, and prejudice. Kenneth Wilber, an advocate of transpersonal psychol- ogy, described this ability of being nonattached to one's ego as transpersonal awareness (Wilber, 2000; Wilber, Engler, & Brown, 1986). David Ho (1995), a Chinese psychologist, termed this process of transcending egocentricity "psychological decentering." In therapy, helping clients to achieve this tran- scended consciousness or transpersonal awareness is helpful when dealing with issues associated with overattachment to intense emotions, lofty desires, worldly possessions, or enmeshed relationships.

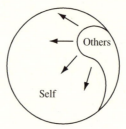

FIGURE **9.4a.** Restoring balance for a "self" overshadowed by egoism.

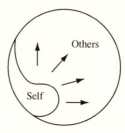

FIGURE **9.4b.** Restoring balance for a "self" overshadowed by other-centeredness.

Restoring Balance

As discussed, overemphasis on both the individualist and subdued "self" has its own shadows. To help the "self" to regain balance, the submissive domain in the "self–other dynamic" has to expand, and the aggressive domain has to be restrained. For those whose "self" is overshadowed by individualism and egoism, psychological decentering (mindful detachment of the self-ego) and connecting with others are helpful strategies (Figure 9.4a). For those whose "self" is overshadowed by other-centeredness, the mindfulness practice of "centering the self" is instrumental in regaining balance and groundedness (Figure 9.4b).

Centering the Self

"Centering the self" is a difficult concept to describe in words. Playing with a roly-poly toy closely simulates the meaning of "centering." When you apply a force on a roly-poly toy, it lies low. It will then bounce back, moving back and forth for a while, and finally regain its balance. If you observe the shape and structure of a roly-poly toy, you will find that its base is ball shaped and made of solid material so that it can be easily grounded. The inside of the upper part of the roly-poly toy is empty so that it is light on top. Likewise, a "centered" person tends to have a mind more or less emptied of craving, hatred, greed, and personal judgment. Such a mind is also freed from the burden of preoccupations or worries. It is therefore calm and clear. Gunaratana (1991) used the analogy of a cup of muddy water to describe our

---

A Story about Mother Teresa

One evening in a slum area of Calcutta, Mother Teresa was with a group of children who had not eaten anything for a long time. Hunger was written all over their faces. She brought the children to a nearby bakery and asked for some bread. She said to the bakery owner: "Sir, these children are very hungry. They have not had anything to eat for some time. Would you kindly give some bread for them?" The bakery owner took a look at the children. He then turned to Mother Teresa, spat on her face, and went on with his work. Mother Teresa took out her handkerchief, wiped her face, and said to the bakery owner: "Sir, This is for me. Thank you. How about bread for the children?"

---

mind. The mud represents our wandering mind. By keeping a cup of muddy water still, the mud settles and the water becomes clear. Focusing our mind is like keeping the muddy water still: It helps the mind to settle down and become clear. Very often, our mind focuses on our past experiences or on our expectations of future experiences. When "centered," the mind settles down, focuses on the moment, and the individual becomes fully aware of his or her own physical experience and psychological activity. In this state, when any thoughts and emotions come up, the person simply lets them come and go and remains peaceful and calm. The tranquility and peacefulness brought forth by "self-centering" not only benefits individuals who practice it, but it can also be felt and experienced by other people. Great spiritual leaders often possess extraordinary charisma that people around them can feel, like peaceful vibrations expanding outwards from them. Mother Teresa is one well-known example.

> If we were humble, nothing would change us—neither praise nor discouragement. If someone were to criticize us, we would not feel discouraged. If someone were to praise us, we also would not feel proud.
>
> Mother Teresa (Gonzalez-Balado, 1996, p. 53)

Mother Teresa did not do much talking, but when she spoke, her words were convincing. Whatever happened, she was not disturbed. This state of tranquility is one of the benefits of "centering the self." In Eastern Zen practice, it is called *anzhu* (安住). *An* means a feeling of calm and peace. *Zhu* has a connotation of stillness and is referred to as the state of being present in the moment. *Anzhu*, or "centering the self," is the state of having a clear, focused, and calm mind. Individuals in this state are able to congruently choose a response or action for incoming stimulus rather than being trapped in compulsive and habitual reactions (Gunaratana, 1991). They are responsive, but not reactive, have internal freedom, and therefore are at peace with themselves and others most of the time.

USE OF "CENTERING" IN TRANSFORMING NEGATIVE EMOTIONS

Despite the fact that the facilitation of spiritual growth in individuals and families is a key component in the treatment process, Integrative Body–Mind–Spirit Social Work has no intention of shaping clients to become like Mother Teresa or any other spiritual figure. We believe that each individual has a unique spiritual journey. Here, we would like to talk about how the mindfulness practice of "centering the self" helps in transforming negative emotions, such as anger, fear, frustration, anxiety, and sadness.

The mindfulness practice of "centering the self" involves four major components: awareness, acceptance, appreciation, and transformation. Using anger as an example, when there is anger, a person who is mindful or centered would not repress or deny it but observe it with a calm mind. She or he will look into the anger and see how it comes, grows, and eventually, goes. The same mental process could be applied for other emotions which one wants to transform.

1. Awareness: We can transform our anger only if we are aware of it and acknowledge its existence. Observing our breathing helps us to get in touch with our feelings. Breathing actually reflects our emotions—when we are angry, our breaths become short and shallow. When we are calm, our breaths are deep and slow. By focusing our attention on breathing, we can be aware of the feelings that surface. Name the feeling by saying to yourself, "I am angry. Anger is now inside me." Below is a meditation by Thich Nhat Hanh (1991) on mindfulness practice to address anger, which therapists can practice with their clients in dealing with anger.

   > Breathing in, I know that anger is here.
   > Breathing out, I know that the anger is me.
   > Breathing in, I know that anger is unpleasant.
   > Breathing out, I know this feeling will pass.
   > Breathing in, I am calm.
   > Breathing out, I am strong enough to take care of this anger. (p. 61)

   We can add two statements: "Breathing in, I have the capacity to transform this anger." "Breathing out, I can turn anger into acts of benevolence."

2. Acceptance: In order to observe our own anger, we must accept the fact that we are angry. We cannot examine our negative emotions without

accepting that they are inside us. In a state of mindfulness, we simply accept what is there and are aware that it is simply life's occurrence at that moment—what is there is there. No judgment, only acceptance. Thich Nhat Hanh (1991) stated that this mindfulness practice helps to prevent anger from monopolizing our consciousness. When angry, we are usually inclined to think about the person (and his or her words or behavior) who we believed made us angry. The more we think about him or her, the more our anger flares. The root of the problem is indeed the anger itself, which is inside us (Nhất Hạnh, 2001). So when we do not think about the "outside" person but attend to our "inside," that is, when we get centered, we find that anger is not so powerful; we can accept our anger.

3. Appreciation: When we know that we are capable of taking care of our anger, it is not so overwhelming. We can let go of it and even appreciate it. We can appreciate anger as a teacher that helps us to discover aspects of our "self" of which we were previously unaware. Turn inward and ask yourself: "What triggers my anger? What is the root of my anger? Is it fear? Disappointment? Unmet expectations? Hurt feelings?" Anger is associated with a lack of understanding of ourselves. When we look deeply into anger, we find that it is rooted in desire, pride, agitation, suspicion, and insecurity.

4. Transformation: We are transforming anger into peace the very moment we bring acceptance of anger into ourselves. When we look deeply inside, we can see our own cravings and attachments, which are common to ordinary human beings, hiding behind the anger. With this understanding, we can watch anger and related thoughts rise with a feeling of serene detachment. In this way, we see our own reactions without being caught up in the reactions themselves. Instead, we see them with calmness and clarity. This frees us from obsessive, compulsive reactions. Also, with this understanding of ourselves, we can see our own humanity. This understanding of human existence fosters compassion toward oneself and others (Gunaratana, 1991). We feel love toward others and can then transform our anger into love and compassion or acts of benevolence for the disadvantaged and oppressed.

We recommend doing deep-cleansing breathing with "centering." In deep-cleansing breathing, one breathes in deeply and visualizes breathing in the positive energy of love through the nose. Then, one holds the breath for a while and then breathes out. While breathing out one visualizes oneself emptying the lungs and taking out all negative energies through the mouth. Repeat the process until feeling that all the negative energies have been transformed into positive energies or when feeling joyful and peaceful.

A SUMMARY: NURTURING THE "SELF" FOR BALANCE AND CONNECTEDNESS

Integrative Body–Mind–Spirit Social Work emphasizes nurturing and redis-covering the "self" in the treatment process. It adopts an expanded conception of that "self" that is more than just individuality. We believe that helping clients to affirm and appreciate individuality is very important, but we also recognize and emphasize the importance of nurturing the social and spiritual "self." As such, treatment goals in relation to nurturing and discovering the "self" in Integrative Body–Mind–Spirit Social Work include helping clients to become "centered"—to focus and initiate self-healing abilities so as to restore balance, as well as to make meaningful interpersonal connections and to enhance spiritual growth. Treatment in Integrative Body–Mind–Spirit Social Work therefore navigates across the intrapersonal sphere, the interper-sonal sphere, as well as the spiritual sphere of the "self" in attaining balance and connectedness (Figure 9.5).

In a therapeutic context, the intrapersonal sphere of the "self" is associated with unconditional self-acceptance, self-actualization, self-valuation, and the dynamic interplay of "psychological decentering" and "centering." Treatment tasks related to nurturing this sphere include, but are not limited to, helping clients to address and transform negative emotions, helping clients to accept and harmonize the different personality parts of self, helping clients to develop

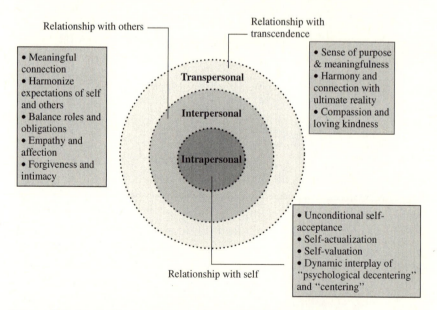

FIGURE **9.5.** Intervention components of Integrative Body–Mind–Spirit Social Work in relation to the intrapersonal, interpersonal, and spiritual domains of the "self."

self-appreciation, helping clients to maximize their potential and utilize their inner strengths, helping clients to express themselves in whatever way that suits them, and helping clients to develop transcendent consciousness.

The social or interpersonal sphere of the "self" is about developing meaningful connections with others in the social world. Treatment tasks related to this domain may include helping clients to harmonize the different expectations of them from others and from themselves; helping clients to integrate and balance different social roles and the obligations that go with them; helping clients to give and receive love, empathy, affection; and helping clients to experience intimacy and forgiveness.

The spiritual "self" is concerned with developing connectedness with nature, God, or the ultimate reality, as idiosyncratically defined by individuals; having a sense of purpose and meaningfulness; and developing the capacity to have compassion and loving kindness toward themselves and other beings. Love, altruism, appreciation, a sense of gratitude, compassion, perseverance, inner tranquility, and conviction are all qualities associated with a fulfilling spiritual self. As discussed extensively in different parts of this book, we believe that focused breathing, mindfulness practices, and meditation are ways to nurture the spiritual sphere of the "self." Yet, the journey varies for different individuals. For some, spiritual transformation may be an enlightenment experience after surviving an unexpected life event, reading a book, encountering someone special, or visiting a place.

Chapter 4 discusses utilizing multiple entry points in Integrative Body–Mind–Spirit Social Work when formulating a treatment plan with a client. The intrapersonal, interpersonal, and transpersonal spheres of the "self" are

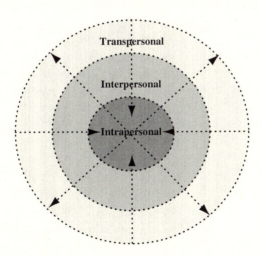

FIGURE **9.6.** The dynamic process of weaving back and forth within the different domains of the "self" in the treatment process.

different entry points in our intervention framework. The three domains of the "self" have fluid boundaries. The treatment process is extremely flexible and highly individualized and may weave back and forth among the different spheres in helping clients to restore balance and harmony (Figure 9.6).

TERMINATING TREATMENT

Integrative Body–Mind–Spirit Social Work believes that clients are able to move on with life on their own when their self-healing and self-balancing capacities are back in place. The decision of ending treatment is made collaboratively between the therapist and the client. There are a number of indicators that the therapist can look for when suggesting termination.

1. The Presenting Problem. Like other approaches, Integrative Body–Mind–Spirit Social Work also goes back to the presenting problem for evaluation. However, we believe that the end of treatment does not necessarily rest on solving the problem, for we believe that problems are a normal part of living and that they will come and go. Our concern here is whether clients have made internal changes that allow them to regain balance and self-healing abilities. If clients are able to look at the problem in a new way, have developed a different perception of the problem, or have a new feeling and relationship with the problem, they will respond and cope differently. Clients may ultimately solve the problem, or they may just embrace the problem and live with it without being disturbed by it. The critical point is when individuals and families can move on with life without being blocked by the problem.

2. Strengths and Resources. Integrative Body–Mind–Spirit Social Work believes that people get stuck because they are disconnected from their own internal strengths and resources. The ability to reconnect with and utilize their own inner strengths and resources signifies a restoration of the self-healing capacities of the client.

3. Plans for the Future. When a client is able to articulate and make realistic plans for the future, it is a good indicator that she or he is ready to move on.

4. The Perception of Problems in Life. As problems will come and go, if clients develop the insight that problems are a part of normal living, or even the insight that problems are teachers in life, they may appreciate problems in their lives, develop an enhanced capacity to cope, and even embrace problems in their lives in the future.

5. The "Self." Integrative Body–Mind–Spirit Social Work believes that the solution to the problem of living does not lie outside but within the

clients. If clients are able to discover new aspects of them, develop a new description of self (Lee et al., 2003), and are affirmative and appreciative of them, we believe that they have an increased capacity to face future challenges.

The key tasks of the therapist include: firstly, conducting an evaluation with the client on the impact of the presenting problem on his or her life at the moment; and secondly, reviewing and anchoring the positive changes in the client. The therapist should facilitate the client in identifying positive changes in any aspects of him or herself. Sometimes, we utilize the body and meditative techniques to help the client access and verbalize new meaning, insights, or discoveries. It is useful to ask how the client sees him or herself after the experience. Personal growth and transformation always accompanies a new perception of the "self." Verbalizing and articulating growth and transformation in the "self" can help anchor the changes. In addition, it is helpful to ask the client how the body feels about his or her own change. The therapist can use body scan as a useful activity for such a purpose. This utilizes the felt body and facilitates the body–mind–spirit connection and groundedness. For example, after treatment, a female client who was lacking confidence may tell the therapist that she feels that her feet are more grounded and she has more strength. She may also walk out of the therapist's office with better posture and grounded steps. A client who was overburdened with responsibility at the beginning may report feeling lighter and relaxed in the shoulders at the end. Therapists can help clients to anchor these changes in the physical body by a meditation in which the whole body is filled with this renewed feeling and energy. Whenever the client needs energy and support in the future, she or he can go into this meditative state and get in touch with her or his inner strengths again. The third key task is inviting the client to make plans for the future. This includes discussing with the client how to apply the changes in his or her life in the future. This task usually goes along with helping the client to develop short- and long-term plans to integrate changes and prevent a relapse. The therapist may also help clients to develop long-term support systems that foster continuous self-development and growth: Discussing with clients the possibility of helping others and engaging in altruistic acts is a commonly used strategy in Integrative Body–Mind–Spirit Social Work. Also, it is always helpful to prepare the client to identify early signs of symptoms and relapses, and to discuss with the client what he or she can do to cope with the situation. An open-door policy should be communicated to clients in case they need help in the future. Lastly, the therapist should provide a context for clients to realize that life challenges are ceaseless and that we can appreciate problems and difficulties, as they help us grow in our process of becoming.

In our experience, when clients feel largely rebalanced and reconnected, they demonstrate some or all of the indicators listed above. The last two indicators are more difficult to achieve. However, when the first three of the above indicators are present, we are quite confident that clients are ready to be on their own again in their life journey.

Clients and families are likely to have mixed feelings and emotions about termination. They are likely to be proud of their accomplishment, but also anxious about leaving a therapeutic relationship, or feel a sense of attachment to the therapist. Psychodynamic-based approaches usually emphasize that a successful resolution of these transference issues is important for successful and sustainable positive treatment effect. Brief approaches do not explicitly attend to these issues possibly because the treatment is so brief that transference issues and dependence issues should not be major concerns. Integrative Body–Mind–Spirit Social Work is a strengths-based approach that emphasizes empowering clients and reducing any long-term psychological dependence on professionals. However, we do recognize the presence of mixed emotions and feelings at termination. In this approach, we engage in the following tasks for termination purposes: (1) We encourage and facilitate ongoing self-evaluation of progress by clients and families so that termination would not come as a surprise, (2) Termination is a collaborative decision discussed by the clients and the therapist, (3) We explicitly discuss potential feelings and mixed emotions about termination with clients and families, and address any issues as arise, (4) We routinely share with clients and families our open-door policy. We take a developmental perspective of life and that life challenges are ceaseless. Clients and families learn new skills and move on with their lives and it is okay to come back when life present different challenges; (5) We encourage and collaboratively design a "graduation ceremony" or any other helpful termination rituals with clients and families so that they have a beneficial way to metaphorically anchor their successes and bring a closure to the treatment.

To end this section on body–mind–spirit therapeutic techniques, we would like to share the words of Daisy, one of the participants in an Integrative Body–Mind–Spirit Social Work group for bereaved widows. Daisy was a newly bereaved widow. Prior to joining our group, she had uncontrollable crying spells and she literally hid in the house. In the last session of the group, she shared her experience: "It was like I was in a pit after my husband passed away. I did not know how to get out of it. I could not see any future. I was very sad and just stayed home and cried every day. The therapist was the "ladder constructor." She constructed the ladder with me so that I could climb up from the pit. I still miss my husband although I have a different perspective about life. Now, I can move on with my life and am no longer stuck in the pit."

SUMMARY

Integrative Body–Mind–Spirit Social Work believes that personal growth and transformation is possible while coping with and surviving life challenges, changes, and crises. While the client is taking charge of his or her own process of becoming and transforming, therapy serves to provide the context to facilitate this transformative experience. An expanded conception of the "self" that speaks of a larger self, a self that is connected to others, to the community, the environment and the ultimate being, as espoused by Integrative Body–Mind–Spirit Social Work, allows therapists and clients to address problems of living in different ways. This understanding of the self complements a Western conception of the self as practiced in mainstream social work, which serves to widen our therapeutic repertoire in helping individuals and families.

Integrative Body–Mind–Spirit Social Work treatment helps client not only to deal with the problems at hand but also aims to nurture the "self" and enhance the self-healing and self-balancing abilities of individuals and families. Even when treatment ends, the process of becoming continues. After all, the end of treatment opens up a new phase of becoming for the client.

III

Applications and Treatment Effectiveness

10

The Efficacy of the Integrative Body–Mind–Spirit Group and Social Support Group on Female Breast Cancer Patients

INTRODUCTION

Breast cancer is the most common form of cancer diagnosed among women in Hong Kong (Hong Kong Cancer Registry, Hospital Authority, 2004). Not only is breast cancer a menacing threat to physical health, but it also disrupts the harmony of our physical bodies, our emotions, and our spiritual well-being. Unfortunately, rarely is the disruption confined to just the physical level. Emotional health consequently deteriorates and threatens our spiritual beliefs, values, and meanings of life.

METHODS

This is a randomized controlled trial study that examines the feasibility of an Integrative Body–Mind–Spirit group (I-BMS) for improving psychosocial outcomes in female breast cancer patients in Hong Kong. Given that social support is an important aspect in group interventions for cancer patients (Helgeson, Cohen, Schulz, & Yasko, 2000, 2001), this study aims to identify effects of Integrative Body–Mind–Spirit intervention other than the effects of social support in group treatment. For this purpose, the study used social support group (SS group) as a comparison group. The study hypothesized that participants in the I-BMS group would have better mental adjustment to cancer, emotional control, posttraumatic growth, and quality of life than participants in the SS group. Salivary cortisol was used as the physiological measure representing the physiological stress level and healthy functioning of the hypothalamus-pituitary-adrenal (HPA) axis. It was considered a major indicator of an altered physiological state in response to stressful stimulation (Kirschbaum & Hellhammer, 1989) such as stress experienced by cancer patients (Turner-Cobb, Sephton, Koopman, Blake-Mortimer, & Spiegel, 2000; Van der Pompe, Antoni, Visser, & Garssen, 1996).

Treatment Conditions

Intervention group

The intervention group adopted Integrative Body–Mind–Spirit model in treatment (Chan, Ho et al., 2001). Participants met consecutively for 5 weekly sessions, each lasting 3 hours. The focus of treatment is placed on empowering participants for self-healing and opportunities for growth and transformation. Participants were encouraged to face cancer positively, to realize the interconnectedness of their physical health with their emotions and their spiritual well-being, to help themselves and others, and to learn ways to develop a healthy lifestyle. Table 10–1 summarized the themes and objectives of each group session.

TABLE 10–1. Summary of Session Themes and Objectives

SESSION THEMES	OBJECTIVES
Session one: The Interconnectedness of Body, Mind, and Spirit	Introducing the concept of holistic health: emotions, thoughts and physical health can affect each other. Regaining autonomy to heal oneself.
Session two: Letting Go	Letting go and accepting mishaps in life. Evaluating gains and losses from cancer.
Session three: Forgiveness	Forgiveness and self-love as the keys to joy and peace of mind. Accepting mishaps in life.
Session four: Self-Transformation	Appreciation for oneself. Sharing transformations and growth. Planning and commitment to goals.
Session five: Helping Others	Giving as a means to happiness. Planning and taking action to help self and others.

Control group

A social support group served as the control group. Participants met consecutively for 5 weekly sessions, each lasting 3 hours. A social worker, who takes part in all five sessions, would first explain the importance of peer social support. Aside from that, participants were not offered any structured program or educational materials and were free to decide what they would like to do or discuss in their scheduled time.

Research Participants

From September 2002 to February 2005, female breast cancer patients were recruited from the oncology units of two hospitals in Hong Kong into this randomized study. Formal consent was obtained from patients prior to their participation in the study. Exclusion criteria for research participation included the following: (1) central nervous system metastases, (2) stage IV breast cancer or life expectancy of less than 3 months as assessed by the treating oncologist, (3) recurrence prior to study, (4) presence of other cancers, (5) major psychiatric illness (other than depression or anxiety) within 1 year prior to the study, and (6) pregnancy or serious illnesses (including concomitant or systemic diseases) that limit life expectancy to less than 10 years.

Eligible participants who completed the Integrative Body–Mind–Spirit intervention ($N = 27$) were diagnosed on average 20 months before recruitment, and their mean age was 48. In the SS group ($N = 36$), participants had a mean age of 47 and were diagnosed on average 23 months prior to recruitment. There were no significant differences between the two groups on all demographic variables (Table 10–2).

Method of Data Collection

All eligible patients were assessed before the intervention in a pre-group individual interview, primarily aimed at clarifying expectations and psychologically preparing them for the five intervention sessions. Baseline psychosocial outcome measurements were taken at this point by the following self-administered questionnaires:

The Chinese posttraumatic growth inventory (PTGI)

Adapted from Tedeschi and Calhoun's (1996) Posttraumatic Growth Inventory, the Chinese PTGI consists of 21 items tapping on perceived positive changes in life as a result of the cancer crisis (Ho, S. M. Y., Chan, & Ho, 2004). The six-point Likert scale covers four dimensions of posttraumatic

TABLE **10–2.** Patients' Demographic and Clinical Information

	I-BMS ($N=27$)		%	SS ($N=36$)		%	t	χ^2
	N	MEAN (SD)		N	MEAN (SD)			
Age (years)	27	47.9 (5.9)	–	35	46.9 (5.7)	–	.66	–
Months since diagnosis	27	19.8 (14)	–	35	22.5 (12)	–	–.83	–
Mastectomy *(those who did not have mastectomy had lumpectomy)*	13	–	66	20	–	62.7	–	0.5
Income (HK$ per month)	25	7280 (12,000)	–	32	12,641 (12,300)	–	–1.6	–
Employment								9.07
Retired	4	–	14.8	1	–	2.9	–	–
Homemaker	9	–	33.3	11	–	31.4	–	–
Part-time	4	–	14.8	5	–	14.3	–	–
Full-time	7	–	25.9	18	–	51.4	–	–
Other	3	–	11.1	0	–	0	–	–
Education								0.29
Primary school	4	–	14.8	5	–	14.3	–	–
Lower secondary school	4	–	14.8	4	–	11.4	–	–
Upper secondary school	11	–	40.7	16	–	45.7	–	–
Matriculated	2	–	7.4	3	–	8.6	–	–
University	6	–	22.2	7	–	20	–	–
Number of children								5.48
None	7	–	25.9	14	–	40	–	–
One	6	–	22.2	5	–	14.3	–	–
Two	10	–	37	10	–	28.6	–	–
Three or more	4	–	14.8	6	–	17.2	–	–
Marital status								1.33
Single	5	–	18.5	9	–	25.7	–	–
Married	21	–	77.8	24	–	68.6	–	–
Divorced/separated/ widowed	1	–	3.7	2	–	5.8	–	–

I-BMS–denotes Integrative Body–Mind–Spirit group, SS–denotes social support group.

growth: Interpersonal (score range: 0–15), Life Orientation (score range: 0–10), Spiritual (score range: 0–15), and Self (score range: 0–35). Confirmatory factor analysis further introduced the Intrapersonal subscale (score range: 0–60). Total scores range from 0 to 105, and higher scores indicate greater growth. The Chinese version has been validated and demonstrates good internal consistency.

Chinese mini-mental adjustment to cancer scale (Mini-MAC)

The Mini-MAC identifies attitudes and coping styles of cancer patients toward their illness on a four-point Likert scale (Ho, Wong, Chan, Watson, & Tsui, 2003). The Chinese version of the original Mini-MAC (see Watson, Greer et al., 1988) holds a three-factor structure including Negative Emotions (score range: 0–48), which includes helpless, hopeless, and preoccupied coping styles, and Positive Attitudes (score range: 0–27), including fighting spirit and fatalistic coping. The third subscale, Cognitive Avoidance (score range: 0–12), measures avoidance in thinking about cancer.

Chinese emotional control scale (CECS)

CECS measures the degree to which the participant controls the expression of negative emotional reactions (Ho, R. T. H., Chan, & Ho, 2004). Its three sub-factors include the control of anger (score range: 7–28), anxiety (score range: 7–28), and depressed mood (score range: 7–28), otherwise known as depression. Higher scores indicate a greater suppression of the emotion. Designed primarily for cancer patients, the scale proved to be largely free of social desirability, and the Chinese version had reliabilities comparable to the English one (Watson & Greer, 1983).

Chinese 12-item short form health survey (SF-12)

The study administered the Chinese SF-12 Health Survey (Lam, Tse, & Gandek, 2005) to measure health-related quality of life in participants. The standard SF-12 was abbreviated from the original SF-36 and yields the Physical Component Score and the Mental Component Score. The two components respectively measure one's physical functioning and emotional well-being. Higher scores indicate more favorable health and quality of life. The mean score for either component in the Hong Kong population is 50 (SD = 9.5).

Salivary cortisol

Salivary cortisol was used as a physiological stress marker. Participants were asked to provide a saliva sample at five prescribed times (on waking up, 45 min after waking up, 12 p.m., 5 p.m., and 9 p.m.) on two consecutive days before and after the program. Salivary cortisol was determined using an enzyme-linked immunoabsorbent assay kit (EIA) (Salimetrics, Inc.). Cortisol levels were presented in mean, total level (area under the curve), and diurnal slope.

Following baseline assessment, participants were randomized into their respective intervention groups. Randomization was performed by manual selection of sealed envelopes containing numbers representing the participants by a member of staff who was blind to the research project in our center. Both the I-BMS group and the SS group consist of five consecutive weekly sessions, each lasting for 3 hrs. After the final session, participants were once again asked to complete the questionnaires above.

Method of Data Analyses

Analyses were only performed on participants who attended all five intervention sessions of either group. The effect of each intervention was examined using t-test and effect size between baseline and post-intervention measurements for each outcome measure. Comparisons between intervention effects were analyzed by analysis of variance between the magnitude of score changes in each group (as calculated by the difference between pre-intervention and post-intervention scores).

RESULTS

Integrative Body–Mind–Spirit Group

Baseline levels of psychosocial well-being

Table 10–3 summarizes the baseline and post-intervention levels of the psychosocial well-being of the Integrative Body–Mind–Spirit group. Baseline scores indicate that, in general, participants were doing average in most psychosocial measurements prior to intervention. Scores on the PTGI and SF-12 were middle ranged or proximal to general population levels. The baseline Mini-MAC indicated that participants were not inclined toward any particular coping style, although there was a slight bias toward positive rather than negative coping. CECS was near average (mean = 55.9), although much higher scores were reported by Iwamitsu et al. (2003) on Japanese breast cancer patients (mean = 31.7). This expands on the popular notion that Chinese cancer patients tend to be more suppressive than their counterparts from different cultures, even other Asians.

Intervention effects

Psychosocial effects.   Integrative Body–Mind–Spirit intervention demonstrated positive improvements in all four psychosocial domains being measured, including posttraumatic growth, cancer coping, emotional expressiveness, and quality of life (Table 10–3).

TABLE **10–3.** Baseline and Post-Intervention Scores of the Integrative Body–Mind–Spirit Group

		Body–Mind–Spirit Intervention						
		Baseline (T0)		Post-Intervention (TP)			t	p
	N	MEAN	SD	MEAN	SD	ES		
Posttraumatic Growth								
Interpersonal	23	9.7	2.5	10	1.7	0.1	−0.74	.47
Intrapersonal	26	37.7	7.5	41.6	7.9	0.5	−2.94	.01**
Life Orientation	23	5.5	1.9	5.7	1.5	0.1	−0.52	.61
Spiritual	26	9.1	2.2	10.3	2.1	0.6	−2.61	.02*
Self	25	23.2	5.1	25.6	5.5	0.5	−3.36	.00**
Total Score	23	65.5	13.3	71.9	12.4	0.5	−3.51	.00**
Mini-Mental Adjustment to Cancer								
Positive Attitude	26	18.5	3.6	20	3.6	0.4	−2.05	.05*
Negative Emotions	23	17.8	9.1	14.4	7.5	0.4	1.98	0.06
Cognitive Avoidance	24	7.1	2.1	7.5	2.8	0.2	−0.83	.42
Chinese Emotional Control Scale								
Anger	24	19.8	4.2	18.9	3.2	0.3	1.21	.24
Anxiety	23	19	3	18.1	3	0.3	1.18	.25
Depressed Mood	23	16.9	5.2	15	3.5	0.4	2.38	.03*
Total Score	23	55.9	11.2	51.9	7.8	0.4	2.18	.04*
Quality of life (SF-12)								
Physical Component	23	43.6	6.8	48.8	5.7	0.8	−3.05	.01**
Mental Component	23	47.3	7.6	50.8	7.3	0.5	−1.88	.07
Salivary Cortisol								
Mean (ln nmol/l)	18	1.20	0.35	1.24	0.33	0.03	−0.38	.71
AUC (nmol/l)	18	57.12	24.19	54.31	21.66	0.03	0.51	.62
Diurnal Slope (nmol/l/hr)	18	−0.13	0.04	−0.12	0.04	0.26	−0.76	.46

Note: *$p \leq .05$, **$p \leq .01$.

1. Posttraumatic growth: Integrative Body–Mind–Spirit group participants demonstrated significant improvements in posttraumatic growth ($ES = 0.5$) particularly in the areas of "Self" ($ES = 0.5$) and "Spiritual" ($ES = 0.6$). The Self dimension refers to the cognitive dimension of growth (Ho, S. M. Y., Chan, & Ho, 2004), for instance, self-confidence, ability to express feelings, appreciation and acceptance of life, or formulating new directions. The greatest improvement, nevertheless, took

place in the Spiritual subscale. This subscale refers not to one's connection with God or supreme power but rather one's philosophical understanding of life, such as the beauty of life, feelings of self-reliance, and an understanding of spiritual matters. Improvements in this subscale echo the spiritual element of the Integrative Body–Mind–Spirit model, which also stresses building inner strength and looking at things from a positive light.

Both the Self and Spiritual dimensions fall under the Intrapersonal subscale ($ES = 0.5$), indicating that growth was focused more on oneself rather than being relational. Ho, S. M. Y., Chan, & Ho, (2004) suggested that posttraumatic growth among cancer survivors could be broadly separated into the two dimensions of Intrapersonal and Interpersonal growth. Interpersonal growth refers to feelings of closeness and compassion for others. Despite encouraging altruism, Integrative Body–Mind–Spirit intervention did not appear to be as successful in promoting Interpersonal growth as it did the other domains of growth.

2. Cancer coping: Upon group completion, Positive Attitude, which depicts positive coping styles, including proactive spirit and acceptance of fate, significantly improved ($ES = 0.4$). It should be noted that items pertaining to acceptance of fate do not refer to a passive acceptance of cancer but rather an acceptance that life is not entirely under our control and, because of this, we should enjoy every moment of it. With that in mind, participants after the I-BMS group became more determined not to succumb to cancer while also accepting their own limitations.

Negative coping styles (Negative Emotions) fell with equivalent effect size ($ES = 0.4$), despite being only near significance ($p = .06$), indicating a decrease in ruminating over cancer and a sense of helplessness.

3. Emotional Control: Despite scoring the lowest of the subscales, the depression factor experienced a further significant drop after Integrative Body–Mind–Spirit intervention ($ES = 0.4$). Anger ($ES = 0.3$) and anxiety ($ES = 0.3$) subscales also decreased with a mild–moderate effect size; however, their declines did not reach significance. Nonetheless, total the CECS score decreased ($ES = 0.4$). In short, participants after Integrative Body–Mind–Spirit intervention were generally less suppressive of their negative affect, particularly depressed mood.

4. Quality of Life: Participants' quality of life remarkably improved following intervention. The physical component score drastically improved ($ES = 0.8$), implying amelioration in general physical health and functioning. Similarly, the mental component score showed marked improvement ($ES = 0.5$) but was not significant ($p = .07$).

5. Physiological Effects, Salivary Cortisol: The three indices of salivary cortisol level—mean, total level (AUC), and diurnal slope—did not show significant changes after the intervention, suggesting a stable cortisol level and HPA axis functioning presented in this group of cancer patients; or the changes were neutralized within the group.

In order to explore the relationship between psychosocial and physiological variables, correlation studies were conducted firstly on cross-sectional relationship in pre-group data and secondly on longitudinal relationship between pre-group and post-group data. Results are shown in Tables 10–4a and 10–4b. Negative coping style was the only psychosocial variable showing relationships to cortisol variables both before and after intervention. Higher negative emotion toward cancer associated with more total cortisol secretion (AUC) before intervention ($r = .50$, $p = .01$). After intervention, significant correlations were still found between negative emotion and total cortisol level ($r = .59$, $p = .007$). Daily mean cortisol concentration had the same relationship with negative emotion ($r = .52$, $p = .02$), implying a negative influence or negative coping style on physiological stress level. In addition, the mental component score of the quality of life measure was found to associate with diurnal cortisol slope after intervention ($r = .55$, $p = .02$). A higher score related to a steeper cortisol slope (more negative), indicating better HPA axis functioning (Table 10–4).

Social Support Groups

Baseline levels of psychosocial well-being

Table 10–5 shows the baseline and post-intervention psychosocial measures of SS Group. Psychosocial measures at baseline were about average and demonstrated patterns similar to the intervention group at baseline. However, despite randomization, baseline comparisons between I-BMS group and SS group revealed that the I-BMS group had significantly lower suppression of depressive affect ($ES = 0.2$) as well as posttraumatic growth in spirituality ($ES = 0.5$) prior to intervention.

Social support groups—intervention effects

Psychosocial effects. Compared with I-BMS group, SS group demonstrated less distinct improvements after the group intervention. The physical component score of SF-12 was the only measurement with statistically significant amelioration ($ES = 0.6$). The control over anxiety expression notably increased ($ES = 0.4$), although it was not statistically significant. Apart from those changes, no other changes in psychosocial measurements could

TABLE 10–4a. Correlations of Mean Cortisol Levels, Total Cortisol Levels, Diurnal Slope, and Psychosocial Variables before Intervention (N = 26)

	PTGI	INTER	INTRA	MAC	NEGE	POSA	CA	ECS	ECA	ECX	ECD	SF_P	SF_M
Pre_Mean	-.10	.00	-.10	.24	.28	-.07	.07	-.03	-.18	.08	.05	-.13	-.15
Pre_AUC	-.14	.02	-.16	.45*	.50*	-.17	.28	.05	-.03	-.07	.17	-.20	-.32
Pre_Slope	-.05	-.21	.01	.01	.12	-.19	-.13	.16	.06	.34	.11	.16	.33

Note: *p ≤ .05, **p ≤ .01. Pre_—pre-intervention data, mean—log transformed mean cortisol concentration (ln nmol/l), AUC—total cortisol level (area under the curve, nmol/l), Slope—diurnal cortisol slope (nmol/l/hr), PTGI—Posttraumatic Growth Inventory, Inter—interpersonal, intra—intrapersonal, NegE—Negative emotions, PosA—positive attitude, CA—cognitive avoidance, MAC—mental adjustment of cancer, ECS—Courtauld emotional control scale, ECA—control of anger, ECX—control of worry, ECD—control of depressed mood, SF_P—physical dimension of short form-12, SF_M—mental dimension of short form-12.

TABLE 10–4b. Correlations between Pre-Group Psychosocial Variables and Post-Group Mean Cortisol Level, Total Cortisol Level, and Diurnal Slope (N = 19)

	PTGS	INTER	MAC	NEGE	POSA	CA	ECS	ECA	ECW	ECD	SF_P	SF_M
Pt_Mean	-.21	.18	.46*	.52*	-.13	.14	.05	.07	.04	.03	.15	-.43
Pt_AUC	-.24	.18	.55**	.59**	-.20	.31	.22	.25	.17	.18	-.03	-.30
Pt_Slope	.17	.14	.35	.34	.04	.15	-.05	.19	-.27	-.11	-.24	-.55*

Note: *p ≤ .05, **p ≤ .01, Pt—post-intervention data.

TABLE **10–5.** Baseline and Post-Intervention Scores of Social Support Groups

				Social Support Groups				
		Baseline (T0)		Post-Intervention (TP)			t	p
	N	MEAN	SD	MEAN	SD	ES		
Posttraumatic Growth								
Interpersonal	33	9.2	3.3	9.2	3.1	0	0.13	0.9
Intrapersonal	32	34.2	12.8	35.7	10.2	0.1	−0.88	0.38
Life Orientation	34	5.7	2.8	5.8	2.4	0	−0.24	0.81
Spiritual	33	7.7	3.5	8.4	2.7	0.2	−1.46	0.15
Self	34	20.8	7.6	21.3	6.7	0.1	−0.44	0.66
Total Score	31	59.7	22.5	62.4	18.1	0.1	−0.92	0.36
Mini-Mental Adjustment to Cancer								
Positive Attitude	33	18.9	4.2	18.7	3.9	0	0.3	0.77
Negative Emotions	33	16.1	7.7	16.5	7.4	0.1	−0.55	0.58
Cognitive Avoidance	34	6.9	2.9	7	3	0	−0.33	0.74
Chinese Emotional Control Scale								
Anger	33	18.9	3.7	18.9	4.1	0	0.04	0.97
Anxiety	34	16.7	2.6	17.7	2.4	0.4	−1.85	0.07
Depression	33	15.5	3.6	16.1	4.3	0.1	−0.75	0.46
Total Score	33	51.3	8.2	52.7	9.2	0.2	−0.88	0.39
Quality of life (SF-12)								
Physical Score	32	40.3	6.1	44.6	8	0.6	−2.7	0.01*
Mental Score	32	47.7	6.6	48.6	7.6	−0.1	−0.53	0.6
Salivary Cortisol								
Mean (ln nmol/l)	34	1.18	0.39	1.24	0.32	0.17	−0.78	0.44
AUC (nmol/l)	34	62.55	21.26	59.13	17.59	0.20	0.78	0.44
Diurnal Slope (nmol/l/hr)	34	−0.12	0.07	−0.12	0.04	0.14	0.78	0.44

Note: *$p \leq .05$.

be observed. In short, participants after SS group enjoyed better health and functioning but became slightly more suppressive of feelings of anxiety (Table 10–5).

Physiological effects. As in I-BMS group, SS group did not demonstrate any effect on any of the cortisol indices. A correlation study on pre-intervention data indicated positive copying attitude related to diurnal cortisol slope ($r = .36$, $p = .03$) (Table10–6a). Higher fighting spirit and fatalistic attitude associated with higher diurnal slope (flatter). Pre-intervention Negative Emotion also related significantly but reversely to post-intervention

TABLE 10–6a. Correlations of Mean Cortisol Levels, Total Cortisol Levels, Diurnal Slope, and Psychosocial Variables before Intervention (n = 35)

	PTGI	INTER	INTRA	MAC	NEGE	POSA	CA	ECS	ECA	ECX	ECD	SF_P	SF_M
Pre_Mean	-.07	-.05	-.08	.01	.05	-.13	.10	.14	.24	-.02	.08	.06	-.06
Pre_AUC	-.03	.04	-.05	-.11	-.03	-.15	-.08	.21	.29	.10	.11	-.05	-.00
Pre_Slope	-.10	-.21	-.10	.20	-.07	.36*	.33	.02	.03	-.09	.10	.23	.08

Note: *p ≤ .05, Pre_—pre-intervention data, mean—log transformed mean cortisol concentration (ln nmol/l), AUC—total cortisol level (area under the curve, nmol/l), Slope—diurnal cortisol slope (nmol/l/hr), PTGI—Post-traumatic Growth Inventory, Inter—interpersonal, intra—intrapersonal, NegE—Negative emotions, PosA—positive attitude, CA—cognitive avoidance, MAC—mental adjustment of cancer, ECS—Courtauld emotional control scale, ECA—control of anger, ECX—control of anxiety, ECD—control of depressed mood, SF_P—physical dimension of short form-12, SF_M—mental dimension of short form-12.

TABLE 10–6b. Correlations between Pre-Group Psychosocial Variables and Post-Group Mean Cortisol Level, Total Cortisol Level, and Diurnal Slope (n = 34)

	PTGS	INTER	INTRA	MAC	CA	NEGE	POSA	ECS	ECA	ECX	ECD	SF_P	SF_M
Pt_Mean	-.14	-.05	-.15	-.28	-.06	-.31	-.08	.08	-.01	-.11	.27	-.05	.41*
Pt_AUC	-.11	-.04	-.13	-.51**	-.20	-.54**	-.12	-.08	-.14	-.17	.10	-.04	.29
Pt_Slope	-.08	-.08	-.07	.14	.38*	-.03	.12	.12	.15	-.01	.11	.07	-.16

Note: *p ≤ .05, **p ≤ .01, Pt—post-intervention data.

overall levels of cortisol ($r = .54$, $p = .00$), indicating discrepancy or changes that happened during or after intervention that might lead to changes in the way that coping style could normally affect physiological stress (Table 10–6b). Similar things might happen to the participants with better mental functioning at baseline, leading to higher mean cortisol level after intervention ($r = .41$, $p = .02$). Cognitive avoidance at baseline had a moderate but significant relationship with diurnal cortisol slope after intervention ($r = .38$, $p = .03$). An avoidance coping attitude tended to have adverse effects on HPA axis functioning (flatter slope), or result in higher evening cortisol level.

Comparing Integrative Body–Mind–Spirit Group and Social Support Group

There was initial empirical evidence that participants of the I-BMS groups experienced significantly greater improvements in more psychosocial domains compared with participants of the SS groups. Further analysis using ANOVA identified areas where the intervention effects of the two groups statistically differed. Details are listed in Table 10–7.

Emotional control

Emotional control is the area where the two intervention effects differed most, particularly in the anxiety ($F_{(1, 55)} = 4.35$, $p = .04^*$) and sadness control ($F_{(1, 54)} = 4.69$, $p = .03^*$). Whereas the I-MBS group decreased in the suppression of these emotions (total score decreased by about 5 percent), suppression levels increased in the SS group (2 percent increment). It is evident that peer support groups discourage participants from displaying feelings of anxiety and sadness. With appropriate directive psychosocial intervention, participants demonstrate a higher readiness to express negative affect. Integrative Body–Mind–Spirit intervention eases participants into a deeper understanding of their emotions, confronts their sources of pain, and offers those who are less verbally explicit of their emotions other media of expression such as drawing or breathing exercises.

Cancer coping

Changes in negative cancer coping, despite not reaching statistical significance for individual intervention effects, demonstrated distinct trends between I-BMS group and SS group ($F(1, 54) = 4.94$, $p = .03$). The negative emotions subscale of the former group declined by 7 percent as opposed to a 1 percent increment in the SS group.

TABLE **10–7.** ANOVA Results of Comparing Integrative Body–Mind–Spirit Group and Social Support Group

Differences between Groups: Changes in Scores						
		N	MEAN	SD	F	P
Posttraumatic Growth						
Interpersonal	I-BMS	26	−0.31	2.1	0.21	.65
	SS	33	0.09	4		
Intrapersonal	I-BMS	23	−3.87	6.3	1.2	.28
	SS	32	−1.44	9.2		
Life Orientation	I-BMS	26	−0.23	2.3	0.05	.82
	SS	32	−0.09	2.2		
Spiritual	I-BMS	24	−1.21	2.3	0.44	.51
	SS	34	−0.74	2.9		
Self	I-BMS	25	−2.4	3.6	2.43	.12
	SS	33	−0.42	5.5		
Total Score	I-BMS	23	−6.43	8.8	0.98	.33
	SS	31	−2.71	16.3		
Mini-Mental Adjustment to Cancer						
Positive Attitude	I-BMS	25	−1.48	3.6	3.08	.08
	SS	33	0.18	3.5		
Negative Emotions	I-BMS	23	3.39	8.2	4.94	.03*
	SS	33	−0.45	4.7		
Cognitive Avoidance	I-BMS	24	−0.46	2.7	0.2	.66
	SS	34	−0.15	2.6		
Emotional Control						
Anger	I-BMS	24	0.96	3.9	0.73	.4
	SS	33	0.03	4.2		
Anxiety	I-BMS	23	0.96	3.9	4.35	.04*
	SS	34	−0.94	3		
Depressed Mood	I-BMS	23	1.87	3.8	4.69	.03*
	SS	33	−0.58	4.4		
Total Score	I-BMS	23	3.96	8.7	4.83	.03*
	SS	33	−1.39	9.1		
Quality of life (SF-12)						
Physical Score	I-BMS	23	−5.25	8.2	0.16	.69
	SS	32	−4.3	9		
Mental Score	I-BMS	23	−3.55	9	1.2	.28
	SS	32	−0.85	9		
Salivary Cortisol						
Mean Cortisol	I-BMS	18	0.04	0.41	0.03	.86
	SS	34	0.06	0.44		
Total Cortisol (AUC)	I-BMS	18	−2.81	23.32	1.14	.29
	SS	34	−3.42	25.46		
Diurnal Slope	I-BMS	18	0.01	0.06	0.01	.93
	SS	34	−0.01	0.06		

Note: *$p \leq$ .05, I-BMS denotes Integrative Body–Mind–Spirit group, SS denotes social support group.

Negative emotions encapsulate apprehensive and helpless attitudes toward cancer. Such negative attitudes are prevalent among cancer patients in remission, including vulnerability toward the limitations due to the cancer or a haunting anxiety toward recurrence (Fawzy, 1999). Unfortunately, these defeating thoughts are found to be positively correlated with anxiety and depression in women with breast cancer (Ho et al., 2003).

Our results suggest that the Integrative Body–Mind–Spirit intervention effectively alleviated participants' helplessness and ruminating thoughts toward cancer and relapse, which peer support alone cannot account for. Through learning ways to help themselves, such as acupressure or breathing techniques, a sense of autonomy can be fostered. As some patients remarked after the intervention (and we paraphrase): "I learned that cancer is not terminal disease . . . it is up to me to plan my own life." However, beyond the areas one has control over, such as the possibility of recurrence or various inevitable mishaps in life, acceptance and letting go are the keys to better adjustment.

Quality of life

Physical well-being as measured by SF-12 improved in both I-BMS group and SS group and hence is not attributable to unique elements of either group. The Integrative Body–Mind–Spirit model acknowledges the importance of physical health to mental and spiritual well-being, and hence various physical exercises and acupressure points are taught every session. Also, there has been a growing trend for cancer survivors to look for alternative therapies such as herbal supplements, or *taiji*. Peer support often involves information exchange regarding nutrition, exercise, and other ways to improve health. Consequently, it is not surprising why SS group also experienced a similar improvement in physical health. Ganz et al. (1996), in a study on breast cancer survivors' quality of life, found that physical health attains maximum recovery in the first year post-treatment, a period comparable to that of the participants of our study.

Posttraumatic growth

Likewise, posttraumatic growth showed general improvement after both I-BMS group and SS group interventions, despite the effect being comparatively less salient in the latter group. However, between-group differences were not enough to reach statistical significance. It is therefore likely that Integrative Body–Mind–Spirit intervention may have enhanced the process.

Salivary cortisol

None of the three salivary cortisol indices showed between-group differences in I-BMS group and SS group in ANOVA analysis.

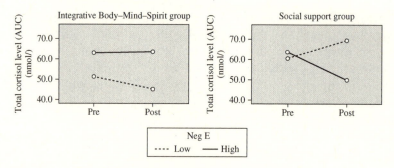

FIGURE 10.1. Negative emotions and cortisol levels, by interventions.

Negative coping style and salivary cortisol

Correlation studies indicate that negative coping style related significantly with salivary cortisol indices, in particular, the overall cortisol levels (AUC). A General Linear Model (GLM) analyses for repeated measures was then carried out to examine the effect of negative emotion on the changes of cortisol level in two intervention groups. Pre-total and post-total cortisol level (AUC) was used as the within-subjects factor, and different treatment group (I-BMS group and SS group) and baseline Negative Emotion (median split into High and Low groups) were the between-subject factors. Figure 10.1 is the graphical presentation of the results. In the group, participants with lower negative coping style benefited more than those who had a higher negative coping style. In the SS group, those who had a high negative coping style at baseline had a declined salivary cortisol level after the group. However, those who had a low negative coping style at the beginning showed increased cortisol level after the intervention. ANOVA analyses indicated a significant interaction effect for AUC × Groups × Negative Emotion $(F(1, 48) = 4.22, \; p = .04)$, indicating distinct differences in AUC in participants with high and low negative coping style in two intervention groups.

DISCUSSION

This chapter reports findings of a study that examines the psychosocial efficacy of BMS Group and SS group in a population of Hong Kong female breast cancer survivors. Findings provides initial empirical evidence of the effectiveness of I-BMS group in promoting posttraumatic growth, effective coping styles, expression of negative effect, and maintaining stable stress hormone level in female breast cancer survivors. By using social support groups as a comparison, we were also able to identify the positive effects of Integrative

Body–Mind–Spirit interventions in reducing negative coping and emotional suppression, maintaining stable stress hormone level in some participants; these outcomes are not due to the effects of peer support alone.

Literature extensively discuss cancer coping styles and the expression of emotions as predictors of psychosocial adjustment, which form the basis of various psychosocial interventions (Cameron, Booth, Schlatter, Ziginskas, & Harman, 2007; Classen et al., 2001). According to the theory of stress and coping (Lazarus & Folkman, 1984), the way one copes with a stressor is associated with subsequent psychological distress. Positive ways of coping, including acceptance and positive reappraisal, result in lower mood disturbances (Carver et al., 1993). Conversely, negative coping has been linked to clinical anxiety and depression and, therefore, this subscale of the Mini-MAC is deemed most useful in evaluating psychosocial intervention programs in outcome studies (Ho et al., 2003).

Similarly, the detrimental effects of excessively suppressing negative emotions have been largely emphasized in literature. Although negative emotions and stress are common in the aftermath of cancer, suppressing them is found to be highly correlated to poor coping, depression, or even mortality (Iwamitsu et al., 2003; Temoshok, 1987; Weihs, Enright, Simmen, & Reiss, 2000). Eastern philosophy, however, does not merely encourage emotional expressiveness but stresses the need to find a moderate level at which affect should be expressed (Chan, Ho et al., 2001). Being overly conservative or expressive can exert negative effects on our organs. When designing psychosocial interventions for Chinese cancer patients, there is a need to take into account such imbedded cultural elements. Instead of simply indulging in an exploration and sharing of feelings, psychosocial interventions should aim to help members to find a proper balance and medium in which emotions can be effectively released.

Findings of this study indicated that peer support alone is insufficient to produce psychosocial improvements among women with breast cancer. Fawzy (1999), in a review of psychosocial interventions for cancer patients, pointed out the importance of professional guidance in group interventions. Peer support, which mainly involves discussions of immediate problems, may not be helpful unless there is appropriate guidance to help members manage the concerns raised. Moreover, conversations in support groups often become too engrossed in information sharing. Despite an obvious advantage of having members actively take care of their health, this can become overwhelming and stress inoculating for some, as different patients may have different information preferences (Meredith et al., 1996)—possibly explaining the rise in negative cancer adjustment following our SS group. However, the pertinence of this notion to our study is possibly confounded by the fact that the SS group had lower posttraumatic growth in Spirituality as well as the control of depressive affect at baseline, which may have contributed to its relative inefficacy.

Physiological outcome measure did not show any marked changes in either the I-BMS group or the SS group. However, results revealed a close relationship between negative coping style and salivary cortisol indices. Integrative Body–Mind–Spirit intervention could not reduce stress hormone level right after the intervention, but it did not cause any increase either. For those who had negative coping style, Integrative Body–Mind–Spirit intervention could help to decrease cortisol level slightly, whereas for others, cortisol level was kept stable before and after intervention. Promotion of inner peace and harmony in I-BMS group, leading to less emotional fluctuation, might contribute to this result. In the SS group, inconsistent effects on salivary cortisol level were observed. Group gathering seemed to benefit only those participants with higher negative coping style. Participants who are less negative in coping received adverse effects from the group. This finding echoes some of the previous studies about the adverse or even harmful effects of self-help or social support groups (Gray, Fitch, Phillips, Labrecque, & Fergus 2000; Helgeson et al., 2000; Ray, 1992). Disclosure of negative feelings without working on them might induce anxiety and distress in some members. Nonetheless, caution has to be taken to avoid over-interpretation of the results because of the small sample size. A larger sample in a future study may help verifying the findings.

Limitations in this study include between-group variations in baseline psychosocial measures, in particular, the posttraumatic growth in spirituality and the suppression of sadness. Although this difference is largely arbitrary after our randomization procedure, it could be a confounding factor to the study's findings. Whether one's susceptibility to group psychosocial interventions is adversely affected by a relatively lower suppression of sadness and less changes in posttraumatic spiritual growth as observed in the SS group has yet to be confirmed by replication studies and by exploring the effects on the interventions over a longer time span.

Overall, this study focuses on the immediate effects of Integrative Body–Mind–Spirit intervention; further studies are underway to investigate its maintenance efficacy. Future efforts can expand the realms of posttraumatic growth to enhance interpersonal growth and compassion for others and the impacts on physiological variables such as hormones and immunity. Furthermore, this study calls for an exploration of a greater arena of psychosocial and physiological domains in which the intervention model can benefit breast cancer patients.

Acknowledgments

We would like to express our sincere gratitude to all the participants in this study. Special thanks have to be made to Prof. Peter W. H. Lee, Dr. Samuel M. Y. Ho, Dr. Louis W. C. Chow, Dr. William Foo, and Dr. Jonathan S. T. Sham for their contributions to this project. We would also like to acknowledge all the people who provided help and support for the study: the staff in the Department of Clinical Oncology, Queen Mary Hospital; The Cancer Center, Queen Mary Hospital, and Patients Resource Center, Queen Elizabeth Hospital.

This study is supported by the CERG Grant of the Hong Kong Research Grants Council (RGC) (HKU7212/03H) and the Hong Kong Cancer Fund.

11

Improving the Quality of Life and Psychological Well-being of Patients with Colorectal Cancer

INTRODUCTION

Colorectal cancer (CRC) is a life-threatening disease that took the lives of 1,538 Hong Kong people in 2004 alone, and an average of 1,000 people per year since year 1999 (Hong Kong Cancer Registry, Hospital Authority, 2004). CRC was recently ranked as the second most common form of cancer and the second leading cause of cancer-related death. An average of 2,050 new CRC cases was registered yearly between 1999 and 2003, and 3,582 new cases were registered in 2004. Such an upward trend in both incidence rate and mortality rate observed over the past few years is alarming and poses much public health concern. While medical advances have brought about tremendous success in prolonging the lives of CRC patients, treatments are usually both invasive and traumatic, posing a wide range of negative effects on the physical and psychological health of the patients including respiratory and cardiac complications, chronic fatigue, and leakage (Bokey et al., 1995), depression, anxiety, and impaired concentration (Walker et al., 1997), and fear of recurrence and metastasis, death anxiety, anger and frustration, disruption in work and social activities, and strains in family relations (Cheung, Molassiotis, & Chang, 2003; Lee-Jones, Humphris, Dixon, & Hatcher, 1997; Mak, 2001; Sprangers, Taal, Aaronson, & Te Velde, 1995).

Such psychosocial distresses, in turn, further debilitate patients' physical well-being, leading to a vicious cycle of demoralization among the lives of CRC patients.

Conventional psychosocial treatment is usually based on cognitive-behavioral approaches (Tatrow & Montgomery, 2006) and physical exercise (McNeely et al., 2006), although findings regarding their effectiveness are mixed and inconclusive. Models that adopt the social cognitive framework, which recognizes the crucial interplay between physical and psychosocial factors in affecting the overall health status of cancer patients, have been found to be more effective (Graves, 2003; Meyer & Mark, 1995).

METHODS

This is a small randomized controlled trial study that examines the feasibility of an Integrative Body–Mind–Spirit (I-BMS) intervention group for improving the quality of life and psychological well-being among colorectal cancer patients in Hong Kong. The study hypothesized that participants in the I-BMS group would have better mental adjustment to cancer, emotional control, posttraumatic growth, and quality of life than participants in the control group.

Treatment Conditions

Participants met consecutively for 5 weekly sessions, each last 3 hours. The Integrative Body–Mind–Spirit (I-BMS) intervention consisted of specific thematic emphases such as normalization of traumatic experiences, letting go of the need for absolute attachments and acceptance of the unpredictability of life, forgiveness and self-love as the key to joy and peace of mind, and reinforcement and stabilization of long-term effects to change through social support and commitment to help others. Each session centred on a particular theme (refer to Table 10–1). The principle therapeutic components included in-depth sharing, emotional expression, meditation, and physical exercise. The I-BMS intervention aimed to foster a sense of control and independence and promote a positive and empowering spirit among CRC patients.

Each group consisted of 10 to 12 members and was led by two leaders, including one co-investigator and one medical social worker, both of whom were experienced in leading group therapy and in using the I-BMS intervention model.

Participants in the control group were provided with health education materials on CRC and its treatment, and no active interventions were offered at any stage of the study.

Research Participants

Patients were recruited from the Departments of Surgery and the Clinical Oncology Units from three hospitals in Hong Kong. Inclusion criteria included patients diagnosed with CRC, aged between 18 and 74 and with the ability to read and speak Cantonese. Patients with central nervous system metastases, serious concomitant disease and nonmalignant systemic disease, a history of psychiatric illness and those who were hospitalized or medicated for symptoms other than depression or anxiety, life expectancy of less than 3 months as assessed by the treating oncologist, a presence of other cancers, or presence of other major medical problems likely to limit life expectancy to less than 10 years were excluded from this study.

Finally, 172 patients were successfully recruited and randomized into the I-BMS intervention group ($n = 86$) and the control group ($n = 86$). There were no significant differences between the intervention and control group on all demographic variables. The mean age of the entire sample was 59.7 years (SD $= 10.7$), and ages ranged between 28 and 85 years. Although the mean age of the intervention group (mean $= 58.9$, SD $= 10.5$) was slightly lower that that of the control group (mean $= 60.5$, SD $= 10.8$), the difference was not statistically significant. Moreover, and as shown in Table 11–1, no significant difference was found in all other demographic characteristics between the intervention group and the control group.

TABLE **11–1.** Comparison of Demographic Characteristics between Participants in the Intervention and Control Groups

Demographics	Intervention ($n = 86$)		Control ($n = 86$)		t	p	χ^2	p
	MEAN (SD)	%	MEAN (SD)	%				
Age (years)	58.87 (10.53)		60.45 (10.82)		−.96	.34		
Sex							.563	.520
Male		36.4		31.0				
Female		63.6		69.0				
Marital status							.421	.963
Single		3.5		3.5				
Married/cohabiting		90.7		88.4				
Divorced/separated		1.2		2.3				
Widowed		4.7		4.7				
Number of children	2.31 (1.30)		2.47 (1.35)		−.77	.44		

			4.04	.671
Education				
None	4.7	5.9		
Primary	24.4	27.1		
Form 1 to 3	22.1	23.5		
Form 4 to 5	31.4	21.2		
Form 6 to 7	3.5	3.5		
Tertiary or above	14.0	16.5		
Other	–	2.4		
Work			4.89	.429
Full-time	12.8	21.7		
Part-time	4.7	8.4		
Retired	54.7	45.8		
Homemaker	23.3	19.3		
Other	4.7	4.8		

Method of Data Collection

Participants of the intervention group were assessed before the I-BMS intervention in a pre-group individual interview, primarily aimed at clarifying expectations and psychologically preparing them for the five intervention sessions. Participants of the intervention and control group completed the following self-administered questionnaires at pre-test (T0) and post-test (T1).

The Chinese version of the posttraumatic growth inventory (PTGI)

Originally developed by Tedeschi and Calhoun (1996), the PTGI, comprising 21 items, is one of the most popular instruments for measuring posttraumatic growth in research. Participants were asked to take their cancer diagnosis as their starting point and thereafter assess the degree of change that this negative life event has contributed to on a six-point Likert scale that ranged from 0 "not at all" to 5 "to a very great extent." The Chinese PTGI assess participants on four dimensions of growth: Self (seven items), Spiritual (three items), Life Orientation (two items), and Interpersonal Relationships (three items), the higher scores indicating greater growth. Reported internal consistency ranged from 0.43 to 0.80, and construct validity was well established (Ho, S. M. Y., Chan, & Ho, 2004).

The Chinese version of the mini-mental adjustment to cancer scale (Mini-MAC)

Originally developed by Watson, Greer, Young, Inayat, Burgess, & Roberston (1988), the Mini-MAC is a reliable and widely used instrument to assess coping with cancer among cancer patients. Comprising 29 items scored on a four-point Likert scale that ranges from 0 "Strongly Disagree" to 4 "Strongly Agree," the Chinese Mini-MAC assesses patients on the three dimensions of

Negative Emotions (16 items), Positive Attitude (nine items), and Avoidance Coping (four items), higher scores indicating better adjustment. Reported internal consistency ranged from 0.65 to 0.91, and construct validity was well established (Ho et al., 2003).

The Chinese (Hong Kong) SF-36 health survey

The SF-36 is a self-reporting instrument that is brief and has been widely validated as a summary measure of health status and quality of life (Ware & Sherbourne, 1992). Comprising 36 items, the Chinese Mini-MAC was aggregated into eight subscales: Mental Health (MH), Role limitation due to Emotional problems (RE), Vitality (VT), Social Functioning (SF), Bodily Pain (BP), General Health (GH), Physical Functioning (PF), and Role limitation due to Physical problems (RP). Scores are expressed in a standardized t-score metric, and each subscale is scored from 0 to 100, higher scores indicating better functioning. Reported internal consistency ranged from 0.65 to 0.87 and construct validity was well established (Lam, Gandek, Ren, & Chan, 1998).

Socio-demographic characteristics, including age, sex, education level, marital and employment status, as well as cancer stage were collected.

Method of Data Analyses

Repeated-measures ANOVA on each outcome measure were conducted to assess the effect of the I-BMS intervention. Specifically, main effects of Time (differences at baseline-T0 and post-test-T1), Group (differences existing between the intervention and control groups), and possible Time × Group interactions were tested for statistical significance.

RESULTS

Intervention Effects

Out of the total of 172 recruited participants, 157 patients successfully completed the study from T0 to T1, (75 in the intervention group and 82 in the control group), rendering an attrition rate of 19 percent. The main reasons for dropout were death (26 percent) and deteriorating health status (74 percent), which prevented the patients from continuing participation in the study. An attrition analysis shows no significant difference between those who completed the study and those who did not, in age, sex, cancer stage, education level, marital and employment status.

Table 11–2 summarizes the comparisons between the baseline (T0) and post-test (T1) scores of all the subscales of the three outcome measures of

TABLE 11-2. Repeated-Measures ANOVA of Pre-Test and Post-Test Measure of Intervention and Control Groups

| | Intervention Group | | | | | Control Group | | | | | Repeated-Measures ANOVA | | |
| | | T0 | | T1 | | | T0 | | T1 | | TIME (×) GROUP | | |
	n	MEAN	SD	MEAN	SD	n	MEAN	SD	MEAN	SD	p	F	df
Measures for Patients													
PTGI (Chinese)													
Life Orientation	64	4.22	2.14	5.08	2.27	64	3.84	2.31	3.59	2.07	.000**	13.01	1
Spiritual	64	3.67	2.59	5.69	2.20	64	3.14	2.38	3.16	1.90	.000**	29.01	1
Interpersonal	64	5.16	3.73	8.73	2.80	64	4.80	3.17	4.75	2.95	.000**	57.56	1
Self	64	10.45	7.20	19.17	5.03	64	9.02	6.74	9.13	6.27	.000**	71.93	1
Mini-Mac (Chinese)													
Positive Attitude	64	18.86	4.48	19.19	3.29	77	18.39	4.37	17.60	3.80	.05*	3.95	1
Negative Emotion	61	16.34	8.34	15.59	8.29	77	16.71	9.43	17.66	7.94	.10	2.69	1
Cognitive Avoidance	65	7.08	2.76	7.25	222	78	7.23	2.06	6.85	1.80	.06	3.54	1
SF-36													
Physical Functioning	68	75.81	20.49	79.56	19.14	80	78.44	20.20	75.88	16.40	.002**	10.35	1
Role Physical	67	54.48	43.94	54.48	39.63	80	60.63	41.29	60.00	35.49	.91	.01	1
Bodily Pain	67	20.15	20.93	20.90	21.09	79	19.87	20.10	21.27	18.35	.83	.05	1
General Health	66	52.19	20.94	52.58	9.86	78	57.24	21.22	51.15	10.53	.16	2.00	1
Vitality	69	59.28	20.02	64.71	18.65	79	62.03	21.99	61.77	20.65	.008**	7.17	1
Social Functioning	69	92.39	21.67	95.65	21.63	78	91.67	22.76	90.22	20.71	.034**	4.60	1
Role Emotional	68	66.67	37.77	61.76	41.64	80	64.58	39.81	65.42	37.29	.33	.954	1
Mental Health	69	73.68	18.32	77.51	25.89	79	73.32	17.22	72.91	16.13	.137	2.24	1

Note: * $p < .05$, ** $p < .01$.

241

PTGI, Mini-MAC, and SF-36. Findings indicated that there were significant Time × Group interaction effects in PTGI, the Positive Attitude subscale of Mini-MAC, and the Physical Functioning, Vitality, and Social Functioning subscales of SF-36. Positive changes in the intervention group from T0 to T1 were significantly greater than the changes observed in the control group.

Specifically, scores on all four subscales of the PTGI displayed significant Time × Group interaction effect. These included Life Orientation [$F_{(1, 126)} = 13.01$, $p = .000$], Spiritual [$F_{(1, 126)} = 29.01$, $p = .000$], Interpersonal [$F_{(1, 126)} = 57.56$, $p = .000$], and Self [$F_{(1, 126)} = 71.93$, $p = .000$]. In addition, the Positive Attitude subscale of Mini-MAC showed significant Time × Group interaction effect [$F_{(1, 139)} = 3.95$, $p = .05$]. Three subscales of SF-36 also showed significant Time × Group interaction effects. These include the Physical Functioning [$F_{(1, 146)} = 10.35$, $p = .002$], Vitality [$F_{(1, 146)} = 7.17$, $p = .008$], and Social Functioning [$F_{(1, 145)} = 4.60$, $p = .034$] subscales.

DISCUSSION

The purpose of this study is to evaluate the efficacy of the I-BMS intervention model for improving the psychological well-being and quality of life in patients with CRC. Findings provide initial empirical evidence of the effectiveness of I-BMS intervention to introduce significant positive changes in CRC patients. In particular, the impact was most prominent in facilitating growth after the traumatic cancer experience, in enhancing positive attitude, and in improving physical functioning.

Significant increase on the Positive Attitude subscale of the Mini-MAC in patients in the intervention group was observed, which was significantly higher than that in the control group. This highlights that I-BMS intervention, which focuses on the promotion of self-love, forgiveness, and acceptance, was effective in enhancing CRC patients' positive self-appraisal in relation to their illness. This finding could be important in reducing the many psychological symptoms often reported by CRC patients, including depression, death anxiety, anger and frustration, and social and family relational strain (Cheung et al., 2003; Lee-Jones et al., 1997; Sprangers et al., 1995).

Regarding quality of life, significant Time × Group interaction effect on the Physical Functioning, Vitality, and Social Functioning subscales of the SF-36 was found. This suggests that the core physical exercise component of the I-BMS intervention, which includes moderate activities, such as *taiji* and meditation, could improve CRC patients' physical health, energy level, and liveliness. The positive gains in physical health may also result from improvement in psychological well-being brought about by I—BMS intervention, as emotional health and physical health are intricately intertwined. The improvement in physical functioning and vitality is of particular importance, as critical functional impairments such as cardiac complications and chronic fatigue are often reported to complicate the recovery process in CRC patients (Walker et al., 1997). These in turn contribute to strained social life and poor quality of life (Cheung et al., 2003; Lee-Jones et al., 1997; Mak, 2001). The ability of I-BMS intervention to improve CRC patients' physical functioning and vitality is not only important in its own right but is also significant in other aspects of patients' lives. As our results show, participants in the intervention group demonstrated a marked increase in the subscale of Social Functioning compared to the control group. This may well suggest that, as a result of increased functional capacity and vivacity, CRC patients are more open to joining social activities, are more socially active, and at the same time feel less need to withdraw from the outside world and from human contact (Cheung et al., 2003; Sprangers et al., 1995). These promising results provide further evidence that the Integrative Body–Mind–Spirit model, which adopts a group modality to therapy and incorporates both Western therapeutic techniques and Eastern philosophies and practices, is effective in improving the quality of live of CRC patients.

Overall, perhaps the greatest contribution of the Integrative Body–Mind–Spirit model lies in its impressive ability to facilitate posttraumatic growth. As the findings show, various dimensions of growth were facilitated by I-BMS intervention in CRC patients. These include improvements in the life orientation dimension, which signified positive changes in life priorities; the spiritual dimension, which implied stronger faith, better understanding of spiritual matters, and feeling of self-reliance; the interpersonal dimension, which implied enhanced feeling of closeness and compassion to others; and the self-dimension, which reflected improved self-confidence, willingness to accept and express emotions, and better appreciation of life. In circumstances in which health problems are beyond the individual's control or ability to change, acceptance and willingness to endure pain are paramount in bringing about a more positive outlook of the illness as well as one's well-being. Moreover, the concept of letting go and forgiveness is another important component of the Integrative Body–Mind–Spirit model. By helping clients to let go of their bitterness and resentment toward their illnesses and the array of problems that accompany them, individuals will be able to resolve anger, destructive impulses, and grudges so as to attain emotional tranquility (Chan & Palley, 2005). The spiritual components of the Integrative Body–Mind–Spirit model may well have brought about the impressive overall life orientation changes that other forms of intervention may not be capable of achieving.

Despite all the promising results, I-BMS intervention was not successful in bringing about more positive changes in the Negative Emotion and Cognitive

Avoidance subscales of the Mini-MAC, as well as the five other subscales of the SF-36 among the participants. A comparison of the current study with an earlier study on breast cancer patients (Ho & Chan, 2002) shows a strikingly similar pattern of findings.

Although the preliminary results from this study are encouraging, some caveats should be kept in mind. Similar to other psychosocial intervention studies, findings from this study are negatively affected by the problem of attrition. Nonetheless, a synopsis of the aforesaid attests to the efficacy of I-BMS intervention for improving the psychological well-being and quality of life in CRC patients. The immediate impact on positive attitude, growth through life crisis, physical and social functioning, and vitality is most prominent. The findings from this study have clear implications for clinical applications. Further studies should focus on the maintenance of positive changes over time. Process research to identify specific intervention components and mechanisms that contribute to therapeutic success should also be conducted.

Acknowledgments

The project was funded by a grant from the Health and Health Services Research Fund, Health, Welfare, and Food Bureau, Hong Kong SAR Government (Ref no: 02030111), and the Small Project Funding Program of the CRGC of the University Grant Council of the University of Hong Kong (Ref no: 10205189/12172/30300/323/01). The authors gratefully acknowledge and thank all the patients who participated in the study and the hospital staff for their heartfelt support and assistance in making this project successful.

12

Instilling Hope: The Efficacy of Integrative Body–Mind–Spirit Group Treatment for Female Patients with Depressive Disorders

INTRODUCTION

Depression is the one of the most prevalent mental health conditions affecting millions of people around the globe. The Global Burden of Disease study (Murray & Lopez, 1996) states that depression is a leading cause of disability and will account for 15 percent of diseases worldwide by the year 2020. In Taiwan, various treatment programs and approaches have been developed for treating depression. The Integrative Body–Mind–Spirit model (Chan, 2001) integrates concepts and practices from Western therapy, Eastern philosophies of Buddhism, Daoism, as well as Traditional Chinese Medicine (TCM) to create positive changes in clients. This chapter introduces and discusses findings of the efficacy of this model for Taiwanese patients with depressive disorders.

METHODS

This is a single-group pre-test and post-test study that used multiple methods to examine the feasibility of Integrative Body–Mind–Spirit group treatment with female patients with diagnoses of depressive disorders. Quantitative data measured the feasibility of this treatment in reducing symptoms of depression and improving quality of life in participants. Qualitative data collected from semi-structured interviews explored the complexity of participants' experiences of Integrative Body–Mind–Spirit treatment. A combination of quantitative and qualitative methods allowed us to develop a more comprehensive understanding of the mechanisms of change associated with Integrative Body–Mind–Spirit treatment for depression patients.

Treatment Conditions

The intervention group adopted Integrative Body–Mind–Spirit model for treatment (Chan, Ho et al., 2001). Participants met consecutively for 12 weekly sessions, each lasting 2 hr. An Integrative Body–Mind–Spirit group for treating clients with depressive disorders is characterized by four components:

(1) Treatment emphasizes the normalization of traumatic experiences and the view that suffering is a disguised opportunity for growth. We help clients accept and appreciate the meaning of suffering. We provide a context for patients to discover positive role models who have transformed themselves through working through life challenges and reinforce the wisdom of "no pain, no gain."

(2) Treatment provides a space for participants to explore and discuss the meaning of suffering, attachment, and letting go.

(3) Strategies for practicing forgiveness and self-love constitute key components to attaining joy and peace of mind. Clients are taught that negative emotions are derived from persistent grudges held in the mind. Thus, forgiving oneself and others helps to free one from negative energy and to learn self-love.

(4) Social support and a commitment to help others are ways to facilitate and maintain clients' efforts to find meaning in their suffering. The clients' sense of isolation and loneliness is therefore reduced.

Table 12–1 describes the objectives and content of Body–Mind–Spirit (BMS) treatment for patients with depressive disorders. The session themes included "growth through pain," "letting go and forgiveness," "loving yourself," and "transforming yourself." Body–mind–spirit group treatment consisted of 12 two-hour sessions, and participants met once every week.

Research Participants

Female outpatients who had a diagnosis of depressive disorders were recruited to participate in a 3-month Integrative Body–Mind–Spirit treatment group that

TABLE **12–1.** Integrative Body–Mind–Spirit Group for Female Patients with Depressive Disorders

SESSION THEMES	OBJECTIVES	CORE CONTENT OF THE PROGRAM
Growth through pain	Introduce the Integrative Integrative Body–Mind–Spirit concept and holistic health Understand the nature of loss and learn positive thinking attitudes Establish the positive attitudes of "transformation through suffering" and "gain through loss"	*Theme of the first session*: Regarding suffering from depression as a gift of life and growing through pain • Introduction to the course: introduce the goal of establishing holistic well-being • Make friends: introduce participants, personal favorites, and personal strengths • Share suffering from depression and learning goals for participating in group • The wisdom of "no pain no gain" • Breathing exercise • Homework assignment: road of life and picture of emotions *Theme of the second session*: Understanding the nature of emotions and loss, and thinking positively • Breathing exercise • Sharing assignment: picture of emotions • Power of thought • Sharing assignment: road of life • Loss and gain • Homework assignment: creative management of emotion and favorite song *Theme of the third session*: Introduction to effective emotion management • Breathing exercises • Sharing assignment: creative management of emotion • Guided imagery: integration with nature • Ways to be happy • Sharing assignment: favorite song

TABLE **12–1.** (*continued*)

SESSION THEMES	OBJECTIVES	CORE CONTENT OF THE PROGRAM
		• Hand massage exercises • Homework assignment: a self-love letter and appreciation of life
Loving yourself	Instill the importance of self-acceptance and self-love Affirm mastery of life skills Increase the sense of restoring comfort and joy in life Facilitate mutual learning and support Increase sensitivity to our own needs and the energy of our body Learn to love yourself	*Theme of the fourth session*: Understanding and caring for one's own needs • Breathing exercise • Sharing assignment: a self-love letter • Roots of happiness • Learn to love yourself • Hand massage exercises • Sharing assignment: appreciation of life • Homework assignment: my photos at different life stages *Theme of the fifth session*: Understanding personal strengths • Breathing exercises • Sharing assignment: my photos • Guided imagery: obtaining the power through yellow light • Hand massage exercises • Positive attitude toward life • Homework assignment: mirror exercises and a gift to myself *Theme of the sixth session*: Accepting oneself • Breathing exercises • Sharing assignment: mirror exercises • Positive attitude toward self • Sharing a gift to self • The ten techniques to longevity • Homework assignment: making a rainbow of forgiving
Letting go and forgiveness	Share insights of letting go and the barriers to forgiveness	*Theme of the seventh session*: Understanding impacts of rage and love on life

Facilitate positive views of one's emotional management skills

Identify strengths and positive coping strategies

Let go and accept the mishaps of life

Forgiveness for freedom from pain, to experience peace of mind and personal transformation

- Breathing exercises
- Sharing assignment: Rainbow of Forgiveness
- The roots of frustration
- Rage emotions and health
- Beliefs in forgiveness
- Homework assignment: a letter to him or her

Theme of the eighth session: Expressing rage and understanding the importance of letting go

- Breathing exercises
- Sharing assignment: a letter to him or her
- Chinese meanings of rage (怒) and Chinese wisdom of forgiveness (恕)
- Letting go exercises
- One-second hand techniques
- Homework: methods of forgiveness

Theme of the ninth session: Learning ways to forgive and to live a peaceful life

- Breathing exercises
- Sharing assignment: methods of forgiveness
- About letting-go story
- Guided image: love and forgiveness
- Shoulder massage
- Homework: A second gift to self and my support network

Transforming yourself

Appreciate and reinforce the action of self-love

Assist in transformation at the individual and interpersonal levels

Facilitate plans for further commitment to help others

Reinforce supportive networks in the future

Theme of the tenth session: Facilitating self-love

- Breathing exercises
- Sharing assignment: a second gift to self
- Group massage: shoulder massage
- Sharing assignment: my support network
- Homework: my growth and strengths

TABLE **12–1.** (*continued*)

SESSION THEMES	OBJECTIVES	CORE CONTENT OF THE PROGRAM
		Theme of the eleventh session: Recognizing strengths that were used to heal suffering from depression
		• Breathing exercises • Sharing assignment: my growth and strengths • Group massage: back massage • My new life now • Positive attitude toward life • Homework: blessing card for self
		Theme of the twelfth section: Developing future plans for future hope
		• Breathing exercises • Sharing assignment: blessing card for self • Toward transformation: my future goals and plans • Mutual support and encouragement among group members

was conducted from September 2004 to October 2004. With the approval of the head of the department of psychiatry and the patients' primary medical practitioners, the potential subjects obtained information about this study from psychiatrists of the outpatient department of psychiatry. With the permission of clients, psychiatrists provided the researcher with client contact numbers. The researcher contacted each client and arranged an in-person interview in a place determined by the client: the client's house, a restaurant near his or her home, or the researcher's office. During the interview, the subjects gave their written consent to participate in the study, after the purposes, risks, and benefits of the study were explained to them verbally and in writing. Those who reported current problems with substance abuse were excluded.

Fourteen participants completed the program. The average age was 35.79 (SD = 9.82). The majority of participants had attained a college education (71.6 percent). The majority of participants were also diagnosed with major depressive disorders (64.5 percent) (Table 12–2).

TABLE **12–2.** Demographics of Participants ($N = 14$)

	N	%
Marital status		
Single	6	42.9
Married	7	50.0
Divorced	1	7.1
Education level		
Junior high school	1	7.1
Senior high school	2	14.2
Bachelor's degree	10	71.6
Master's degree	1	7.1
Different types of depressive disorders		
Major depressive disorder	9	64.5
Major depressive disorder/recurrent	2	14.2
Neurotic depression	3	21.3
First onset?		
Yes	7	50.0
No	7	50.0

Quantitative inquiry

Method of data collection

Participants completed the Beck Depression Inventory (BDI) (Beck, Steer, & Garbin, 1988) and the Taiwanese version of the World Health Organization Quality of Life abbreviated version (QOL) (Yau, 2000) at pre-treatment and post-treatment. The BDI is a self-administered 21-item measure that is designed to assess the severity of the symptoms of depression, to monitor the beneficial or adverse effects of treatment, and to assess symptom changes over time. Statements denote symptom severity along with an ordinal continuum from absent (scored as 0) to mild (scored as 1) to severe (scored as 3). The responses are summed to determine possible scores ranging from 0 to 63, higher scores indicating a greater level of symptoms. Based on the study of psychiatric patients, BDI indicates a high internal consistency. Cronbach's alpha ranged from 0.76 to 0.95.

The Taiwanese version of the World Health Organization QOL abbreviated version is a 28-item self-administered instrument that assesses respondents' health status and responses to treatment. Participants are asked to assess their quality of life subjectively based on their experiences during the last 2 weeks. Statements denote five levels of satisfaction with quality of life and range from "not satisfied at all" (scored as 1), "somewhat satisfied" (scored as 2), "moderately satisfied" (scored as 3), "very satisfied" (scored as 4), to "extremely satisfied" (scored as 5). The total score is computed by summing the responses to the 28 items. A high score indicates a higher quality of life. Cronbach's alpha for the internal consistency of this instrument is 0.90.

Method of data analysis

Quantitative data was managed by the SAS system. The Wilcoxon signed-rank test was performed to examine the difference in reducing symptoms of depression and in improving quality of life before and after participating in the group program.

Qualitative Inquiry

Method of data collection

A semi-structured interview was conducted with each group's participants upon completion of the program. Open-ended questions were used to explore participants' perception of their experience of the program and effective treatment components for treating depressive disorders. Open-ended questions included "What leads you to think that the therapy was helpful or not helpful?" and "What do you think was the most impressive and interesting event that occurred during the therapy? Can you tell me why you think that it was the most impressive and interesting event?"

Method of data analyses

Content analysis (Miles & Huberman, 1994) was conducted to analyze the qualitative data. Themes emerged through examining qualitative data for the meanings of patents' views of the efficacy of BMS group therapy. Three members of the research team and an independent reviewer, who was invited to verify the validity and reliability of analysis, were involved in developing a thematic scheme. We reviewed randomly selected passages from all verbatim transcripts to explore their meanings and then discussed the meanings of emerging themes until agreement was reached. Thirty percent of interview transcripts were analyzed for distinguishing themes, which illustrated different aspects of therapeutic mechanisms. The themes illustrated how group therapy worked to reduce symptoms of depression and to improve BMS holistic well-being in Chinese patients with depressive disorders.

RESULTS

Quantitative Data

Findings showed a decrease in the mean scores of the BDI from 33.0 at pre-treatment to 10.0 at program completion (Figure 12.1). In other words,

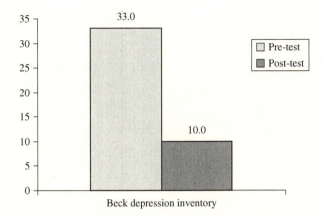

FIGURE **12.1.** Beck depression inventory BDI ($N = 14$).
Note: Wilcoxon signed-rank test $S = -52.5$, $p < 0.001$.

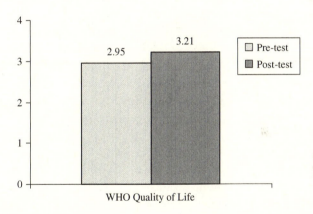

FIGURE **12.2.** Taiwanese version of the World Health Organization Quality of Life-abbreviated version ($N = 14$).
Note: Wilcoxon signed-rank test $S = 31.5$, $p = 0.04$.

the level of depression changed from severe to mild among participants. There was an increase in the mean scores of the Taiwanese version of the World Health Organization QOL from 2.95 at pre-treatment to 3.21 at program completion (Figure 12.2). The results showed that there was an increase in participants' life satisfaction from "somewhat satisfied" to "moderately satisfied."

Findings of the Wilcoxon signed-rank test indicated that there were significant differences in participants' level of depression ($S = -52.5$, $p < 0.001$) and quality of life ($S = 31.5$, $p = 0.04$) from pre-treatment to program completion. The observed changes were in the desirable direction.

Qualitative Data

In the pre-group individual interviews, participants were invited to describe their experiences of suffering from depressive disorders. The common reasons for suffering were struggling to fulfill expectations of appropriate behaviors in the family, while wishing to have autonomy. Participants who were in their late thirties and over reported that after they were married, they had worked hard and had sacrificed themselves to achieve expectations of their husbands and parents-in-law. Suppression of emotions was their common coping strategy in dealing with suffering. Their own needs and thoughts were not expressed, in order to maintain harmony in the family. Therefore, participants reported that they wanted to participate in the group to express their emotions and find solutions to their suffering. Those participants who were in their twenties and thirties described that they felt guilty for failing to fulfill expectations of their parents to be a good daughter. Their desire to be obedient and submissive as a filially pious daughter conflicted with their desire to be assertive and autonomous. Suppression was their way of maintaining the desired self-identity in the family. Thus, the reason for them to participate in the group was to have a place to share their suffering and to discover their true natures. In summary, the group participants wanted to release their suppressed emotions, uncover their unrevealed selves, and balance themselves between autonomy and harmony in the family.

During the semi-structured interviews, participants unanimously reported improvement in their holistic well-being, upon program completion. Emerging themes were identified pertaining to beneficial treatment components that helped transform participants' suffering into healing experiences. Each theme was clearly defined to ensure its distinct meanings from other themes. Eight emerging themes were identified: (1) depression as an opportunity for growth; (2) learning to relax physically; (3) understanding and expressing emotions and oneself; (4) viewing life stress positively; (5) uncovering inner strengths; (6) learning forgiveness, letting go, and living in the moment; (7) learning to love self and others; and (8) developing a helpful social support system.

Depression as an opportunity for growth

When participants tried to accept their illness and explore the meanings of suffering, they found they were better able to face their problems and to accept themselves and their lives.

Participant 1.   "After I fell ill, I had the opportunity to revisit many things in my life. Many things I had previously ignored came to mind, such as my relationship with family members and study problems. I had written two letters and read them in our group class. Did I say that there was a secret I could not tell anyone? After I saw a movie (that was showed in the group), I realized that it didn't need to be a secret. I told my therapist, my parents, and my friends about this secret. I saw the same thing from a different perspective. If I had not been depressed and ill, I would not have had the courage to face this."

Participant 2.   "I moved from resisting to accepting treatment under the professional and safe guidance of my therapist, who showed me how, using a special calm feeling, I could reveal depression and accept its meanings in life. After all I had been through, like the therapist said, suffering from depression is not awful; rather, it is a special gift. Due to the presence of depression in my life, I have had a good opportunity to explore feelings of uneasiness, agitation, and fear deep within my mind, to be fond of and cherish the child who had been ignored, held in a dark corner for a long time, and hurt mentally. Through these things, I learned to love myself."

Learning to relax physically

Participants found that relaxation methods combined with Western guided imagery and breathing and Chinese medical massage and acupressure points could help them relax and to focus on positive feelings.

Participant 3.   "Because of our children, I had a quarrel with my husband. My neck and shoulders were stiff. I tried the relaxation method taught by my therapist in the last group therapy session. After the children fell asleep, I went back to my room. I played the record player and made hot tea. I imagined myself as a single woman who did whatever she liked to do and felt free. After doing these exercises for about ten minutes, I felt better in my neck and shoulders."

Participant 4.   "When I feel *yu-men* (stagnation and pressure) in my chest, I stand in front of a window in our house and practice deep breathing. Sometimes, when I take deep breaths, I close my eyes and imagine a soft breeze blowing on me. I feel very cool and comfortable. So, when I feel annoyed, I close my eyes and enjoy the breeze."

Participant 5.   "The therapist taught us about hand exercises. This reminds me that it is good for me to massage my acupuncture points to release pressure."

Understanding and expressing emotions and self

Participants saw that group treatment helped them to understand the meanings of emotions and the impact of self-suppression on negative emotions. Such an understanding allowed them to accept and express the negative emotions and thoughts. They were healed after they expressed themselves truly and honestly.

Participant 3.   "People's emotions are wonderful things that are the symbol of honesty, of the 'inner self.' I realized that the reason I was able to gradually recover from depression was that the therapist persistently taught me to 'understand and accept emotions' (including the darker side of the self). When I stopped resisting and fully accepted my bad thoughts, I found myself becoming tougher and gradually recovering from depression. Of course, my family members are obviously aware of my 'change' into a 'hedgehog.' My reaction and power to fight back are stronger. I am no longer an obedient person, because I want to be honest, to face my feelings and not suppress them. By doing this, I can make myself healthier. When I recover from my illness, of course I will adjust to my 'sheep-like' character. But this sheep will be different from what it used to be. Even though I will still get angry, when I quarrel with others, I will be more assertive in attitude and tone. This is how my powerful depression 'forced' me to change my character."

Participant 6.   "Not like earlier, when I swallowed other people's emotions, I now express my own thoughts. I told my sister-in-law that, although I worked in the hospital, it was not my fault that I didn't know her daughter was admitted to the hospital. Rather, she should have taken the initiative to let me know about it. It is important to clarify the truth. I used to blame myself. Do you know how much I would do for her? I would call her and ask her if she took her medicine and if she felt better. I used to do these things, but this is the response I got: As long as I did not do well, I would be blamed for having made mistakes."

Participant 2.   "As I experienced high and low emotions during the treatment process, my therapist was there for me and helped me to deal with each uneasy thought and problem. We developed coping strategies step by step. In addition to 'speaking our thoughts inside our minds,' 'singing our inner feelings out,' and 'writing about reasons for problems,' we learned to clear the mind and spirit through engagement with the natural environment, doing exercises, receiving the love given by family members, staying in the safest situations, and seeing ourselves and our lives in a satisfactory way." (Case 2)

Viewing life stress positively

Narratives of participants described the benefit of sharing that helped them to reappraise their situations in a positive way. Positive emotions emerged when they were able to view their situations positively. Moreover, helping others not only can influence participants to consider their lives worthwhile and meaningful but also expanded their views of the world. Some examples are described below.

Participant 11.   "If we do not go out and do not talk to others, we will be isolated and feel miserable. But when we hear other people's situations, we feel that ours might not be the worst in the world. For example, other group members did not perceive my situation as too bad. At least my husband hands me his income. I am the one who controls the finance of my family. I feel better when I view my situation positively."

Participant 13.   "It is important for me to think about things positively. I think that I can change ways of thinking about things. For example, being a volunteer helps me distance from my unhappy life, engages in good deeds, and allows me to understand the outside world, which broaden my view of the world."

Uncovering inner strength

The therapist, by guiding participants to believe in their own power of healing their suffering, creates a space for them to be aware of and reconnect with their inner strengths. Participants' narratives showed that their inner strengths were uncovered when they began to understand their suppressed needs and emotions. They found that their discovered strengths helped them to manage their emotional and interpersonal distress.

Participant 7.   "Today the therapist pointed out that 'we are our own doctors' and that 'people have their own self-healing powers.' I have benefited from these ideas a lot."

Participant 3.   "I brought a painting of my emotions drawn with heavy black lines to the class. The therapist unexpectedly interpreted that 'the tree nearby appears to show fresh spirit. It seems to reveal the message that, although a person is currently experiencing the darkest time of life, there is still a strong and powerful base, like a vigorous tree. We need to make an effort to uncover our own inner supportive power, through which we will recover from illness.' The therapist's sharing is inspirational."

Participant 9.   "The therapist helps me to understand my emotional problems, thoughts, and values. I was influenced by others a lot of the time; I was confused. As a result, I could not understand what I really wanted and what my real feelings were . . . With the therapist's help, my strength and the powerful side of me emerged. After my positive self appeared, I began to think that the outside environment was not so bad. Subsequently, I began to feel happy and to develop good communication with my husband."

Learning forgiveness, letting go, and living the moment

Participants learned about the impact of practicing forgiveness on positive emotions through exploring meanings of tolerance as they engaged with their natural environments. Moreover, exploring meanings of existence and emphasizing living in the moment contributed to more positive emotions and views of self. Expressing suppressed anger and guilt to significant others was considered by participants an essential method of forgiveness.

Participant 3.   "The therapist asked me to find things related to the time I lived overseas. I found some photos and books. One of them was a photo of a field. The therapist wanted me to write a reflection on the field with the title of forgiveness. After I wrote it, I realized that there were many varied places on the good earth, which seemed to reveal that this world could tolerate different people and things. People could learn tolerance from nature to make them feel better."

Participant 5.   "With tears in my eyes, I asked my husband, 'When you understand your time in life is limited, will you still push your son to prepare for examinations, to put things in the right places, to clear shit up—these trivial things? Should we not emphasize the importance of how to cherish affection?' Live the moment is the significant change of life values after I got sick. Happiness, confidence, and healthy minds are priceless!"

Participant 6.   "About the group assignment on methods of forgiveness, I tried to tell my mom that father has been dead for many years. Every year, on my father's death anniversary, she would always tell me that I am a bad daughter. I was not there when my father died. I feel like I'm the one who is responsible for father's death. It makes me feel that I was always wrong, whatever I did. Recently, I brought all the letters that I had written to my father for the past 7 years to his grave. I had been not able to look at my father's photo on his grave, as I felt guilty. After paying respect to my father, when I turned my head, I saw the moon. It's full moon and the sky was so bright. The moment was just inspiring and touching. I did not realize that it was the fifteenth day of the eighth lunar month (Chinese mid-Autumn Festival). I knelt down in front of my father's grave so that I could look at his photo. I felt peaceful and calm. I told my father that I had brought him a book and would burn this book to him because he did not have time to read books when he was alive . . . One day when I left my house, I met the person whom I did not want to see, my father-in-law. As usual, he was leaving the place where he often drank. I did not know where my power came from. I just walked toward him and said hello to him . . . I found that I could be calm when I was with him. Before that, I felt angry whenever seeing him. But now I can forgive him. I think this is because I have reconciled with myself after the encounter with my father. I had told my father what I had wanted to say to him."

Learning to love self and others

Participants discovered that the assignment of writing a self-love letter could enhance their exploration of their unrevealed needs and strengths and their family members' needs. Exploring their strengths in the process of writing a letter to themselves could improve their emotional distress and relationships with their significant family members. This study also illustrated that, during group therapy, participants learning to love themselves could reaffirm their positive selves and enhance effective communication with themselves and their family members. Here are transcript examples of the findings.

Participant 4.   "I am quite sensitive about expressing my emotions and observing my surroundings. I have written the following in a letter to myself. I wrote that, when I held my daughter, I realized my eagerness for being cuddled as a child. Time flies very fast, so sometimes I forget to express my feelings in an intimate way. Now I can make myself stop to see and listen to my needs. I can also try to understand the needs of my children. In fact, right now, I am not really sure what I need. But I think I may need a sense of security."

Participant 10.   "Thank you for asking me to do this wonderful assignment, 'a love letter to myself.' I did not know what to write because love letters are supposed to be filled with good words, good parts of myself. I did not know what my strengths were. Last night, I talked to my husband about my worries. He suggested to me that I could imagine that I was writing it to him. I said no, because his strengths were different from mine. I could not find the strength with which to word the letter, so I wanted him to help me out. Because this was an assignment, I needed to take it seriously and be honest with myself. This was the first time I wrote a love letter to myself after living in this world for 42 years. It was a hard job for me. . . As my husband washed dishes, he told me about my strengths, including 'being skillful in teaching children,' 'being naturally optimistic,' 'being considerate of others' needs,' 'not being vainglorious,' and so on. I found that some went beyond the truth, but some were close to the truth. I was surprised by the compliments he gave me, as he never says them to me. I felt the old self coming back. Maybe this was because he confirmed my strengths. I enjoyed very much the process of writing this assignment, which has surprised me."

Participant 6. "At the beginning, the death of my father made me feel that I did not do my duty as a daughter. Because of this, I thought God was punishing me. My life was getting worse. I thought that I was being punished for not fulfilling the role of a good daughter. Nevertheless, after I took these classes, I now tell myself that I am a loving daughter... You may not know that I used to have a problem with cutting myself. I worked very hard to recover from this illness. I learned from the therapist that I am not a bad person; rather, I am a good person. Even if I am judged by outside standards of other people, I believe that there is no reason I should give up on myself."

Participant 3. "After receiving the reminder from the therapist last week, I have continually done what the therapist asks me to do, 'to have five to ten minutes everyday living life like a queen,' and let my husband understand that I need to be taken care of. Expressing my feeling helps to calm me down."

Developing a helpful social support system

Participants described improved relationships with their family members. By sharing their feelings with family members, participants helped their families to better understand reasons for their negative emotions and their vulnerable self.

Participant 3. "Now, my husband helps me look after the children. After I became sick, we talked more. I shared with him about what my therapist told me. I also discussed with him my feelings and changes of emotion. He also benefits from that. Before, he thought that my negative emotions were directed toward him and he became defensive, which usually ended in a big fight between us."

Participant 5. "My husband often said, 'you are not a good daughter-in-law because you do not love my mother...' He did not allow me to explain, so the only thing I could do was cry. He did not know that I cried as I don't want him to see me being vulnerable. Crying incessantly made me suffer from depression. Now I let him know that I cry. When I stay awake the whole night, I also let him know. Ha! Ha! He cannot sleep when I cannot sleep. Now, when I cannot sleep he puts his arms around me. I cherish this feeling very much. The change is huge. I think what the therapist says is right, to let him know about me! In fact, I am the kind of person who feels touched easily. I used to not cry in front of him. I did not want him to know I cried. In fact, I am very vulnerable."

Participant 6. "One day I suddenly told my mother, 'I feel that you have not been fond of me since I was a child.' I told her about all of the unfair ways she treated me. I told her about my dissatisfaction. My mother felt very sad. Suddenly, I felt that she was vulnerable. After revealing my negative feeling toward mom, I found that there were many different ways to express love. I think that I was lucky to have this experience of talking to my mother. There were many things she had kept in her thoughts. She had no one with whom to talk. Now I can listen to her, which makes me feel so grateful. This can hardly be described in words."

DISCUSSION

This study provided initial empirical evidence of the effectiveness of a BMS group in reducing symptoms of depression and improving quality of life among female participants with diagnoses of depressive disorders. There was a significant decrease in the level of depression from severe to mild among participants from pre-treatment to program completion. In addition, there was a significant increase in participants' life satisfaction from "somewhat satis-fied" to "moderately satisfied" as measured by the World Health Organization QOL Scale.

Findings of the qualitative data further elucidated the impact of the BMS group and beneficial treatment components that helped heal participants from their suffering. The identified themes were: (1) depression as an opportunity for growth; (2) learning to relax physically; (3) understanding and express-ing emotions and self; (4) viewing life stress positively; (5) uncovering inner strengths; (6) learning forgiveness, letting go, and living the moment; (7) learning to love self and others; and (8) developing a helpful social support system. Normalizing experiences of depression helped participants to view suffering from depression as an opportunity for growth in their lives. The positive view of suffering facilitated the participants' positive features, such as hope, courage, wisdom, and spirituality. The positive features enhanced participants' inner powers to deal with their distress. For example, the posi-tive view of depression facilitated participants' courage to explore what gift they would obtain from depression. Their process of exploration helped them to uncover suppressed thoughts, needs, feelings, and trauma in their lives. Their discovered new selves led them to accept and appreciate negative emo-tions, to love themselves and others, to make changes in their character, and to find meaning in life. Participants' positive views of themselves and the use of their inner powers could reduce symptoms of depression such as a sense of hopelessness and helplessness.

In sum, Integrative Body–Mind–Spirit treatment create a therapeutic con-text for participants to accept depression in their lives, appreciate the beauty of emotions, express appreciation for the contributions of the body, learn self-love, forgive, and let go. Through practicing these empowerment strategies, they found inner strength in their minds, which helped them to be in control of their health and relieve their sense of helplessness. They also worked through their sense of hatred and understood the meaning of suffering and the existence of life. Their acceptance of depression as a life challenge and efforts to solve problems arising from misfortune contributed to their ability to gain from loss and transform their suffering into a process of growth. Their experiences of suffering became "family treasure."

Limitations of the study need to be acknowledged. First, the study used a purpose sample, and no control group was included in this study. Second, the sample size was relatively small. Third, the study focused only on a female population. As such, the generalizability of the findings of this study to other populations is limited. Nevertheless, this pilot study provided initial empirical evidence for the effectiveness of BMS group therapy in reducing depression and improving quality of life in participants. Moreover, findings based on qualitative data advanced our understanding of beneficial therapeutic mechanisms involved in BMS group treatment. Implications of the study for future research include: (1) use a larger sample for more precise and refined statistical analysis; (2) use randomization with control groups that include conventional treatment modalities such as cognitive-behavioral models or psychodynamic approaches for a more conclusive findings regarding effectiveness of the approach; (3) include both female and male populations in the study; (4) develop several research sites that include participants from both Eastern and Western cultures to examine cultural adaptability of the model to populations from diverse ethnic and racial backgrounds.

13

Integrative Body–Mind–Spirit Approach to Enhance Women's Well-being

INTRODUCTION

In the early 1980s, research on the effects of multiple roles on women's health focused on the number of roles women engaged in. Within the context of two competing hypotheses, women's psychological well-being may be increased by less life involvement, that is, the scarcity hypothesis, or increased by more life involvement, that is, the expansion hypothesis, (Froberg, Gjerdingen, & Preston, 1986). In later years, the direction of research on women's multiple roles shifted to analyzing the effects of specific role combinations. Individuals tend to internalize the multiple roles they play and the statuses they occupy in their social networks; however, there are fewer psychological advantages of holding multiple roles for women than there are for men. Numerous studies have been done on examining the distressing aspects of enacting the specific primary roles of worker, wife, and mother. Among women, simultaneously attending to the demands of multiple roles showed immediate negative effects on their psychological well-being (Williams, Suls, Alliger, Learner, & Wan, 1991). This gender difference in distress may contribute to male–female differences in perception of the nature of work–parent conflict, attributions of responsibility for marital problems (Chan, Chan et al., 2001), feelings of guilt, and self-evaluation as parents and spouses (Simon, 1995).

Jenny, a 40-year-old married mother of two sons under 10, works as a clerk in a mid-size company. Like most working mothers, in addition to striving hard to stay competitive in the employment world, Jenny is expected to take up the role of caregiver for her family members. In another case, Betty, a housewife with a daughter aged 12, lives with her parents-in-laws. She is expected not only to take care of her husband and daughter but also be responsible for the caregiving of the older family members at home. In the gerontology literature, women are always found to be the primary caregivers for older people in the family. The number of women with multiple role responsibilities, such as wife, mother, employee, and caregiver to the elderly, is on rise. This is especially the case in Hong Kong, where, because of the influence of Chinese culture, the role of caregiver was presumed to be shouldered by the female members in the family.

Women's well-being is one of the important health issues that have been specifically researched in the last few decades. Although it is well known that diet and exercise promotes physical health, the status of one's mental health would be seriously affected by overall well-being. Those who are under immense stress or who are depressed are more likely to be ill than those who are not (Ader, Felten, & Cohen, 1990). Conventional health and mental health interventions often have the problem of compartmentalization, that is, each intervention focuses on a narrowly defined domain only. Ng and Chan (2005) argue that such an intervention model is ineffective. Health is a manifestation of one's physical, psychological, and spiritual well-being and of their interaction with one another (Chan, Ho et al., 2001).

METHODS

The study used a single-group, longitudinal design to examine the feasibility of Integrative Body–Mind–Spirit treatment in improving the mental health and quality of life among female group participants. The study hypothesized that women who attended the Integrative Body–Mind–Spirit group would experience improved mental health and quality of life outcomes.

Treatment Conditions

Inspired by the Integrative Body–Mind–Spirit model (Chan, Chan et al., 2001; Ho & Chan, 2003), this 3-hr, five-session group was developed with the goal of improving the overall well-being of women. The health intervention for well-being enhancement is elaborated from the Body–Mind–Spirit (BMS) model in health (Chan et al., 2001), which comprises nine main therapeutic areas: (1) understanding emotions, (2) stress management, (3) loving yourself, (4) love and forgiveness, (5) relationship with children and family, (6) diet and nutrition in accordance with the concept of Traditional Chinese Medicine (TCM), (7) meditation, (8) physical exercise, and (9) body massage and TCM acupressure. Table 13–1 presents the detailed session plan.

TABLE **13–1.** Session Plans of the Integrative Body–Mind–Spirit Treatment Group

SESSION THEMES	CONTENT

Session one: Understanding emotions and stress	1. Physical warm-up exercise
	2. Introduce the concept of Integrative Body–Mind–Spirit model
	3. Contracting: "I will attend with an open-heart."
	4. Ice-breaking game
	5. Understanding emotions
	6. Talk: Connection between body and mind
	7. Understanding stress and stress management, including massage, regular exercise, and meditation
	8. Music: Singing songs
	9. Homework:
	  a. Prepare an affirmation statement or drawing for other group members
	  b. Do one thing that can make you happy

Session two: To love and be loved	1. Physical warm-up exercise
	2. Group sharing: What really makes me happy?
	3. Relationship with children
	4. Diet and nutrition I
	5. Practice massage I
	6. Discussion: How often do women forget to treat themselves well?
	7. Discussion: What is the way to express love correctly?
	8. Music: Singing songs
	9. Homework:
	  a. Exercise every day
	  b. Do one thing that can make you happy (it can be different from the previous one)
	  c. Construct a family tree with family members
	  d. Bring a family photo that records happy times

Session three: Love and forgiveness	1. Physical warm-up exercise 2. Group sharing: Relationship with family 3. Discussion: Over-attachment and letting-go 4. Practice massage II 5. Discussion: Which is harder? Forgiving others or forgiving yourself?

TABLE **13–1.** (*continued*)

SESSION THEMES	CONTENT
	6. Meditation
	7. Activities: Pick an affirmation statement for a group member
	8. Music: Singing songs
	9. Homework:
	a. Do one thing that can make you happy
	b. Forgiving your family members: Do one thing to represent this
Session four: Love yourself	1. Physical warm-up exercise
	2. Group sharing: What can help you forgive others, especially your family members
	3. Timeline: Share significant incidents in life and the ability to overcome such incidents
	4. Practice massage III
	5. Discussion: What are my favorites?
	6. Discussion: Ways to love yourself: An action plan
	7. Music: Singing songs
	8. Homework:
	a. Exercise regularly
	b. Practice the action plan scheduled
	c. Bring some nice food to share with group members
	d. Think: A woman you appreciate very much
Session five: Living a life with dreams and goals	1. Physical warm-up exercise
	2. Group sharing: The woman you appreciate: What are the characteristics that make her so special?
	3. Meditation: I love myself
	4. Group sharing:
	5. Discussion: My goals and my plans
	6. Discussion: What have I gained from this experience?
	7. Concluding ceremony: Distribution of the Certificate of Attendance, group photos.

Research Participants

The sample included participants of six Integrative Body–Mind–Spirit treatment groups. Group participants were recruited from clients of 11 Social Services Units operated by the Tung Wah Group of Hospitals Social Services in Hong Kong. Each group consisted of 10–12 members and the groups were facilitated by therapists who had received a 3 day training in the Integrative Body–Mind–Spirit model at The Center on Behavioral Health, The University of Hong Kong. All 71 participating women had completed the 5 week

TABLE **13–2.** Demographic Characteristics of Research
Participants ($N = 42$)

DEMOGRAPHICS	MEAN (SD)	%
Age (years)	38.3 (7.3)	
Marital status		2.4
Single		97.6
Married/cohabiting		
Number of children	1.8 (0.73)	
Education		
College or above		21.4
High School		47.7
Middle School		14.3
Primary or below		16.7
Work		
Full-time		23.8
Part-time		2.4
Homemaker		69
Unemployed		
<6 months		2.4
>6 months		2.4

intervention, but only 42 women had returned the questionnaire at all three
points of assessment. Only data from these 42 participants were included in
the present analyses. Statistical analyses were conducted to examine whether
there were any significant differences between women who completed the
questionnaire at all three points of assessment and those who did not. There
were no significant differences between the two groups regarding age, marital
status, educational level, and employment status.

Table 13–2 described the demographic characteristics of the women who
participated in this study. The age of participants ranged from 21 to 57, and the
mean was 38.3 years (SD = 7.30). The majority of participants were married
(98 percent) with an average number of children of 1.8. Diverse educational
backgrounds were observed, 16.7 percent completed elementary education or
below, 14.3 percent middle school, 47.7 percent high school, and 21.4 percent
college or above.

Method of Data Collection

Baseline (pre-test T0) measures were taken prior to the group treatment. Subsequent assessments were taken immediately after the completion of the group
(post-test T1). The final assessment, which attempted to examine the maintenance of the intervention effects, was taken 5 weeks after the intervention
(maintenance T2).

Body–mind–spirit well-being inventory (BMSWBI)

Body–Mind–Spirit Well-being Inventory (BMSWBI) (Ng et al., 2005) is a self-report scale that consists of four domains related to physical distress, daily functioning, affect (sub-domains: positive and negative), and spirituality (sub-domains: tranquility, disorientation, and resilience). All items in each scale are assessed with a 10-point response scale.

The scores of Physical Distress Scale range from 0 to 140. The mean score is 29.7, in which the lower the score the better the physical health. The scores of Daily Functioning Scale range from 0 to 100. The mean score is 59.2. The higher the score, the better the health. The Affect Scale consists of 2 subscales: (1) The scores of Positive Affect Subscale range from 0 to 80, and the mean score is 42.3. The higher the score, the more positive the affect is; (2) The scores of Negative Affect subscale range from 0 to 110. The mean score is 40.7. The higher the score, the more negative the affect is. The Spirituality Scale consists of three subscales: (1) The scores of Tranquility subscale range from 0 to 50, and the mean score is 28.6. The higher the score, the better the spiritual health; (2) The scores of Disorientation Subscale range from 0 to 50. The mean score is 14.5. The higher the score, the worse the spiritual health; (3) The scores of Resilience subscale range from 0 to 30, and the mean score is 21.5. The higher the score, the better the spiritual health.

Each scale of this inventory has been validated in the original paper (Ng et al., 2005). Cronbach's alpha was found to range from .76 to .95, indicating the scales and subscales are internally reliable.

General health questionnaire (GHQ-12)

General Health Questionnaire is a 12-item version with a four-point response scale (Goldberg, 1972; Shek, 1987). GHQ-12 is internationally and widely used in screening for common mental disorders. This scale ranges from 0 to 12, and higher scores indicate a better health condition.

Short form 12-item version (SF-12)

Short Form 12-item version assesses the health-related quality of life (HQOL) (Health Assessment Lab, 1995), yielding subscores on physical and mental health. According to Lam et al. (2005), the Chinese version of SF-12 was found to be valid in the Chinese population. According to the specific encoding methods, a high score indicates good physical and mental health.

The Chinese version of the hospital anxiety and depression scale (HADS)

The Chinese version of the Hospital Anxiety and Depression Scale (HADS) (Leung, Ho, Kan, Hung, & Chen, 1993) is a 14-item scale measuring the anxiety and depression status of the participants. This scale is designated to assess the psychological state of people with physical problems. It is recommended in addition to the general quality of life assessment scale (Fossa & Dahl, 2002). Both the anxiety and the depression subscales range from 0 to 21. The higher the score, the worse the health.

Method of Data Analyses

The effect of intervention was examined using repeated-measures ANOVA on each outcome measure. The main effects of time between T0, T1, and T2 were measured, and a series of pairwise comparisons was performed between T0 and T1, between T0 and T2, and between T1 and T2 in each variable. The comparison between T0 and T2 and between T1 and T2 in each measure served as an indication of any maintenance effect of each variable.

RESULTS

Intervention Effects

The physical and psychological characteristics of participating women at each point of assessment are presented in Table 13–3. A repeated-measure ANOVA was performed to examine the intervention effect. As hypothesized, a significant main effect of time was found between time and participant groups in the total BMSWBI score [$F_{(2,52)} = 8.729, p < .001$], indicating that the well-being of women was found to be significantly different over time. In fact, 11 out of the 15 psychosocial variables included in this study demonstrated such significant overall differences over the three time-points of assessment, including daily functioning [$F_{(2,68)} = 6.377, p < .01$], positive affect [$F_{(2,66)} = 7.549\ p < .001$], and tranquility subscale in spirituality [$F_{(2,74)} = 7.622, p < .001$], and mental health [$F_{(2,66)} = 7.73, p < .001$]. With an attempt to examine the immediate intervention effect and the maintenance of the intervention effect over 5 weeks, further analyses, that is, pairwise comparison, was also conducted between T0 (baseline), T1 (immediately after), and T2 (5 weeks after). Findings showed that, in comparison with T0, the total BMSWBI score increased significantly at T1 [$t_{(37)} = 3.787, p < .005$] and T2 [$t_{(36)} = 1.357, p < .05$] from T0. Such findings indicate significant improvement in the overall well-being of women immediately after the intervention. In addition, such an improvement was maintained five weeks after the completion of the intervention. The pattern of findings also demonstrates positive changes in other psychosocial variables like daily functioning [T0:T1, $t_{(34)} = 2.653, p < .05$; T0:T2, $t_{(38)} = 3.346, p < .005$], positive affect [T0:T1,

TABLE 13–3. Repeated-measures ANOVA of Pre-test (T1), Post-test (T1), and Maintenance (T2) Measures ($N = 42$)

	T0		T1		T2		Main Effect of Time	Pairwise Comparison		
								T0:T1	T1:T2	T0:T2
	MEAN	SD	MEAN	SD	MEAN	SD	p	p	p	p
Measures for patients										
BMSWBI										
Physical distress	25.66	23.89	25.03	21.85	30.31	27.20	.229	.098	.660	.619
Daily functioning	68.5	16.29	70.44	18.62	61.43	22.63	.031*	.012*	.390	.002**
Affect										
Positive	38.50	16.39	54.33	17.69	51.94	16.52	.001**	.001**	.376	.003**
Negative	29.37	19.58	26.40	19.21	26.74	20.66	.583	.400	.726	.329
Spirituality										
Tranquility	30.00	10.99	35.79	9.69	35.55	10.49	.001**	.003**	.712	.011*
Disorientation	13.23	10.48	9.58	8.81	11.19	11.66	.031*	.008**	.555	.354
Resilience	19.87	6.66	23.24	5.04	21.74	6.12	.012*	.005**	.122	.224
BMSWBI total	357.2	59.62	397.3	61.41	381.6	77.49	.002**	.002**	.932	.010*
GHQ	1.76	2.39	.97	1.72	1.32	2.48	.296	.074	.485	.501
SF12										
Physical	45.74	7.87	46.56	5.85	45.96	9.30	.350	.279	.525	.074
Mental	45.03	7.08	45.77	7.98	46.81	5.75	.001**	.018*	.838	.024*
HADS										
Anxiety	14.78	3.54	16.36	3.37	15.94	4.09	.026*	.011*	.394	.078
Depression	16.08	3.34	17.74	2.95	16.82	3.18	.001**	.002**	.032*	.030*

Note: * $p < .05$, ** $p < .01$.

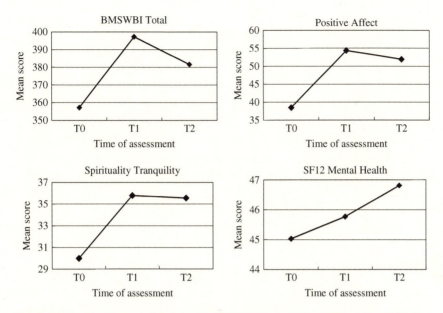

FIGURE **13.1.** Mean scores of each scale of BMSWBI at pre-test (T1), post-test (T1), and maintenance (T2). ($N = 42$).

$t_{(34)} = 4.357$, $p < .005$; T0:T2, $t_{(38)} = 3.147$, $p < .01$], tranquility [T0:T1, $t_{(37)} = 3.227$, $p < .001$; T0:T2, $t_{(39)} = 2.677$, $p < .05$], and mental health [T0:T1, $t_{(36)} = 2.489$, $p < .05$; T0:T2, $t_{(38)} = 2.354$, $p < .05$]. Figure 13.1 shows the trajectory of changes across T0, T1, and T2 of these variables.

DISCUSSION

This study evaluated the effectiveness of Integrative Body–Mind–Spirit group treatment in enhancing the well-being of women. Findings of the study provide initial empirical evidence that support the effectiveness of Integrative Body–Mind–Spirit treatment in bringing out significant positive changes in daily functioning; psychosocial and spiritual characteristics of women, including positive affect, ability to remain tranquil, and mental health; from pre-treatment to post-treatment. In addition, some of these positive changes were maintained 5 weeks after group treatment.

The stress created by multiple roles in women can weaken internal resources and negatively affect their cognitive appraisal abilities. By building a resourceful inner-self, women learn to appreciate their own selves, regardless of the unpredictability of life and the feeling of being out of control. This can be achieved only when the comprehensive approach of health is taken into account. The BMS integrative treatment group model focuses on the holistic concept of health, which is grounded in the belief of body–mind–spirit connectedness. Upon completion of the group, women showed significant immediate improvement primarily in three areas, and such improvement was maintained five weeks after treatment. The areas are: (1) daily functioning, (2) positive affect, and (3) ability to remain inwardly tranquil in the face of external turmoil.

Daily functioning of women was improved by raising their awareness of the importance of being in touch with their bodies. Body–mind connectedness has been well documented in different cultural settings over the years (e.g., Chan, C. L. W., Chan, & Lou, 2001; Ray, 2004). In our group, treatment included exercises such as body massage, acupressure, body scan, and mindfulness training. This new experience of nurturing one's own body can improve mood and augment a sense of satisfaction (Chan, Sham, & Wei, 1993).

Although there were positive changes in women's daily functioning from pre-treatment to post-treatment, no maintenance effect in daily functioning was found 5 weeks after completion of the group. In other words, positive changes in daily functioning were not sustained after treatment. One plausible reason is that the improvement in physical aspects during treatment maybe a result of positive social influence within the group. As described in the session plan, activities like physical exercises and group massage were included in the group. Motivation to engage in these activities could be relatively greater while receiving group treatment, because of peer influence. How to motivate participants to maintain the habit of engaging in regular healthy exercise on their own after treatment is a challenge for social work professionals to address.

A large body of literature illustrates the influence of the state of affect on one's physical well-being and coping strategy in the face of stressful events. Positive affect was found to be strongly associated with the activeness of one's coping skills (Lyubomirsky, King, & Diener, 2005). It is worth noticing that positive and negative affects are not mutually exclusive: The presence of positive affect is not equivalent to the absence of negative affect, or vice versa. Findings of this study are consistent with previous literature regarding the concept of positive and negative affects. Based on the concept introduced by Watson, Clark, and Tellegen (1988), high positive affect refers to the energetic stage of full concentration and pleasurable engagement, and low positive affect is characterized by sadness. However, high negative affect also includes various states of aversive moods, such as anger, guilt, fear, and nervousness, in contrast to low negative affect as a state of calmness and serenity. The divergence between the positive and negative affect should not be interpreted as a single bipolar dimension. Ng (2003) further explicated, "positive affect is not simply the reverse of negative affect, or vice versa. Conceptually, it is important to recognize that polarity is distinct from dimensionality. Methodologically, it is more appropriate to represent positive and negative affect on two unipolar dimensions, rather than on a single bipolar dimension" (p. 45). With the intention of improving women's stage of affect, several exercises were introduced in the group: (1) training of stress management, (2) techniques to improve relationships with family and children, (3) activities to understand the nature of emotions, and (4) discussion pertaining to topics such as "loving yourself." Compared to the initial assessment of psychological characteristics of participants, regardless of the statistical indifference of the negative affect across time, the positive affect of women was significantly improved immediately and five weeks after the intervention.

Spirituality, in particular tranquility, is intimately related to one's ability to see beyond the vulnerability of life and the unchangeable circumstances. Although measuring spirituality is still a controversial topic, the attempt to measure spirituality in this study indicates our strong belief in the central role of spirituality in the concept of holistic health, which is largely neglected in other psychosocial intervention models. The acknowledgment of the fact that life is vulnerable may help individuals to appraise stressful situations as less threatening, hence diminishing the distress experience (Bonanno, 2004). Chan et al. (2006) further elaborated the concept by suggesting that only when one can appreciate the meaning of suffering can one learn the essence of "letting-go" and then "gain strength" to face misfortunes, turmoil, and loss. In order to promote a sense of peace and tranquility for women, numerous psychosocial techniques were employed during the BMS integrative treatment group, including a series of meditations, life story review, and discussion of topics such as over-attachment and letting go. Women who participated in this study demonstrated a significant improvement in their ability to stay tranquil when encountering stress and tension induced by their multiple-role responsibilities and other external stressors.

Nevertheless, limitations of the study should also be addressed. Firstly, due to the small sample size, control group was not included in the study. There is a possibility that the positive changes in participants were due to the spurious effect of social support. To address this problem, we adopted a longitudinal design to measure the maintenance effect of the treatment as a way to compensate for the potential effect of social support. The second limitation is the relatively high attrition rate recorded in this study. Almost 40 percent of the women who enrolled in the group did not complete all three points of assessment. Most of the nonresponse cases were marked at the 5-week follow-up. On the other hand, we had conducted statistical analyses to examine whether there were significant differences between the completers and noncompleters.

Findings showed that there were no significant differences between the two groups regarding their age, educational level, and marital and employment status.

One primary premise of Integrative Body–Mind–Spirit treatment is a belief in holistic well-being that can only be achieved by a state of harmonious balance between body, mind, and spirit. Findings of this study provide initial empirical evidence supporting the efficacy of this approach in enhancing women's well-being. Future research adopting a more rigorous design will be needed to further establish its effectiveness. It will be helpful to (1) use an experimental design, (2) include a larger and more representative sample, (3) further refine measurements, especially instruments for measuring spirituality, (4) address problem of attrition, and (5) include a qualitative study design to carefully explore mechanisms of change associated with the treatment model.

14

Meditation and Treatment of Female Trauma Survivors

INTRODUCTION

Posttraumatic stress disorder (PTSD) became a formal diagnosis included in *DSM-III* only in 1980 on account of the organized efforts of Charles Figley, Chaim Shatan, and other advocate groups for veterans and trauma survivors. Trauma has pervasive and devastating impacts on individuals. Trauma survivors, especially those with prolonged histories of interpersonal abuse, typically suffer from other "co-morbid conditions." These include, but are not limited to, diagnoses related to substance abuse problems, mood disorders (e.g., depression and manic-depressive disorders), and dissociative identity disorder (Mueser et al., 1998). According to the "self-medication" hypothesis (Khantzian, 1990), people drink to cope with negative emotions and stressors. PTSD clients also have unusually high utilization rates of psychiatric services. Macy (2002) examined records of 384,000 Medicaid recipients in Massachusetts between 1997 and 1998 and reported that PTSD and depression were the most common psychiatric diagnoses among this population. Patients with a PTSD diagnosis spent 10 times as much time in the hospital as patients with a diagnosis of depression only.

While PTSD is being fully recognized now as a mental health condition, helping professionals are still struggling to find viable and evidence-based treatments for PTSD (Foa, Keane, & Friedman, 2000). Conventional treatment efforts involve mostly cognitive-behavioral therapy, which has received the greatest research attention and support for its efficacy (For detailed reviews please refer to Foa & Meadows, 1997; Rothbaum, Meadows, Resick, & Foy, 2000). Cognitive-behavioral therapeutic interventions include prolonged exposure treatment (Cooper & Clum, 1989; Foa & Rothbaum, 1998; Foa, Rothbaum, Riggs, & Murdock, 1991; Lombardo & Gray, 2005), stress inoculation training (Veronen & Kilpatrick, 1983), cognitive process-ing therapy (Resick & Schnicke, 1992, 1993), and cognitive therapy (Ehlers & Clark, 2000). While cognitive-behavioral approaches have made significant contributions to treatment with this client population, some evidence suggests that these approaches may not be helpful for PTSD clients with prolonged histories of interpersonal abuse. McDonagh-Coyle et al. (1999) conducted a randomized controlled trial of combined prolonged exposure and cognitive restructuring versus "present-centered therapy" with clients who had PTSD diagnoses. Findings revealed that PTSD subjects with prolonged histories of interpersonal abuse responded adversely to prolonged exposure and cognitive restructuring treatments. Treatment was related to increased severity in PTSD symptoms primarily because of psychophysiological reactivity of clients to trauma memories (McDonagh-Coyle et al., 2001).

Bessel van der Kolk, the Medical Director and Founder of the Trauma Center in Massachusetts, has identified important evidence in neurobiology research that questions the utility of cognitive-behavioral approaches with PTSD clients who have experienced prolonged interpersonal abuse (van der Kolk, 1994; van der Kolk, McFarlane, & Weisaeth., 1996). Research regard-ing the neurobiology of trauma shows that trauma disrupts the stress-hormone system, influences the entire nervous system, and prevents people from pro-cessing and integrating trauma memories into conscious mental frameworks. Because of these complex physiological processes, traumatic memories stay in the brain's "nether regions," the nonverbal, nonconscious, subcortical regions (amygdala, thalamus, hippocampus, hypothalamus, and brain stem) where they are not accessible to the frontal lobes, the understanding, thinking, and reasoning parts of the brain (van der Kolk, 1994). Thus, prolonged expo-sure and cognitive restructuring approaches may not be helpful and can even be harmful to some trauma survivors because when encouraged to reexperi-ence the trauma (a routine procedure in prolonged exposure), they could be so overwhelmed by intense negative emotions they can no longer consciously process the trauma (Ford & Kidd, 1998; van der Kolk, 2002; van der Kolk & van der Hart, 1991).

Traumas fundamentally disrupt the affect modulation ability of an individ-ual. Severe or extreme distress elicits intense emotions such as fear, anger, and/or pain. PTSD describes the development of a cluster of symptoms following a psychologically distressing event that is outside the range of usual human experience and is most often experienced with intense fear, terror, and helplessness. The characteristic symptoms as described in *DSM-IV-TR* include: (a) distressing and intrusive thoughts, feelings, and images that recapitulate the traumatic event, (b) psychological and/or physiological reactivity to internal or external cues that symbolize an aspect of the traumatic event, (c) persistent avoidance of stimuli associated with the trauma and numbing of general responsiveness, and (d) persistent symptoms of increased arousal and vigilance (American Psychiatric Association, 2000). These symptoms describe a situation in which the trauma survivor is still living in the past trauma. Psychologically and physiologically, trauma survivors react to present-time experiences with diminished emotion regulating ability—they react as if they are presently experiencing the original trauma/s.

PTSD symptoms can be partly perceived as the consequences of clients being trapped in the past traumas and not able to live in the present. A clinical challenge in treatment is how to enhance clients' capacity to recognize and attend to current experiences as well as to differentiate them from trauma-based emotional and behavioral responses so they can make choices that are responsive and beneficial to their current needs and situations.

MEDITATION AND TREATMENT OF TRAUMA SURVIVORS

Meditation is an integral intervention used in Integrative Body–Mind–Spirit Social Work. Through meditation, clients learn to discipline and calm their minds, develop the ability to observe, be openly aware, and attend to emotions, even distressing ones, and accept them for what they are. In doing so, meditation should enhance clients' capacity to develop psychological resources that allow them to increase self-regulation of their emotions in a beneficial way (Linehan, 1993; Martin, 1997). Meditation practice should be helpful for trauma survivors to accomplish the following tasks and goals in treatment:

1. Foster clients' capacity to recognize and attend to current experiences as well as to differentiate them from past traumatic experiences so that clients have increased ability to uncouple current physical/psychological sensations from trauma-based emotional and behavioral responses.
2. Enhance clients' ability to stay physiologically calm, which constitutes a necessary condition for clients to engage beneficially in treatment and assists them in processing and integrating their trauma experiences.
3. Enhance clients' self-regulating abilities so they make choices that are responsive and beneficial to their current needs and situations.

METHODS

This study used an experimental design to examine the feasibility of using meditation as an intervention for treating trauma survivors. The study tested the following hypotheses: (1) A 6-week meditation curriculum will be effective in reducing PTSD symptoms of research participants, (2) A 6-week meditation curriculum will be effective in increasing positive emotions in research participants, (3) A 6-week meditation curriculum will be effective in improving emotion regulation abilities of research participants, and (4) A 6-week meditation curriculum will be effective in increasing a mindful state in research participants.

The development of the study framework is guided by the existing literature on the physiological impact of meditation (Lazar et al., 2000); self-determination theory, postulated by Deci and Ryan, that examines the importance of self-awareness to facilitate positive self-regulative behaviors for individual well-being (Deci & Ryan, 1980; Ryan & Deci, 2000); and a systems perspective that describes how the self-regulation process occurs through the operation of feedback mechanisms (Bateson, 1972, 1979; Becvar & Becvar, 2003). Figure 14.1 illustrates the framework of the study.

Treatment Conditions

Treatment conditions consisted of a 6-week meditation curriculum with the first 2 weeks devoted to Breathing Meditation, the second 2 weeks to Nying-je (Loving kindness meditation), and the final 2 weeks to Tonglen (Compassion meditation). Breathing meditation focuses on training for mindfulness and calmness, while Loving kindness meditation and Compassion meditation teach empathy skills in terms of sensitivity to one's own affect and sensitivity

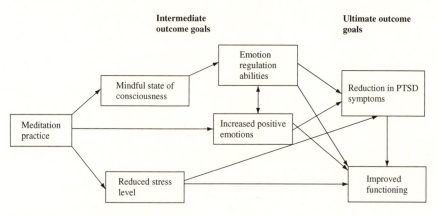

FIGURE **14.1.** Framework of the study.

to another's affect and teach development of compassion for oneself and others (please refer to Chapter 5 for a detailed description of the meditation practice). The meditation class met twice every day for 1 hr, 5 days a week, consecutively for 6 weeks for a total of 60 hr. Geshe Kalsang Damdul, Assistant Director of the Institute of Buddhist Dialectics in Dharamsala, India (which is under the direct administration of His Holiness the Dalai Lama), assisted in developing the meditation curriculum and provided the meditation instruction.

Research Participants

The meditation class was conducted between October 8 and November 16, 2007. Seventeen clients participated in the meditation group and 15 clients in the comparison group. Research participants were clients at a substance abuse treatment and housing program for homeless women and their children in a Midwestern cosmopolitan city. All clients have experienced different types of traumas and interpersonal abuses in addition to their alcohol use disorders. Participation in the study was voluntary and formal consent was obtained from all participants. Clients who consented to participate in the study were randomly assigned to the meditation or the comparison group. Researchers consulted with agency staff regarding the appropriateness of the assignment. The assignment of four clients was changed from the meditation group to control group because of scheduling problems, and another four clients were changed from the control group to the meditation group because agency staff expressed concerns regarding therapeutic benefits. Residents with comorbid conditions of schizophrenia and severe depression or who were actively suicidal were excluded from participation. This exclusion is based on literature that shows meditation can be counter-therapeutic for these clients. The Institutional Review Board at The Ohio State University reviewed and approved the study.

Data analyses were based on 17 participants in the meditation group and 15 participants in the comparison group. All participants were female. The age of the program participants ranged from 22 to 56 years (mean = 40.5, SD = 7.9). Program participants were predominantly Caucasian (59.4 percent) with 40.6 percent African Americans. Participants had attained an average of 12.6 years of education (SD = 1.5; range = 9–19). Regarding the marital status of program participants, 50 percent were never married, 3.1 percent married, 12.5 percent separated, 31.3 percent divorced, and 3.1 percent widowed. The majority of participants were unemployed (78.1 percent), only 3.1 percent were employed on a part-time basis, 12.5 percent were students and 6.3 percent identified themselves as disabled. There were no significant differences between the two groups on demographic characteristics including age, educational attainment, employment, and marital status.

TABLE **14–1.** Participants' Demographic Information

	Mediation Group ($N = 17$)		%	**Comparison Group ($N = 15$)**		%	t	χ^2
	N	MEAN (SD)		N	MEAN (SD)			
Age (years)	17	39.4 (8.5)	–	15	41.3 (7.3)	–	.69	–
Employment								1.2
Employed Part-time	0		0	1		6.7	–	–
Unemployed	14		82.4	11		73.3	–	–
Student	2		11.8	2		13.3	–	–
Disabled	1		5.9	1		6.7	–	–
Education								8.0
Some High School	0	–	0	3	–	20	–	–
High School Grad.	2	–	11.8	4	–	26.7	–	–
Some College	11	–	64.7	8	–	53.3	–	–
College Graduate	2	–	11.8	0	–	0	–	–
Graduate work	2	–	11.8	0	–	0	–	–
Ethnicity								7.9**
White American	14	–	82.4	5	–	33.3	–	–
African American	3	–	17.6	10	–	66.6	–	–
Marital status								3.5
Never married	9	–	52.9	7	–	46.7	–	–
Married	0	–	0	1	–	6.7	–	–
Separated	1		5.9	3		20.0		
Divorced	6		35.3	4		26.7		
Widowed	1	–	5.9	0	–	0	–	–

Note: $^* p \leq .05,$ $^{**} p \leq .01.$

However, there was significant difference between the two groups in terms of their ethnicity. In the meditation group, 82.4 percent were white and 17.6 percent African Americans; in the control group, 66.3 percent of participants were African American. (Table 14–1).

The study also collected information regarding participants' childhood and trauma-related experiences. Of the participants, 40.6 percent experienced parental divorce or separation, 71.9 percent were children of alcoholics, and 50 percent had witnessed domestic violence between parents. Regarding their trauma-related experiences, 87.5 percent had experienced physical abuse (56.5 percent happened in childhood, 13.0 percent in teenage, and 30.4 percent adulthood), 78.1 percent had experienced sexual abuse (72.0 percent happened in childhood, 8.0 percent in teenage, and 20.0 percent adulthood), and 87.5 percent had experienced emotional abuse (67.9 percent happened in childhood, 17.9 percent in teenage, and 14.3 percent adulthood). There were no significant differences between the two groups on their childhood and trauma-related experiences, including parental divorce; parental violence; family alcoholism; and physical, sexual, and/or emotional abuses.

Method of Data Collection

Assessment of participants' PTSD symptoms, state of mindfulness, positive emotions, and emotion regulation abilities were made at pre-treatment and post-treatment. The following instruments were used for data collection.

Modified PTSD Symptom Scale (MPSS). MPSS is a 17-item instrument developed by Falsetti and her associates (Falsetti, Resnick, Resick & Kilpatrick, 1993) to measure the frequency and severity of current PTSD symptoms occurring during the past 2 weeks in respondents. MPSS has three subscales: Reexperiencing Subscale (items 1,2,3,4,17), Avoidance/numbing Subscale (items 5–11), and Arousal Subscale (items 12–16). Because the items correspond directly to DSM-IV PTSD symptoms, MPSS can be scored dichotomously to determine if diagnostic criteria for PTSD are met (Falsetti, 1997). MPSS has demonstrated excellent reliability and validity (Falsetti, 1997; Falsetti, Resnick, Resick & Kilpatrick, 1992; Wilson & Keane, 1997).

Structured Interview for Disorders of Extreme Distress (SIDES). SIDES is a 45-item instrument developed by Pelcovitz et al. (1997) to assess respondents' past and current functioning in six domains of (1) disorders of affect regulation, (2) amnesia and dissociation, (3) somatization, (4) disruptions in self-perception, (5) disorders in relationships with others, and (6) disrupted systems of meaning. These six domains are represented in the DSM-IV under Associated Features of PTSD and describe the areas of impairment of the Disorders of Extreme Stress construct (Luxenberg, Spinazzola, & van der Kolk, 2001). SIDES has demonstrated good reliability and validity (Pelcovitz et al., 1997). Research supports the construct validity of SIDES; the instrument discriminated individuals with histories of PTSD from individuals with no history of PTSD (van der Kolk et al., 1996), and rape victims with chronic PTSD from anxiety disorders or depressed controls (Spinazzola et al., 1994). This study used the self-report version of SIDES that has excellent full-scale internal consistency (Cronbach's alpha = .93).

The Intensity and Time Affect Survey (ITAS). ITAS is a 24-item survey developed by Lucas, Diener, and Larsen (2003) to measure the frequency of 24 emotional experiences based on respondents' self-reports. Respondents are asked to rate the intensity and frequency of the measured emotions on a seven-point Likert-type scale from 1-(Never); 4-(About half of the time); to 7-(Always). The Overall Positive Emotions Scale is comprised of the Love Subscale and the Joy Subscale. The scores of Overall Positive Emotions Scale range from 8 to 56 with a higher score indicating increased positive emotions experienced by respondents.

Mindfulness Attention Awareness Scale (MAAS). MAAS is a 15-item questionnaire developed by Brown and Ryan (2003) to measure the level of mindfulness of respondents. The items are distributed across cognitive, emotional, physical, interpersonal, and general domains. Respondents rate how frequently they have the experience described in each statement using a 6-point Likert scale where higher scores reflect higher levels of mindfulness. Brown and Ryan (2003) reported evidence for the psychometric adequacy and validity of MAAS through exploratory factor analysis and confirmatory factor analysis. Cronbach's alpha of MAAS with seven populations ranged from 0.80 to 0.87. The test–retest reliability coefficients for the stability of the MAAS over a 4-week period was .81.

DATA ANALYSES

The study used a series of paired-sample t-tests to compare the pre-treatment and post-treatment measures of the assessment instruments regarding research participants' PTSD symptom severity, emotional experiences, and mindful states of consciousness. The study used repeated measures of analysis of variance to assess the "within subjects" changes during the two assessments.

Results

Findings of this study provided initial empirical evidence of the positive impact of the meditation curriculum on clients' mental health outcomes. Findings based on paired sample t-test showed significant reduction in overall PTSD symptoms from pre-treatment to post-treatment [$t = 3.17$, $df = 14$, $p < .01$], in particular in avoidance symptoms [$t = 3.31$, $df = 14$, $p < .01$] and hyperarousal symptoms [$t = 2.82$, $df =$, $p < .05$] in clients who had attended the meditation curriculum. In addition, there were significant increases in positive emotions including love [$t = -2.61$, $df = 16$, $p < .01$] and joy [$t = -4.55$, $df = 16$, $p < .05$]; significant reduction in negative emotions of fear [$t = 2.38$, $df = 16$, $p < .05$], shame [$t = 2.33$, $df = 16$, $p < .05$], and sadness [$t = 2.61$, $df = 16$, $p < .05$]; significant increase in mindfulness [$t = -2.04$, $df = 16$, $p < .05$]; and significant decrease in affect dysregulation [$t = 2.46$, $df = 16$, $p < .05$] among clients in the meditation group from pre-treatment to post-treatment (Table 14–2). Nonsignificant changes in all evaluated dimensions were observed among clients in the control group (Table 14–3).

TABLE **14–2.** Paired-Sample t-tests at Pre-Treatment and Post-Treatment: Meditation Group ($N = 17$)

	PRE-TREATMENT	POST-TREATMENT	t	df	p
PTSD Symptoms: MPSS					
Total Score	50.58	25.67	3.17	14	.007
	(SD = 29.61)	(SD = 22.48)			
Intrusion subscale	13.08	8.07	1.90	14	.079
	(SD = 9.12)	(SD = 6.69)			
Avoidance/Numbing	22.79	10.73	3.31	14	.005
subscale	(SD = 13.39)	(SD = 10.63)			
Hyperarousal	13.90	6.87	2.82	14	.014
subscale	(SD = 9.33)	(SD = 7.07)			
Positive Emotion: ITAS					
Total	65.55	78.12	−3.75	16	.002
	(SD = 17.19)	(SD = 16.27)			
Love subscale	34.24	39.18	−2.61	16	.019
	(SD = 8.25)	(SD = 8.59)			
Joy subscale	30.29	38.94	−4.55	16	.000
	(SD = 9.57)	(SD = 8.37)			
Fear subscale	33.82	27.41	2.38	16	.030
	(SD = 10.90)	(SD = 9.22)			
Anger subscale	28.18	25.94	.82	16	.423
	(SD = 11.06)	(SD = 9.88)			
Shame subscale	34.24	27.37	2.33	16	.033
	(SD = 9.31)	(SD = 11.97)			
Sad subscale	34.53	26.41	2.61	16	.019
	(SD = 11.21)	(SD = 8.97)			
Mindfulness: MAAS					
MAAS	57.29	62.53	−2.04	16	.050
	(SD = 10.23)	(SD = 8.22)			
Emotional Regulation: SIDES					
Disorders of Affect	.83	.36	2.46	16	.026
Regulation subscale	(SD = .58)	(SD = .57)			

The study used repeated measures of analysis of variance to assess the "within subjects" changes during the two assessments. Figures 14.2 to 14.5 show the comparisons between the pre-treatment and post-treatment scores of the outcome measures of MPSS, ITAS, MAAC, and SIDES between the meditation and the control groups. Findings indicate there are significant Time × Group interaction effects in MPSS Total Score [$F_{(1, 25)} = 4.73$, $p = .039$], MPSS Avoidance Subscale [$F_{(1, 25)} = 4.12$, $p = .05$],

TABLE **14–3.** Paired-Sample t-Tests at Pre-Treatment and Post-Treatment: Comparison Group ($N = 15$)

	PRE-TREATMENT	POST-TREATMENT	t	df	p
PTSD Symptoms: MPSS					
Total score	35.51	32.96	.43	11	.675
	(SD = 22.74)	(SD = 20.21)			
Intrusion subscale	12.33	11.81	.18	11	.861
	(SD = 8.50)	(SD = 6.01)			
Avoidance/Numbing	14.00	11.08	1.38	11	.195
subscale	(SD = 11.50)	(SD = 9.11)			
Hyperarousal	8.90	10.03	−.51	11	.618
subscale	(SD = 6.13)	(SD = 7.07)			
Positive Emotion: ITAS					
Total	80.62	82.00	−.43	13	.672
	(SD = 16.02)	(SD = 13.45)			
Love subscale	41.14	42.29	−.72	13	.484
	(SD = 8.76)	(SD = 6.91)			
Joy subscale	39.52	39.71	−.11	13	.917
	(SD = 8.00)	(SD = 7.47)			
Fear subscale	29.71	31.21	−.49	13	.634
	(SD = 12.00)	(SD = 12.77)			
And subscale	25.88	27.71	−.78	13	.450
	(SD = 12.36)	(SD = 12.60)			
Shame subscale	29.57	29.14	−.22	13	.832
	(SD = 11.89)	(SD = 11.97)			
Sad subscale	30.29	28.07	−.66	13	.518
	(SD = 14.75)	(SD = 12.76)			
Mindfulness: MAAS					
MAAS	51.57	51.86	−.093	13	.927
	(SD = 16.89)	(SD = 12.85)			
Emotional Regulation: SIDES					
Disorders of Affect	.24	.52	−1.20	14	.249
Regulation subscale	(SD = .31)	(SD = .80)			

and MPSS Hyperarousal Subscale [$F_{(1, 25)} = 5.68$, $p = .025$]; ITAS Positive Emotion Score [$F_{(1, 29)} = 6.11$, $p = .020$], ITAS Joy Subscale [$F_{(1, 29)} = 10.12$, $p = .003$]; and SIDES Disorders of affect regulation Subscale [$F_{(1, 30)} = 6.29$, $p = .018$]. Positive changes in the meditation group from pre-treatment to post-treatment were significantly greater than the changes observed in the comparison group.

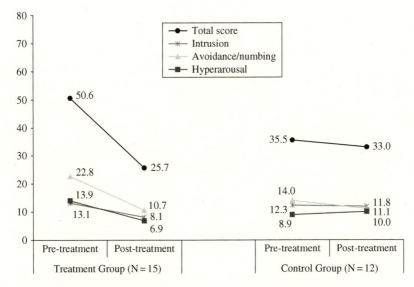

FIGURE **14.2.** Paired-sample *t*-tests at pre-treatment and post-treatment: MPSS.

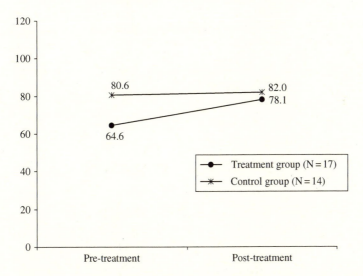

FIGURE **14.3.** Paired-sample *t*-tests at pre-treatment and post-treatment: positive emotions ITAS.

DISCUSSION

Findings of this study provided initial empirical evidence of the positive impact of meditation on clients' mental health outcomes. Findings showed a significant reduction in overall PTSD symptoms, in particular in avoidance and hyperarousal symptoms from pre-treatment to post-treatment in clients who had attended the meditation classes. In addition, there were significant

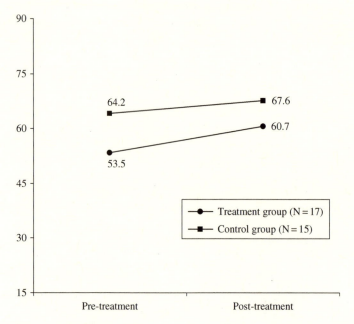

FIGURE **14.4.** Paired-sample *t*-tests at pre-treatment and post-treatment: mindfulness MAAS.

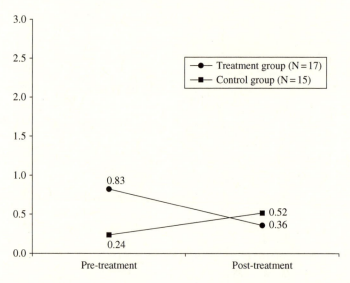

FIGURE **14.5.** Paired-sample *t*-tests at pre-treatment and post-treatment: disorder of affect regulation, SIDES.

increases in positive emotions including love and joy; significant reduction in negative emotions of fear, shame, and sadness; significant increase in mindfulness; and significant decrease in affect dysregulation among clients in the meditation group from pre-treatment to post-treatment. Findings also indicated that there were significant Time × Group interaction effects in PTSD symptoms, positive emotions, and emotion regulation abilities with positive changes in the meditation group from pre-treatment to post-treatment were significantly greater than the changes observed in the control group.

Limitations of the study need to be acknowledged. First, the sample size was relatively small. Second, there were no significant differences between the meditation and the comparison group on demographic characteristics including age, educational attainment, employment, and marital status, as well as childhood and trauma-related experiences including parental divorce, parental violence, family alcoholism, physical, sexual, and/or emotional abuses. However, there were significantly more African American clients in the comparison group than the meditation group. Regarding the studied variables, there were no significant differences in the two groups on PTSD symptoms at *pre-treatment*, but there were significant differences between the two groups regarding their emotional states, emotional dysregulation, and state of mindfulness. Clients in the meditation group were significantly less mindful [53.53 vs. 64.20, $t = -2.29$, $df = 30$, $p < .05$], had less positive emotion [64.55 vs. 80.85, $t = -2.80$, $df = 30$, $p < .01$], and more severe emotional dysregulation [1.31 vs. .33, $t = 4.14$, $df = 30$, $p < .001$] than clients in the comparison group. In other words, clients in the meditation group were worse off than clients in the comparison group at pre-treatment. Findings of the study showed significant improvement of the meditation group on all studied variables at *post-treatment*. However, there was no significant difference in the post-treatment scores between the two groups, due to the different levels of pre-treatment scores. Finally, while there were no drop-outs from the meditation and control group from pre-treatment to post-treatment, findings might still be influenced by the problem of measurement attrition as we did not have complete data from clients on all measurements at pre-treatment and post-treatment (Fraser, 2004).

Findings of the study provided initial empirical evidence of the feasibility of meditation as an intervention. Future research using a more rigorous and robust research design is needed to establish the effectiveness of meditation as an intervention. Specific recommendations for the future large scale effectiveness study include: (1) the use a larger sample size; (2) the use of more rigorous, randomized assignment procedures; (3) the use of observation-based rating systems for data collection where appropriate, (4) the development of a treatment manual for training purposes and fidelity analyses, and (5) the inclusion of research sites that serve diverse PTSD client populations.

CONCLUSION

Trauma has pervasive and devastating impacts on individuals. Many trauma survivors use mind-altering substances to numb their feelings, calm their anxiety, and cope with their depression. The biggest challenge for trauma survivors is learning how to live beneficially in the present and not under the shadow of trauma. While cognitive-behavioral approaches have made significant contributions to advancing treatment with trauma survivors (Rothbaum et al., 2000), there are particular concerns for trauma survivors with prolonged histories of interpersonal abuse who respond negatively to prolonged exposure and cognitive restructuring treatments. When clients cannot stay psychologically and physiologically calm to beneficially process and integrate their trauma experiences in treatment, exposure or cognitive structure techniques might bring harm instead of help. Clinical challenges encountered by trauma survivors revolve primarily around recognizing and differentiating current emotional experiences and physical cues from trauma-based responses as well as learning how to regulate emotions and behaviors that allow beneficial fulfillment of needs and goals as defined by *current* life context and not past trauma.

From an Integrative Body–Mind–Spirit Social Work perspective, meditation utilizes the power of mind in a nonconventional manner and provides a different and complementary "technology" in conceptualizing and providing treatment to trauma survivors. Meditation initiates cognitive change at the meta-cognitive level. Instead of focusing on the rational and conscious mind and directly addressing and focusing on the "content" of trauma, meditation trains individuals to "discipline" their mind, that is, changing one's relationship to thoughts, without directly focusing on the problems (Marlatt et al., 2004). By training clients to attend to the present, by enhancing clients' ability to stay physiologically calm, and by increasing positive emotions, meditation practice allows clients to unfold their internal and personal resources and strengths to address the problems of trauma. If meditation practice proves effective in enhancing clients' capacity to attend to the present, to stay calm, and to better regulate their emotions and behaviors based on current life demands and needs, clients will have a better chance to benefit from treatment and integrate their trauma experience. Effective treatment of PTSD clients with prolonged history of interpersonal abuse should also reduce their need for psychiatric services.

One major significant, potential contribution of meditation is the way meditation practice empowers trauma clients in the process of recovery. Meditation is, in itself, a low-cost, nonintrusive, and empowering intervention. Clients can practice meditation on a regular basis individually once they learn how to do it and if they find it beneficial. Meditation can be practiced any time, anywhere, and is not dependent on costly medication, equipment, facilities, or professional assistance. Meditation does not even require the client to share their trauma experiences as it is a private, internal practice. The focus is on facilitating clients' ability to unfold their internal and personal resources and strengths in addressing the problems of trauma. Meditation could be a complementary and empowering treatment approach for helping trauma survivors in their recovery process.

IV

Learning and Using Integrative Body–Mind–Spirit Social Work in Practice

15

Ethics and Integrative Body–Mind–Spirit Social Work

Integrative Body–Mind–Spirit Social Work combines Western and Eastern philosophies and practices to help develop effective and competent social work practices; such an approach embraces a holistic approach to treatment and focuses on the body–mind–spirit connection. Although the social work profession has begun to embrace and celebrate a holistic approach to social work practice in recent years, issues concerning ethical practice have been raised regarding respect for spiritual diversity and clients' self-determination (Canda, Nakashima, & Furman, 2004; Cnaan, Wineburg, & Boddie, 1999; Hodge, 2003). In addition, there are ethical issues pertaining to using treatment techniques involving body process work that will need to be thoughtfully considered. Besides addressing boundary issues between clients and social work professionals, we have to attend to boundary issues between social work practice and other disciplines, such as the fields of medicine, healthcare practice, and physiotherapy.

ETHICS OF INTEGRATIVE BODY–MIND–SPIRIT SOCIAL WORK

Integrative Body–Mind–Spirit Social Work builds upon the established ethical guidelines of the National Association of Social Workers (NASW)

(NASW, 1999), The International Federation of Social Workers (IFSW), and The International Association of Schools of Social Work (IASSW) (IFSW/IASSW, 2004). These codes and principles of ethics are based on social work's core values of service, social justice, human rights and dignity, importance of human relationships, integrity, and competence (IFSW/IASSW, 2004; NASW, 1999). These principles set forth ideals to which Integrative Body–Mind–Spirit Social Work embraces and aspires. Building upon these ethical guidelines, Integrative Body–Mind–Spirit Social Work particularly emphasizes the role of spirituality and body process work to aid in the developing of a client's strengths and to help create change (Ellor, Netting, & Thibault, 1999; Koening & Spano, 1998). As such, Integrative Body–Mind–Spirit Social Work also believes that it is our ethical responsibility to (1) treat clients in a holistic manner that respects the connectedness of the body, the mind, and the spirit, and to (2) respect clients by developing and using treatment techniques that build upon their strengths, initiate self-healing potential, and effectively create change in their lives.

Human Rights and Dignity

Ethical principle: Social workers respect the inherent dignity and worth of a person.

Social work is based on respect for the inherent worth and dignity of all people, and the rights that follow from this. Social workers should uphold and defend each person's physical, psychological, emotional, and spiritual integrity and well-being. This means: (1) respecting the right to self-determination, (2) promoting the right to participation, (3) treating each person as a whole, and (4) identifying and developing strengths (IFSW/IASSW, 2004).

Social workers treat each person in a caring and respectful fashion, mindful of individual differences and cultural and ethnic diversity. Social workers promote clients' socially responsible self-determination and seek to enhance clients' capacity and opportunities to address their own needs and to change. Social workers are cognizant of their dual responsibility to clients and to society: They seek to resolve conflicts between clients' interests and society's interests in a socially responsible manner consistent with the values, ethical principles, and ethical standards of the profession (NASW, 1999).

Integrative Body–Mind–Spirit Social Work regards respect for dignity and worth of a person as the fundamental value, and this value constitutes the cornerstone of our values and ethics. Because of individual differences as well as cultural and ethnic diversity, Integrative Body–Mind–Spirit Social Work strives for the development of cultural competence in practitioners, which was founded on respect for and appreciation of differences. Integrative Body–Mind–Spirit Social Work believes in the innate strength and beauty of individuals, and consequently, Integrative Body–Mind–Spirit Social Work respects clients' needs and interests, trusts their motivation for fostering interest in benefiting themselves and others, and respects their self-determination and freedom of choice. Integrative Body–Mind–Spirit Social Work believes in clients' right to participate and views clients as collaborators and equal participants in the treatment process. The client–social worker relationship is collaborative and nonhierarchical. Instead of perceiving social work professionals as experts, we believe that clients are experts of their lives and social workers are experts on the change process.

Social Justice

Ethical principle: Social workers challenge social injustice.

Social workers pursue social change, particularly with and on behalf of those who are vulnerable and oppressed. Their social change efforts focus primarily on the ever-present issues of poverty, unemployment, discrimination, and other forms of social injustice. These activities seek to promote sensitivity to and knowledge about oppression and cultural and ethnic diversity. By engaging in such efforts, social workers strive to ensure access to needed information, services, resources, quality of opportunity, and meaningful participation in decision making for all people (NASW, 1999).

Besides an explicit emphasis on social workers' responsibility to promote social justice in relation to society and the people with whom they work, IFSW and IASSW (2004) further breakdowns the principles of social justice into: (1) Challenging negative discrimination, (2) recognizing diversity, (3) distributing resources equitably, (4) challenging unjust policies and practices, and (5) working in solidarity.

Integrative Body–Mind–Spirit Social Work affirms the values regarding social justice as exemplified by these principles of ethics. Based on a yin–yang perspective, change is constant and dynamic with contrasting forces working mutually and complementarily to strike for a dynamic equilibrium of the system. When social injustice is observed in society, the social work profession has the ethical and professional responsibility to become a dynamic and contrasting force to strive for a healthy balance in the society by challenging negative discrimination, distributing resources equitably, and challenging unjust social policies and practices. It should be done in a way that respects the diversity of values and opinions and with a stated goal of achieving solidarity in society.

Service

Ethical principle: A social worker's primary goal is to help people in need and to address social problems.

Social workers elevate service to others above self-interest. They draw on their knowledge, values, and skills to help people in need and to address social problems and are encouraged to volunteer some portion of their professional skills with no expectation of significant financial return (*pro bono* service) (NASW, 1999).

Our values in service are grounded in compassion toward others and ourselves. In addition, Integrative Body–Mind–Spirit Social Work is influenced by a yin–yang perspective, which emphasizes the interconnectedness and complementary existence of phenomena, as well as the ever-changing nature of reality. Consequently, serving clients is not a linear process. We learn from clients, who can be our teachers in many ways. Professionals are served through the process of serving others. Consequently, Integrative Body–Mind– Spirit Social Work views that it is a privilege to be in a helping profession. Every opportunity to serve is an honor, as professionals learn and grow from the experience as well.

As change is constant and movement is an integral process of dynamic balance and change, social work professionals should not be complacent about the status quo, even when service seems to be well developed and implemented, for a stagnant system will ultimately become unbalanced. Instead, Integrative Body–Mind–Spirit Social Work firmly believes in continuous creative development, design, and the implementation of service that keeps pace with the dynamic changes of life. Like running water that continuously races to a lower level, creativity and joy lubricate the dynamic system for a continuous flow.

Importance of Human Relationships

Ethical principle: Social workers recognize the central importance of human relationships.

Social workers understand that relationships between and among people are an important vehicle for change and seek to engage clients and others as partners in the helping process. The goal of every social worker is to strengthen relationships among people in a purposeful effort to promote, restore, maintain, and enhance the well-being of individuals, families, social groups, organizations, and communities (NASW, 1999).

Integrative Body–Mind–Spirit Social Work focuses on the importance of community and collectivity in addition to an emphasis on more immediate human relationships. It views that individuals' well-being cannot be separated from and is complementary to collective well-being: As the old saying goes, "It takes a community to raise a child." Here, we are talking about the reciprocity between people, compassion toward others, and the sustainability of the community. Underlying this value of human relationship is not just compassion for established relationships but also a respect for unfamiliar people. In other words, the passion for human relationships embraces diversity and focuses on social inclusion and cohesion. Therefore, social workers denounce discrimination and acts of exclusion.

Integrity

Ethical principle: Social workers behave in a trustworthy manner.

Social workers should act with integrity. This includes not abusing the relationship of trust with the people using their services, recognizing the boundaries between personal and professional life, and not abusing their position for personal benefit or gain (IFSW/IASSW, 2004). Social workers are continually aware of the profession's mission, values, ethical principles, and ethical standards, and practice in a manner consistent with them. They act honestly and responsibly and promote ethical practices in the organizations with which they are affiliated (NASW, 1999).

Besides affirming integrity in social work professional practice, Integrative Body–Mind–Spirit Social Work believes in the importance of the use of the self in professional practice. From the perspective that things are interconnected, our professional self cannot be totally separated from our private self. Integrity implies a certain level of consistence between what social work professionals believe personally and how they relate to clients in their professional roles. Integrative Body–Mind–Spirit Social Work upholds a holistic perspective that emphasizes body, mind, and spirit connectedness for well-being in one's life context. The assumptions of Integrative Body–Mind–Spirit Social Work exemplify simplicity, the appreciation of life, balance, harmony, tranquility, and peace. Consequently, Integrative Body–Mind–Spirit Social Work perceives the continuous personal growth and development of the social work professional, including in the spiritual domains, as an integral part of upholding integrity.

Competence

Ethical principle: Social workers practice within their areas of competence and continually develop their professional expertise.

Social workers are expected to develop and maintain the required skills and competence to do their jobs (IFSW/IASSW, 2004). Social workers continually strive to increase their professional knowledge and skills and to apply them in practice. They aspire to contribute to the knowledge base of the profession (NASW, 1999).

A holistic perspective assumes a parallel process between the development of the professional and personal selves of social work professionals. When the use of the self is an eminent part of social work practice, the development and enhancement of competence is no longer limited to professional knowledge and skills. Social work professionals aspire not only to the development of professional knowledge and skills but also to a continuous personal development that includes the enrichment of and growth in the self, including the spiritual domain.

A holistic perspective also emphasizes the utilization of a wide range of treatment techniques in the domain of the body, mind, and spirit. Without setting unrealistic standards or crossing professional boundaries with other disciplines, it is helpful for social work professionals to pursue a wider range of knowledge, to develop creative arts, skills, and hobbies, and to develop personal skills that they can utilize for therapeutic purposes.

PRACTICE ETHICS OF INTEGRATIVE BODY–MIND–SPIRIT SOCIAL WORK

A holistic perspective in social work practice brings a new set of considerations in ethical practice, because of the inclusion of therapeutic techniques pertaining to body process work and the spiritual domain, both of which are rather new to most models of conventional social work practice. A thoughtful review is therefore necessary for ensuring ethical professional practice. There are issues pertaining to respecting clients' self-determination and ethical considerations regarding the use of treatment techniques related to body process and spiritual interventions. In addition to addressing boundary issues between clients and social work professionals, we have to attend to boundary issues between social work and other disciplines such as the fields of medicine, healthcare, and physiotherapy.

Respect for Self-Determination

Consistent with the fundamental values of social work practice, Integrative Body–Mind–Spirit Social Work respects the client's self-determination in the treatment process. While doing so, it is important to recognize that Integrative Body–Mind–Spirit Social Work is not about religious or spiritual conversion or promotion. We have no interest in convincing clients to accept whatever religious beliefs or practices we may hold. For instance, people may associate mediation with Zen Buddhism, but Integrative Body–Mind–Spirit Social

Work utilizes meditation practices primarily for therapeutic purposes and has nothing to do with Buddhism as a religion. In addition, we use modified and simplified versions of meditation practices for treatment purposes. The following principles guide our policy concerning respecting clients' self-determination:

- Integrative Body–Mind–Spirit Social Work respects religious and spiritual diversity in clients.
- Integrative Body–Mind–Spirit Social Work utilizes clients' religions in treatment; that is, we utilize the values and practices of clients' spiritual or religious beliefs in treatment. For instance, for Christian clients, the love of Christ could be referenced in forgiveness work or in motivating clients to address challenges and appreciate life.
- Integrative Body–Mind–Spirit Social Work assesses the client's spirituality and asks for the client's consent prior to any interventions related to spirituality.

Ethics of Treatment Techniques Related to Body Process

Treatment techniques related to body process as utilized in Integrative Body–Mind–Spirit Social Work involve many senses and primarily include the following activities:

- Treatment techniques related to breathing exercises
- Kinesthetic: physical movement and exercises, dance, massage, and stretching
- Taste: bitter tea, the mindful eating of rice, and herbal drinks
- Visual: mental imagery, color imagery, eye massage, and mental camera
- Touch: drumming, percussion, hand massage, and acupressure
- Sound: singing, mantra, humming, bells, and music
- Diet: healthy eating habits, mindful appreciation of food, and balanced and simple meals

Ethical considerations primarily exist at two levels: (1) ethics relating to the selection of body process activities, and (2) ethics relating to the implementation of body process activities.

Ethics relating to the selection of body process activities

The selection of appropriate treatment techniques relating to body process activities is both an art and a science. The pertinent questions are: (1) how professionals select any particular treatment technique from a wide range of available choices, and (2) how professionals decide what types of body process activities would be helpful for clients. Here, the following principles guide Integrative Body–Mind–Spirit Social Work.

Effectiveness in treating clients.   We choose body process techniques that can effectively address what clients would like or need to accomplish at that point in the treatment process. The selected techniques should also align with the overall treatment goals as determined by clients and families. For instance, Susan came in with a red face, swollen lips, and was panicky. She had just found out that her husband had had an extramarital affair, and she was very emotional and angry. The therapist briefly explored the situation and asked Susan what would be most helpful to her at that moment. Susan said that she was very confused, angry, and just wanted to have a clear mind to decide on the next step. With her consent, the therapist decided to help Susan engage in the following two activities: (1) replenish herself with iced green tea or a drink of her choice, and (2) help her engage in a breathing exercise. The purpose of these two activities was to help Susan calm down so that she could beneficially engage in a therapeutic dialogue regarding her presenting problem pertaining to her marital relationship.

Safety.   Safety is a primary criterion for professionals to select any potential body process activities. Integrative Body–Mind–Spirit Social Work endorses and encourages only the use of body process techniques that are safe and within acceptable social norms. For instance, we teach clients to use light massage and not therapeutic massage, which is only taught and practiced by licensed healthcare professionals. When we utilize touching during group activities, we suggest only activities that are within acceptable social norms. For instance, we may ask group members to shake hands as a gesture of encouragement but not to hug each other.

Nonintrusion.   Integrative Body–Mind–Spirit Social Work promotes nonintrusive techniques for treatment purposes. We use the principle of parsimony in our practice, meaning that we take a minimalist approach to treatment. We think that a minimalist approach is respectful of clients' strengths, is empowering, and economical. We are concerned that major interventions will disturb the system in an unpredictable or an unanticipated way because of reiteration of the feedback mechanism. Based on such a position, we choose acupressure or light massage, which clients can self-administer, but not the more intrusive interventions such as acupuncture. When suggesting light massage activities, we limit our suggestion to socially acceptable body parts such as the head, shoulders, limbs, back, and face.

> Bob, an 85-year-old colon cancer patient who had had his tumor removed, did not dare to move around after his surgery and sat on a sofa watching television all day long. Both of his feet were heavily swollen, painful, and uncomfortable. He became depressed and threw temper tantrums at his wife. After the therapist taught Bob's wife how to massage his feet and to elevate them, the edema in his feet subsided within 15 min. Bob was very pleased and began to talk to the therapist about his discharge plans.

Self-administration. Integrative Body–Mind–Spirit Social Work also chooses body process activities that clients can self-administer. We believe that self-administrable body process activities are empowering and efficient, and both criteria are consistent with the fundamental values of the treatment orientation of Integrative Body–Mind–Spirit Social Work. When clients are able to learn and master the body process activities, they do not need to depend on professionals to engage in those activities. Clients are more likely to engage in those activities when they can do them at any time or at any pace that is viable in their life context.

Simple, easy, and quick to learn. Clients and families are much more likely to engage in body process activities when they can master the activities and feel competent about doing them. We believe that activities that are simple, easy, and quick to learn are more conducive to mastery and competence. For instance, we favor acupressure over acupuncture, because (1) acupressure is self-administrable, whereas only licensed healthcare professionals can administer acupuncture; and (2) one does not need to press the exact acupressure points for treatment to be effective. Hence, it is easier and safer for clients to learn how to do it themselves.

Culturally appropriate and sensitive. Because the way a person experiences his or her problem and solution reality is culturally embedded (Lee, M. Y., 1996), it is imperative to select body process activities that are culturally appropriate, respectful, and acceptable for the clients and families. While social work professionals must possess adequate cultural knowledge of the particular groups that he or she works with, it is always important to engage the client in designing culturally appropriate body process activities in a collaborative manner (Lee, M. Y., 2003). Because Integrative Body–Mind–Spirit Social Work is strongly influenced by Eastern philosophies and practices, the suggested body process activities are inevitably based on cultural wisdoms and practices of the East. While the effectiveness of some activities, such as breathing exercises, meditation, and acupressure are well-documented, social work professionals will still need to pay attention to the process of cultural adaptability of using these interventions in treatment. In addition, a belief in clients' strengths, resources, and innate healing abilities constitutes a fundamental value premise of Integrative Body–Mind–Spirit Social Work. Consequently, it is imperative to explore and utilize clients' unique cultural experiences and wisdom in designing effective and appropriate body process activities in the treatment process. For instance, "What would be some good advice a trusted person in your community would have for you to help you feel better?"

Ethics relating to the implementation of body process activities

The other set of ethical considerations pertains primarily to the implementation of body process activities. These issues focus on a client's self-determination, informed consent, and boundary issues. We routinely adopt the following procedures when introducing clients to and engaging clients in body process activities.

Introduction of activities.   When introducing the selected activities to clients and families, we carefully explain the benefits and potential consequences of the selected body process activities as well as what procedures are involved. Many of the exercises we introduce are commonly practiced movements that can be taught within 5 to 10 min. The therapist should provide clients with as much information as possible and handouts or simple instructions so that they can practice at home after the session. The therapist also answers any questions that clients might have so that they can provide informed consent.

Consent.   The therapist should actively seek the client's consent to engage in the activities by asking them whether they are comfortable with trying the activities. The therapist should routinely let clients know that they can discontinue the activities at any time, even if they gave consent at the beginning.

Self-administration.   The therapist should demonstrate the activities and ask clients to do the body process activities themselves for the following purposes:

- Explain ethical issues regarding boundaries, particularly those relating to body touch
- Minimize dependency
- Enhance self-mastery so that clients can regularly practice the activities in their natural environment.

Clinical judgment.   We carefully observe clients' behavioral and emotional reaction to the selected activities. We ask clients to discontinue the activities if discomfort is observed, based on the therapist's clinical judgment. In addition, we routinely seek feedback from clients about their reaction to and effectiveness of the activities. Most selected activities are simple or familiar to the client. For example, appropriate physical movements, breathing exercises, guided imagery, or relaxation techniques are usually helpful ways for making shifts in clinical processes, especially in situations when verbal interactions do not help. However, the social work professional should not assume the effectiveness of these activities but should carefully observe and track clients' responses and solicit feedback from them.

Touching as a way to express care and concern.   Touching clients is a sensitive issue that our profession has shied away from because of ethical considerations. However, we know that there are situations when we would offer a client a hand, shake hands with him or her, or give a pat on the shoulder. In addition, Integrative Body–Mind–Spirit Social Work adopts a developmental perspective of emotional regulation, meaning that a person learns how to regulate emotion from external encounters before such abilities can be internalized to the extent that the person can regulate the emotions internally in an appropriate and effective manner.

Instead of classifying all types of touch as inappropriate, Integrative Body–Mind–Spirit Social Work endorses body touch that is appropriate at times under the following conditions:

- The therapist uses it for the expression of care and concern, especially in emotional situations such as a crisis or during moments of great success and accomplishment for clients and families.
- The client consents to the encounter.
- Touching is strictly limited to socially acceptable "public parts," such as shoulders and hands.
- The encounter must be brief.

Ethics relating to the competent practice regarding body process activities.   There are situations when one should not use body process activities with clients and families:

- Imagery or meditation should not be used with clients who have active psychotic symptoms such as hallucinations and delusions.
- Body process activities can be used with people with severe or terminal illness, but the therapist must clearly explain the purposes of the body process activities (such as massage) and get clients' consent and consult with their healthcare professionals prior to the activities.

Ethical considerations pertaining to treatment on diet and life style

Based on our belief of mind–body connectedness, Integrative Body–Mind–Spirit Social Work views that clients' diet and living habits constitute significant factors that affect their well-being. However, social work professionals are not dieticians or health professionals. We only encourage clients to seek balance in their diets and daily lives instead of being prescriptive in our approach. Oftentimes, we ask constructive questions that help clients to evaluate their diets and daily habits. When we make recommendations pertaining to diets or life styles, we ask them, "How healthy is your lifestyle?" and "What is the first small thing that you can do to make it more balanced?" We use the following criteria in the process:

- Affordable and accessible: For instance, foods that are available at the grocery store, supermarket, etc., or activities and exercises that clients can self-initiate
- No recommendation or marketing of any product at the treatment facility, either by social work professionals or by group members
- We only recommend daily food or herbs but not any medicinal herbs or products.

ETHICAL CONSIDERATIONS PERTAINING TO COMPETENT PRACTICE

Integrative Body–Mind–Spirit Social Work interprets competent practice as developing and using treatment techniques that effectively and quickly create positive change in the lives of clients and families, as determined by the clients. In doing so, we abide by the principle of parsimony: We use the least intrusive intervention required to accomplish treatment goals, which is generally to create positive changes, as determined by the clients. In addition, the therapist should not ask for information or get into detail regarding clients' lives more than is needed for therapeutic purposes and should particularly avoid re-traumatizing clients by asking them to retell their traumatic experiences more than necessary. Competent practice requires ongoing and life long learning. Social workers are expected to develop and maintain the required skills and competence to do their job and continually develop their professional expertise (IFSW/IASSW, 2004; NASW, 1999).

Ethical Considerations Pertaining to Cultural Competence and Social Diversity

Integrative Body–Mind–Spirit Social Work affirms the ethical standard regarding cultural competence and social diversity in that (1) social workers should have a knowledge base of their clients' cultures and be able to demonstrate competence in the provision of services that are sensitive to their clients' cultures and to differences among people and cultural groups (NASW, 1999), and (2) social workers should recognize and respect the ethnic and cultural diversity of the societies in which they practice, taking into account individual, family, group and community differences (IFSW/IASSW, 2004).

The development of Integrative Body–Mind–Spirit Social Work was inspired by a vision to bring eastern philosophies and practices into conventional social work practice. Its origin is a live example of an appreciation of "differences." Integrative Body–Mind–Spirit Social Work believes that human behaviors, understanding, and experiences are embedded in one's culture. Effective treatment must be based upon social work professionals' cultural sensitivity, appreciation of differences, cultural knowledge, and ability to connect with and respect clients from diverse backgrounds. Because the way a client experiences his or her problem and solution reality is culturally embedded, it is imperative for the therapist to explore, understand, and utilize clients' unique cultural experiences and wisdom in designing culturally appropriate and sensitive interventions in the treatment process (Lee, 2003). While different social and cultural groups have their unique cultural beliefs, values, and practices, Integrative Body–Mind–Spirit Social Work affirms the importance and values of cross-cultural learning, which is accomplished through respectful dialogues and encounters with diverse groups.

ETHICS RELATED TO SPIRITUAL-BASED PRACTICE

Canda and Furman (1999, p. 264) have listed comprehensive, explicit, and thoughtful guidelines regarding spiritual-based social work practices with clients. They have listed six options: (1) implicit spiritually sensitive relationship and context-meaning qualities such as genuine respect and passion for people, etc.; (2) private spiritually based activities by social workers, such as praying for a client's well-being in an open and compassionate manner; (3) referral to outside spiritual support systems; (4) collaboration with outside spiritual support systems; (5) direct use of spiritual activities at client's request; and (6) direct use of spiritual activities at the social work professional's invitation. Canda and Furman suggested that social work professionals could use the first four spiritual-based activities when clients have expressed an interest in incorporating spiritual-based treatment; the first five activities when a spiritually sensitive relationship is well established with an interested client; and all activities when a social work professional also possesses relevant qualifications for spiritual-based treatment activities. When a client has not expressed interest, professionals should limit any use of spiritual-based activities to only the first two listed options. However, sound clinical judgment, cautious usage, and thoughtful ethical reflection are recommended for using any spiritual-based activities for any client scenario.

Richards and Bergin (1997, p. 252) suggest that there are at least four situations in which a healthcare practitioner should refrain from applying religious and spiritual interventions, and the American Psychological Association has adopted their position. The four situations are: (1) when clients do not want to participate in such interventions; (2) when clients have active psychotic symptoms, such as auditory hallucination and delusion; (3) when spiritual issues are irrelevant to the client's presenting problem; and (4) when clients are minors and their parents have not given permission for spiritual interventions.

Integrative Body–Mind–Spirit Social Work adopts these ethical guidelines in using spiritual-based interventions/activities in our practice.

ETHICS REGARDING THE USAGE OF PRACTICES FROM SOURCES OTHER THAN MAINSTREAM SOCIAL WORK

Integrative Body–Mind–Spirit Social Work uses techniques and ideas from diverse sources and traditions in formulating its own theoretical and practical base. It is imperative for practicing professionals to acknowledge the original source of the tradition. For instance, *Ha* breathing is based on the theory and practices of *qigong*, acupressure from Traditional Chinese Medicine (TCM), health exercises from Chinese medicine meridian theory, meditation practices and breathing exercises from Buddhism and Daoism, movement techniques from dance therapy, etc. Integrative Body–Mind–Spirit Social Work firmly believes that it is unethical to use or modify techniques from other traditions without acknowledging the source or tradition.

Another primary ethical concern pertains to criteria for learning or selecting techniques from other disciplines or traditions for treatment purposes. Integrative Body–Mind–Spirit Social Work adopts the following criteria regarding learning techniques from other disciplines:

- Integrative Body–Mind–Spirit Social Work views competent and effective practice as our primary ethical concern to clients and families. Consequently, the treatment techniques to be learned, adopted, or modified should have clinical relevance to positive treatment outcomes. Clinical relevance can be assessed based on empirical evidence of effectiveness (e.g., meditative practices for reducing stress), clinical experiences, and theoretical or empirical evidence provided by other disciplines (e.g., acupressure based on TCM).
- Integrative Body–Mind–Spirit Social Work affirms the use of self in the treatment process. Consequently, we encourage self-exploration and

self-awareness in social work professionals so that they can discover their own interests and passion. In doing so, they can maximize their own creativity in the learning process. For instance, a therapist who is interested in and passionate about dance can explore how she or he can modify dance into movement-related body process activities in treatment.

- Integrative Body–Mind–Spirit Social Work believes in the importance of developing a broad spectrum of treatment techniques that can touch many senses and dimensions of the human experience. For example, movement, visual, metaphors, breathing, touch, and so on affect different areas.
- Integrative Body–Mind–Spirit Social Work views that change is an integral part of living and encourages lifelong learning on the part of social work professionals in their professional pursuits. What one considers lifelong learning will be different from what another considers lifelong learning. Active engagement in living a healthy life style, engaging in activities for spiritual growth, and searching to cultivate compassion and loving kindness can be some pathways towards an integrative life style, but the choices are endless, depending on one's aspirations, beliefs, and life experiences.
- Integrative Body–Mind–Spirit Social Work is strengths-based and emphasizes empowerment. The learned treatment techniques should be empowering for both individual clients and families. Clients will feel empowered if the techniques are simple and easy to learn, can be self-administered, are inexpensive, and are effective at treating problems. We particularly avoid learning or adopting techniques that are expensive or highly commercialized.

BOUNDARY ISSUES WITH OTHER DISCIPLINES

Because of the holistic perspective adopted by Integrative Body–Mind–Spirit Social Work, as well as its tradition regarding learning and adopting techniques from other disciplines, there is bound to be overlapping and collaboration between Integrative Body–Mind–Spirit Social Work and other disciplines, primarily with healthcare professionals. Instead of shying away from such collaboration or negatively focusing on "turf issues," Integrative Body–Mind–Spirit Social Work embraces a connected and concerted effort in treatment that promotes body–mind–spirit connectedness in human existence. Integrative Body–Mind–Spirit Social Work adopts the following position in collaborating with and learning from other disciplines:

- Integrative Body–Mind–Spirit Social Work considers other professions, including their scope of services, missions, expertise, and practices, as essential in establishing professional boundaries and collaborating relationships. For instance, when discussing diet and life styles with clients and families, we only inquire into daily eating habits or recommend food or herbs that are available at groceries. We thoroughly refrain from recommending any medicinal products or herbs, which is the job of healthcare professionals.

- Integrative Body–Mind–Spirit Social Work views a mutual understanding of the nature, scope, expertise, practices, and expertise of collaborating disciplines as paramount in facilitating a collaborating and mutually respectful relationship.
- Integrative Body–Mind–Spirit Social Work does not perceive a holistic perspective and specialization as mutually exclusive. We routinely refer clients for specialized treatment if deemed beneficial. We maintain respect to professionals that clients are already consulting with, unless unethical practices are observed.

SUMMARY

Ethical considerations pertaining to Integrative Body–Mind–Spirit Social Work are particularly important because of its holistic approach to practice, which addresses the body–mind–spirit connection as well as the introduction of Eastern philosophies and practices in social work treatment. Although Integrative Body–Mind–Spirit Social Work practice is based on mainstream social work practice, the new practice orientation and techniques deserve careful consideration pertaining to ethical issues. Integrative Body–Mind–Spirit Social Work affirms the ethical principles of social work practice as stated in the NASW Code of Ethics (1999) and The International Federation of Social Workers and The International Association of Schools of Social Work (IFSW/IASSW, 2004). We also expand on the meaning of values pertaining to service, social justice, dignity and worth of humans, importance of human relationships, integrity, and competence. We outline in detail ethical considerations pertaining to body process activities at the level of selecting useful body process activities and implementing these activities in treatment sessions. Integrative Body–Mind–Spirit Social Work selects body process activities that are culturally appropriate and sensitive, effective at treating clients, are safe, can be self-administered to empower clients, and are simple, easy, and quick to learn. We thoroughly introduce the activities, explain the benefits and potential consequences, seek consent, teach the activities, and carefully observe clients' reactions when engaging them in a particular body process activity. We give consideration to ethical guidelines pertaining to body touch because of the potentially powerful therapeutic effect, as well as the potential danger of crossing socially acceptable boundaries.

Because Integrative Body–Mind–Spirit Social Work introduces eastern philosophies and practices into conventional social work practice, we specifically address the importance of cultural competence and respect for diversity. In addition to attending to cultural adaptability when introducing interventions that might be culturally different from the clients' original culture, it is imperative for the therapist to explore, understand, and utilize clients' unique cultural experiences and wisdom in designing culturally appropriate and sensitive interventions in the treatment process.

Ethical considerations regarding spiritual-based practice are based on guidelines provided by Canda and Furman (1999) as well as Richards and Bergin (1997). These are positions widely adopted by social work professionals and psychologists. Canda and Furman (1999) provide positively stated guidelines to decide when to provide spiritual-based interventions and what types of spiritual-based interventions to provide. Richards and Bergin state under what conditions not to provide spiritual-based treatment. These ethical guidelines are important because of the traditional downplaying of spirituality in social work practice and, consequently, a lack of clear guidelines pertaining to its use.

Because of the holistic orientation of Integrative Body–Mind–Spirit Social Work, there are also ethical considerations regarding the usage and learning of techniques and ideas from other disciplines and traditions, as well as boundary issues with them. We feel that thorough and explicit acknowledgment of the original source of techniques is a solution to this ethical issue. We also describe specific criteria for learning and ethical considerations pertaining to setting appropriate boundaries with other disciplines and traditions.

16

Learning Integrative Body–Mind–Spirit Social Work

Learning Integrative Body-Mind-Spirit Social Work requires interested professionals to acquire skills and knowledge relevant to a holistic approach that incorporates body, mind, and spirit in social work practice. We believe that there are some prerequisite skills and knowledge that professionals should possess prior to learning this approach. In addition, integrating holistic techniques into social work treatment involves revisiting values in addition to learning a new set of knowledge and skills. This chapter systematically describes the essence of each component and provides useful information and thinking pertaining to acquiring these skills. Integrative Body-Mind-Spirit Social Work believes in the strengths and inherent potential of individuals. Consistent with such a stance, we focus on how social work professionals can utilize, build, and expand upon their existing expertise and strengths to further develop a creative and beneficial therapeutic repertoire.

PREREQUISITE SKILLS AND KNOWLEDGE

Integrative Body-Mind-Spirit Social Work is built upon established social work practice knowledge. We therefore assume that professionals will have basic background training in their own disciplines regardless of whether it is in the area of social work, psychology, human services, counseling, nursing, and so on. Consequently, we assume that learners should have basic knowledge and skills in working with individuals and families in the following areas. This list is not meant to be exhaustive; it should be viewed as a guide instead.

Basic Knowledge

- Knowledge pertaining to a developmental perspective of the individual and family life cycle that also includes knowledge about different stages of development, tasks to be learned at each stage, and challenges to be addressed. Examples of these developmental theories/perspectives include, but are not limited to, the eight stages of psychosocial development of individuals as postulated by Erikson (1963) and family life cycle development discussed by Carter and McGoldrick (1998).
- A basic understanding and appreciation of power and control in human relationships, particularly in a family context.
- A basic understanding of the relationships between people and the environment as postulated by, for example, an ecological perspective or systems perspective: How does social policy affect individual and family well-being? There should also be some understanding of the impact of the broader socio-cultural-political environment on individual behavior and well-being.
- A basic understanding of the impact of cultural influences on individuals' development and behavior.
- A basic knowledge of mental health issues and psychopathology.
- Knowledge regarding treatment or therapy, informed by individual disciplines. For instance, professionals with backgrounds in counseling, psychology, and social work should possess knowledge regarding family and/or individual psychotherapy. Professionals with a background in health care should have knowledge about medical treatment and its biopsychosocial impact on patients.

Basic Skills

- Self-awareness of power and control issues in the therapeutic process.
- Relational skills, including empathy, joining, and engagement.
- Basic interviewing skills, including active listening, paraphrasing, restating, and engaging clients in therapeutic dialogues for change.
- Basic skills regarding treatment as determined by an individual's professional training. These skills should include problem identification, goal

setting, treatment planning, treatment, and termination skills, as based on individual expertise.

• Basic skills in providing culturally competent and appropriate services to clients.

REVISITING VALUES

The evolution of Integrative Body-Mind-Spirit Social Work includes development of its own knowledge and practice base. However, Integrative Body-Mind-Spirit Social Work is more than a set of techniques: It embraces a way of thinking and values about human life and change. We do not believe that a professional can provide effective and authentic treatment to clients and families if they do not, at least to a certain extent, understand, embrace, or agree with these values and orientations. Consequently, competent practice of Integrative Body-Mind-Spirit Social Work does involve a revisiting and a personal reevaluation of values and perspectives regarding human behavior and change.

The practice of Integrative Body-Mind-Spirit Social Work is informed by Eastern philosophies in addition to mainstream social work practice. These philosophies include, but are not limited to, Daoism, Buddhism, and theories of Traditional Chinese Medicine (TCM). Underlying these philosophies are values that we believe should be made explicit for readers to revisit and critically examine. The following are examples of these cores values and perspectives of Integrative Body-Mind-Spirit Social Work.

Because change is constant and phenomena are interconnected, forces of diverse natures often work together in a complementary and dynamic manner that contributes to the evolving and changing reality. Such a view leads to the following values and perspectives regarding problems and solutions:

• A perspective of problems as opportunities for growth, which leads to the following perspectives regarding pain and problems:

  ○ Discomfort and uneasiness can be catalysts for change in disguise.
  ○ Individuals are invited to move outside of their comfort zone for growth and change.
  ○ Crises, problems, and challenges are opportunities for change.
  ○ The treatment goal is not just problem eradication or symptoms reduction but transformation and growth through problems and crises.

• Embracing adversity and tolerating pain and uncertainty as potential passages for growth and transformation (versus the conventional wisdom of avoiding pain and pursuing happiness).

- A holistic view that recognizes the interconnectedness of diverse phenomena contributes to the following values, which are exemplified in treatment and intervention:

  ○ Reclaiming the role of body and spirituality in the process of change
  ○ Reclaiming the connection between body, mind, and spirit in the context of our broader sociocultural environment

- The holistic perspective that what is functional and what is dysfunctional, wellness and disease, and individual well-being and collective well-being are complementary and in a dynamic balance rather than dichotomous, mutually exclusive phenomena.

The described values, assumptions, and perspectives fundamentally influence how Integrative Body-Mind-Spirit Social Work approaches assessment, construes the treatment process and interventions, and defines treatment goals. Although some of these values are similar to those promoted by other theories of mainstream social work practice, others are quite different from existing values, beliefs, and assumptions. We strongly and sincerely encourage readers to critically examine these ways of thinking in their learning process. Providing treatment for individuals and families is rarely a purely technical process. It always involves values, judgment, and assumptions about human behavior, change, and what is defined as healthy or pathological. We believe that it is much more helpful to make these values and assumptions explicit so that they can be openly scrutinized, clarified, and revisited, so that treatment can best serve the interest of informed clients and their families.

EXPANDING THE KNOWLEDGE BASE

Building upon existing social work treatment approaches and skills, the Integrative Body-Mind-Spirit Social Work practice also involves an additional set of treatment techniques, which require an expanded knowledge base. This knowledge primarily focuses on treatment techniques pertaining to integrating body process and spirituality as an integral part of treatment. Although such knowledge is theoretically unlimited, Integrative Body-Mind-Spirit Social Work views competent and effective practice as our primary ethical concern when providing treatment for clients and families. Consequently, knowledge regarding treatments should have clinical relevance to positive treatment outcomes. Clinical relevance can be assessed based on empirical evidence of effectiveness (e.g., meditative practices for reducing stress), clinical experiences, and theoretical and empirical evidence provided by other disciplines (e.g., effectiveness of acupressure based on TCM). Currently, we have expanded our knowledge base to include TCM and other selected complementary or alternative therapies.

Traditional Chinese Medicine

It is helpful to understand the basic core theories and assumptions of Chinese medicine in conceptualizing health and disease. In particular, Chinese medicine's holistic, systemic perspective is highly relevant to Integrative Body-Mind-Spirit Social Work. Health is seen as a state of dynamic equilibrium, whereas disease is primarily a state of disequilibrium. Interventions strive to restore balance rather than reduce symptoms.

It is also helpful to have a basic understanding of the meridian theory of Chinese medicine, because the concept is quite often used in Integrative therapy body process work, such as massage and acupressure. Because Integrative Body-Mind-Spirit Social Work emphasizes empowerment and self-mastery, we use the meridian theory and techniques in the most simplified manner. It is not necessary to spend a year learning everything about meridian theory, and it would require even more time to learn about the complicated meridian network and the 360 or so acupuncture points all over the body. For Integrative Body-Mind-Spirit Social Work, we have selected 10 useful acupressure points at the head and limbs that can be located and self-administered to easily. We have also selected a few easy-to-learn massage activities that are safe and fun.

We certainly encourage readers who are interested in Chinese medicine to further pursue such an interest. Useful books on Chinese medicine can easily be found in libraries and bookstores. Moreover, helpful resources can be readily found on the Internet (Appendix B).

Complementary and Alternative Therapies/Practices

Integrative Body-Mind-Spirit Social Work utilizes a wide range of techniques in the assessment and treatment process, including those that are borrowed from complementary and alternative therapies or practices. Most of the selected techniques focus on integrating body process work and spirituality in treatment, as these dimensions have traditionally been downplayed in social work practice. Examples of these techniques are:

- Movement therapy, including dance and psychodrama
- Eastern-based health practices, such as *taiji* (tai chi), *qiqong*, and yoga
- Expressive art, focusing mostly on art and music
- Play therapy, especially with children and adolescents
- Meditation-based practices focusing primarily on breathing and visualization

It is important to note that Integrative Body-Mind-Spirit Social Work does not use these techniques as an independent mode of treatment but rather as an integral part of treatment. Despite the fact that we have therapists who are experts, for instance, in dance therapy, Integrative Body-Mind-Spirit Social Work does not claim expertise or specialization in any of these areas. We expand our knowledge and skills base primarily to include treatment techniques related to body process and spirituality. We usually modify and adapt helpful techniques from these sources to be used in the treatment process, oftentimes, in a simplified manner that is easy to learn and self-administrable by both the therapist and the client.

We view these techniques as constantly evolving, and there are almost infinite possibilities of cross-learning. Readers will have to be careful in selecting appropriate techniques to develop and use in treatment. We have described in detail the ethical guidelines of selecting techniques in Chapter 15. In addition, these techniques have to be culturally appropriate and viable, as clients and families from diverse backgrounds will certainly find some techniques more personally and culturally meaningful and relevant than others. For instance, visualizing the love of Christ in a meditation practice is surely more appropriate for clients who believe in Christ than those who do not. Similarly, *taiji* movements will make more sense to clients who practice or are interested in *taiji*, whereas walking meditation is more viable to most people, as all people walk and breathe.

LEARNING THE TECHNIQUES

We have given much thought to the learning process involved in acquiring this approach to practice. Of course, reading this book constitutes a useful and important start. Interested professionals can also read other books or the references recommended in this book. However, learning any set of skills involves much more than cognitive knowing. Simply put, learning involves multiple modalities (Kolb, 1976) and implicit learning (Polanyi, 1962). At the Centre on Behavioral Health, we have designed an experiential learning 3-day retreat, 5-day practitioner training course.

Other useful sources include the book *An Eastern Body–Mind–Spirit Approach: A Training Manual With One-Second Techniques*, written by Cecilia Chan, Department of Social Work and Social Administration, The University of Hong Kong, in 2001. Readers are also encouraged to visit the Web site http:\\www.cbh.hku.hk, which provides current information about useful resources and references pertaining to learning Integrative Social Work.

The Centre on Behavioral Health of the University of Hong Kong runs experiential workshops for professionals who would like to learn the Body–Mind–Spirit (BMS) holistic approach for the promotion and betterment of their own physical, mental, emotional, and spiritual well-being and that of the individuals and families that they serve. Participants include people working in various helping professions, such as counselors, social workers, medical doctors, nurses, and so on.

Workshop participants are provided with references to the approach and are invited to review the materials before attending the training. The workshop is primarily experiential based; thus, involvement on the part of participants is stressed. There are individual and group exercises, usually followed by small-group sharing. Short lectures on specific topics such as the interconnectedness of body, mind, and spirit are provided. Traditional Eastern health techniques such as massage, *qigong*, and bodily exercises are taught and practiced in groups. Participants should then be able to master these hands-on techniques and practice them with their clients afterwards. Guided meditation and mindfulness practice are scheduled over the 3-day workshop, enabling participants to go inside and get in touch with themselves. The workshop highlights the three major themes of the Integrative Body–Mind–Spirit approach, which are *Growth Through Pains; Loss, Death, and Life*; and *Forgiveness and Appreciation*. Most of the tools and exercises that are presented and practiced during the workshops are discussed in previous chapters of this book. (Table 16–1).

The approach of the workshop is experiential; the exercises are designed to allow participants to venture into deep personal reflection, to take risks to get in touch with their vulnerabilities and untapped potentials, and to gain access to their hearts and souls. Thus, it provides a space for participants to venture into a spiritual retreat and a journey for personal growth.

In general, the workshop runs for 3 days. As the workshop lasts for only 3 days, participants will neither learn all the techniques of Integrative Social Work nor complete their search for meaning and spirituality. There are two key messages in the workshop. Firstly, the body, mind, and spirit of a person are interconnected and each dimension can be utilized for healing. Secondly, it is absolutely important for participants to be in touch with themselves so that they can utilize their inner resources and their own unique strengths to help others in their work. Participants are therefore encouraged to continue their personal journey of meaning searching and utilize the holistic integrative approach in their own innovative ways.

Use of Self

We cannot emphasize enough the importance of the use of the self in Integrative Social Work. In the age of scientificism, people are increasingly trained to believe in the objectivity of skills and techniques that have no face but just proven effectiveness, regardless of who administers the techniques or provides the treatment. Integrative Body-Mind-Spirit Social Work emphasizes

TABLE **16–1.** Outline of the 3-Day Body–Mind–Spirit Experiential Training Workshop

DAY 1	DAY 2	DAY 3
Theme: Growth through pain	*Theme: Loss, Death and Life*	*Theme: Forgiveness and Appreciation*
Warm-up exercise	Exercise with hands and *qigong*	Sound *qigong* exercise
Introduction and overview of the BMS approach	The lesson of death – *Loss and unpredictability in life*	Loving mind – *I am thankful to. . .*
Small group sharing – *Myself: I am who I am*	Meditation – *Imagery on the growth of a seed*	Group exercise – *Cognitive Map*
Nurturing the body – *Face massage*	Small-group sharing – *Life imprints*	A wounded healer – *The letter of forgiveness*
Mindful eating	Spiritual journey – *Chapters in your autobiography*	Meditation – *Loving kindness*
Lunch break	Lunch Break	Lunch Break
Body-mind connection – *Body scan meditation*	Mindful walking – *Visiting the cemetery*	Nurturing the body – *Neck & shoulder massage*
Small-group sharing – *I am in touch with my pains*	Mindful drinking	Affirmation of self – *Signature strengths*
Nurturing the body – *Back massage, acupressure points*	Life lessons – *Letter to your 3-year old*	Small group sharing – *Integrating BMS in your own practice*
Homework assignment	Homework assignment	Feedback and evaluation

empirically based practice and does not downplay the importance of being accountable and effective. However, we do not think that professionals should or can lose sight of the importance of the self, which constitutes a significant venue for change. The importance of the use of self has been reiterated by numerous highly respected therapists such as Virginia Satir, Carl Rogers, and others (e.g., Baldwin, 2000; Lammert, 1986; Real, 1990; Satir, 1988). Integrative Body-Mind-Spirit Social Work accords great significance to professionals because of a holistic and systems perspective in viewing change. The "self" of the therapist is inseparable with how she or he relates to clients and families, how she or he understands a client's situation and makes clinical judgment in assessment and treatment, what she or he views as effective treatment, and what she or he does in a session. In other words, the same treatment technique may result in different therapeutic outcomes if adopted by two therapists with different styles and orientations. Because of the importance of the use of self in social work treatment, learning Integrative Body-Mind-Spirit Social Work necessarily involves keen self-awareness and ongoing self-reflection pertaining to the interfacing between the personal self and professional self of the social work professional.

Utilization of One's Own Expertise, Interests, and Hobbies, Personal Experience

A systems perspective suggests an isomorphic process between connected systems. We believe that, when a therapist authentically utilizes his or her strengths, expertise, and resources in the treatment process, there will be a parallel process of strengths-identification and utilization in clients and families. The therapist's holon and the client's holon are not distinctly separate. For example, at the Center on Behavioral Health, one of the developers of Integrative Body-Mind-Spirit Social Work, Rainbow, a talented dancer who is also a therapist, utilized her personal interest and expertise in dance to develop movement therapy with clients and families, which has been effective and inspiring. Siu-Man, one of the coauthors of this book, has been a renowned psychiatric social worker for more than 20 years. Because of his personal interest in Chinese culture and Chinese medicine, he pursued a degree in TCM and is currently a qualified Chinese medicine doctor. Upon joining the Center, he integrated his knowledge of TCM into clinical practice with clients and families and has developed a wide range of useful body process-related techniques in treatment.

Although it is important to enrich our professional development through learning from external sources, we sincerely believe that it is crucial, if not more important, for professionals to identify, discover, and reconnect with their personal strengths, interests, and expertise in expanding and refining their therapeutic repertoire.

Nurture Body–Mind–Spirit Well-Being

Integrative Body-Mind-Spirit Social Work promotes a holistic approach to treatment that emphasizes the well-being of a connected body–mind–spirit system. In our experience, it is very hard to foster body–mind–spirit well-being in clients and families when the therapist is disconnected, exhausted, and burnt out. Consistent with our belief in isomorphic processes, we believe that professionals need to nurture their own body–mind–spirit well-being in order to be authentic and effective.

Integrative Body-Mind-Spirit Social Work recognizes the existence of a delicate boundary between the professional and personal self, and respects the diverse interpretations of body–mind–spirit well-being. Professionals who come from different cultures, embrace diverse religious beliefs or spirituality, or grew up in different backgrounds will, of course, develop their own meaning of and ways to nurture body–mind–spirit well-being. However, we believe that it is important to contemplate the following:

- Being mindful and living in the moment
- Nurturing the well-being of the body–mind–spirit in an integrated manner
- Enriching and embracing life as a process of being with opportunities for growth and transformation
- Appreciating the beauty of life in small ways
- Developing peer support and "a community of others"

THE PARADOX OF LEARNING

Daoism describes true knowledge, as "knowing is knowing, not-knowing is not-knowing." What this means is that there are always things that we can know and things that we cannot know. There are always situations that we are familiar with and others that are unfamiliar, foreign, and strange. True knowledge is not about knowing everything and having answers for all questions or problems. True knowledge is about being at ease when we know and at ease when we do not know, at peace when we have the answer and at peace when there is no immediate solution. Similarly, learning does not imply that we will have the answers for every question or problem. Learning involves patience so that we will not rush to develop immature, inappropriate, or irrelevant answers or solutions to the questions or problems at hand. Learning is a paradox that entails knowing the unknown and trusting it in times when we do not know. The spirit of learning is an aspiration for and curiosity toward knowing the unknown but also being at peace with times of not-knowing, without losing curiosity toward knowing or rushing to come up with premature answers.

SUMMARY

In this chapter, we share with readers our thinking pertaining to the process of learning Integrative Body-Mind-Spirit Social Work. We assume that readers have already developed or possess knowledge and skills, based on their respective disciplines, regarding human development and change, mental health, and treatment with individuals and families. In addition to the prerequisite knowledge and skills, Integrative Body-Mind-Spirit Social Work requires learners to expand their knowledge and skill bases primarily in the area of assessment and treatment techniques pertaining to integrating body process and spirituality as an integral part of treatment. However, Integrative Body-Mind-Spirit Social Work is more than a set of techniques. It is a way of thinking about human behavior and changes. We have succinctly described the values and assumptions underlying Integrative Body-Mind-Spirit Social Work and strongly encourage readers to critically revisit and examine these ways of thinking in their learning process. The assumptions and values regarding the nature and mechanisms of change and the interconnectedness of phenomena lead to a distinctive view of problems and treatment goals, in addition to a body–mind–spirit focus in treatment. It is of crucial importance for readers to carefully revisit their personal values as well as professional values related to social work practice. When learning this approach, readers can benefit from reading this book as the first step, and engage with other modes of learning, such as training courses offered at the Center on Behavioral Health, experiential learning courses in alternative therapies, or utilize other resources that are provided in this book. We strongly advocate the importance of the use of the self in the learning process. Nurturing the body–mind–spirit constitutes part of the parallel process in which professionals create a context for clients and families to do the same. Consistent with a focus on strengths, we sincerely believe that it is of paramount importance for social work professionals to discover, reconnect, and utilize their personal strengths, expertise, and experiences in developing and creating their practice styles and expertise. Similar to what has been described earlier in the book about the process of change, learning involves a dynamic balance of knowing and not-knowing that keeps the learner moving to a new level of knowledge and understanding. The journey itself is a paradox that brings out our creativity, our passion, and appreciation of life when working with clients and families.

Appendix A: Additional Information on Yin–Yang Perspective, Buddhism, and Daoism

THE YIN–YANG PERSPECTIVE

The concepts of yin and yang have been described as fundamental to the Chinese view of the world. No one knows any historical details about the people who first formulated such ideas, nor do we have any ancient texts that set forth their ideas. However, there is general consensus that these ideas were developed among students of *The Book of Change* (*Yijing*, formerly known as *I Ching*). *The Book of Change* is another significant legacy of the Chinese philosophical tradition, and it was devised by ancient sages who observed the processes that operate in the ever-changing world and discovered underlying principles that allowed people to bring their activities into alignment with the natural processes (Höchsmann, 2001; Kirkland, 2004; Wong, 1997). *The Book of Change* is perceived as "the foundation for later developments in divination, geomancy, astronomy, music, medicine, and other arts and sciences. Its influence on the metaphysics and astronomy of east Asia is comparable to the influence of Plato in the West" (Lee, 1979, p. 2). Later, the yin–yang school blended with proponents of ideas of the Five Elements, which interpreted life's processes by five distinct aspects of reality instead of two (Wong, 1997). The development of the Five Elements explanatory system has traditionally been attributed to a thinker named Tsou Yen, but his writings were lost in ancient times. The yin–yang perspective was largely suppressed during the Qin times, formerly known as Ch'in (B.C. 221–B.C. 206), but it became very influential during the Han period (B.C. 206–221 A.D.) (Kirkland, 2004).

The yin–yang perspective can be perceived as a systems perspective described in ancient Chinese terminology. Based on the perception and long-term observation of nature, ancient Chinese scholars believed that all things in the world could be classified into two broad categories, yin and yang. Yin and yang are the two fundamental forces or building blocks of all things that define, make up, and are in life (Höchsmann, 2001; Wong, 1997). Yin is the dark principle, represented by darkness, softness, stillness, and receptive energy. It is frequently symbolized by the moon, night, winter, earth, and women. Yang is the light principle, represented by brightness, hardness, movement, and creative energy. It is oftentimes symbolized by the sun, day, summer, heaven, and men. Common examples of yin–yang pairs are earth and sky, night and day, moon and sun, cold and heat, winter and summer, and women and men. There is constant interplay between the yin and yang forces: As the sun goes down, the moon rises, which brings an end to the day but also the anticipation of a new day.

It is important to recognize that, although yin and yang are contrasting forces, they are also mutually facilitating and mutually repressing. In fact, both yin and yang originate from the same universal and nontransient force, the *Dao*, from which life originates and from which one can never truly be separated. As such, the dualistic holism conceptualization of the yin–yang perspective is embedded within a monistic and nondual conception of reality (Canda & Furman, 1999). The dynamic interaction and mutuality of yin–yang is beautifully symbolized and described in *The Book of Change*. The Chinese title of *The Book of Change* is *Yijing* (*I Ching*). The Chinese character for *Yi* is 易, which means change. The word 易 is made up of two characters: 日 (sun) and 勿 (not, i.e., not sun), thereby, meaning moon. In other words, the Chinese character 易 already depicts the inseparability of the yin and yang forces despite their differences.

The symbols of yin and yang as depicted in *The Book of Change* further elucidate the fascinating synchronicity of these two concepts and the Chinese view of change. Yin, as the dark principle, is represented by a broken line "__ __" to suggest its soft nature. Yang, as the light principle, is represented by an unbroken line, "__" to suggest its firm and strong nature. Yin and yang are the two fundamental components of change, although they do not force the other to become the same. Instead, the relationship leading to change is complementary, continuous, and interconnected. The pattern of change, movement, and development, as depicted in ancient symbols in *The Book of Change* is a continuous movement of one force contracting while the other is expanding. Yin is considered new and incomplete when there is a presence of yang. The incomplete yin is symbolized by ▀▀ ▀▀; it continues to expand and reaches full maturity as yang completely contracts. The old yin is symbolized by ▀▀ ▀▀. At the state of old yin, it begins to yield to the expansion of new yang, symbolized by ▀▀▀. Yang becomes mature and complete ▀▀▀ before yielding to the new yin ▀▀ ▀. The ever-evolving cycle describes a systematic movement of change in time.

The classic yin–yang symbol further illustrates the dynamic interplay, intricate balance, complementarity, and inseparability of diverse and contrasting life forces (Figure 1.1). The boundary between yin and yang is not a rigid line.

Instead, the boundary is moving and changing, as depicted by the smooth and curving line. Also, no matter where you attempt to divide this circle in half, the divided section will always contain both yin and yang. There is always the presence of yin in the yang half and the presence of yang in the yin half, even if it is just a small dot. It represents balance, mutuality, change, and interdependence. The inseparability of yin and yang is grounded in the belief that yin and yang forces originate from the *Dao*.

DAOIST TEACHINGS

Daoism, previously known as Taoism, is an ancient Chinese philosophy that is primarily about how one can live a harmonious or true life. *Dao* literally means "the way." Daoism consists of heterogeneous traditions. Scholars studying Daoism usually distinguish Daoist traditions into "philosophical Daoism" and "religious Daoism" (Kirkland, 2004; Livia, 2000; Oldstone-Moore, 2003). Recent scholars such as Russell Kirkland proposed using a hermeneutic approach to understand Daoism (Kirkland, 2004). Livia Kohn (2001) suggested that, within the Daoist tradition, one could distinguish three types of organization and practice: (1) Literati Daoists are members of the educated élite who focus on Daoist ideas as expressed by ancient thinkers. They use these concepts to personally create meaning in their world and exert socio-political influence for greater universal harmony. (2) Communal Daoists are members of organized Daoist groups that have priestly hierarchies, formal initiations, and regular rituals and prayers to God. These people practice Daoism as religion. (3) Self-cultivationists practice Daoism for personal attainment of health, longevity, peace of mind, and spiritual benefits. The practice of Integrative Social Work is primarily influenced by philosophical Daoism and the self-cultivationist tradition.

The Book of Change, Yijing, was a prime inspiration for Daoism. *Yijing* symbology, which contained the ancient sages' understanding of the world, provided useful metaphors for Daoist followers to explain and navigate life's subtle forces and processes. Daoist teachings primarily originated in three texts: The *Daodejing* (previously known as *Tao-te-ching*), *Zhuangzi* (previously known as *Chuang-tzu*), and *Neiyang* (previously known as *Nei-yeh*). The *Daodejing* and *Zhuangzi* were universally renowned as the primary texts of classical Daoism. They are perceived as the most influential cultural roots of the Chinese mind and their influence is still profound nowadays, both in the East and the West. In fact, the *Daodejing* is the most often translated book among the European Sinologue, and it is estimated that 200 versions in different Western languages have been translated, the first Latin translation appearing before 1788 (Cheng, 1995). The focuses of these three texts are diverse and different, although all share the idea that one can live one's life wisely only if one learns how to live in accord with life's natural but unseen forces and subtle processes, and not based on society's established ideals and concerns.

The *Daodejing*

The *Daodejing* is a collection of poetry and aphorisms that set forth the basic teachings of *Dao*. Laozi (formerly known as Lao Tzu), who lived in ancient China around 5 BCE, is believed to have written this text. The *Daodejing* describes a universal, nontransient force, the *Dao*, from which life originates and from which one can never truly be separated.

> Dao produced the One.
> The One produced the two.
> The two produced the three.
> And the three produced the ten thousand things.
> The ten thousand things carry the Yin and embrace the Yang,
> and through the blending of the material force they achieve harmony.
>
> (Chan, 2000)

There is unity amidst differences and diversity as *Dao* gives life to all things and brings them into harmony. *Dao* is everlasting and changing at all times. One can easily observe the influence of *Yijing* and the yin–yang perspective in how the *Daodejing* describes the *Dao*. The nature of the *Dao* is dynamic, interconnected, mutual, and relative.

> If you want to shrink something, you must first allow it to expand. If you want to get rid of something, you must first allow it to flourish. If you want to take something, you must first allow it to be given. This is called the subtle perception of the way things are" (Mitchell, 1988, p. 36).

> If you want to become whole, let yourself be partial. If you want to become straight, let yourself be crooked (Mitchell, 1988, p. 22)

Making value judgments regarding the nature of any attribute has no place in Daoist teachings, as nothing is inherently good or bad. Being straight is not preferred to being crooked, because both states are connected in a constant process of change. Instead, maintaining a dynamic balance between contrasting forces is considered beneficial.

> As it acts in the work, the *Dao* is like the bending of a bow. The top is bent downward; and the bottom is bent up. It adjusts excess and deficiency so that there is perfect balance. It takes from what is too much and gives it to what isn't enough (Mitchell, 1988, p. 77).

The *Daodejing* also revealed the transient, unreliable, but inevitable, nature of language, which primarily transmits and supports socially constructed standards of all kinds:

> The Dao that can be told is not the eternal Dao; the name that can be named is not the eternal name. The Nameless is the origin of Heaven and Earth; the Named is the mother of all things (Chan, 2000).

Because of the nature of dynamic revertism of the *Dao* and the transient nature of all earthly things as described by language, one should not be bound by socially constructed standards, such as moral or immoral, good or bad, existing or nonexisting, difficult or easy, and so on, as these standards are relative and transient. When in harmony with the *Dao*, one transcends from the self and secular pursuits that are unreliable, transient, and perishable.

> Honor and disgrace are alike a cause of excitement. The great trouble of man lies in the love for self (*Lao Tzu* Chapter 13, trans. Cheng, 1995).

> The pursuit of pleasures deranges the mind of man. The love for wealth perverts the conduct of man. Wherefore the Sage attends the inner self, and not to the outward appearance (Cheng, 1995, Chapter 12).

Instead, one should learn to perceive the unseen reality, which is the source of our life and our sustenance. By being in harmony with nature, the *Dao*, one can be freed from unnecessary competition, struggle, and confusion and better return to behaviors that are "natural" for us. Daoism maintains a deep trust in the intelligence, inner wisdom, healing capacities, and goodness of human beings, and such a trust also extends to the nature and the cosmos. *Wu-wei*, an important teaching in the *Daodejing*, means nonaction or noninterference. Nonaction represents a trust in the universal rhythm of nature to do what it will do. Nonaction does not mean passivity—it denotes activity in harmony with the natural course of human life and nature. Through nonaction and being in harmony with the natural forces, our behavior flows out of the core of who we are and is in harmony and in balance with ourselves, others, and the ever-changing life force (*Dao*) (Koening & Spano, 1998).

> The Master acts without doing anything and teaches without saying anything. Things arise and she lets them come; things disappear and she lets them go (Mitchell, 1988, p. 2).

> The Master does his job and then stops. He understands that the universe is forever out of control, and that trying to dominate events goes against the current of the *Dao* (Mitchell, 1988, p. 30).

When a person does not focus or force an act but practices *wu-wei*, she or he will be able to perceive reality and understand the world more holistically. Daoist teachings promote a simultaneous and unconscious knowledge that fosters spontaneity, respects instinct, intuition, and mystery (Watts, 1957). This intuitive and spontaneous knowledge contrasts with the linear, abstract thinking that can be presented only sequentially. When living in harmony with the *Dao*, a person can relax and let go of his or her self-conscious and goal-driven work. He or she will be able to make decisions spontaneously based on experience and trust the mind and body to know what needs to be done.

When a person has learned to practice nonaction, be in harmony with the natural forces in life, and functions spontaneously in a holistic way, his or her mind will begin to show a certain effectiveness or power, like the healing power of a plant (Koening & Spano, 1998). The *Daodejing* defines this healing power as *te*, which means virtue. Each person is entrusted with this virtue when in harmony with the *Dao*. This virtue does not come from socially based morality, which is relative and transient. In fact, the *Daodejing* showed a deep mistrust of social and political rules and regulations, which mostly reflect linear thinking and are based on a desire to control, monitor, and intervene. Virtue comes about when we connect to the *Dao* and act upon our intuition based on direct experience.

> Throw away holiness and wisdom, and people will be a hundred times happier. Throw away morality and justice, and people will do the right thing. Throw away industry and profit, and there won't be any thieves. If these three aren't enough, just stay at the center of the circle, and let all things take their course (Mitchell, 1988, p. 19).

Keeping in tune with the nature, which is forever moving, renewing, and immortal, helps a person to attain absolute happiness.

> When one has attained the utmost humility and abided in the state of extreme quiescence, he can observe the cycle of changes in the simultaneous growth of all animate creation. Things appear multitudinous and varied, but eventually they return to the common root, quiescence (*Lao Tzu* Chapter 16, trans. Cheng, 1995).

> The whole universe may be compared to a bellow. It is hollow, but not empty. It is moving and renewing without cease (Cheng, 1995, Chapter 5).

The *Daodejing* proposed a life orientation that transcends the self, social standards, and the unreliable and perishable pursuits of wealth and objects (Chan, 2000). Instead, one should understand, attend to, and tune in to the *Dao* so that one can be in harmony with the natural forces of the universe and attain the ultimate peace and unity with the *Dao*. In addition, the *Daodejing* suggested a way for one to link with the *Dao* through meditative introspection.

Zhuangzi

Zhuangzi is a 33-chapter text that contains fascinating parables and stories. *Zhuangzi* advocates reverting to a boundless "heavenly mechanism" of life that is independent of the psycho-cultural constructs of good or bad. The primary thesis is that life can never be fully predicted (Chang, 1990). If we just simply enjoy and adjust our life as it unfolds, our life can be pleasant and enjoyable. A "real person" simply abides and flows with the life processes rather than trying to manage, plan, and control life's events. "To see things from the light of Heaven, means to see things from the point of view that which transcends the finite, which is Dao" (*Zhuangzi*, Chi'I Wu Lun, in Chang, 1983). Such a person is in accord with the reality that is boundless and unending. Similar to the *Daodejing*, *Zhuangzi* emphasizes transcendence from worldly attachments and struggles. A person who understands "the way" transcends emotions and limitations.

> At the very beginning, she was not living, having no form, nor even substance. But somehow or other there was then her substance, then her form, and then her life. Now by a further change, she has died. The whole process is like the sequence of the four seasons, spring, summer, autumn, and winter. While she is thus lying in the great mansion of the universe, for me to go about weeping and wailing would be to proclaim myself ignorant of the natural laws. Therefore, I stop. (*Zhuangzi*, in Fung, 1948)

She or he also transcends the self and perceptions.

> The perfect man has no self, the spiritual man has no achievement, and the true sage has no name (*Zhuangzi*, Happiness Excursion, in Chang, 1990).

Consequently, the life orientation suggested by *Zhuangzi* transcends socially based constructs, such as good or bad, desirable or undesirable, and useful or useless. The ideal depicted in *Zhuangzi* has always appealed to many Eastern and Western readers. One does not really have to solve any problems. We simply have to see life as it truly is and allow life's surprises to unfold (Chang, 1990; Kirkland, 2004). *Zhuangzi*, unlike the *Daodejing*, does not concern itself with political or moral issues. It primarily contains a philosophical description of "truth and boundless living." *Zhuangzi* also does not provide any specific directions as to how one might attain the described ideal.

Neiyang

Neiyang literally means *inner cultivation*. Whereas *Zhuangzi* raises epistemological issues and the *Daodejing* raises moral and political issues,

Neiyang is primarily concerned with biospiritual cultivation and offers advice and directions for guiding one to cultivate oneself (Kirkland, 2004; Oldstone-Moore, 2003). The teaching of *Neiyang* begins with the assumption of a powerful life reality called *qi*, or life energy. This life energy, *qi*, is present both within all things and all around them. It is fundamental to our living world as well as to each living being. In fact, *qi* forms a fundamental concept in Traditional Chinese Medicine (TCM), including the practice of acupuncture. The opening lines of *Neiyang* reads:

> The vital essence of all things—
> This is what makes life come into being;
> Below, it generates the five grains,
> Above, it brings about the constellated stars.
> When it flows in the interstices of Heaven and Earth,
> It is called "spiritual beings";
> When it is stored up inside [a person's] chest,
> It is called "sageliness."

Apparently, the opening lines of *Neiyang* recognizes the existence and the importance of an unseen life force that is generative in nature, operates within the world, and transcends things of diverse natures. Yet, the idea that different entities with their own distinct identities are filled with the same life force reinforces a holistic perspective of the world and the belief that all things are interconnected. To summarize succinctly, *Neiyang* proposed that the "heart–mind" is the center of an individual's existence. Our "heart–mind" oftentimes becomes confused as our thoughts and passions are intensified by diverse desires, such as wealth, status, and love. *Neiyang* suggested practices for a person to keep his or her mind–heart balanced and tranquil and to not be overwhelmed by excessive desires or emotions. If one can maintain a tranquil "heart–mind," one can naturally receive and retain healthy life energies and live a long, healthy, and pleasant life (Kirkland, 2004).

Neiyang describes *Dao* in almost exactly the same way as does the *Daodejing*: "What gives life to all things and brings them to perfection is call *Dao*." However, it is obvious that "the way" described in *Neiyang* is rather different from "the way" depicted in either *Zhuangzi* or the *Daodejing*. The key to life, as proposed by *Neiyang*, is a person's diligent effort to receive the life force, *qi*, whereas the key to a good life suggested by *Zhuangzi* or the *Daodejing* is about the transcendence of socially based constructs and the alignment with natural life processes (Kirkland, 2004; Oldstone-Moore, 2003).

BUDDHIST TEACHINGS

Buddhism is a philosophy that originated in ancient India. "Buddhism" literally means "the way of enlightenment," and "Buddha" means "enlightened person." Seeing life as full of suffering, Buddhism is primarily concerned about freeing people from such sufferings (Huston, 2003; Nhất Hạnh, 1999).

The Law of Dependent Origination

The Buddha's teachings are a model of the elimination of suffering built on the Law of Dependent Origination, which he discovered while mediating under a bodhi tree, just before attaining enlightenment (Rahula, 1974; Sik, 2005a; Sik, 2005b). The Buddha was not satisfied with the suffering in life and had a genuine desire for himself and for others to be liberated from such sufferings. "This world has fallen into troubles, in that it is born, ages, and dies, it passes away and is reborn, yet it does not understand the escape for this suffering. When now will an escape be discerned from this suffering?" (Bhikkhu Bodhi, 2000, p. 601). The Buddha perceived human existence and the endless process of cyclic existence as a long path of suffering, which is undesirable. True liberation from suffering comes only when one is freed from this endless cyclic process. Buddha was sincere in understanding life, and he questioned the origins of this cyclic process of suffering. Through *bhikkhus* (careful attention), the Buddha was enlightened and realized that "When there is birth, aging-and-death comes to be; aging-and-death has birth as the condition" (Bhikkhu Bodhi, 2000, p. 601). What the Buddha noticed was that phenomena were conditional; that is, the coming of one phenomenon will bring about the arising of the next. Paticcasamuppada (the Law of Dependent Origination), which represents the awareness of the dependent nature of all phenonmena, is fundamental to the teachings af the Buddha (Nhất Hạnh, 1999; Sik, 2005b).

The 12 Links of the Process of Cyclic Existence

The Buddha further observed that life is a process of cyclic existence, which is supported by 12 connecting links, in which one leads to the rising of the next. In addition, all links are ultimately interdependent on each other. The twelve links are aging and death, birth, existence, grasping, attachment, feeling, contact, the sense spheres, name and form, consciousness, volitional action, and ignorance (Nhất Hạnh, 1999; Sik, 2005a; Rahula, 1974). As such, birth leads to aging and death, existence leads to birth, grasping to existence, and so on. The Buddha observed that ignorance is the fuel of this cyclic existence and thus the root of suffering. Consequently, the key to eliminating suffering is to eliminate ignorance through the development of true knowledge and wisdom.

The Buddha further noticed that, of the twelve links, the interdependent triangle of name, form, and consciousness was the most important in understanding the development of existence and suffering (Nhất Hạnh, 1999; Sik, 2005a). The Buddha saw a person as composed of five domains: form, feeling, thoughts, volitional action, and consciousness. Form is the physical body.

Feeling, thought, volitional action, and consciousness belong to the psychological domains of a person. In this triangle, name represents the aggregation of feeling, thought, and volitional action. The interdependent triangle of name, form, and consciousness thereby represents the five domains that form a person. Only with "consciousness" can there be "name and form," and only with "name and form" can there be "consciousness." The Buddha realized that he had found a way to bring an end to suffering, because "with the cessation of 'name and form' comes the cessation of consciousness; with the cessation of consciousness comes the cessation of 'name and form;' with the cessation of 'name and form,' the whole mass of suffering ceases to be" (Nhất Hạnh, 1999; Rahula, 1974; Sik, 2005a; Sik, 2005b).

From the causal chain of the 12 links, consciousness ceases when ignorance and volitional action ceases. The Buddha, through the wisdom and knowledge developed from realizing the Law of Dependent Origination and the workings of the 12 links of cyclic existence, discovered a way to eliminate ignorance, and as a result, all factors that depended on ignorance ceased to be (Sik, 2005a).

The Enlightenment: True Vision, Knowledge, and Wisdom

The Buddha was enlightened when he realized the universal Law of Dependent Origination that described the coming and cessation of all phenomena:

> When there is this, that comes to be;
> With the arising of this, that arises.
> When there is not this, this does not come to be;
> With the cessation of this, that ceases.

This apparently simple observation is far-reaching in its meanings. It is imperative to understand the law itself as well as the nature/characteristics of the phenomena that come to existence according to the conditions set by the law. The Buddha did not create the Law of Dependent Origination but only discovered it. According to the Buddha, this is the natural law of the universe that explains the coming of all phenomena. Phenomena are not created independently but come into existence when the cause and necessary conditions are present. For instance, one does not make an apple. Instead, one plants the seed (cause) and facilitates its growth by providing water, soil, and sunlight (conditions). According to the Law of Dependent Origination, when the cause (seed) and the conditions (water, sunlight, good soil, etc.) are present, the phenomenon (apple) arises. Consequently, any phenomenon is a synthesis of cause and condition, and therefore, there is nothing that exists independently or substantially as "a thing" (Sik, 2005a). In addition, phenomena are interdependent, much like the seed and the apple, which are different but interdependent. The Law of Dependent Origination suggests the following nature and characteristics of phenomena (Sik, 2005a):

- Impermanence: Phenomena are always changing, depending on the gestalt of cause and condition.
- "No-self": All phenomena are inherently empty in nature, because it is always a consequence of something else and therefore do not have an independent, distinguishable, or permanent "self." Such a view avoids emotional or sensory attachment because of the illusionary nature of reality.
- Phenomena exist interdependently and relatively, based on a "cause and effect" relationship: The Law of Karma.
- Middle path: The similar and different relationships between phenomena (such as the seed and the apple) promote a middle position that avoids the notion of duality, an either-or position, or a rigid attachment to the notions of "there definitely is" or "there definitely is not."

The Two Darts of Suffering

The Buddha further differentiates two types of suffering, known as the two darts of suffering (Bhikkhu Bodhi, 2000, p. 1263). The Buddha explained that, when the "well-taught noble disciplines" and the "untaught worldlings" encounter stimulus through their senses, both experience the same physical feeling. However, when the "untaught worlding" experiences a painful feeling, he "worries and grieves, he laments, beats his chest, weeps and is distraught" (Bhikkhu Bodhi, 2000, p. 1263). For an enlightened person, when she or he is afflicted with a painful feeing, she or he only experiences the bodily pain but not the mental aguish. However, for other people, they can experience two types of suffering—physical suffering and mental suffering. In those situations, a person would be hit by a second dart of mental suffering after being pierced by the first dart of physical pain.

Mindfulness

Being mindful has a unique place in the Buddha's teachings to attain true vision, knowledge, and wisdom, which can lead to the cessation of ignorance. The Buddha himself attained enlightenment and the development of knowledge and wisdom by observing and learning, which he did by paying careful attention—mindfulness practices. In his teachings about the interdependent triangle of "name-and-form" and "consciousness," consciousness is the condition for the development of the body, feeling, thoughts, and actions.

In the *Dhammapada Sutta*, the Buddha explained that a person's thoughts and actions are the causes and conditions that will shape his or her future:

> Mind is the forerunner to all things. It directs and makes them. If someone speaks and acts with a deluded mind, suffering will follow him, as the wheels follow the footsteps of the animal that draws the cart.
> Mind is the forerunner to all things. It directs and makes them. If someone speaks and acts with a pure mind, happiness will follow him, as the shadow follows the body. (*Dhammapada Sutta*)

In the *Satipathanna Sutta* (The Discourse on the Four Foundations of Mindfulness), the Buddha explained the essentials of practicing mindfulness as, "A monk dwells contemplating the body in the body, ardent, clearly comprehending and mindful, overcoming covetousness and grief in the world." "Dwell contemplating" implies the person should be at ease and comfortable with the objects of his or her mindfulness. "Body in the body" means that, when contemplating the body (or emotions, thoughts, etc), the person should not differentiate or add any subjective interpretation to what has been observed or comprehended. The person should stay mindful in the moment and without judgment. "Ardent" represents the attitude with which one practices mindfulness—with diligence and enthusiasm so that the mind will stay focused and not be distracted. "Clear comprehending" is related to the development of knowledge and wisdom. Besides developing concentration, mindfulness practices focus on the development of awareness and comprehension of the nature and characteristics of the object of mindfulness, which will facilitate the development of vision, knowledge, and wisdom (Nhất Hạnh, 1999; Sik, 2005a; Sik, 2005b). Nyanaponika Thera (1972) describe mindfulness, "The clear and single-minded awareness of what actually happens to us and in us at the successive moments of perception." (p. 5). Mindfulness (*sati*) literally means *remembering* in Pali. "Clear comprehending" allows the mind to observe and remember the experiences of one's awareness, and consequently, to discern what is truly beneficial and helpful.

According to the Buddha's teachings, mindfulness practices allow one to develop vision, knowledge, and wisdom (Sik, 2005a). "Vision" emphasizes a person's ability to be aware of and recognizes objects that she or he might not have been aware of before. In the *Satipathanna Sutta*, the Buddha described four foundations of objects of mindfulness: the body, feelings, consciousness, and Dharma. The suggested focus is on the person, because we are usually accustomed to focus our attention on objects in the outside, illusory world, instead of in our inner, real world. Vision undistorted by delusion or illusion leads to awareness, recognition, and information, which constitutes the foundation of true knowledge about the way events and phenomena in our life and world work and function. It fosters wisdom in a person to differentiate, sort out confusion, and make beneficial decisions (Sik, 2005a; Sik, 2005b).

In sum, the Buddha perceives that thoughts and actions dictate a person's well-being and future. Deluded emotions, thoughts, and actions fueled by ignorance are the primary cause of suffering. The practice of mindfulness permits a person to stop ignorance and develop true knowledge, which liberates a person from suffering.

Appendix B: Internet Resources

Meditation and Yoga

1. Bhavana Society, The Buddhist Meditation Center: www.bhavanasociety. org/
2. The World Community for Christian Meditation: www.wccm.org/
3. The Plum Village: www.plumvillage.org/
4. The Centre for Mindfulness in Medicine, Health Care, and Society, University of Massachusetts Medical School: www.umassmed.edu/

Web sites on Mind–Body medicine/Alternative medicine/Body processes

1. Centre for Mind–Body Medicine: www.cmbm.org
2. The Alternative Medicine Foundation: www.amfoundation.org/ mindbodymed.htm
3. Association for Comprehensive Energy Psychology: www.energypsych. org/

Web sites on Meaning and Spirituality

1. International Network of Personal Meaning: promoting health, peace, and spirituality through meaning: www.meaning.ca/
2. The Center for Spirituality and Social Work: http://csisw.cua.edu

Traditional Chinese Medicine

1. A good overview on Wikipedia (http://en.wikipedia.org/wiki/ Main_Page). Search for "Chinese medicine."

2. http://www.acupuncture.com.au/

   This is a regularly updated Web site on Chinese medicine based in Australia.

3. http://ejournals.worldscientific.com.sg/ajcm/ajcm.shtml

   This is the Web site of the American Journal of Chinese Medicine, which covers both basic and intervention research, and emphasizes an evidence-based approach in clinical practice.

4. http://www.aaom.org/

   This is the Web site of the American Association Oriental Medicine. It provides information on training courses available in North America.

5. http://www.nccaom.org/

   This is the Web site of National Certification Commission for Acupuncture and Oriental Medicine.

6. http://nccam.nih.gov/

   The National Center for Complimentary and Alternative Medicine (under the National Institutes of Health of the United States) provides information on acupuncture, herbals, and other popular forms of complementary and alternative medicine practiced in the United States.

Dance and Movement Therapy

1. American Dance Therapy Association: http://www.adta.org/
2. The Association for Dance Movement Therapy UK: http://www.admt.org.uk/
3. Dance-Movement Therapy Association of Australia: http://dtaa.org.au/

References

Abels, S. L. (Ed.). (2000). *Spirituality in social work practice: Narratives for professional helping*. Denver, CO: Love Publishing.

Ader, R., Felten, D., & Cohen, N. (1990). Interactions between the brain and the immune system. *Annual Review of Pharmacology and Toxicology, 30*, 561–602.

American Psychiatric Association. (2000). *Diagnostic and statistical manual of mental disorders* (4th ed. Text Rev.). Washington, DC: American Psychiatric Association.

Anandarajah, G., & Hight, E. (2001). Spirituality and medical practice: Using the HOPE questions as a practical tool for spiritual assessment. *American Family Physician, 63*(1), 81–88.

Asay, T. P., & Lambert, M. J. (1999). The empirical case for the common factors in therapy: Quantitative findings. In M. A. Hubble, B. L. Duncan, & S. Miller (Eds.), *The heart and soul of change: What works in therapy*. Washington, DC: American Psychological Association.

Astin, J. A. (1997). Stress reduction through mindfulness meditation. *Psychotherapy and Psychosomatics, 66*, 97–106.

Baldwin, M. (Ed.). (2000). *The use of self in therapy* (2nd ed.) New York: Haworth.

Barreiro, M. A., & James, G. D. (2005). A prospective, observational study of patients with functional disorders in Binghamton, NY. Paper presented at the 6th International Symposium on Functional Gastrointestinal Disorders, Milwaukee, WI.

Bateson, G. (1972). *Steps to an ecology of mind*. New York: Ballantine Books.

Bateson, G. (1979). *Mind and nature: A necessary unity*. New York: Dutton.

Beck, A. (1976). *Cognitive therapy and emotional disorders*. New York: Meridian.

Beck, J. S. (1995). *Cognitive therapy: Basics and beyond*. New York: Guilford Press.

Beck, A. T., Rush, A. J., Shaw, B. F., & Emery, G. (1979). *Cognitive therapy of depression*. New York: Guilford Press.

Beck, A. T., Steer, R. A., & Garbin, M. G. (1988). Psychometric properties of the Beck Depression Inventory: Twenty-five years of evaluation. *Clinical Psychology Review, 8*(1), 77–100.

Becvar, D. S. (Ed.) (1988). *Family, spirituality and social work*. Binghamton, NY: Haworth.

Becvar, D. S., & Becvar, R. J. (2003). *Family therapy: A systemic integration* (5th ed.). Boston, MA: Allyn & Bacon.

Beit-Hallahmi, B. (1987). The social work practice subculture: Practice and ideology. *Social Science Information, 26*, 475–492.

Benson, H. (1975). *The relaxation response.* New York: William Morrow.

Benson, H., Berry, J. F., & Carol, M. P. (1974). The relaxation response. *Psychiatry, 37,* 37–46.

Berg, I. K. (1994). *Family-based services: A solution-focused approach.* New York: W. W. Norton.

Berg, I. K., & Kelly, S. (2000). *Building solutions in child protective services.* New York: W. W. Norton.

Berg, I. K., & Miller, S. (1992). *Working with the problem drinker: A solution-focused approach.* New York: W. W. Norton & Co.

Bertalanffy, L. V. (1968). *General System theory: Foundations, development, applications.* New York: George Braziller.

Bhikkhu, B. (Trans.). (2000). *The connected discourses of the Buddha. A new translation of the Samyutta Nikaya* (Vol. II). Somerville, MA: Wisdom Publications.

Bohm, D. (1998) *On creativity* (Ed. L. Nichol). New York: Routledge.

Bohm, D., & Peat, D. F. (2000). *Science, order, and creativity: A dramatic new look at the creative roots of science and life* (2nd ed.). London: Routledge.

Bokey, E. L., Chapuis, P. H., Fung, C., Hughes, W. J., Koorey, S. G., Brewer, D. et al. (1995). Postoperative morbidity and mortality following resection of the colon and rectum for cancer. *Dis Colon Rectum, 38,* 480–486.

Bonanno, G. A. (2004). Loss, trauma, and human resilience: How we underestimated the human capacity to thrive after extremely aversive events. *American Psychologist, 59*(1), 20–28.

Bordin, E. S. (1979). The generalizability of the psychoanalytic concept of the working alliance. *Psychotherapy: Theory, Research and Practice, 16,* 252–260.

Bower, J. E., Kemeny, M. E., Taylor, S., & Fahey, J. (1998). Cognitive processing, discovery of meaning, CD4 decline, and AIDS-related mortality among bereaved HIV-seropositive men. *Journal of Consulting and Clinical Psychology, 66*(6), 979–986.

Bower, J. E., Kemeny, M. E., Taylor, S., & Fahey, J. (2003). Finding positive meaning and its association with natural killer cell cytotoxicity among participants in a bereavement-related disclosure intervention. *Annals of Behavioral Medicine, 25*(2), 146–155.

Bowlby, J. (1982). *Attachment and loss* (2nd ed.). New York: Basic Books.

Bowlby, J. (1979). *The making and breaking of affectional bonds.* London: Tavistock.

Brady, M. J., Peterman, A. H., Fitchett, G., Mo, M., & Cella, D. (1999). A case for including spirituality in quality of life measurement in oncology. *Psycho-Oncology, 5*(8), 417–428.

Brandon, D. (1976). *Zen in the art of helping.* New York: Delta/Seymour Lawrence.

Brazier, D. (1997). *Zen therapy: Transcending the sorrows of the human mind.* New York: John Wiley and Sons.

Briggs, J., & Peat, D. F. (1999). *Seven life lessons of Chaos: Timeless wisdom from the science of change.* New York: HarperCollins Publishers

Brooks, J. (2002). Ayurveda. In S. Shannon (Eds.), *Handbook of complementary and alternative therapies in mental health* (pp. 453–474). San Diego, CA: Academic Press.

Brown, K. W., & Ryan, R. M. (2003). The benefits of being present: Mindfulness and its role in psychological well-being. *Journal of Personality and Social Psychology, 84,* 822–848.

Bullis, R. K. (1996). *Spirituality in social work practice.* Washington, DC: Taylor & Francis.

Burnet, J. (1964). *Greek philosophy: Thales to Plato.* London: Macmillan.

Busseri, M. A., & Tyler, J. D. (2004). Client-therapist agreement on target problems, working alliance, and counseling outcome. *Psychotherapy Research, 14,* 77–88.

Butler, K. (September/October 2003). Living on purpose. *Social work practice Networker, 27,* 28–37.

Cai, J. (1995). *Advanced textbook on traditional Chinese medicine and pharmacology* (Vol. 1). Beijing: New World Press.

Caldwell, C. (Ed.) (1997) *Getting in touch: The guide to new body-centered therapies.* Wheaton, IL: Quest Books.

Cameron, L. D., Booth, R. J., Schlatter, M., Ziginskas, D., & Harman, J. E. (2007). Changes in emotion regulation and psychological adjustment following use of a group psychosocial support program for women recently diagnosed with breast cancer. *Psycho-Oncology, 16,* 171–180.

Canda, E. (1997). Spirituality. In R. L. Edwards (Ed.), *Encyclopedia of social work 19th edition supplement* (pp. 299–309). Washington, DC: National Association of Social Workers.

Canda, E. R. (1998). Afterword: Linking spirituality and social work: Five themes for innovation. In E. R. Canda (Ed.), *Spirituality in social work: New directions* (pp. 97–106). New York: The Haworth Pastoral Press.

Canda, E. R. (2002). Wisdom from the Confucian classics for spiritually sensitive social welfare. *Currents: New scholarship in the human services, 1*(1), 31 pp., http://fsw.ucalgary.ca/currents/articles/canda2_v1_n1.htm

Canda, E. R., & Furman, L. D. (1999). *Spiritual diversity in social work practice: The heart of helping.* New York: Free Press.

Canda, E. R., Nakashima, M., & Furman, L. D. (2004). Ethical considerations about spirituality in social work: Insights from a national qualitative survey. *Families in Society, 85,* 1–9.

Canda, E. R., & Smith, E. D. (Eds). (2001). *Transpersonal perspectives on spirituality in social work.* Binghamton, NY: Haworth Press.

Carmody, J., & Baer, R. A. (2007). Relationships between mindfulness practice and levels of mindfulness, medical and psychological symptoms and well-being in a mindfulness-based stress reduction program. *Journal of Behavioral Medicine, 31*(1), 23–33.

Carroll, M. M. (1998). Social work's conceptualization of spirituality. In E. R. Canda (Ed.), *Spirituality in social work: New directions* (pp. 1–13). New York: The Haworth Pastoral Press.

Carroll, M. M. (1997). Spirituality and clinical social work: Implications of past and current perspectves. *Arete, 22,* 25–34.

Carter, E. A., & McGoldrick, M. (Eds.). (1998). *The expanded family life cycle: Individual, family, and social perspectives* (3rd ed.). Needham Heights, MA: Allyn & Bacon.

Carver, C. S., Pozo, C., Harris, S. D., Noriega, V., Scheier, M. F., Robinson, D. S. et al. (1993). How coping mediates the effect of optimism on distress: A study of women with early stage breast cancer. *Journal of Personality & Social Psychology, 65,* 375–390.

Carver, C. S., & Scheier, M. F. (1981). *Attention and self-regulation: A control-theory approach to human behavior.* New York: Springer-Verlag.

Carver, D. J., & Wallace, M. J. (Eds.). (1995). *Collins gem English learner's dictionary.* London: Collins.

Chan, A. (2000). The *Daodejing* and its tradition. In L. Kohn (Ed.), *Daoism handbook* (pp. 1–29). Leiden, Boston, MA: Brill.

Chan, C. L. W. (2001). *An Eastern body-mind-spirit approach: A training manual with one-second techniques.* Hong Kong: Department of Social Work and Social Administration, The University of Hong Kong.

Chan, C. L. W., Chan, Y., & Lou, V. W. Q. (2001). Evaluating an empowerment group for divorced Chinese women in Hong Kong. *Research on Social Work Practice, 12,* 558–569.

Chan, C. L. W., Ho, P. W. Y., & Chow, E. (2001). A body-mind-spirit model in health: An Eastern approach. *Social Work in Health Care, 34*(3/4), 261–282.

Chan, C. L. W., Lo, M., & Leung, P. P. Y. (2000). An empowerment group for Chinese cancer patients in Hong Kong. In C. L. W. Chan & R. Fielding (Eds.), *Psychosocial oncology & palliative care in Hong Kong: The first decade* (pp. 167–188). Hong Kong: Hong Kong University Press.

Chan, C. L. W., Ng, S. M., Ho, R. T. H., & Chow, A. Y. M. 2006. East meets West: Applying Eastern spirituality in social work practice with individuals and families. *Journal of Clinical Nursing, 15,* 822–832.

Chan, C. L. W., & Palley, H. A. (2005). The use of traditional Chinese culture and values in social work helath care related interventions in Hong Kong. *Health & Social Work, 30*(1), 76–79.

Chan, C. L. W., Sham, J., & Wei, W. (1993). Contribution of self-help to mental health of larygectomees in Hong Kong. *Asia Pacific Journal of Social Work, 3*(1), 24–35.

Chandler, C. K., Holden, J. M., & Kolander, C. A. (1995). Counseling for spiritual wellness: Theory and practice. In M. T. Burke & J. G. Miranti (Eds.), *Counseling: The spiritual dimension* (pp. 41–58). Alexandria, VA: American Counseling Association.

Chang, W. Y. (1983). *Lao Tzu: Text, interpretation and meaning.* Hong Kong: Chung Wah Publishers [in Chinese].

Chang, W. Y. (1990). *Chuan Tzu: Text and meaning.* Hong Kong: Chung Wah Publishers [in Chinese].

Cheng, L. (1995). *The work of Laozu: Truth and nature* (8th ed.). Hong Kong: The World Book Company.

Cheng, W. K., & Macfarlane, D. J. (2001). Effects of a modified tai chi programme on the physical and psychological wellbeing of elderly Chinese. Paper presented at the 2nd International Symposium on Chinese Elderly, Shanghai.

Cheung, Y. K., Molassiotis, A., & Chang, A. M. (2003). The effect of progressive muscle relaxation training on anxiety and quality of life after stoma surgery in colorectal cancer patients. *Psycho-Oncology, 12,* 254–266.

Chibucos, T. R., & Leite, R. W. (2005). *Readings in family theory.* Thousand Oaks, CA: Sage Publications.

Chodorow, N. (1978). *The reproduction of mothering.* Berkeley: University of California Press.

Chung, D., & Haynes, A. W. (1993). Confucian welfare philosophy and social change technology: An integrated approach for international social development. *International Social Work, 36,* 37–46.

Clark, J. (1994). Should social work education address religious issues? No! *Journal of Social Work Education, 30,* 11–16.

Classen, C., Butler, L. D., Koopman, C., Miller, E., DiMiceli, S., Ciese-Davis, J. et al. (2001). Supportive-expressive group therapy and distress in patients with metastatic breast cancer—a randomized clinical intervention trial. *Archives of General Psychiatry, 58*(5), 494–501.

Cnaan, R., Wineburg, R. J., & Boddie, S. C. (1999). *The newer deal: Social work and religion in partnership.* New York: Columbia University Press.

Collins, S. (1982). *Selfless person: Imagery and thoughts in Theranada Buddhism.* Cambridge: Cambridge University Press.

Cooper, N. A., & Clum, C. A. (1989). Imaginal flooding as a supplementary treatment for PTSD in combat veterans: A controlled study. *Behavior Therapy, 20*, 381–391.

Cowley, A. (1993). Transpersonal social work: A theory for the 90s. *Social Work, 38*, 527–534.

Cromer, A. (1993). *Uncommon sense: The heretical nature of science.* New York: Oxford University Press.

Crompton, M. (1998). *Children, spirituality, religion and social work.* Brookfield, VT: Ashgate Publishing Company.

Culliford, L. (2002). Spirituality and clinical care. *British Medical Journal, 325*, 1434–1435.

Cushman, P. (1995). *Constructing the self, constructing America: A cultural history of psychotherapy.* Reading, MA: Addison-Wesley.

d'Angelo, R. (2002). Aromatherapy. In S. Shannon (Eds.), *Handbook of complementary and alternative therapies in mental health* (pp. 71–92). San Diego, CA: Academic Press.

Dalai Lama, & H. C. Cutler. (1998). *The art of happiness: A handbook for living.* New York: Riverhead Books.

Damian, P., & Damian, K. (1995). *Aromatherapy: Scent and Psyche.* Rochester, VT: Healing Arts Press.

Davidson, B., & Thomas, A. (2002). Buddhism and group analysis. *Group Analysis, 25*(1), 57–71.

Deci, E. L., & Ryan, R. M. (1980). Self-determination theory: When mind mediates behavior. *The Journal of Mind and Behavior, 1*, 33–43.

DeJong, P., & Berg, I. K. (2002). *Interviewing for solutions* (2nd ed.). Pacific Grove, CA: Brooks/Cole.

DeJong, P., & Berg, I. K. (2007). *Interviewing for solutions* (3rd ed.). Pacific Grove, CA: Brooks/Cole.

Descartes, R. (1641/1990). *Meditations on first philosophy: Meditationes de prima philosophia* (G. Heffernan ed., trans., and indexed). Notre Dame, Ind:University of Notre Dame Press.

de Shazer, S. (1991). *Putting difference to work.* New York: W. W. Norton.

de Shazer, S. 1994. *Words were originally magic.* New York: W. W. Norton.

Dinerman, M., & Geismar, L. (Eds.). (1984). *A quarter century of social work education.* Washington, DC: Council on Social Work Education.

Doherty, W. J. (1995). *Soul searching; why social work practice must promote moral responsibility.* New York: Basic Books.

Donzelot, J. (1979). *The policing of families.* New York: Pantheon Books.

Dossey, L. (1985). *Beyond illness: Discovering the experience of health.* Boston, MA: Shambhala Publications.

Dossey, L. (1993). *Healing words: The power of prayer and the practice of medicine.* San Francisco: Harper.

Dossey, L. (1996). *Prayer is good medicine: How to reap the healing benefits of prayer.* San Francisco: Harper.

Dossey, L. (1997). *Be careful what you pray for—you just might get it: What we can do about the unintentional effects of our thoughts, prayers, and wishes.* San Francisco: Harper.

Dossey, L. (2001). *Healing beyond the body: Medicine and the infinite reach of the mind.* Boston, MA: Shambhala Publications.

Ehlers, A., & Clark, D. M. (2000). A cognitive model of posttraumatic stress disorder. *Behavioral Research Therapy, 38*(4), 319–345.

Eisenberg, D. M., Davis, R. B., Ettner, S. L. Appel, S., Wilkey, S., Van Rompay, M, et al. (1998). Trends in alternative medicine use in the United States, 1990–1997: Results of a follow-up survey. *Journal of the American Medical Association, 280*, 1569–1575.

Eisenberg, D. M., Kessler, R. C., & Foster, C. (1993). Unconventional medicine in the United States. *New England Journal of Medicine, 328*, 246–252.

Elliot, A. J., & Church, M. A. (2002). Client-articulated avoidance goals in the therapy context. *Journal of Counseling Psychology, 49*, 243–254.

Ellis, A. (1996). *Better, deeper, and more enduring brief therapy: The rational emotive behavior therapy approach.* New York: Brunner/Mazel.

Ellis, A., & Dryden, W. (1987). *The practice of rational emotive therapy (RET).* New York: Springer.

Ellor, J. W., Netting, F. E., & Thibault, J. M. (1999). *Religious and spiritual aspects of human service practice.* Columbia, SC: University of South Carolina Press.

Epstein, M. (1998). *Going to pieces without falling apart: A Buddhist perspective on wholeness.* London: T. Thorsons Berry.

Erikson, E. H. (1963). *Childhood and society.* New York: W. W. Norton.

Espenak, L. (1981). *Dance therapy: Theory and application.* Springfield, IL: Charles C Thomas.

Falsetti, S. A. (1997). A review of the Modified PTSD Symptom Scale. Paper presented at the International Society of Traumatic Stress Studies 13th Annual Meeting, November 6–10, Montreal, Quebec, Canada.

Falsetti, S. A., Resick, P. A., Resnick, H. S., & Kilpatrick, D. G. (1993). The Modified PTSD Symptom Scale: A brief self-report measure of posttraumatic stress disorder. *Behavioral Assessment Review,* June 1993, 161–162.

Fawzy, F. I. (1999). Psychosocial interventions for patients with cancer: What works and what doesn't. *European Journal of Cancer, 35*(11), 1559–1564.

Fechner, G. T. (1906). *On life after death, from the German of Gustav Theodor Fechner, by Dr. Hugo Wernekke.* Chicago, The Open Court Publishing Company.

Fife, B. L. (1994). The conceptualization of meaning in illness. *Social Science & Medicine, 38*(2), 309–316.

Fitchett, G., Burton, L. A., & Sivan, A. B. (1997). The religious needs and resources of psychiatric patients. *Journal of Nervous and Mental Disease, 185*, 320–326.

Foa, E. B., Keane, T. M., & Friedman, M. J. (Eds.) (2000). *Effective treatments for PTSD: Practice guidelines from the International Society for Traumatic Stress Studies.* New York: Guilford Press.

Foa, E. B., & Meadows, E. A. (1997). Psychosocial treatments for post-traumatic stress disorder: A critical review. In J. Spence, J. M Darley, & D. J. Foss (Eds.), *Annual Review of Psychology* (Vol. 48, pp. 449–480). Palo Alto, CA: Annual Reviews.

Foa, E. B., & Rothbaum, B. O. (1998). *Treating the trauma of rape: Cognitive-behavioral therapy for PTSD.* New York: Guilford Press.

Foa, E. B., Rothbaum, B. O., Riggs, D. S., & Murdock, T. B. (1991). Treatment of post-traumatic stress disorder in rape victims: A comparison between cognitive-behavioral procedures and counseling. *Journal of Consulting and Clinical Psychology, 59*, 715–723.

Ford, J. D., & Kidd, T. P. (1998). Early childhood trauma and disorders of extreme stress as predictors of treatment outcome with chronic posttraumatic stress disorder. *Journal of Traumatic Stress, 114*, 743–761.

Fossa, S. D., & Dahl, A. A. (2002). Short Form 36 and Hospital Anxiety and Depression Scale: A comparison based on patients with testicular cancer. *Journal of Psychosomatic Research, 52*(2), 79–87.

Foster, S., & Mash, E. (1999). Assessing social validity in clinical treatment research: Issues and procedures. *Journal of Consulting and Clinical Psychology, 67*, 308–319.

Frankl, V. (1967). *Psychotherapy and existentialism.* New York: Simon and Schuster.

Fraser, M. (2004). Intervention research in social work: Recent advances and continuing challenges, *Research on Social Work Practice, 14*, 210–222.

Freud, A. (1936). *The ego and the mechanisms of defense.* New York: International Universities Press.

Freud, S. (1961). The ego and the id. In J. Strachey (Trans. and ed.), *The standard edition of the complete psychological works of Sigmund Freud.* London: Hogarth Press. (Original work published 1923.)

Froberg, D., Gjerdingen, D., & Preston, M. (1986). Multiple roles and women's mental and physical health: What have we learned? *Women's Health, 11*(2), 79–96.

Fung, Y. L. (1948). *A short history of China.* New York: Macmillan.

Gadamer, H. G. (2002). *The beginning of knowledge.* Translated by Rod Coltman. New York: Continuum.

Gall, T. L., & Cornblat, M. W. (2002). Breast cancer survivors give voice: A qualitative analysis of spiritual factors in long-term adjustment. *Psycho-Oncology, 11*, 524–535.

Gambrill, E. (2003). Evidence-based practice: See change or the emperor's new clothes. *Journal of Social Work Education, 39*, 3–23.

Ganz, P. A., Coscarelli, A., Fred, C., Kahn, B., Polinsky, M. L., & Petersen, L. (1996). Breast cancer survivors: Psychosocial concerns and quality of life. *Breast Cancer Research and Treatment, 38*, 183–199.

Gelder, M., Gath, D., Mayou, R., & Cowen, P. (1996). *Oxford textbook of psychiatry* (3rd ed.). Oxford, New York, Melbourne: Oxford University Press.

Gendlin, E. T. (1979). *Focusing.* New York: Everest House.

Gergen, K. J. (1999). *An invitation to social construction.* Thousand Oaks, CA: Sage Publications.

Germain, C. B., & Gitterman, A. (1980). *The life model of social work practice.* New York: Columbia University Press.

Germain, C. B., & Gitterman, A. (1996). *The life model of social work practice: Advances in theory & practice.* New York: Columbia University Press.

Gibbs, L. (2005). *Evidence-based practice for the helping professions: A practical guide with integrated multimedia.* Pacific Grove, CA: Brooks/Cole.

Gilliland, B. E., & James, R. J. (1997). Chapter 1 in *Crisis intervention strategies* (3rd ed.). Pacific Grove, CA: Brooks/Cole.

Goin, M., Yamamoto, J., & Silverman, J. (1965). Therapy congruent with class-linked expectations. *Archives of General Psychiatry, 13*, 133–137.

Goldberg, D. (1972). *The detection of mental illness by questionnaire.* London: Oxford University Press.

Goldberg, D., Benjamin, S., & Creed, F. (1994). *Psychiatry in medical practice* (2nd ed.). London: Routledge.

Goldstein, E. G. (1995). *Ego psychology and social work practice* (2nd ed.). New York: The Free Press.

Goleman, D. (2003). *Healing emotions: Conversations with the Dalai Lama on mindfulness, emotions, and health.* Boston, MA: Shambhala Publications.

Goleman, D., & Gurin, J. (1993). *How to use your mind for better health.* New York: Consumer Reports Books.

Gondolf, E. W. (1997). Expanding batterer program evaluation. In G. K. Kantor & J. L. Jasinski (Eds.), *Out of the darkness: Contemporary perspectives on family violence* (pp. 208–218). Thousand Oaks, CA: Sage.

Gonzalez-Balado, J. L. (Compiler). (1996). *In my own words: Mother Teresa.* New York: Gramercy Cooks.

Goorich, T. J., Rampage, C., Ellman, B., & Halstead, K. (1988). *Feminist family therapy: A casebook.* New York: Norton.

Graves, K. D. (2003). Social cognitive theory and cancer patients' quality of life: A meta-analysis of psychosocial intervention components. *Health Psychology, 22,* 210–219.

Gray, R. E., Fitch, M., Phillips, C., Labrecque, M., & Fergus, K. (2000). To tell or not to tell: Patterns of disclosure among men with prostate cancer. *Psycho-Oncology, 9*(4), 273–282.

Green, J. W. (1998). *Cultural awareness in the human services: A multi-ethnic approach* (3rd ed.). Needham Heights, MA: Allyn & Bacon.

Green, E., & Green, A. (1977). *Beyond biofeedback.* New York: Delacorte Press/ S. Lawrence.

Greenstein, M., & Breitbart, W. (2000). Cancer and the experience of meaning: A group psychotherapy for people with cancer. *American Journal of Psychotherapy, 54,* 486–500.

Gu, Z. (1995). *Lao Tzu: The book of Tao and Teh.* Beijing: Peking University Press.

Gunaratana, H. (1991). *Mindfulness in plain English.* Boston, MA: Wisdom Publications.

Haley, J. (1990). *Strategies of social work practice* (2nd ed.). New York: Triangle Press.

Halprin, D. (1998). Creativity, art, and therapy. In D. Halprin (Ed.), *The expressive body in life, art and therapy—working with movement, metaphor, and meaning* (p. 92). London and Philadelphia: Jessica Kingsley Publishers.

Hameroff, S. (1998). Did consciousness cause the Cambrian evolutionary explosion? In S. Hameroff, A. Kaszniak, & A. Scott (Eds.), *Toward a science of consciousness II: The second Tucson discussions and debates* (pp. 421–437). Cambridge, MA: MIT Press.

Hameroff, S. R., Kaszniak, A. W., & Scott, A. C. (1996). *Toward a science of consciousness: The first Tucson discussions and debates.* Cambridge, MA: MIT Press.

Hameroff, S. R., & Penrose, R. (1996). Conscious events as orchestrated spacetime selections. *Journal of Consciousness Studies, 3*(1), 36–53.

Hamilton, E. (1973). *The Greek way.* New York: Avon. (Original work published 1930)

Hansen, C. (1983). *Language and logic in ancient China.* Ann Arbor: University of Michigan Press.

Hartmann, H. (1939). *Ego psychology and the problem of adaptation.* New York: International Universities Press.

Health Assessment Lab. (1995). *The Chinese (Hong Kong) SF-12 Health Survey— Standard Version 1.* Boston, MA: Health Assessment Lab.

Helgeson, V. S., Cohen, S., Schulz, R., & Yasko, J. (2000). Group support interventions for women with breast cancer: Who benefits from what? *Health Psychology, 19*(2), 107–114.

Helgeson, V. S., Cohen, S., Schulz, R., & Yasko, J. (2001). Long-term effects of educational and peer discussion group interventions on adjustment to breast cancer. *Health Psychology, 20*(5), 387–392.

Herman, J. L. (1992). *Trauma and recovery.* New York: Basic Books.

Ho, D. Y. F. (1995). Selfhood and identity in Confucianism, Taoism, Buddhism, and Hinduism: Contrasts with the West. *Journal for the Theory of Social Behaviour, 25*(2): 115–139.

Ho, D. Y. F., Chan, S. F., & Zhang, Z. X. (2001). Metarelational analysis: An answer to "What's Asian about Asian social psychology?" *Psychology in Chinese Societies, 2*(1): 7–76.

Ho, D. Y. F., Peng, S. Q., Lai, A. C., & Chan, S. F. (2001). Indigenization and beyond: Methodological relationalism in the study of personality across cultures. *Journal of Personality, 69*, 925–953.

Ho, R. T. H., & Chan, C. L. W. (2002). The effect of Eastern psychosocial intervention support group in breast cancer patients in Hong Kong: A pilot study on salivary cortisol, GHQ12 and HADS. Paper presented at the 6th Psycho-oncology Conference, Hong Kong.

Ho, R. T. H., & Chan, C. L. W. (2003). The effect of Eastern psychosocial intervention support group in breast cancer patients in Hong Kong: A pilot study on salivary cortisol, GHQ12 and HADS. *Psycho-Oncology, 13*, 377–389.

Ho, R. T. H., Chan, C. L. W., & Ho, S. M. Y. (2004). Emotional control in Chinese female cancer survivors. *Psycho-Oncology, 13*, 808–817.

Ho, S. M. Y., Chan, C. L. W., & Ho, R. T. H. (2004). Posttraumatic growth in Chinese cancer survivors. *Psycho-Oncology, 3*(6), 377–389.

Ho, S. M. Y., Wong, K. F., Chan, C. L. W., Watson, M., & Tsui, Y. K. Y. (2003). Psychometric properties of the Chinese version of the Mini Mental Adjustment to Cancer (Mini-MAC) Scale. *Psycho-Oncology, 12*, 547–556.

Hodge, D. R. (2001a). Spiritual assessment: A review of major qualitative methods and a new framework for assessing spirituality. *Social Work, 46*(3), 203–215.

Hodge, D. R. (2001b). Spiritual genograms: A generational approach to assessing spirituality. *Families in Society, 82*(1), 35.

Hodge, D. R. (2003). The challenge of spiritual diversity: Can social work facilitate an inclusive environment? *Families in Society, 84*, 348–358.

Hodge, D. R. (2005a). Spiritual ecograms: A new assessment instrument for identifying clients' strengths in space and across time. *Families in Society, 86*(2), 287–297.

Hodge, D. R. (2005b). Spiritual lifemaps: A client-centered pictorial instrument for spiritual assessment, planning, and intervention. *Social Work, 50*(1), 77–88.

Höchsmann, H. (2001). *On Chuang Tzu.* Belmont, CA : Wadsworth/Thomson Learning.

Hoffman, L., Paris, S., & Hall, E. (1994). *Developmental psychology today* (6th ed.). New York: McGraw Hill, Inc.

Holland, J., & Neimeyer, R. A. (2005). Reducing the risk of burnout in end-of-life care settings: The role of daily spiritual experiences and training. *Palliative & Supportive Care, 3*, 173–181.

Hollis, F. (1964). *Casework: A psychosocial therapy.* New York: Random House.

Hong Kong Cancer Registry, Hospital Authority. (2004). *Fast stats for female breast cancer 2003.* Retrieved September 20, 2006, from http://www3.ha.org.hk/cancereg/eng/stat.asp

Hovdestad, W. E., & Kristiansen, C. M. (1996). Mind meets body: On the nature of recovered memories of trauma. *Women & Therapy, 19*(1), 31–45.

Huston, S. (2003). *Buddhism : A concise introduction.* New York : HarperCollins.

IFSW/IASSW (2004). *Ethics in social work, statement of principles.* Bern, Switzerland: International Federation of Social Workers and International Association of Schools of Social Work

Imbrogno, S., & Canda, E. R. (1988). Social work as an holistic system of activity. *Social Thought, 14*(1), 16–29.

Iwamitsu, Y., Shimoda, K., Abe, H., Tani, T., Kodama, M., & Okawa, M. (2003). Differences in emotional distress between breast tumor patients with emotional inhibition and those with emotional expression. *Psychiatry and Clinical Neurosciences, 57*, 289–294.

Janoff-Bulman, R. 1989. Assumptive worlds and the stress of traumatic events: Applications of the schema construct. *Social Cognition, 7*, 113–136.

Johanson, G. & Kutz, R. S. (1994). *Grace unfolding: Psychotherapy in the Spirit of Tao-te ching.* New York: Harmony/Bell Tower.

Johnson, E. L., & Sandage, S. J. (1999). A postmodern reconstruction of psychotherapy: Orienteering, religion, and the healing of the soul. *Psychotherapy, 36*, 1–15.

Johnson, L. N., Wright, D. W., & Ketring, S. A. (2002). The therapeutic alliance in home-based family therapy: Is it predictive of outcome? *Journal of Marital and Family Therapy, 28*, 93–102.

Johnstone, A. A. (1992). The bodily nature of the self or what Descartes should have conceded Princess Elizabeth of Bohemia. In M. Sheet-Johnstone (Ed.), *Giving the body its due* (pp. 16–47). Albany, NY: State University of New York Press.

Jung, C. G., Adler, G., & Hull, R. F. C. (Eds.). (1977). *Collected works of C. G. Jung, Vol. 18: The symbolic life: Miscellaneous writings.* Princeton, NJ: Princeton University Press.

Jung, C.G., & Wolfgang, P. (1955). *The interpretation of nature and psyche.* New York: Pantheon Books.

Kabat-Zinn, J. (1990). *Full catastrophe living: Using the wisdom of your body and mind to face stress, pain, and illness.* New York: Delta Books.

Kabat-Zinn, J., Lipworth, L., & Burney, R. (1985). The clinical use of mindfulness meditation for the self-regulation of chronic pain. *Journal of Behavioral Medicine, 8*, 162–190.

Kabat-Zinn, J., Massion, A. O., Kristeller, J., Peterson, L. G., Fletcher, K. E., Pbert, L. et al. (1992). Effectiveness of a meditation-based stress reduction program in the treatment of anxiety disorders. *American Journal of Psychiatry, 149*, 936–943.

Katz, J. (1985). The sociopolitical nature of counseling. *Counseling Psychologist, 13*, 615–624.

Kearney, M. (2000). *A place of healing: Working with suffering in living and dying.* Oxford: Oxford University Press.

Keefe, T. (1975). A Zen perspective on social casework. *Social Casework, 56*(3), 140–144.

Keeney, B. P., & Thomas, F. N. (1986). Cybernetic foundations of family therapy. In F. P. Piercy & D. H. Sprenkle (Eds.), *Family therapy sourcebook* (pp. 262–287). New York: Guilford Press.

Kepner, J. I. (1993). *Body process: Working with the body in social work practice.* San Francisco, CA: Jossey-Bass.

Khantzian, E. J. (1990). Self-regulation and self-medication factors in alcoholism and the addictions: Similarities and differences. In M. Galanter (Ed.), *Recent development in alcoholism* (Vol. 8, pp. 255–271). New York: Plenum Press.

Kim, Y., & Seidlitz, L. (2002). Spirituality moderates the effect of stress. *Personality and Individual Differences, 32*, 1377–1390.

Kirkland, R. (2004). *Taoism: The enduring tradition.* New York: Routledge.

Kirschbaum, C., & Hellhammer, D. (1989). Response variability of salivary cortisol under psychological stimulation. *Journal of Clinical Chemistry and Clinical Biochemistry, 27*(4), 237.

Kissman, K. & Maurer, L. (2002). East meets West: Therapeutic aspects of spirituality in health, mental health, and addiction recovery. *International Social Work, 45*(1), 35–43.

Koenig, H. G. (2002). The role of religion and spirituality at the end of life. *The Gerontologist, 42*, 20–23.

Koening, T. K., & Spano, R. N. (1998). Taoism and the strengths perspective. In E. R. Canda (Ed.), *Spirituality in social work: New directions* (pp. 47–65). New York: The Haworth Pastoral Press.

Kohn, L. (Ed.) (2000). *Daoism handbook.* Leiden; Boston, MA: Brill.

Kohn, L. (2001). Chinese religion. In R. C. Neville (Ed.), *The Human condition* (pp. 21–48). Albany: State University of New York Press.

Kohut, H. (1971). *The analysis of self.* New York: International Universities Press.

Kohut, H. (1977). *The restoration of self.* New York: International Universities Press.

Kolb, D. A. (1976). *Learning style inventory: Technical manual.* Boston, MA: McBer and Company.

Kutz, R. (1997). *Body-centered psychotherapy: The Hakomi method: The integrated use of mindfulness, nonviolence and the body.* Mendocino, CA: Life Rhythm.

Laird, J. (2001). Theorizing culture: Narrative ideas and practice principles. *Journal of Feminist Family Therapy, 11*, 99–114.

Lam, C. L, Gandek, B., Ren, X. S., & Chan, M. S. (1998). Tests of scaling assumptions and construct validity of the Chinese (HK) version of the SF-36 health survey. *Journal of Clinical Epidemiology, 51*, 1139–1147.

Lam, C. L., Tse, E. Y. Y., & Gandek, B. (2005). Is the standard SF-12 health survey valid and equivalent for a Chinese population? *Quality of Life Research, 14*(2), 539–547.

Lambert, M. J., & Ogles, B. M. (2004). The efficacy and effectiveness of pyschotherapy. In M. J. Lambert (Ed.), *Bergin & Garfield's handbook of psychotherapy and behavior change* (5th ed.). New York: Wiley.

Lammert, M. (1986). Experience as knowing: Utilizing therapist self-awareness. *Social Casework, 67*, 369–376.

Langer, E. J. (1990). *Mindfulness.* Jackson, TN: Perseus Publishing.

Lantz, J. (1993). *Existential family therapy.* Northvale, NJ: Jason Aronson Inc.

Lax, W. D. (1996). Narrative, social constructivism, and Buddhism. In H. Rosen & K. T. Kuehlwein (Eds.), *Constructing realities: Meaning-making perspectives for psychotherapists* (pp. 195–220). San Francisco: Jossey-Bass.

Lazar, S. W., Bush, G., Gollub, R. L., Fricchione, G. L., Khalsa, G., & Benson, H. (2000). Functional brain mapping of the relaxation response and meditation [Autonomic Nervous System]. *NeuroReport, 11*(7), 1581–1585.

Lazare, A., Eisenthal, S., & Wasserman, L. (1975). The customer approach to patienthood: Attending to patient requests in a walk-in clinic. *Archives of General Psychiatry, 32*, 553.

Lazarus, R. S., & Folkman, S. (1984). *Stress, appraisal, and coping.* New York: Springer.

Lebow, J. (2006). *Research for the psychotherapist: From science to practice.* New York: Routledge.

LeCroy, C. W., & Goodwin, C. C. (1988). New directions in teaching social work methods: A content analysis of course outlines. *Journal of Social Work Education, 24*, 43–49.

LeDoux, J. (1998). *The emotional brain.* London: Weidenfeld & Nicolson.

Lee, G. W. (1996). Defining traditional healing. *Justice as healing.* Newsletter of The Native Law Centre of Canada, Saskatoon, Saskatchewan, Canada: University of Saskatchewan. In *Alternative medicine sourcebook,* 2nd eds. D. D. Mattews, 113–120. Detroit, MI: Omnigraphics.

Lee, J. Y. (1979). *The theology of change: A Christian concept of God in an Eastern perspective.* Maryknoll, NY: Orbis Books.

Lee, M. Y. (1996). A constructivist approach to the help-seeking process of clients: A response to cultural diversity. *Clinical Social Work Journal, 24,* 187–202.

Lee, M. Y. (2003). A solution-focused approach to cross-cultural clinical social work practice: Utilizing cultural strengths, *Families in Society, 84,* 385–395.

Lee, M. Y. (2005). The complexity of indigenization of clinical social work knowledge and practice. *Hong Kong Journal of Social Work, 39,* 3–31.

Lee, M. Y. (2007). Discovering strengths and competencies in female domestic violence survivors: An application of Roberts' continuum of the duration and severity of woman battering. *Brief Treatment and Crisis Intervention, 7*(1). http://www.10.1093/brief-treatment/mhm002 102–114.

Lee, M. Y., Uken, A., Sebold, J. (2007). Role of self-determined goals in predicting recidivism in domestic violence offenders. *Research on Social Work Practice, 17,* 30–41.

Lee, M. Y., Greene, G. J., Solovey, A., Grove, D., & Fraser, S. (in press). Utilizing family strengths and resilience: Integrative Family and Systems Treatment (I-FAST) with children and adolescents with severe emotional and behavioral problems. *Family Process.*

Lee, M. Y., Greene, G. J., Solovey, A., Grove, D., Fraser, S., & Washburn, P. (2009). Intensive community-based treatment of children, adolescents, and their families: The effectiveness of family-community systems therapy (I-FAST). *New Research in Mental Health, 2006–2008 Biennium* (Vol. 18). Columbus, OH: The Ohio Department of Mental Health.

Lee, M. Y., Sebold, J., & Uken, A. (2003). *Solution-focused treatment with domestic violence offenders: Accountability for change.* New York: Oxford University Press.

Lee, M. Y., Zaharlick, A., & Akers, D. (2009). Treatment of trauma survivors: Effects of meditation practice on clients' mental health outcomes. *New Research in Mental health, 2006–2008 Biennium* (Vol. 18). Columbus, OH: The Ohio Department of Mental Health.

Lee-Jones, C., Humphris, G., Dixon, R., & Hatcher, M. B. (1997). Fear of cancer recurrence—a literature review and proposed cognitive formulation to explain exacerbation of recurrent fears. *Psycho-Oncology, 6,* 95–105.

Leung, C. M., Ho, S., Kan, C. S., Hung, C. H., & Chen, C. N. (1993). Evaluation of the Chinese version of the Hospital Anxiety and Depression Scale: A cross-cultural perspective. *International Journal of Psychosomatics, 40,* 29–34.

Leung, P. P. Y. (1997). Stress management for cancer patients: A psycho-educational-support group. In C. L. W. Chan & N. Rhind (Eds.), *Social work intervention in health care: The Hong Kong scene* (pp. 85–103). Hong Kong: Hong Kong University Press.

Leung, P. P. Y., & Chan, C. L. W. (2006a). The combined use of narrative and experience-near techniques in an investigation of meaning in women with breast cancer. *Psycho-Oncology, 15*(1), S5.

Leung, P. P. Y., & Chan, C. L. W. (2006b). Reconstructing the self: A qualitative study of the experience of Hong Kong Chinese breast cancer survivors. Paper presented at the 3rd Annual Conference of American Psychosocial Oncology Society, Florida.

Linehan, M. M. 1993. *Cognitive-behavioral treatment of borderline personality disorder.* New York: Guilford Press.

Linehan, M. M., Cochran, B. N., & Kehrer, C. A. (2001). Dialectical behavior therapy for borderline personality disorder. In D. H. Barlow (Ed.), *Clinical handbook of psychological disorders: A step-by-step treatment manual* (3rd ed., pp. 470–522). New York: Guilford Press.

Linley, P. A., & Joseph, S. 2004. Positive change following trauma and adversity: A review. *Journal of Trauma Stress, 17*(1), 11–21.

Lloyd, G. E. R. (Ed.). (1991). The invention of nature. *Methods and problems in Greek science* (pp. 417–434). Cambridge: Cambridge University Press.

Loehr, J., & Schwartz, T. (2003). *The power of full engagement; Managing energy, not time is the key to high performance and personal renewal.* New York: Free Press.

Logan, R. F. (1986). *The alphabet effect.* New York: Morrow.

Lombardo, T .W., & Gray, M. J. (2005). Beyond exposure for posttraumatic stress disorder (PTSD) symptoms. *Behavior Modification, 29,* 3–9.

Long, J. R. (2001). Goal agreement and early therapeutic change. *Psychotherapy, 38,* 219–232.

Lowen, A. (1967). *The betrayal of the body.* New York: Macmillan.

Lowen, A. (1973). *Depression and the body.* Baltimore, MD: Penguin.

Lu, H. C. (1994). *Chinese natural cures: Traditional methods for remedies and preventions.* New York: Black Dog and Leventhal Publishers.

Lucas, R. E., Diener, D., & Larsen, R. J. (2003). Measuring positive emotions. In S. J. Lopez & Snyder, C. R. (Eds.), *Positive psychological assessment: A handbook of models and measures* (pp. 201–218). Washington, DC: American Psychological Association.

Luxenberg, T., Spinazzola, J., & Van der Kolk, B. A. (2001). Complex trauma and disorders of extreme stress DESNOS diagnosis, Part one: Assessment. *Direction in Psychiatry, Vol. 21, Lesson 25,* 373–387. New York: Norton.

Lyons, A., & Petrucelli, R. (1987). *Medicine: An illustrated history.* New York: Harry N. Abrams.

Lyubomirsky, S., King, L., & Diener, E. (2005). The benefits of frequent positive affect: Does happiness lead to success? *Psychological Bulletin, 131*(6), 803–855.

Macy, R. D. (2002). *On the epidemiology of posttraumatic stress disorder: Period prevalence rates and acute service utilization rates among Massachusetts Medicaid program enrollees: 1993–1996.* Unpublished doctoral dissertation, Union Institute and University.

Mahler, M. (1968). *On human symbiosis and vicissitudes of individuation.* New York: International Universities Press.

Mahoney, M. J. (1995). Continuing evolution of the cognitive sciences and psychotherapies. In R. A. Neimeyer, & M. J. Mahoney (Eds.), *Constructivism in psychotherapy* (pp. 39–67). Washington DC: American Psychological Association.

Mak, M. H. J. (2001). Awareness of dying: An experience of Chinese patients with terminal cancer. *Omega: Journal of Death and Dying, 43,* 259–279.

Maple, F. F. (1998). *Goal-focused interviewing.* Thousand Oaks, CA: Sage Publications.

Marlatt, G. A. (2002). Buddhist philosophy and the treatment of addictive behavior. *Cognitive and Behavioral Practice, 9,* 44–50.

Marlatt, G. A., Witkiewitz, K., Dillworth, T. M., Bowen, S. W., Parks, G. A., Macpherson, L. M., et al. (2004). Vipassana meditation as a treatment for alcohol and drug use disorders. In S. C. Hayes, V. M. Follette, & M. M. Linehan (Eds.), *Mindfulness and acceptance: Expanding the cognitive-behavioral tradition*(pp. 261–287). New York: The Guilford Press.

Martin, J. R. (1997). Mindfulness: A proposed common factor. *Journal of Psychotherapy Integration, 7*, 291–312.

McClain, C. S., Rosenfeld, B., & Breitbart, W. (2003). Effect of spiritual well-being on end-of-life despair in terminally ill cancer patients. *The Lancet, 361*(9369), 1603.

McDonagh-Coyle, A., McHugo, G. J., Ford, H. D., Mueser, K., Demment, C., & Descamps, M. (1999). *Cognitive-behavioral treatment for childhood sexual abuse survivors with PTSD.* Paper presented at the 15th Annual Meeting of the International Society for Traumatic Stress Studies, Miami, Florida.

McDonagh-Coyle, A., McHugo, G. J., Friedman, M. J., Schnurr, P. P., Zayfert, C., & Descamps, M.(2001). Reactivity in female sexual abuse survivors. *Journal of Traumatic Stress, 14*, 667–683.

McNeely, M. L., Campbell, K. L., Rowe, B. H., Klassen, T. P., Mackey, J. R., & Courneya, K. S. (2006). Effects of exercise on breast cancer patients and survivors: A systematic review and meta-analysis. *Canadian Medical Association Journal, 175*(1), 34–41.

McSherry, W. (2000). *Making sense of spirituality in nursing practice: An interactive approach.* Edinburgh: Churchill Livingstone.

Meichenbaum, D. (1977). *Cognitive behavior modification.* New York: Plenum.

Meichenbaum, D. (1995). Changing conceptions of cognitive behavior modification: Retrospect and prospect. In M. J. Mahoney (Ed.), *Cognitive and constructive psychotherapies: Theory, research, and practice* (pp. 20–28). Washington, DC: American Psychological Association.

Meredith, C., Symonds, P., Webster, L., Lamont, D., Pyper, E., Gillis, C. R. et al. (1996). Information needs of cancer patients in west Scotland: Cross-sectional survey of patients' views. *British Medical Journal, 313*, 724–726.

Meyer, T. J., & Mark, M. M. (1995). Effects of psychosocial interventions with adult cancer patients: A meta-analysis of randomized experiments. *Health Psychology, 14*,101–108.

Miles, M. B., & Huberman, A. M. (1994). *Qualitative data analysis: An expanded sourcebook* (2nd ed.). Thousand Oaks, CA: Sage Publications.

Miller, G. (1997). *Becoming miracle workers, Language and meaning in brief therapy.* New York: Aldine de Gruyter.

Milulas, W. L. (2002). *The Integrative helper: Convergence of Eastern and Western traditions.* Pacific Grove, CA: Brooks/Cole.

Minuchin, S., & Fishman, H. C. (1981). *Family therapy techniques.* Cambridge, MA: Harvard University Press.

Minuchin, S., Nichols, M. P., & Lee, W. Y. (2007). *Assessing families and couples: From symptom to system.* New York: Ally and Bacon.

Mitchell, S. (Trans.). (1988). *Tao te ching (Lao Tzu).* New York: HarperCollins. (Original work published *c.* 400 BCE.)

Moody, H. R. (2006). The link between religion and health: Psychoneuroimmunology and the faith factor. *Gerontologist, 46*(1), 147–149.

Morris, B. (1994). *Anthropology of the self: The individual in cultural perspective.* London: Boulder.

Moser, D. J. (1996). *Abstract thinking and thought in anceint Chinese and early Greek.* Unpublished doctoral dissertation, University of Michigan, Ann Arbor.

Motl, J. M. (2002). Acupuncture. In S. Shannon (Eds.), *Handbook of complementary and alternative therapies in mental health* (pp. 431–452). San Diego, CA: Academic Press.

Mueser, K. T., Goodman, L. B., Trumbette, S. L., Osher, F. C., Vidaver, R., Auciello, P., & Foy, D. W. (1998). Trauma and posttraumatic stress disorder in severe mental illness. *Journal of Consulting and Clinical Psychology, 66,* 493–499.

Munro, D. J. (1969). *The concept of man in early China.* Stanford, CA: Stanford University Press.

Munro, D. J. (1985). Introduction. In D. J. Munro (Ed.), *Individualism and holism: Studies in Confucian and Taoist values* (pp. 1–34). Ann Arbor: Center for Chinese Studies, University of Michigan.

Murray, C.J., & Lopez, A. D. (1996). *The global burden of disease.* Cambridge, MA: Harvard University Press.

Nakamura, H. (1985). *Ways of thinking of Eastern peoples.* Honolulu: University of Hawaii Press. (Original work published 1964)

Nakashima, M., & Canda, E. R. (2005). Positive dying and resiliency in later life: A qualitative study. *Journal of Aging Studies, 19,* 109–125.

National Association of Social Workers. (1999). *The NASW Code of Ethics.* Washington, DC: NASW.

Neimeyer, R. A. (2001). *Meaning reconstruction and the experience of loss.* Washington, DC: American Psychological Association.

Neimeyer, R. A. (2002). *Lessons of loss: A guide to coping* (2nd ed.). New York: Brunner Routledge.

Neimeyer, R. A. (2006). Narrating the dialogical self: Toward an expanded toolbox for the counselling psychologist. *Counselling Psychology Quarterly, 19*(1), 105–120.

Neimeyer, R. A., & Mahoney, M. J. (1993). *Constructivism in psychotherapy.* Washington, DC: American Psychological Association.

Ng, S. M. (2003). *Chinese medicine yangsheng and body/mind/spirit wellness.* Hong Kong: Veritas Book House [in Chinese].

Ng, S. M., & Chan, C. L. W. (2005). Social work intervention to embrace holistic well-being. In R. Adams, L. Dominelli, & M. Payne (Eds.), *Social work futures—crossing boundaries, transforming practice* (pp. 68–82). Basingstoke, UK: Palgrave Macmillan.

Ng, S. M., Chan, C. L. W., Ho, D. Y. F., Wong, Y. Y., & Ho, R. T. H. (2006). Stagnation as a distinct clinical syndrome: Comparing "yu" (stagnation) in traditional Chinese medicine with depression. *British Journal of Social Work, 36,* 467–484.

Ng, S. M., Chan, T. H. Y., Chan, C. L. W., Lee, A. M., Yau, J. K. Y., Chan, C. H. Y. et al. (2006). Group debriefing for people with chronic diseases during the SARS pandemic: Strength-focused and meaning-oriented approach for resilience and transformation (SMART). *Community Mental Health Journal, 42*(1), 53–63.

Ng, S. M., Yau, J. K. Y., Chan, C. L. W., Chan, C. H. Y., & Ho, D. Y. F. (2005). The measurement of body-mind-spirit well-being: Toward multidimensionality and transcultural applicability. *Social Work in Health Care, 41*(1), 33–52.

Nhất Hạnh, T. (1991). *Peace is every step: The path of mindfulness in everyday life.* New York: Bantam Books.

Nhất Hạnh, T. (1999). The heart of the Buddha's teaching: Transforming suffering into peace, joy, and liberation. New York: Broadway Books.

Nhất Hạnh, T. (2001). *Anger: Wisdom for cooling the flames.* New York: Riverhead Books.

Nhất Hạnh, T. (2002). *Our appointment with life: The Buddha's teaching on living in the present.* Taiwan: Oak Culture Publisher [in Chinese].

Nisbett, R. E. (1998). Essence and accident. In J. Cooper & J. Darley (Eds), *Attribution processes, personal perception, and social interaction: The legacy of Ned Jones* (pp.169–200). Washington, DC: American Psychological Association.

Nisbett, R. E., Peng, K., Choi, I., & Norenzayan, A. (2001). Culture and systems of thought: Holistic versus analytic cognition. *Psychological Review, 108*(2), 291–310.

Oldstone-Moore, J. (2003). *Taoism: Origins, beliefs, practices, holy texts, sacred places.* New York: Oxford University Press.

Pachuta, D.M. (1989). Chinese medicine: The law of five elements. In A. A. Sheikh & K. S. Sheikh (Eds.), *Healing East & West: Ancient wisdom and modern psychology* (pp. 64–90). New York: John Wiley & Sons.

Pardini, D. A., Plante, T. G., Sherman, A., & Stump, J. E. (2000). Religious faith and spirituality in substance abuse recovery: Determining the mental health benefits. *Journal of Substance Abuse Treatment, 19*, 347–354.

Parry, C. (2003). Embracing uncertainty: An exploration of the experiences of childhood cancer survivors. *Qualitative Health Research, 13*(2), 227–246.

Patel, N., Naik, D., & Humphreys, B. (Ed.). (1997). *Visions of reality: Religion and ethnicity in social work.* London: Central Council for Education and Training in Social Work.

Pelcovitz, D., van der Kolk, B. A., Roth, S. H., Mandel, F. S., Kaplan, S. J., & Resick, P. A. (1997). Development of a criteria set and a structured interview for disorders of extreme stress SIDES. *Journal of Traumatic Stress, 10*, 3–16.

Peng, K., & Nisbett, R. E. (1999). Culture, dialectics, and reasoning about contradiction. *American Psychologist, 54*, 741–754.

Penrose, R. (1997). On understanding understanding. *International Studies in the Philosophy of Science, 11*(1), 7–20.

Penrose, R. (1994). *Shadows of the Mind.* Oxford, UK: The Oxford Press.

Penrose, R., & Hameroff, S.R. (1995). What gaps? Reply to Grush and Churchland. *Journal of Consciousness Studies, 2*(2), 99–112.

Perlman, H. H. (1957). *Social casework: A problem-solving process.* Chicago: University of Chicago Press.

Perls, F. (1969). *Gestalt therapy verbatim.* Lafayette: Real People Press.

Pert, C. B., Dreher, H. E., & Ruff, M. R. (1998). The psychosomatic network: Foundations of mind-body medicine. *Alternative Therapies in Health and Medicine, 4*(4), 30–41.

Peterson, C., & Park, M. (2004). Classification and measurement of character strengths: Implications for practice. In P. A. Linley & S. Joseph (Eds.), *Positive psychology in practice.* Hoboken, NJ: John Wiley & Sons.

Polanyi, M. (1962). *Personal knowledge: Towards a post-critical philosophy* (corrected ed.). Chicago: The University of Chicago Press.

Rahula, W. (1974). *What the Buddha taught: Revised and expanded edition with texts from Suttas and Dhammapada* (2nd Ed.). New York: Grove Press.

Ramaswami, S., & Sheikh, A. (1989). Buddhist psychology: Implications for healing. In A. Sheikh & K. Sheikh (Eds.), *Eastern and Western approaches to healing: Ancient Wisdom and modern knowledge* (pp. 91–123). New York: Wiley-Interscience.

Ray, C. (1992). Positive and negative social support in a chronic illness. *Psychological Reports, 71*(3), 977–978.

Ray, O. (2004). How the mind hurts and heals the body. *American Psychologist,* (January) *59*, 29–40.

Real, T. (1990). The therapeutic use of self in constructionist/systemic therapy. *Family Process, 29*, 255–272.

Reamer, F. G. (1992). Social work and the public good: Calling or career? In P. N. Reid & P. R. Popple (Eds.), *The moral purposes of social work* (pp. 11–33). Chicago: Nelson-Hall Publishers.

Reber, A. S. (1993). *Implicit learning and tacit knowledge: An essay on the cognitive unconscious*. New York: Oxford University Press.

Reid, W. J. (1998). The paradigms and long-term trends in clinical social work. In R. A. Dorfman (Ed.), *Paradigms of clinical social work* (Vol. 2, pp. 337–351). New York: Brunner/Mazel.

Reid, W. J., & Esptein, L. (1972). *Task-centered casework*. New York: Columbia University Press.

Resick, P. A., & Schnicke, M. K. (1992). Cognitive processing therapy for sexual assault victims. *Journal of Consulting and Clinical Psychology, 60*, 748–756.

Resick, P. A., & Schnicke, M. K. (1993). *Cognitive processing therapy for rape victims: A treatment manual*. Newbury Park, CA: Sage Publications.

Ricard, M. (2006). *Happiness: A guide to developing life's most important skill*. New York: Little, Brown & Company.

Richards, P. S., & Bergin, A. E. (1997). *A spiritual strategy for counseling and psychotherapy*. Washington, DC: American Psychological Association.

Rogers, C. (1961). *On becoming a person*. Boston, MA: Houghton Mifflin.

Rogers, C. R. (1965). *Client-centered therapy: Its current practice, implications, and theory*. Boston, MA: Houghton Mifflin.

Rosen, H., & Kuehlwein, K. T. (Eds.) (1996). *Constructing realities: Meaning-making perspectives for psychotherapists*. San Francisco: Jossey-Bass Publishers.

Rothbaum, B. O., Meadows, E. A., Resick, P., & Foy, D. W. (2000). Cognitive-behavioral therapy. In E. B. Foa, T. M., Keane, & M. J. Friedman (Eds.), *Effective treatments for PTSD: Practice guidelines from the International Society for Traumatic Stress Studies* (pp. 60–83). New York: Guilford Press.

Rothschild, B. (2000) *The body remembers: The psychophysiology of trauma and trauma treatment*. New York: Norton.

Rubin, J. B. (1996). *Psychotherapy and Buddhism: Toward integration*. New York, London: Plenum Press.

Ryan, R. M., & Deci, E. L. (2000). Self-determination theory and the facilitation of intrinsic motivation, social development, and well-being. *American Psychologist, 55*, 68–78.

Russel, R. (1998). Spirituality and religion in graduate social work education. In E. R. Canda (Ed.), *Spirituality and social work: New directions*. Hazleton, PA: Haworth Press.

Saari, C. (1992). The person-in-environment reconsidered: New theoretical bridges. *Child and Adolescent Social Work Journal, 9*, 205–219.

Saleebey, D. (1997). Introduction: Power in the people. In D. Seleebey (Ed.), *The strengths perspective in social work practice* (2nd ed., pp. 3–19). New York: Longman.

Satir, V. (1988). The tools of the therapist. In J. K. Zeig & S. R. Lankton (Eds.), *Developing Ericksonian therapy: State of the art* (pp. 513–523, C30). New York: Brunner/Mazel.

Schacter, D. L. (1987). Implicit memory: History and current status. *Journal of Experimental Psychology: Learning, Memory, and Cognition, 13*, 501–518.

Schmidt, S. (2004). Mindfulness and healing intention: Concepts, practice, and research evaluation. *Journal of Alternative and Complementary Medicine, 10* (Suppl 1), S7–S14.

Schneider, J. M. (2000). *Grief's wisdom: Quotes for understanding the transformation process*. Traverse City, MI: Seasons Press.

Schneider, R. H., Alexander, C. N., Staggers, F. Rainforth, M., Salerno, J. W., Hartz, A. et al. (2005). Long-term effects of stress reduction on mortality in persons over 55 years of age with systemic hypertension. *The American Journal of Cardiology, 95*, 1060–1064.

Schneider, J. M., & Zimmerman, S. K. (2006). *Transforming loss—a discovery process.* East Lansing, MI: Integra Press.

Schoop, T., & Mitchell, P. (1994). Reflections and projections: The Schoop approach to dance therapy. In P. Lewis (Ed.), *Theoretical approaches in dance-movement therapy* (Vol. 1, p. 44). Dubuque, IA: Kendall/Hunt Publishing Company.

Schwartz, T. (1995). *What really matters: Searching for wisdom in America.* New York: Bantam Books.

Scott, A. (1996). The Hierarchical Emergence of Consciousness. In S. R., A. Hameroff, W. Kaszniak, & A. C. Scott (Eds.), *Toward a science of consciousness: The first Tucson discussions and debates, 659–676.* Cambridge, MA: MIT Press.

Scott, A. (2000). Modern Science and the Mind. In Velmans, M. (Ed.), *Investigating phenomenal consciousness: New methodologies and maps, 215–232.* Philadelphia: J. Benjamins Publishing Company.

Segal, Z. V., Williams, J. M. G., & Teasdale, J. D. (2001). *Mindfulness-based cognitive therapy for depression: A new approach to preventing relapse.* New York: Guilford Press.

Sephton, S., & Spiegel, D. (2003). Circadian disruption in cancer: A neuroendocrine-immune pathway from stress to disease? *Brain Behavior and Immunity, 17*(5), 321–328.

Shannon, S. (Ed.). (2002). *Handbook of Complementary and Alternative Therapies in Mental Health.* San Diego, CA: Academic Press.

Shapiro, S. L., Schwartz, G. E., & Bonner, G. (1998). Effects of mindfulness-based stress reduction on medical and premedical students. *Journal of Behavioral Medicine, 21*, 581–599.

Sheikh, A. A., Kunzendorf, R. G., & Sheikh, K. S. (1989). Healing images: From ancient wisdom to modern science. In A. A. Sheikh & K. S. Sheikh (Eds.), *Healing East & West: Ancient wisdom and modern psychology* (pp. 470–515). New York: John Wiley & Sons.

Shek, D. T. (1987). Reliability and factorial structure of the Chinese version of the General Health Questionnaire. *Journal of Clinical Psychology, 43*, 683–691.

Shen, G. Q., & Yan, J. T. (2004). *Illustrations of tuina manipulations.* Shanghai, China: Shanghai Science and Technology Publishing [in Chinese].

Sherman, A. C. (2001). *Faith and health: Psychological perspectives.* New York: Guilford Press.

Siegel, D. (1999). *The developing mind: Toward a neurobiology of interpersonal experi-ence.* New York: Guilford Press.

Sik, H. H. (2005a). *Dharma therapy: A therapeutic intervention that builds on the Uni-versal Dharma with mindfulness practice as one of its key components.* Unpublished manuscript, University of Hong Kong.

Sik, H. H. (2005b). *The way out for life: The teachings and footprints of the intellectual.* Hong Kong: Clear-Cut Publishing and Printing Co. [in Chinese].

Simon, R. W. (1995). Gender, multiple roles, role meaning, and mental health. *Journal of Health and Social Behavior, 36*(2), 182–194.

Singer, E. (1970). *Key concepts in social work practice* (2nd ed.). New York: Basic Books.

Siporin, M. (1983). The therapeutic process in clinical social work. *Social Work, 28*(3), 193–198.

Siporin, M. (1986). Contributions of religious values to social wok and the law. *Social Thoughts, 12*, 35–50.

Slife, B. D., Hope, C., & Nebeker, S. (1999). Examining the relationship between religious spirituality and psychological science. *Journal of Humanistic Psychology, 39*(2), 51–85.

Snyder, C. R., Cheavens, J., & Michael, S. T. (1999). Hoping. In C. R. Snyder (Ed.), *Coping: The psychology of what works* (pp. 205–231). New York: Oxford University Press.

Snyder, C. R., Ilardi, S., Michael, S. T., & Cheavens, J. (2000). Hope theory: Updating a common process for psychological change. In C. R. Snyder & R. E. Ingram (Eds.), *Handbook of psychological change: Psychotherapy processes and practices for the 21st century* (pp. 128–153). New York: John Wiley and Sons.

Snyder, C. R., & Taylor, J. D. (2000). Hope as a common factor across psychotherapy approaches: A lesson from the Dodo's verdict. In C. R. Snyder (Ed.), *Handbook of hope: Theory, measures & applications* (pp. 89–108). San Diego, CA: Academic Press.

Speca, M., Carlson, L. E., Goodey, E., & Angen, M. (2000). A randomized, wait-list controlled clinical trial: The effects of mindfulness meditation-based stress reduction program on mood and symptoms of stress in cancer outpatients. *Psychosomatic Medicine, 62*, 613–622.

Spinazzola, J., Roth, S., Derosa, R., Efrom, L., Lifton, N., & Davidson, J. (November 1994). The specificity of the Disorders of Extreme Stress construct. Poster presented at the meetings of the International Society for Traumatic Stress Studies, Chicago, IL.

Sprangers, M. A., Taal, B. G., Aaronson, N. K., & Te Velde, A. (1995). Quality of life in colorectal cancer. Stoma vs. nonstoma patients. *Diseases of the Colon and Rectum, 38*, 361–369.

Stace, W. T. (1969). *A critical history of Greek Philosophy*. London: Macmillan.

Sudsuang R., Chentanez, V., & Veluvan, K. (1991). Effect of Buddhist meditation on salivary cortisol and total protein levels, blood pressure, pulse rate, lung volume and reaction time. *Physiology and Behavior*, 50, 543–548.

Sue, D. W., Carter, R. T., Casas, J. M., Fouad, N. A., Ivey, A., Jensen, M., et al. (1998). *Multicultural counseling competencies: Individual and organizational development*. Thousand Oaks, CA: Sage Publications. Sue, D. W., Carter, R. T., Casas, J. M., Fouad, N. A., Ivey, A., Jensen, M. et al.,

Sullivan, P. (1994). Should spiritual principles guide social policy? No. In H. J. Karger & J. Midgley (Eds.), *Controversial issues in human behavior in the social environment* (pp. 69–74). Boston, MA: Allyn & Bacon.

Stroup, H. (1986). *Social work pioneers*. Chicago, IL: Nelson-Hall.

Tatrow, K., & Montgomery, G. H. (2006). Cognitive behavioral therapy techniques for distress and pain in breast cancer patients: A meta-analysis. *Journal of Behavioral Science, 29*(1), 17–27.

Taylor, S. E., Kemeny, M. E., Reed, G. M., Bower, J. E., & Gruenewald, T. L. (2000). Psychological resources, positive illusions, and health. *American Psychologist, 55*(1), 99–109.

Teasdale, J. D., Segal, Z. V., & Williams, J. M. G. (2003). Mindfulness training and problem formulation. *Clinical Psychology: Science and Practice, 10*, 157–160.

Teasdale, J. D., Segal, Z. V., Williams, J. M. G., Ridgeway, V. A., Soulsby, J. M., & Lau, M. A. (2000). Prevention of relapse/recurrence in major depression by mindfulness-based cognitive therapy. *Journal of Consulting and Clinical Psychology, 68*, 615–625.

Tedeschi, R. G. (1995). *Trauma and transformation: Growing in the aftermath of suffering.* Thousand Oaks, CA: Sage Publications.

Tedeschi, R. G., & Calhoun, L. G. (1996). The posttraumatic growth inventory: Measuring the positive legacy of trauma. *Journal of Traumatic Stress, 9*(3), 455–471.

Temoshok, L. (1987). Personality, coping style, emotional and cancer: Towards an integrative model. *Cancer Surveys, 6*, 545–567.

Thera, N. (1972). *The power of mindfulness.* San Francisco: Unity Press.

Thurman, R. (1998). *Inner revolution: Life, liberty, and the pursuit of real happiness.* New York: Riverhead Books.

Toulmin, S., & Goodfield, J. (1961). *The fabric of heavens: The development of astronomy and physics.* New York: Harper and Row.

Tolson, E. R., Reid, W. J., & Garvin, C. D. (1994). *Generalist practice: A task-centered approach.* New York: Columbia University Press.

Tosevski, D. L., & Milovancevic, M. P. (2006). Stressful life events and physical health. *Current Opinion in Psychiatry, 19*(2), 184–189.

Toulmi, S., & Goodfield, J. (1961). *The fabric of heavens: The development of astronomy and physics.* New York: Harper and Row.

Tu, W. M. (1979). *Humanity and self-cultivation: Essays in Confucian thought.* Berkeley, CA: Asian Humanities Press.

Turner-Cobb, J. M., Sephton, S. E., Koopman, C., Blake-Mortimer, J., & Spiegel, D. (2000). Social support and salivary cortisol in women with metastatic breast cancer. *Psychosomatic Medicine, 62*(3), 337–345.

van der Kolk, B. (1994). The body keeps the score: Memory and the evolving psychobiology of posttraumatic stress. *Harvard Review of Psychiatry,* (Jan/Feb), 253–265.

van der Kolk, B. (2002). The assessment and treatment of complex PTSD. In R. Yehuda (Ed.), *Treating trauma survivors with PTSD* (pp.127–156). Washington, DC: American Psychiatric Press.

van der Kolk, B., McFarlane, A. C., & Weisaeth, L. (Eds.). (1996). *Traumatic stress: The effects of overwhelming experience on mind, body, and society.* New York: Guilford Press.

van der Kolk, B., & van der Hart, O. (1991). The intrusive past: The flexibility of memory and the engraving of trauma. *American Imago, 48*, 425–454.

van Middendorp, H., R., Geenen, M. J., Sorbi, L. J. P., van Doornen, & Bijlsma, J. W. J. (2005). Neuroendocrine-immune relationships between emotion regulation and health in patients with rheumatoid arthritis. *Rheumatology, 44*(7), 907–911.

Varma, V. (1995). *Ayurveda, a way of life.* York Beach, ME: Samuel Weiser.

Veronen, L. J., & Kilpatrick, D. J. (1983). Stress management for rape victims. In D. Meichenbaum & M. E. Jaremko (Eds.), *Stress reduction and prevention* (pp. 341–374). New York: Plenum.

Vitetta, L., Anton, B., Cortizo, F., & Sali, A. (2006). Stress and its impact on overall health and longevity. *Reversal of Aging: Resetting the Pineal Clock, 1057*, 492–505.

Walker, L. G., Walker, M. B., Heys, S. D., Lolley, J., Wesnes, K., & Eremin, O. (1997). The psychological and psychiatric effects of rIL-2 therapy: A controlled clinical trial. *Psycho-Oncology, 6*, 290–301.

Walsh, R. (1989). Toward a synthesis of eastern and western psychologies. In A. Sheikh & K. Sheikh (Eds.), *Eastern and Western approaches to healing: Ancient wisdom and modern knowledge* (pp. 542–55). New York: Wiley-Interscience.

Ware, J. E., & Sherbourne, C. D. (1992). The MOS 36-item short-form health survey (SF-36). Conceptual framework and item selection. *Medical Care, 30,* 473–483.

Watson, D., Clark, L. A., & Tellegen, A. (1988). Development and validation of brief measures of positive and negative affect: The PANAS scales. *Journal of Personality and Social Psychology, 54,* 1063–1070.

Watson, M., & Greer, S. (1983). Development of a questionnaire measure of emotional control. *Journal of Psychosomatic Research, 27,* 299–305.

Watson, M., Greer, S., Young, J., Inayat, Q., Burgess, C., & Robertson, B. (1988). Development of a questionnaire measure of adjustment to cancer: The MAC scale. *Psychological Medicine, 18,* 203–209.

Watts, A. (1957). *The way of Zen.* New York: Pantheon Books.

Watzlawick, P., Weakland, J. H., & Fisch, R. (1974). *Change, principles of problem formulation and problem resolution.* New York: W. W. Norton.

Weihs, K. L., Enright, T. M., Simmen, S. J., & Reiss, D. (2000). Negative affectivity, restriction of emotions, and site of metastases predict mortality in recurrent breast cancer. *Journal of Psychosomatic Research, 49*(1), 59–68.

Weil, A. (1995). *Spontaneous healing.* New York: Fawcett Columbine.

Weisman, E. R. (1997). Does religion and spirituality have a significant place in the Core HBSE cuuriculum? No. In M. Bloom & W. C. Klein (Eds.), *Controversial issues in human behavior in the social environment* (pp. 177–183). Boston, MA: Allyn & Bacon.

Welwood, J. (2000). *Toward a psychology of awakening: Buddhism, psychotherapy, and the path of personal and spiritual transformation.* Boston, MA: Shambhala Publications.

Werner, H. (1965). *A rational approach to social casework.* New York: Association Press.

White, M., & Epston, D. (1990). Narrative means to therapeutic ends. New York: W. W. Norton.

Wilber, K. (Ed.). (1985). *The holographic paradigm.* Boston, MA: Shambhala Publications.

Wilber, K. (2000). *Integral psychology: Consciousness, spirit, psychology, therapy.* Boston, MA: Shambhala.

Wilber, K. (2001). *No boundary: Eastern and Western approaches to personal growth.* Boston, MA: Shambhala Publications.

Wilber, K., & Walsh, R. (2000). An integral approach to consciousness research: A proposal for integrating first, second, and third person approaches to consciousness. In M. Velmans, (Ed.), *Investigating phenomenal consciousness: New methodologies and maps, 301–332.* Philadelphia: J. Benjamins Publishing Company.

Wilber, K. (2001). *No boundary: Eastern and Western approaches to personal growth.* Boston, MA: Shambhala Publications.

Wilber, K., Engler, J., & Brown, D. (1986). *Transformations of consciousness.* Boston, MA: Shambala Publications.

Williams, K. A., Kolar, M. M., Reger, B. E., & Pearson, J. C. (2001). Evaluation of a wellness-based mindfulness stress reduction intervention: A controlled trial. *American Journal of Health Promotion, 15,* 422–432.

Williams, K. J., Suls, J., Alliger, G. M., Learner, S. M., & Wan, C. K. (1991). Multiple role juggling and daily mood states in working mothers: An experience sampling study. *Journal of Applied Psychology, 76*(5), 664–674.

Wilson, J., & Keane, T.M. (1997). *Assessing psychological trauma and PTSD*. New York: Guilford Press.

Witkiewitz, K., Marlatt, G. A., & Walker, D. (2005). Mindfulness-based relapse prevention for alcohol and substance use disorders. *Journal of Cognitive Psychotherapy: An International Quarterly, 19*(3), 211–228.

Wong, M. (Trans.). (1987). *Huang Di Nei Jing Ling Shu*. Paris: Editions Masson.

Wong, E. (1997). *Harmonizing yin and yang*. Boston, MA: Shambhala Publications.

Wong, P. T. P. (1998). Meaning-centered counseling. In P. T. P. Wong & P. S. Fry (Eds.), *The human quest for meaning: A handbook of psychological research and clinical applications* (pp. 359–394). Mahwah, NJ: Erlbaum.

Worell, J., & Remer, P. (1992). *Feminist perspectives in therapy: An empowerment model for women*. New York: John Wiley & Sons.

Wright, L.M. (2005) Spirituality, suffering, and illness—ideas for healing. Philadelphia: F.A. Davis Company.

Yalom, I. D. (1995). The theory and practice of group psychotherapy. New York: Basic Books.

Yau, K. P. (2000). *The development and manual of the World Health Organization Quality of Life—abbreviated version (WHOQOL-BREF Taiwan)*. Taiwan: Department of Psychology, National Taiwan University.

Yip, K. S. (2004). Taoism and its impact on mental health of the Chinese communities. *International Journal of Social Psychiatry, 50*, 25–42.

Zebrack, B. J., & Chesler, M. A. (2002). Quality of life in childhood cancer survivors. *Psycho-Oncology, 11*, 132–141.

Zeig, J. K., & Gilligan, S. G. (Eds.). (1990). *Brief therapy: Myths, methods, and metaphors*. New York: Brunner/Mazel.

Zgierska, A., Rabago, D., Zuelsdorff, M., Coe, C., & Miller, M., & Fleming, M. (in press). Mindfulness meditation for alcohol relapse prevention: A feasibility pilot study. *Journal of Addiction Medicine*.

Index